National Identity ● in Indian Popular cinema

1 9 4 7 – 1 9 8 7

Texas Film Studies Series Thomas Schatz, Editor

Sumita S. Chakravarty

National Identity

University of Texas Press Austin

in • Indian Popular

cinema

1947 – 1987

Library of Congress
Cataloging-in-Publication Data

Chakravarty, Sumita S.
    National identity in Indian popular
cinema, 1947–1987 / Sumita S.
Chakravarty. — 1st ed.
        p.   cm. — (Texas film studies
series)
    Includes bibliographical references
(p.   ) and index.
    ISBN 0-292-75551-1. —
ISBN 0-292-71156-5 (pbk.)
    1. Motion pictures—India.
    2. Motion pictures—Social
aspects—India.   3. India in motion
pictures.   I. Title.   II. Series.
PN1993.5.I8C48   1993
302.23'0954—dc20   93-16985

An earlier version of Chapter 3
appeared as "National Identity and the
Realist Aesthetic: Indian Cinema of the
Fifties," in *Quarterly Review of Film
and Video* 11/3 (1989): 31–48.
Copyright © Harwood Academic
Publishers GmbH. Reprinted by
permission of Gordon and Breach,
Science Publishers S.A.

For Prasun

and in memory of

Kali Prasanna Sinha

Contents

Acknowledgments, ix

Introduction, 1

1 Culture/Nation: Reclaiming the Past, 18

PART ONE. THE EARLY YEARS OF NATIONHOOD

2 The Film Industry and the State: The Dynamics of
Cultural Legitimation, 55

3 National Identity and the Realist Aesthetic, 80

4 New Uses of the Romantic-Mythic Tradition, 119

5 The Recuperation of History and Memory, 157

PART TWO. THE SIXTIES AND BEYOND

6 The National-Heroic Image: Masculinity and
Masquerade, 199

7 The Authenticity Debate: Take Two, 235

8 Woman and the Burden of Postcoloniality:
The Courtesan Film Genre, 269

Conclusion, 307

Notes, 313

Selected Bibliography, 325

Index, 335

Acknowledgments

I would like to thank the Museum of Modern Art/Film Stills Archive, the Asia Society in New York, the National Film Archive of India, and Bimal Roy Productions for providing me with photographic material for this book. I also wish to thank Gordon and Breach Publishers for allowing me to reclaim an earlier draft of Chapter 3 of this study which was originally published in the *Quarterly Review of Film and Video* (1989). For the initial financial support for my research on the Bombay cinema, I am very grateful to the American Institute of Indian Studies. The award of a junior research fellowship by the AIIS in 1983–1984 enabled me to spend many months in India and helped spark what has turned into a long-term scholarly interest in the popular cinema.

I am deeply indebted to my series editor, Tom Schatz, for his painstaking readings of several drafts of this book, and for his valuable suggestions and editorial comments. This project has benefited greatly from his expert guidance. To Bob Stam of New York University I wish to convey my heartfelt thanks for his infinite generosity of spirit and his excellent scholarly advice on many matters pertaining to our common interest in cinema. I am also grateful to Parag Amladi for reading the manuscript and offering insightful comments. For moral support and encouragement through the course of this endeavor, I am much obliged to my friends Ella Shohat, Keya Ganguly, and Susan Heske, as also to Frankie Westbrook, my sponsoring editor. Jyotika Virdi undertook to procure film stills for me at very short notice and, no doubt, at considerable inconvenience to herself. I am very thankful for her help. I have also been lucky to find an enthusiastic helper in Siddananjapp Chandrakala, a graduate research assistant whose services are very timely at the crucial final stages of the production of this book.

To one's family it is difficult to express in a few words what amounts to a deeply-felt, seldom-articulated consciousness of mutual support built up on a daily basis. My parents started this process many years ago; my husband, Prasun, practices thoughtfulness as second nature; my children, Aditi and Anupam, if somewhat baffled as to why it was taking their mom so long to "make" her book, have on the whole been quite generous in accommodating this rival entity in the house. With them all I have shared the joys and challenges of exploring my stake in the signifying world of India's popular cinema.

It was the death of God. Or something very like it; for had not that outsize face, suspended above its devotees in the artificial cinematic night, shone like that of some supernal Entity that had its being at least halfway between the mortal and the divine?
—*Salman Rushdie,* The Satanic Verses

Introduction

In the storm of protest that followed the publication of Salman Rushdie's *The Satanic Verses,* whereby a fictional character's dream became a religious community's "nightmare," readers and reviewers paid scant attention to the identity of the dreamer himself: Gibreel Farishta, a former Bombay film star. That the world's reputedly "trashiest" film industry should provide the vehicle for one of the most evocative explorations and allegorical representations of the postcolonial consciousness is in its own way perhaps as outrageous a fact for cultural purists to digest as the hapless author's forced withdrawal from public life no doubt is for him. And yet, the very force of the parallels demands scrutiny. For

1

if fiction has leaked into (its author's) real life, what Rushdie's book makes abundantly clear is that the (formerly) colonized world, in this case, India, condensed into the metaphor of its supremely hybrid form, the commercial Hindi film, has become composite with, leaked into, the cultural imaginary and vocabulary of the West in ways previously unimaginable. By investing his vision of double alienation, fiction and dream, in a composite icon of the Hindi movies, Rushdie not only provides legitimacy to a despised national-cultural form but underscores the political dimensions of fantasy. As the novel transforms Indian national life into the detritus that we call a global transnational culture, it is the Bombay film as a rear-view mirror that is granted the privilege of capturing this process. Sustained by the life-blood of Bombay Hindi and *desi:* English, this brilliantly inventive, sprawling, and media-incestuous book constructs its parable of death and life, birth and rebirth, love and hatred, destruction and metamorphosis in the very idiom of the *masa:la:* movie.

Gibreel Farishta is the embodiment of memory, an echo-chamber of Indian cinematic and social history. As his story unfolds in the opening pages of the novel, the reader familiar with Bombay film jargon and gossip is teased with a host of references scrambled in the manner of the average commercial film. "Gibreel had spent the greater part of his unique career incarnating, with absolute conviction, the countless deities of the subcontinent in the popular genre movies known as 'theologicals.' It was part of the magic of his persona that he succeeded in crossing religious boundaries without giving offence" (*SV*, 16). Was Rushdie perhaps thinking of Prem Adib, a Muslim who, decades ago, portrayed the Hindu god Rāma on the screen and, as legend has it, devout folk would prostrate themselves before him?[1] Misnaming the "mythological" genre of the Hindi cinema is not just a fictional device; it recalls the conflict-ridden profile of "theological" matters in modern Indian history, the commitment to "secularism" inscribed in the Indian Constitution, and Rushdie's own study of "theocratic" Pakistan in *Shame*. Similarly, Gibreel Farishta's accident on the set of a film is a barely disguised news event from the life of the long-reigning Bombay superstar Amitabh Bachchan:

> The whole of India was at Gibreel's bedside. His condition was the lead item on every radio bulletin, it was the subject of hourly newsflashes on the national television network, and the crowd that gathered

in Warden Road was so large that the police had to disperse it with lathi-charges and tear-gas, which they used even though every one of the half-million mourners was already tearful and wailing. The Prime Minister cancelled her appointments and flew to visit him. Her son the airline pilot sat in Farishta's bedroom, holding the actor's hand. A mood of apprehension settled over the nation, because if God had unleashed such an act of retribution against his most celebrated incarnation, what did he have in store for the rest of the country? (*SV*, 28–29)

Compare this scenario with the account carried by *India Today*, the prestigious weekly magazine, of Amitabh's accident while filming a stunt scene for *Coolie* (*Porter*, 1983):

Bachchan, the near indestructible superstar who had battled seemingly insurmountable odds in thousands of celluloid frames, was fighting the most epic and rivetting battle of all—for his life. . . . Childhood friend Rajiv Gandhi broke off his trip to the United States . . . among Prime Minister Indira Gandhi's first appointments after her return was a flying visit to see the stricken star.[2]

Through density of allusion, Gibreel becomes a cultural transmitter, emanating and capturing countless bits and fragments of a collective national life: political intrigue, lurid journalism, film gossip, Satyajit Ray. Lacking fixity, spatial and psychological, he is as mercurial a narrative surface as the cinematic consciousness he embodies. A composite form par excellence, Gibreel is both Muslim and Hindu, mythological character and romantic hero, Bombay superstar Amitabh Bachchan and South Indian actors-turned-politicians M. G. Ramachandran and N. T. Rama Rao all rolled into one.

Like Gibreel Farishta, too, Indian commercial cinema has come to symbolize an order of psychic investment for immigrants of Indian origin all over the world. Both, in a fundamental sense, evoke the problematic scenario of originary desire: the desire for origins (with the accompanying discomfort, pain, and guilt) that lies at the very heart of the attempt at new identity formations on the part of displaced peoples. There are countless stories and phenomenological accounts of the Bombay film and film song providing the common ground of social intercourse in Indian diasporic gatherings.[3] This in turn is refed into the semiotic chain, as in the opening sequence of Mira Nair's *Mississippi Masala*. But the self-enclosed romanticism of the gesture of recall, the metonymic substitution of the Hindi film for "India," is generally a means of effecting closure, of constructing rigid mental boundaries between past and present, parent culture and adopted culture, belonging and exile, nationality and naturalization. As often as not, "India" is frozen in time, a past to which one cannot or will not return but which comes to represent the self valorized in another place, at another time. It is this closure that Rushdie (through Gibreel) refuses, making the immigrant's glance backward a creative and appropriative one, rather than merely a vehicle of recollection. Structuring his narrative itself as film, with flashbacks, superimpositions, and fantasy scenarios, Bombay talkies become for Rushdie the displaced site of national exploration that he had begun in *Midnight's Children*.

The fall from the skies of Gibreel (and his friend Chamcha), then, not only marks the new immigrant's break (and ironic renewal of acquaintance) with the "hollow booming words *land, belonging, home*" (*SV*, 4) but the passage from one literary-imaginative space to another in the author's oeuvre, and, in retrospect, a turning point in Rushdie's own biography. The gap opened up by this concatenation of events and processes shall serve as the point of entry for the present study of postcolonial Indian popular cinema. Just as the "Rushdie affair" has become symptomatic of nationalisms in the age of multinational and transnational economic and cultural traffic, of migrancy and postmodernity, so the allusive/elusive nature and structured compositeness of Rushdie's central character is a figure for cinematic discourse as a symbolic force in postindependence India.

It is the metaphor of *imperso-nation* that I extrapolate from Rushdie's text to construct my own narrative of Indian popular film and national identity. Concentrated within this metaphor are the notions of changeability and metamorphosis, tension and contradiction, recognition and alienation, surface and depth: dualities that have long plagued the Indian psyche and constitute the self-questionings of Indian nationhood. Indian cinema, caught in the cross-currents of this national dialogue and contributing to it, has made the drama of impersonation its distinctive signature. This is more than a matter of reinforcing the truisms that films impersonate life; characters impersonate real men and women; the film-viewing experience impersonates dream. Impersonation subsumes a process of externalization, the play of/on surfaces, the disavowal of fixed notions of identity. But it also encompasses the contrary movement of accretion, the piling up of identities, the transgression of social codes and boundaries. (A mundane example might be the Hindi film heroine changing sarees in different shots of a single romantic song sequence to signify affluence, freedom, fantasy.) Moreover, impersonation implies a form of subversion, of the illegitimate (even the monstrous) masquerading as the real thing or person, generally with the intention of displacing the legitimate. The dialectics of juxtaposition and contamination thus inform this notion. All these tendencies coalesce in the Bombay film and find expression in an intricate language of iconography and allusiveness. The dynamics of imperso-nation, its ludic possibilities, as well as the anxiety generated by it, characterize the mode of Indian popular cinema's evocation and inscription of Indian national identity.

This book presents both a theoretical elaboration of the concept of imperso-nation and its materialization in Indian popular cinema. Through nationally inflected readings of the Bombay cinema, I explore what British cultural critic Raymond Williams has called the "structure of feeling" of contemporary Indian society, treating the concept (and its use) as a way of apprehending contradictory yearnings of the body politic. As an orienting principle, imperso-nation allows us not only to identify strategies of representation and terms of cinematic address but also to conceive impersonation itself as a metaphoric site of struggle between different conceptions of a national-popular culture. At the heart of this drama are notions of "the people" and which groups can stake a more legitimate claim on defining these notions. The cultural battles over what is an authentic Indian popular culture have centered on the cinema because, as Michael Denning points out, "The great paradox of film and broadcasting has of course been that the genuine democratization of cultural audiences required such large capital investment and technical training as to have restricted greatly the production of films and broadcasts.[4] Moreover, in India, the cinema was the latest entrant on the cultural scene and was responsible for taking over, even eclipsing, earlier forms of cultural production. As such it was both popular (in attracting vast audiences) and antipopular (preventing the actual participation of the vast majority in creating new cultural forms or maintaining the old ones).[5] The cultural elite, as official guardians of "Indianness," labeled the commercial cinema an impersonating, debased, and parasitic form, thereby seeking to maintain and police cultural boundaries. The commercial cinema, meanwhile, has used the masquerade to transgress boundaries with impunity and to inscribe the national itself as the ideal-typical mode of impersonation.

Forms of impersonation and masquerade are of course integral to the symbolic repertoire of all the peoples of the world. The mask has a long cultural history associated with ritual and performance. Masks seem to present a supernatural world and help people to cope with what David Napier has called "the metaphysics of ambivalence," divine power beneficent and malign at the same time.[6] In more secular and mundane settings, disguises and costumes communicate meaning through transforming the wearer. Of particular relevance to this investigation is the *bahuru:pi* (literally, "many appearances") tradition in Indian folk performances. *Bahuru:pi*s were/are itinerant villagers belonging to the lower strata of society who impersonated gods, demons, animals, and other natural forces through dress and makeup and received alms from people as they went from door to door or enacted little scenes in a village square. The art seems to have run in families and was a way of earning a little money or grains in exchange for a bit of visual and/or dramatic entertainment. The image of the goddess Kāli, of *shanī* or Saturn, and of wild animals such as tigers and bears—images that struck momentary terror in the hearts of children and adults—were the favored impersonations of the *bahuru:pi*s, and the period of dusk their time of appearance. They evoked the in-between stage dividing day from night, the human from the sub- and superhuman realms, the socially marginal (the laboring classes and untouchables) from the well-placed and well-to-do. Through poems and songs, but more often through nods and facial expressions, the *bahuru:pi*s evoked new and exciting states of being, breaking the monotony of daily life. There is a description of "Chinā:'t" *bahuru:pi* in Sarat Chandra Chatterjee's novel *Shri:kānta* and a scene of a *bahuru:pi* in Ritwik Ghatak's *Subarnarekha:* (*Golden River*, 1962, released in 1965). The Bombay cinema's possible connections to this form have, to my knowledge, not been mentioned, nor have I been able to locate studies of *bahuru:pi*s as a performing group with a distinct aesthetic. While the Bombay film's connection with other folk performative traditions, such as the Parsee theater, the *ja:tra* and *tama:sha:*, as well as the classical *rasa:* theory, has received some attention from critics, the *bahuru:pi* tradition appears to have been overlooked. Yet it seems to me that masquerade and impersonation are crucial structuring and thematic devices in the popular Bombay film and have fairly wide implications for our understanding of its cinematic codes.

In the spirit of the *bahuru:pi*, then, I adopt the idea of impersonation as a field of mobile signifiers in which acting and image making are at

National Identity in Indian Popular Cinema

once forms of communal address and a reminder of all the socially imposed limitations that can come in the way of such address. As an analytic device, impersonation has the advantage of articulating (in both senses of uttering and joining) the aesthetic and political dimensions of cinematic production, the twin foci of this book. Too often a discussion of the cinema, particularly in a Third World context, tends to be one or the other, either identifying stylistic features and narrative conventions (Satyajit Ray as auteur, for instance) or involving a barely disguised sociological approach where actual events or conditions are read off the surface of the text or are seen as lurking just beneath it. The discussion of cinema becomes either too specific or not specific enough. Alternatively, concepts borrowed from other critical vocabularies may too easily be applied for confirmation and reconfirmation of a preexisting thesis. The concept of impersonation as advanced in this study helps us to avoid these critical paths and to see cinematic language and meaning as a process of *translation* of the existential into the symbolic.

Crucially, I shall be claiming that impersonation is a function of the medium and enunciation of cinema in general and a recurring feature of Indian cultural practice in particular. That is, the illusionist nature of the photographic image and of the mass entertainment film has informed discussions of the topic from the very beginning, while acting bodies and narrative characters as personas are a characteristic feature of the movies, as of all performance. The dialectics of disguise and identity, of presence and absence inform the cinema apparatus, and masquerade must be seen as a privileged mode of articulation. However, the "star text," to use Jeremy Butler's phrase, makes the critique of impersonation particularly germane to the movie star/cultural hero as she or he who precisely embodies and underscores the slippery, indeterminate nature of the relationship of the cinema with "real life." Impersonation, therefore, allows us to see the domain of acting and the domain of social life as at once distinct and integrated. In the context of Indian narrative traditions, impersonation as a parable of social relationships has a long though uncharted history.[7] It is also an empirically observable phenomenon (not just an externally imposed theoretical construct) in the Bombay film, where doubled images, mistaken identities, foundlings, and long-lost returns are the repetitive scenarios that foreground problems of good and evil, outsider and insider, law and lawlessness. The concern of this book is how these, in turn, create, to use Timothy Brennan's phrase, "myths of the nation,"[8] how the overriding official goal of Indian national unity is subject to the work of cultural elaboration. Put another way, one might quote South Asian scholar Edwin Gerow, who stated, "In terms of historical variables relevant to the twentieth century, a national consciousness, 'Indianness,' appears to be a kind of response to awareness of other worlds; civilization becomes an object of consciousness the moment it is perceived historically that value systems are total, self-validating, *and yet in some sense alternative*" (my emphasis).[9] This inherently contradictory relationship and its politics within the cinema are the particular objects of the present study.

Exploring the possibilities embedded in imperso-nation helps us to contribute to the debates on Third World filmmaking which are sadly lacking in an engagement with the popular, the mass entertainment film. Granted that the commercial underpinnings of this cinema preclude any easy identification of popularity (of the people) with widespread distribution and consumption, the question must still be raised why some films and not others "take off" (to borrow a phrase from Iain Chambers),[10] how they allow us to engage with the sense or the feel of a situation. "Culture is constructed from given circumstances . . . but what is more significant is how these conditions are experienced and lived out, how they are moulded, shaped, rearranged, translated and modified to meet particular concerns and needs."[11] Cinematic culture, like other forms of widely disseminated communal discourse, can then be seen as a mediated form of national consciousness.

Viewing the Bombay cinema in this light serves several purposes: academic, cultural, political. First, within the flourishing area of film studies, Indian cinema has in general received little attention, the popular film even less so; if Indian cinema has just passed its historic turning point and is being supplanted by television as the new national medium, it is time to evaluate this cinema as a historical-cultural phenomenon. Second, the Bombay cinema's development alongside India's (high) nationalist phase makes it an eminently contemporary mode of expression implicated in debates regarding national identity. Third, our awareness in recent years of the sphere of mass culture as the dominant terrain of ideological (and, increasingly, multinational) struggle is yet inadequately informed by notions of the national-popular as articulated in the so-called Third World.

In wrenching, as it were, the Bombay cinema out of its native moorings, the context within which it has been viewed so far, and giving it a somewhat globalized profile, I am aware of departing from traditional accounts of this cinema. However, only a larger frame of reference can enable us to explore all the ramifications of this cinema's complex development and its multidimensional appeal. In addition, the larger framework helps us to locate some of the themes of this book: nationalism and internationalism, authenticity and falseness, reality and fantasy, identity and difference, fixity and fluidity. These terms can only function in relation to each other, at the same time developing distinct emphases and trajectories in different national contexts.

This study deals with a forty-year period in the history of Indian cinema, from the time India gained its independence from British colonial rule in August 1947 to the late eighties. Such a time frame (1947 being roughly a mid-point) confers a certain symmetry to Indian film history, whose birth goes back to the early 1900s. A sense of its past, a pride in its achievements, and a consciousness of maturity pervade the Indian film industry by 1947. The politics of film culture in postcolonial India that is treated in this book is also a politics of nostalgia, a genealogy of lost ideals in the nation's cultural and sociopolitical life. I have tried to capture a lived sense of the promise and "tragedy" of postcolonial Indian development, the inability to resolve contradictory self-images. In the process, I have sought to extrapolate meaning from the way doubling as a visual and narrative device in the Bombay cinema serves to reflect and deflect this conflict.

The corpus of Indian films is far too vast for any single study to tackle adequately. The number of "talkie" films produced in the Hindi language alone between the years 1931 (when the first Indian talkie was produced) and 1987 is 6,597; between 1947 and 1987 the number stands at 5,074. Since 1971, India has been leading the world in film production, and over the last decade or so, the film factories have churned out an average of 800 films a year. While the southern states of Tamil Nadu and Andhra Pradesh produce the largest number, films are made in all the major languages used in the country, many states sponsoring films in their own language. In order to handle a manageable and uniform body of work, I shall be concerned only with the corpus of Hindi language feature films produced in Bombay, traditionally one of the three major film production centers in India (Calcutta and Madras being the other two). The Hindi film alone caters to the all-India market and is understood by the majority of the Indian population (an achievement in India's polylingual society for which the Bombay film itself has claimed its fair share of credit).

Although this study spans forty years of filmmaking, the goal is not to present a chronology of events and changes within the film industry nor to "cover" as many films as possible in an effort to be exhaustive. Rather, the study provides an interpretive framework within which the Hindi cinema can be apprehended as a distinct aesthetic and cultural system. My choice of films is meant to reflect both the range and diversity of the Bombay cinema as well as its singularity. This choice is not restricted to box-office hits alone but is fairly eclectic, encompassing works of different genres and styles, popular successes and failures, works by established and esteemed directors (Bimal Roy, Raj Kapoor, Guru Dutt, Hrishikesh Mukerjee, Girish Karnad, and Shyam Benegal) as well as those by unknown and forgotten figures, products of both the "new wave" and the "formula" film. I want to trace patterns, suggest tendencies, view intimations of the Bombay film's (and, by extension, Indian culture's) "love-song to its mongrel self." [12]

On the face of it, any discussion of an *Indian* culture seems a risky undertaking at best. Given the deep divisions within Indian society, the primacy of linguistic, regional, and caste affiliations and loyalties, the idea of a common culture is often treated as meaningless or nonexistent. The violent sectarian and communal upsurge since the early 1980s, including the rise of Hindu fundamentalism, reveals the fragility of a (united, secular) India as a viable concept. While an analysis of these trends is beyond the scope of this book, the more modest aim of the present inquiry is to recuperate the idea of India as nation, not via its traditions of purity and exclusivity (past or present), but precisely by foregrounding the contaminating, masquerading, impersonating impulse at its very heart. Put dramatically, it is the story of self-love through self-hate.

But what is a "nation"? How may it be defined, beyond the familiar and commonplace uses of the term? [13] And how do we identify a "national cinema"? Further, what is the relationship between a "national-popular" culture (a positive term) and "mass culture" (generally a negative term)? Can the two be regarded separately in the age of advanced communications technology and mass media? Since questions such as these underlie the present inquiry, it is useful to mention some of the important work in these areas, to engage these overlapping debates on issues of nationalism, postcolonialism, and cultural production, issues which relate to questions of power, ideology, and representation.

The idea of the nation, we are increasingly aware, is an idea in ceaseless contestation, a point brought out in recent studies which explore the ongoing convulsions of what Marxists had called the "national question." If, as Edwin Gerow asserted, "Political or national consciousness is . . . a basic ingredient of modern life,"[14] what we are witnessing now is an array of perspectives brought to bear on nationalism as a literary and cultural phenomenon. For instance, at the end of his book *Looking Awry: An Introduction to Jacques Lacan through Popular Culture,* Yugoslav scholar Slavoj Žižek expands his analysis of popular commercial culture in the West to include his excursus on the nation. He uses the terms of Lacanian psychoanalysis to designate the nation as a "'pathological' fact."[15] Noting the "aggravation of ethnic tensions and of aggressive affirmations of ethnic particularities" in the Europe of the post-Communist era (tensions by no means restricted to Europe), he explains the "failure" of "formal democracy" by stating that the ideas of democracy and of community are fundamentally at odds. "There is in the very notion of democracy no place for the fullness of concrete human content, for the genuineness of community links: democracy *is* a formal link of abstract individuals."[16]

Žižek's linking of the "nation-thing" with notions of collective enjoyment, desire, and fantasy has, with different theoretical emphases or terminology, been a feature of other studies of the nation as a symbolic force. The most influential of these is Benedict Anderson's *Imagined Communities.* In this classic work, Anderson makes the case that the "profound emotional legitimacy" of the nation rests on its diverse signifying power, and that the concept as experienced is associated with "imagining" and "creation."[17] Yet the nation, by its very nature, is a paradoxical creation, a fact that is explored in Homi Bhabha's edited volume *Nation and Narration.* Bhabha sees the nation as an "impossible unity," wherein lies its paradox. He reiterates British historian Tom Nairn's image of the nation as a "modern Janus" in which progression and regression, rationality and irrationality, individuality and universality coexist uneasily. Bhabha wishes to explore the textual or literary constructions of nationness: what is at work is "the Janus-faced ambivalence of language itself in the construction of the Janus-faced discourse of the nation."[18] His turning of "the familiar two-faced god into a figure of prodigious doubling" reinforces the central image of my own study of the Bombay cinema, although I prefer the notion of imperso-nation with its play on acting and visual structures to the more intellectual idea of ambivalence.

While the insights of Anderson, Bhabha, and others have contributed greatly to our understanding of the nation as a discursive entity, they have to be extended in order to consider questions of a "national" cinema. For in their focus on the processes of literary language, primarily the novel, these studies do not identify the quite different production context, representational strategies, and ideological imperatives governing filmmaking in national situations. The point here is that these different factors affect our terms of analysis. One question in relation to form and content is how cinematic (as opposed to literary) elaborations are "tied to" a coherent recognizable entity called the nation-state (a political and legal entity of spatial boundedness) within which all discourses of the nation are ultimately anchored. Where does "India," a discursive space, intersect with India, a particular spot on the map? As film critic Philip Rosen puts it:

> The discussion of a national cinema assumes not only that there is a principle or principles of coherence among a large number of films; it also involves an assumption that those principles have something to do with the production and/or reception of those films within the legal borders of . . . a given nation-state. That is, the intertextual coherence is connected to a socio-political and/or socio-cultural coherence implicitly or explicitly assigned to the nation.[19]

It is this mapping of a textual coherence onto a sociopolitical coherence that needs to be foregrounded in the context of the cinema.

Let me elaborate further. It is obvious that a nation only really comes into its own when it can designate its own space. At the same time, space alone is never sufficient to signify all the complex emotions, desires, and ideologies (not to mention textual practices) which "create" the nation and grant it legitimacy. Hence it is the dialectic of nation and nation-state that is implicit in the way we apprehend nationness. Bhabha refers at least obliquely to this nexus when he writes: "The boundary is Janus-faced and the problem of outside/inside must always itself be a process of hybridity, incorporating new 'people' in relation to the body politic, generating other sites of meaning and, inevitably, in the political process, producing unmanned sites of political antagonism and unpredictable forces for political representation."[20] In short, not only do narratives of the nation have to deal with questions of internal difference and the dynamics of marginal and mainstream, but they invoke notions of citizenship and civic duty as the communal glue that holds different segments of the population together.

For the cinema, it is at once easier and harder to negotiate these boundaries. Because of the cinema's photographic base, the modalities of representation (whether of a people, a landscape, a style of life, a historical period, or whatever) become recognizable as national/cultural. On the other hand, the cinema is dependent far more than literature on the national economy, the level of industrial development of a nation-state, questions of export and import, quotas, and the like. Thus the cinema's relationship to issues of nationalism may be said to be in its own state of ambivalence. It may find itself suspended between the devil of financial investment and technological infrastructure, national and international, on the one hand, and the deep sea of representation and signification, on the other. For many Third World countries (though not for India), the epithet of a "national cinema" partly defined as it must be in terms of its financing and marketing arrangements is a contradiction in terms. Multinational consortiums and international film crews produce "national" cinemas. Here the question of boundaries takes on an entirely different meaning and hybridity is a fact of cinematic life.

And then there is the question of language. The duality of language also has its own specificity in the cinema. Film language (editing, camera placement, camera angle, mise-en-scène) is "ontologically" more uniform and international than the "babel of tongues" that constitutes the basis of literary narratives. In literature, in other words, the use of a specific language (Russian, French, Bengali) is an assertion and usually a signifier of cultural nationalism. But in the cinema, verbal language is only one aspect of "film language" as a whole. While infinitely adaptable (Japanese filmmaker Ozu's breaking of the Hollywood code provides one example among many),[21] this language is nonetheless fairly standardized, its "rules" having been set in the very early days of cinema. Particularly in the popular cinema, motivated as it is to build structures of familiarity and identification, established cinematic codes of framing and editing are widely used. (The *langue* of cinema is universalized, although the *parole* is culturally determined.) Thus it was the introduction of verbal language that in some sense became a herald of nationality. The advent of sound "national-ized" the motion pictures, and linguistic utterance remains the crucial signifier of difference and national/cultural distinctiveness in films. But it is finally in the conception of the audience that we encounter the most specific instances of what French structuralist Louis Althusser called the ideological "interpellation" of the (national) subject.[22] The popular cinema's narration of the nation includes images of the nation-state through a visual shorthand of landscape, maps, particularities of dress, and utterance used to evoke feelings of identification. Its iconographic condensation of images differs fundamentally from the more expansive rhetorical flourishes of the average work of prose fiction.

It is small wonder, then, that the history of film culture intersects with discourses of nationalism in highly volatile ways. This is particularly true of Third World film movements, which emerged under the regime of imperialism or have been held in conditions of economic and cultural dependency. During the sixties and seventies, alternative film practices were theorized by Latin American and African filmmakers who sought to explore the ideological context of their own work and its reception within their own countries. It is the power and fecundity of such theoretical and cinematic work arising out of specific national contexts that has led to the international concept of "Third Cinema." Originally identified as "Third World" cinema (itself a multinational entity), the phrase "Third Cinema" now denotes a politically conscious, oppositional cinema often (also) produced by "Third World" segments of the population within the First World.[23]

Marxist critic Fredric Jameson wrote a few years ago of the cultural production in ex-colonized countries as "national allegories," opening up the term "national" to positive meanings long absent in leftist circles.[24] Jameson's notion of allegory has been quite influential in the study of national cinemas of the non-Western world. Jameson was also one of the first scholars to recognize the utopian dimension of national commercial culture, the widespread nature of which in all modern societies makes it the primary arena of ideological struggle and therefore worthy of serious attention. As cultural critic Andrew Ross puts it, "The struggle to win popular respect and consent for authority is endlessly being waged, and most of it takes place in the realm of what we recognize as popular culture."[25] Ross's concern is with the dialectics of American popular entertainment in maintaining structures of authority at the same time that it incorporates popular perceptions, aspirations, and resentments. Ross's fine analysis in his book *No Respect: Intellectuals and Popular Culture* considers "the emotional charge of popular culture" together with its inextricable complicity with "American values" represented by American capitalism. The emphases that inform such an analysis of the national-popular inflect my own investigation of popular cinema even as it seeks to develop a differentiated theoretical and empirical account of historical dynamics.

This different history is that of colonization, the structural legacy and psychic effects of which inform national conceptions of popular and official culture. How each postcolonial nation then articulates and regulates its cultural domain varies according to its precolonial history, its "present" socioeconomic context, and its relationship to modernity. In the case of India, the popular cinema has been deeply implicated, if marginalized, in the project of decolonization. Questions of an industrial infrastructure and the economic independence it symbolizes, the struggle over (a national) language (verbal or cinematic) as the "authentic" voice of the people, the desire to control one's own image making: all these impulses coalesce in the cinema more than in earlier nontechnological means of expression. In a poor country like India, where technology is both desired as a symbol of progress and feared as an alien imposition, and where the cinema has no organic connection with indigenous cultural traditions, one cannot help but see films as implicated in nationalist concerns over economic and cultural self-sufficiency. This is complicated in India's case by its ancient, rich, and diverse cultural forms and its postcolonial concerns to revive and encourage them. The cinema's urban base and commercial raison d'être have added to its image of being less than representative of India in either a demographic or an ethicospiritual sense. Nevertheless, the fact that early on Indians revealed a passion for the movies and for moviemaking has meant that, indigenous or not, its status as (some form of) culture could not be denied. The struggle over filmic signification between India's ruling elite and the film industry has been a constant factor over the entire span of the cinema's history.

Moreover, for most Third World countries, including India, the terms of film discussion have perforce included the Hollywood cinema, the locus both of envy and resentment. Ruling elites have demanded of the local product the technical polish and narrative sophistication of Hollywood films, while struggling against American films' domination of their markets and/or the "slavish imitation" of superficial elements of style and content. A creative transformation of the dominant Hollywood codes, resulting in parody and carnival in Brazilian popular cinema or an unabashed though selective assimilation of technical codes and values in Indian films, is one of the tactics of survival adopted by beleaguered or berated film industries.

This study attempts to present a conjunctural picture of cinematic text, historical context, and national intertext along the lines indicated above. Textual analysis allows us to concentrate on the films themselves as elaborated instances of social and cinematic meanings and codes. The notion of imperso-nation as an articulating principle, both joining and expressing diverse cinematic practices, will provide the basis of the selection of films in this study. My focus will be on the visual, narrative, and self-reflexive elements in the films whereby traditions of the masquerade and transformation are either appropriated or invented to provide an ongoing discourse of national identity. The book as a whole tries to weave together various strands of this discourse as they have affected the cinematic one, which is primary for us here. Chapter 1 provides for the general reader a background account of political, social, and cultural life during different phases of Indian history as embodied in a key nationalist text from the colonial period. It also presents an account of the cinema in India as it developed in the colonial era. The rest of the book is divided into two parts, roughly corresponding to what might be called an early and a later phase in postindependence Indian history of the cinema. Part 1 is concerned with the immediate postindependence period (what is often designated as the Nehru era) and Part 2 with the period extending from the sixties to the late eighties. Because the ideas regarding the popular cinema as debased and unauthentic were widely circulated in the fifties and are still in place, Chapter 2 provides a detailed account of the struggle over cinematic meaning waged by the new Indian state and different social groups, including film industry representatives, journalists, and the lay public. The remaining chapters are concerned with film analyses organized around particular modalities of imperso-nation: in Chapters 3 through 5 these modalities take the form of realism, myth, and history; in Chapters 6 through 8 other modalities are embodied in the male action film, the "socially committed" personal film, and the genre of the courtesan film. What I try to examine are ways in which contemporary concerns find "creative utterance" in the commercial cinema, despite the widespread impression that the Bombay film is a hopelessly backward-looking, regressive, and random phenomenon.

The study of Indian cinema has scarcely begun. The sheer bulk of this cinema and contemptuous attitudes, long prevalent, regarding it have proved further deterrents to an informed analysis. But we need several frameworks for the understanding of the mechanisms of the popular cinema. For instance, we need studies of the international reach and popularity of the Bombay film in large parts of the Third World. The present work provides one way of interrogating this cinema and its on-going work of cultural elaboration. Indian cinema is too diverse, Indian culture too complex, Indian artistic traditions too varied and eclectic for any one study to encompass their whole range. But beginnings are and have to be made. My contention is that we must understand the generic workings of the Bombay cinema before we can make any strident calls for change. For, as Ashis Nandy points out, it is the "commercial cinema [that] wittingly or unwittingly, taps the fears, anxieties and felt pressures of deculturation latent among those who are living in the peripheries on the edge of survival. As a consequence most criticism of commercial cinema coming from the urban middle class only increases its appeal among its defiant clientele."[26] An understanding of the lived history of contemporary India may well hinge on the way we interpret (or fail to interpret) the power of Bombay popular cinema.

In India, the search for elusive truth among the contending narratives of national identity is a story at once hoary, young, haggard, and terrifyingly fresh.
—Barbara Stoler Miller, "Presidential Address"

The major audience for a normal Hindi commercial film is people who are in the middle or lower-middle-income groups. But more important than them are the people who live below the poverty line. It's very strange, but most of the people who do odd jobs, or even beggars, will keep their money to see the first show of the new releases. In fact I played a character like that. She was a rag-picker, and whatever money she got from selling rags she would stuff in her blouse, so that she didn't have to give it to her father or mother. She would then use that money to see the first show of the first week of an Amitabh Bachchan film. It really happens; it's not a far-fetched imaginary fantasy or some funny incident. It's the truth.
—Smita Patil, Bombay film actress (deceased)

Culture/Nation

Reclaiming the Past

In 1944, while in prison for his role in the independence struggle, Jawaharlal Nehru, later India's first prime minister, wrote his monumental work *The Discovery of India*. This essentially cinematic book, which was recently serialized in fifty parts for *Doordarshan*, the state-owned national television network, presents a panoramic view of Indian history in order to "delve deep into the sources of India's national personality," according to Nehru's daughter, Indira Gandhi. The journey motif, with its promise of arrival and destination, the enigma there to be resolved, the central consciousness of the narrator who is familiar, beloved, and hence an object of identification, the lush physical and emotional landscape of India, and, above all, the element of conflict symbolized by a succession of colonizations all serve to convey a dynamic and moving narrative. An epistemological quest, *The Discovery* seeks to reclaim India's past for its readers, at the same time providing them with a common past. Nehru tries to extract from roughly six thousand years of recorded Indian history a distilled essence of "national" character, blending political, racial, cultural, and philosophical strains in that history into one composite whole. Addressing the general reader rather than the specialist, this remarkable book of nearly six hundred pages (in which, unfortunately, there is not a single reference to film) is a classic "colonial" text in its mixture of national pride and humiliation, its mythologizing of the motherland and its project of historiographic revisionism. Since all history is contemporary history, Nehru's effort must also be seen as an attempt, in the face of increasing Muslim demands for a separate nation-state, to rally the forces of historical evidence against those demands.

At the heart of *The Discovery* is a paradox: to construct an identity (selfsameness) out of an entity which, being the product of constant historical change, must also be established as having no stable identity. The "national personality," in other words, has no personality; rather, what is distinct about that personality is the fact that it is an accretion over centuries and millennia and is in ceaseless mutation. Like the Hindu gods, most of whom embody several personae, Indians jostle within themselves a number of identities—of region, language, religion, race. For specific groups of Indians one or another of these factors may be, to extend Althusser's phrase, the "structure in dominance." In this context it would be appropriate to give a very recent reaffirmation of "nonidentity" by an intellectual whose views no doubt echo those of many other Indian intellectuals. Distinguished cultural theorist Gayatri Chakravorty Spivak recently said in an interview:

"India," for people like me, is not really a place with which they can form a national identity because it has always been an artificial construct. "India" is a bit like saying Europe. . . . And "Indian-ness" is not a thing that exists. Reading Sanskrit scriptures, for example—I can't call that Indian, because after all, India is not just Hindu. That "Indic" stuff is not India. The name India was given by Alexander the Great by mistake. The name Hindustan was given by the Islamic conquerors. The name Bharat, which is on the passport, is in fact a name that hardly anyone uses, which commemorates a mythic king. So it isn't a place that we Indians can think of as anything.[1]

We are back to E. M. Forster's Marabar Caves, where "India" only sends back an echo. Spivak is, of course, right to caution us against any easy identification of all who live in the Indian nation-state as "Indian" (taken as an essentialism). She is also correct in emphasizing the historicity of all concepts and the dangers of perpetuating colonialist definitions of India which have been responsible for romanticization on the one hand and "divide and rule" policies on the other. Nevertheless, to treat "India" as a blank is to undercut her own attempt at historicizing the phenomenon and to concede power to colonialist imagery, which can "construct" and "erase" India at will. Moreover, it is to deny precisely the historical formation of India's very differentiated demographic composition, the fact that for so many Indians language (or mother tongue) is not coincident with area of residence and for whom, therefore, being Indian is the most approximate self-description. Nationness, as so many theorists have been busy pointing out, is not just a matter of bureaucratic state control or ideological imposition (although it is often that) but also a question of emotional or intellectual affiliation, an attempt to override difference in the name of difference. Nor does regionalism in the case of India dissolve the question of a national identity, as Spivak would have it. "If an Indian asks me what I am, I'm a Bengali, which is very different."[2] To what extent such constructions are viable or a matter of choice is always a historically determined, situationally circumscribed phenomenon.

The region/nation dialectic interacts in complex ways with the culture/nation dialectic in Indian thought and politics. Indian nationalist leaders like Gandhi and Nehru conducting a war of independence, as well as nineteenth-century poets, saints, and social reformers trying to unify the country prior to that effort, attacked separatist identities and argued for what might be called a "boundaryless" conception of identity, a pan-Indian consciousness. While not denying the importance of regional affiliations, they stressed nationalism as appropriate to the needs of the moment. Spivak's view above may therefore be juxtaposed to that of another distinguished Bengali, internationally renowned filmmaker Satyajit Ray. A veritable product of "internationalism" (what film critic Chidananda Dasgupta has termed the "Tagore-Nehru synthesis"), Ray attributes his strengths to the fact of having his "feet planted firmly in both cultures [Eastern and Western]." Yet he has also said in a self-reflexive vein:

> More and more over the last ten years I have been going back and back to the history of my country, my people, my past, my culture. . . . This is Indian tradition. It's very, very important. The presence of the essential thing in a very small detail, which you must catch in order to express the larger things; and this is in Indian art, this is in Rajput miniatures, this is in Ajanta, this is in Ellora, this is in the classics, in Kalidasa, in *Śakuntalā*, in folk-poetry, in folk-singing. This is the essence, I think.[3]

Yet Ray was also the most regional of filmmakers, reluctant to venture out of his native Bengal to make films in other languages, thus highlighting the national/regional dialectic in some instances, downplaying it in others. Nor can we hastily conclude that Ray is referring exclusively to a Hindu tradition, for it is important to remind ourselves of the inextricability of any exclusively Hindu or Muslim artistic strand in Indian art, as art historians have pointed out. Hugo Munsterberg, for instance, notes the close relationship and interdependence between the Rajput and Mughal schools of painting, "for many of the finest Mughal paintings were executed by Hindu artists working at the Islamic courts, while outstanding Islamic artists found employment at the courts of the Hindu rulers after Delhi had ceased to be a great artistic center."[4] Can the discourse of Indian national unity be seen, alternatively, in class terms, as the mind-set of the "modern" upper-class intellectual, of little concern to the bulk of the population? While systematic research would have to be carried out in order for us to be able to answer this question, the point to note here is the attempt on the part of the elite to create bonds of understanding and empathy with a larger national, that is, common, historically shared culture. Thus Ray's statement can be seen as encapsulating in a few words the cultural-national project of Nehru's *The Discovery of India*.[5]

If, as Raymond Williams held, culture is a way of life, Nehru conceives Indian history as the way of life of the people of the subcontinent of India. *The Discovery* seeks to write a popular history of India, going back to the beginnings of known culture and civilization, although inevitably a process of selection takes place governed by a dominant theme. That theme, the oneness and unity of India and its people brought about through the absorption of diversity, finds its corollary in the national/international dynamic. India is most truly national, Nehru asserts, when it is international. India's "downfall" and conquest and slavery came at those periods during its history (conquest by white Huns in the eighth century, by the British in the sixteenth) when the people became "inward-looking" and stopped absorbing new influences. India's destiny, Nehru seems to tell us, lies in change and transformation.

A recounting of Indian history is necessary before we can turn to the more specific history of filmmaking in India and its relationship to national identity. If I have chosen to present this history through Nehru's vision rather than through more specialized history texts or folk forms, it is to refer to the particular place that Nehru held as a national-popular figure rather than to suggest a substitution of Nehru's voice for that of the common people of India (to which unmediated access is in any case not available). Nehru's upper-middle-class background and elite status are not under question here; what his text undertakes, however, is a hegemonic project of appeal to all sections of India's population, primarily Hindus and Muslims, to form one nation and not two. This is the obvious subtext of *The Discovery*. For our purposes, the book serves as a reflection of an epochal nationalist consciousness. (It also enables me to cover, for the non-Indian reader, centuries of Indian history in a relatively straightforward and unfortunately schematic manner.)

The Discovery is conceived in the mode of a grand narrative, leaning on the writings of Orientalist scholars of the Max Müller school of romantic-mystical historiography. Nehru culls from these texts as much evidence as he can of the "spirit" of continuity in Indian history. At one point he observes, "We have been changing continually throughout the ages and at no period were we the same as in the preceding one. Today, racially and culturally, we are very different. . . . Yet I cannot get over the fact that Indian and Chinese civilizations have shown an extraordinary staying power and adaptability and, in spite of many changes and crises, have succeeded, for an enormous span of years, in preserving their basic identity" (*DI*, 144). Unlike the ruptures with the ancient past that characterize the Greek, Egyptian, and Mesopotamian civilizations, India is in touch with its past. In fact, Nehru presents an anthropomorphic India, another Orientalist echo, speaking of the culture's youth, maturity, and old age, the tiredness of the spirit as it submits to British colonialism. However, he implies that with independence will come a new birth, a new life.

From Pre-Aryan Times to the Mughals

Tariq Ali, in his biography of the Nehru dynasty, tells us how the discovery of the ancient archaeological sites of Mohenjo-daro and Harappa in the northwest during the 1920s excited Nehru because India could now claim a pre-Aryan civilization which was far superior to what the Aryans had introduced.[6] Known as the Indus Valley civilization from the third millennium B.C., it was a highly sophisticated urban culture, particularly remarkable for its well-planned streets and houses with modern amenities. Nehru comments that "there is always an underlying sense of continuity, of an unbroken chain which joins modern India to the far distant period of six or seven thousand years ago when the Indus Valley civilization probably began." He adds that much in Mohenjo-daro and Harappa reminds one of "persisting traditions and habits—popular ritual, craftsmanship, even some fashions in dress" (DI, 72).

About a thousand years after the Indus Valley period the Aryan migrations to India from the northwest began. The Aryans were nomadic tribes from Central Asia who came in successive waves and became absorbed in India. "We might say," writes Nehru, "that the first great cultural synthesis and fusion took place between the incoming Aryans and the Dravidians, who were probably the representatives of the Indus Valley civilization" (DI, 73). He adds that out of this synthesis and fusion grew the Indian races and the basic Indian culture, which had distinctive elements of both. In the following ages many other races came to India: Iranians, Greeks, Parthians, Bactrians, Scythians, Huns, Turks (before Islam), early Christians, Jews, Zoroastrians; "they came, made a difference, and were absorbed. India was . . . 'infinitely absorbent like the ocean'" (DI, 73). Some pages later he quotes Max Müller's statement that "there is, in fact, an unbroken continuity between the most modern and the most ancient phases of Hindu thought, extending over more than three thousand years" (DI, 89).

Nehru provides a gloss on the words "Hindu" and "Hinduism," dissociating them from their commonly held association with religion and tracing their descriptive nature:

The word "Hindu" does not occur at all in our ancient literature. The first reference to it in an Indian book is, I am told, in a *Tantrik* work of the eighth century A.C. [*sic*], where "Hindu" means a people and not the followers of a particular religion. But it is clear that the word is a very old one, as it occurs in the Avesta and in old Persian. It was used then and for a thousand years or more later by the peoples of western and central Asia for India, or rather for the people living on the other side of the Indus river. The word is clearly derived from Sindhu, the old, as well as the present, Indian name for the Indus. From this Sindhu came the words Hindu and Hindustan, as well as Indus and India. (*DI*, 74)

Here Nehru's association of India with the imagery of oceans and rivers (an association that is endemic in Indian thought) substitutes a pantheism for religious-cultural terminology. While he later defines India in terms of its people, it is important to note how the attitude to India's past displayed by the "good" Europeans affected the thinking of progressive Indians. Nehru seems aware of the pitfalls of Indic celebration, however. Trying to broach the subject of Indian spirituality and charges of India's otherworldliness, he writes that "every civilization and every people exhibit these parallel streams of an external life and an internal life. Where they meet and keep close to each other, there is equilibrium and stability. When they diverge conflict arises and the crises that torture the mind and spirit" (*DI*, 81). But he also cautions, "A country under foreign domination seeks escape from the present in dreams of a vanished age, and finds consolation in visions of past greatness. That is a foolish and dangerous pastime" (*DI*, 81).

National pride certainly informs the mention of thriving foreign trade and an advanced level of education: Pāṇini's grammar of the Sanskrit language written in the sixth or seventh century B.C., Charak's book on medicine, Sushruta's on surgery, the discovery of the zero sign, the famous university at Taxila in the northwest all attest to a high level of intellectual and cultural attainment. During the Maurya (321 to 232 B.C.) and the Gupta (fourth to sixth centuries A.D.) empires, the whole of India was unified and prosperous. From the seventh century onwards, despite successive invasions from Central Asia, there were periods of stability and national unity. Nehru writes that "the notion that the Pax Britannica brought peace and order for the first time to India is one of the most extraordinary of delusions. It is true that when British rule was established in India the country was at her lowest ebb and there was a break-up of the political and economic structure. That indeed was one of the reasons why that rule was established" (*DI*, 141).

Regarding the Muslim invasions from about A.D. 1000 Nehru writes, "So far, for over 300 years, Islam had come peacefully as a religion and taken its place among the many religions of India without trouble or conflict. The new approach produced powerful psychological reactions among the people and filled them with bitterness" (*DI*, 236). But the Delhi Sultanate (1206–1526) and later Babar, the first of the Great Mughals, paved the way for further Indian unification, particularly under Akbar. The process of synthesis and cultural amalgamation continued during India's medieval period, as Nehru remarks that "the record of the Indo-Afghan, Turkish and Moghul rulers, apart from some brief puritanical periods, is one of definite encouragement of Indian culture, occasionally with variations and additions to it. Indian music was adopted as a whole and with enthusiasm by the Moslem courts and the nobility and some of its greatest masters have been Moslems. Literature and poetry were also encouraged and among the noted poets in Hindi are Moslems" (*DI*, 161). It is obvious that questions of power and conflict between the Hindus and the ruling Muslims are in general written out of the script in order to foreground the notions of synthesis and unity. Thus Nehru decides not to deal with the "communal question." Indeed, it is in presenting the long Muslim interlude that led up to the arrival of the British that Nehru the historian has to confront Nehru the mythologist and nationalist. Because it is his purpose to contrast the attitude of the Mughals to the subject population with that of the Europeans, Nehru's account posits the advent of the Muslims as one more chapter in India's long history. Specificity is sacrificed to preserve the idiom of historical continuity. And so Nehru is unable or unwilling to present a historically informed analysis that could explain the roots of the division that was threatening to break the social fabric apart in the mid-forties. Nehru chose to project Hindu-Muslim differences as a domestic quarrel which would have to be set aside for the larger purpose of turning back the common enemy: British imperialism. He contrasts the Mughals' absorption in Indian social and cultural life with the disruptive effects of the British conquest. "The British remained outsiders, aliens and misfits in India, and made no attempt to be otherwise. Above all, for the first time in India's history, her political control was exercised from outside and her economy was centered in a distant place. They made India a typical colony of the modern age, a subject country for the first time in her long history" (*DI*, 239).

Modern India: British Colonialism

The record of British rule in India emerges as one of unmitigated horror in the pages of *The Discovery*. To those readers whose knowledge of Indian history has been shaped by recent mass cultural products celebrating the "Raj revival," films such as *A Passage to India* and *Gandhi* and Granada Television's *Jewel in the Crown*, Nehru's account provides a much-needed insight into the realities of the British "colonial mission" and its naked exploitation. Europeans (the Portuguese, the Dutch, the French, and the British) made their way to India and established settlements from the end of the fifteenth century. The British East India Company was founded in 1600 by royal charter under Queen Elizabeth I to gain access to the Eastern spice trade. Soon the British succeeded in getting permission to start factories, and Madras was founded in 1639. "For over 100 years no one in India attached any importance to the British." As the Mughal empire was weakening, the British made an organized attempt to increase their possessions in India by war. With the death of Aurungzeb, the last Mughal ruler, in 1707 and the ensuing political and economic collapse (partly the ruler's doing), many independent powers sprang up and vied for political control. More invasions occurred from the northwest, further weakening the country. In 1757, Robert Clive in Bengal won the battle of Plassey "by promoting forgery and treason," and the date marks the beginning of the British Empire in India.

Regarding the colonizers Nehru says, "The British who came to India were not political or social revolutionaries; they were conservatives representing the most reactionary social class in England, and England was in some ways one of the most conservative countries in Europe" (*DI*, 291). They encouraged and consolidated the position of the socially reactionary groups in India and opposed all those who worked for political and social change. If the introduction of the steam engine and the railway was a big step toward a change in India's medieval structure, Nehru reminds us that it was meant to facilitate the exploitation of the interior of the country for their own benefit. As the company plundered and looted in the name of trade, Bengal and other parts of the country became intensely poor, with repeated famines (from 1766 to 1770 and

1943 to 1944) wiping out significant portions of the population. "The Bengal plunder began to arrive in London, and the effect appears to have been instantaneous, for all authorities agree that the 'industrial revolution' began with the year 1770" (*DI*, 298).

To promote British industrial power, Indian goods were excluded from the British market and the Indian market opened to British manufactures. Various measures crushed Indian manufactures, leading to the collapse of the Indian textile industry and affecting vast numbers of weavers and artisans. "The classic type of modern colonial economy was built up, India becoming an agricultural colony of industrial England, supplying raw materials and providing markets for England's industrial goods" (*DI*, 299). The liquidation of the artisan class led to unemployment on a prodigious scale. Tens of millions died. The English governor-general of India, Lord Bentinck, reported in 1834 that "the misery hardly finds a parallel in the history of commerce. The bones of the cotton weavers are bleaching the plains of India" (*DI*, 299). As the remaining artisans drifted to the land, India became progressively ruralized, its balance between industry and agriculture destroyed. "This then," writes Nehru, "is the real, the fundamental cause of the appalling poverty of the Indian people, and it is of comparatively recent origin" (*DI*, 300). As the numbers of landless laborers increased, there ensued a permanent crisis in agriculture. "India was under an industrial-capitalist regime, but her economy was largely that of the pre-capitalist period, minus any of the wealth-producing elements of that pre-capitalist economy." The cost in human suffering for England's industrial development was borne by the masses in India.

Reminiscent of writers like Tom Nairn and Homi Bhabha, who have regarded nationalism as "Janus-faced," Nehru characterizes British national culture as inherently contradictory. While the England of the savage penal code and brutal behavior, of entrenched feudalism and reaction came to India, there was the "other England"—of Shakespeare and Milton, of "noble speech and writing and brave deed, of political revolution and the struggle for freedom, of science and technical progress" (*DI*, 287). The latter influenced the Indian intelligentsia, and the efforts of individual British scholars and early missionaries brought technical inventions like the printing press to the country. "English education brought a widening of the Indian horizon, an admiration for English literature and institutions, a revolt against some customs and aspects of Indian life, and a growing demand for political reform" (*DI*, 319). In general it might be said of such statements in Nehru's *Discovery* that the author is positioned as the "ideal mix" of the values of East and West, an unconscious self-projection that found wide support among the Indian liberal intelligentsia. In common parlance, it has come to be known as the "Tagore-Nehru synthesis," an ethos that governed the construction of postindependence values of humanism, rationality, and technological advancement. However, that language and institutions (particularly those of the colonizer) are not neutral vehicles of "progress" and the creative impulse but are themselves deeply implicated in the way we view the world has been the sobering conclusion of much theoretical work in the human sciences in the latter half of the twentieth century. The "epistemic violence" (Spivak) of colonialism can scarcely be undone or even apprehended through the seamless narrative of "synthesis," and the notion of politics as an art form can have, as we know, sinister underpinnings. Thus the "other England" of Nehru's vision must be seen to have revealed its own Janus face, albeit having staged the scenario of its particular historical mission (both in terms of the *Discovery* as nationalist narrative and of Indian nationhood as a political form).

For the end of the nineteenth century saw the beginnings of the end of British rule in India. Growing demands for autonomy culminated in the founding of the Indian National Congress in 1885, an umbrella organization of varied national interests who demanded more autonomy. We now have several histories of the independence movement, its different phases and facets, its players, elite and subaltern, its emphases and recuperations, and these represent all shades of the political spectrum.[7] While explanations differ, the generally agreed upon perspective, from the point of view of nationhood, may be stated as follows: during the 1920s, Gandhi emerged as the popular leader of the nationalist struggle, with the Congress a motley alliance of the Indian capitalist class, left- and right-leaning intellectuals and politicians, women, and vast numbers of ordinary people. Gandhi's strength lay precisely in being able to manage such an alliance and set independence as its goal. His tactic of nonviolent noncooperation with the colonial power eventually secured the departure of the British. India gained independence on August 15, 1947, although at the cost of the partition of the country accompanied by widespread massacres. The Muslim-dominated sections of the country became East and West Pakistan, with India occupying the central area. Despite the bloodshed and movements across the newly created borders on both sides, 45 million Muslims remained in India. This meant that India now had a significant minority population (a voting bloc), one moreover designated anew as "different," bearing the scars of the actions of their erstwhile fellow-Muslims, now Pakistanis, the members of an "enemy state." The effect of such historical complications on the subjectivity of India's Muslims can scarcely be imagined, the perceived need on the part of state and cultural institutions to "assimilate" them scarcely more acute (and deeply problematic). Is it any wonder, then, that the Bombay cinema, India's foremost cultural manifestation, has broached the subject of Muslims in a curiously self-policing way, afraid to offend and yet anxious to woo? But more on that later.

India's Postcolonial Phase

India declared itself a secular state and adopted a parliamentary form of government with a federal structure following independence. Many of the policies, national and international, that were implemented during Nehru's seventeen-year term as India's elected leader are laid out as plans in the last quarter of *The Discovery of India*. The germs of a split vision are also apparent, a split that Tariq Ali has described well in the biography cited earlier. Francine Frankel, in her book *India's Political Economy 1947–1977*, notes the "paradoxical" blend of socialist values and planning and private enterprise that formed the basis of the Indian state in accordance with the Gandhi-Nehru ideals of national growth and development. Nehru spoke of it as "a third way which takes the best from all existing systems—the Russian, the American and others—and seeks to create something suited to one's own history and philosophy."[8] A series of five-year plans introduced massive industrialization of the country under direct state supervision. Yet the more immediately felt impact may have been the strengthening of the bureaucracy and state apparatus and the growth of the moneyed classes and landed interests. Moreover, existential accounts of the period suggest that the preoccupation with industrialization as an overriding imperative often seemed to drive out all other social visions. Bombay film actor Dilip Kumar recalls telling the prime minister, "Ten years from now we'll have good roads, housing schemes, hospitals, food, buildings, etc., but no culture. We can import technology and knowhow, but we can't import culture. . . . We're not paying any attention to our literature, our education, our teachers. How much can we use Sarat Chandra Chatterjee [a nineteenth-century Bengali novelist heavily drawn upon by Indian filmmakers]?"[9]

And actor-director Vijay Anand, who started his career in the early fifties, asserts, "This country never developed a village in the last thirty-five years. A young villager is driven to the glamor of the city. After the sun goes down, villages die." [10]

If the policies of India's early postcolonial phase were inadequate, the foundations of a capitalist democracy had nevertheless been laid. Indian Marxist historian Bipan Chandra notes that Nehru's government evolved policies for independent economic development, introduced a democratic constitution, fought for secularism and national unity, and yielded to popular pressures and mass movements. Although its policies were seriously flawed in view of the needs of the people and cast in a bourgeois developmental perspective, the government enjoyed wide support. These factors "and perhaps the personality of Nehru gave India certain advantages vis-à-vis imperialism which were not available to the smaller countries of Africa, Asia and Latin America." [11]

The post-Nehru years (1964 to the present) have seen a dimming of the optimism of the early years of independence. While India has been politically stable and economically self-sufficient (no mean achievements), it has failed to eradicate the appalling poverty in which a large part of the population still lives. India since the seventies seems to be in a state of crisis. Demographers (and politicians) point to India's exploding population, now exceeding the 850 million mark, as responsible for swallowing up the gains of the economy; political scientists point to the failure of the British-inherited parliamentary system to sustain order amidst increasing corruption; writers and artists point to Westernization, the clash of modernity and tradition, and a collapse of a moral sense; sociologists point to caste, linguistic, and communal hatreds and passions. A detailed account of these years and the social, political, and economic changes that have taken place is beyond the purview of this book; what I shall attempt to do instead is to indicate briefly the notion of contemporary India that emerges from certain forms of discourse in which, *discursively*, a centrifugal impulse has replaced a centripetal one.

One might point first to the language of contradiction used by scholars to denote India's postindependence scene. Political anthropologist Akhil Gupta writes of "an intriguing mix of conditions," [12] Lloyd Rudolph and Susanne Rudolph call India the "weak-strong state," [13] and Barbara Stoller Miller recounts an ancient folktale to try to make sense of a contemporary Hindu-Muslim conflict, evoking the enigmas of truth/lies, truth/illusion, past/present, narrative/history. [14] "In investigating any store in the ancient, complex sphere of Indian culture," she writes, "it is not only impossible to know where to begin, it is impossible to limit the unit of narration." While scholars decide on the best way to objectively grasp the phenomenon of Indian politics and national identity, filmmakers and writers perceive most keenly the impact of socioeconomic changes on their own spheres of activity. Filmmaker Jabbar Patel, for instance, tries to project the general mood of urban Indians when he reflects, "Before 1947, people had believed that freedom would be the panacea for every ill. Even for some years after independence, they continued to dream that freedom would bring peace, communal harmony, economic and social equality, prosperity and wealth. Freedom was a romantic ideal and on this was built the classic Hindi cinema." He goes on to say that it was only in the early sixties that disillusionment and a realization of the limitations of freedom set in. "What we now see in Indian cinema or for that matter in Indian literature is the projection of this socio-economic turmoil, the confusion of ideologies and the struggle to grasp the reality of the situation." [15]

Some writers refer to the disjunction between their experiences in contemporary India and the lack of a common language (linguistic and conceptual) to communicate that experience. In a 1983 interview, Hindi novelist Nirmal Verma spoke of the "crisis" of the Hindi writer of his time. He felt that what writers like himself should really examine are "the conflicts between the essential nature of the Indian *sā:mska:ra,* or the Indian psyche, and the recurrent influences from the outside, even the influence of a tradition from which the writer felt alienated because of the processes of industrialization. In this sense I feel that Indian literature has not been able to make a very important contribution." Answering the question of why this should be so, Verma said:

I think one of the main reasons for this is that, while the changes that are happening to you and to me are very peculiar to us, the language in which these changes are being reflected is very much a part of our Western—modern—equipment that has been made so easily available to us. In India, it has become difficult to have a sort of living continuity with our tradition. We have tried to compensate for this disruption by ready-made images, concepts of personalities and human relationships, which again are not part of our inherent, innate equipment. So instead of rejuvenating and revitalizing the sources of language, which could probably give answers to the problems and tensions of the modern age, we have tried directly to relate our modern anguish or dilemmas with some of the answers or responses which were given to those dilemmas by the Western writers.

The nature of our social reality, of our social relationships are so quantitatively and fundamentally different from what exists in the West that, surely, we should have felt the challenge of evolving an entirely new form of narrative.[16]

Indian Cinema: The Beginnings

The cinema is widely considered a microcosm of the social, political, economic, and cultural life of a nation. It is the contested site where meanings are negotiated, traditions made and remade, identities affirmed or rejected. The Urdu-Hindi word for screen is *purdah*, or curtain, that which hides rather than reveals. The association with the invisible rather than the visible (which is closer to the link with photography) would seem to govern the popular Indian conception of the cinema. Built into this conception is the notion of ambiguity and transformation, for that which is invisible can only be made visible by some transformative means. But there is a further paradox: how can that which is behind a curtain be "on" the curtain at the same time? In other words, what is the nature and status of the cinematic image? To what extent do the flickering light patterns on a screen serve to *stand in* for, to suggest the absent or hidden? Curiously, in a country with a long-sustained presence of iconographic representations (of dominant Hindu origins, to be sure), the cinema has only partially been integrated into notions of an Indian visual aesthetic. Rather, the screen as duplicitous metaphor has become the ontological dilemma of the Indian cinema, affecting conceptions and discussions of this cinema since its earliest days. How else to explain the fact that India's rich traditions of masquerade, in art, literature, philosophy, and poetry, traditions it has "exported" throughout the world and appropriated by the popular cinema in conscious and unconscious ways, have evoked mostly criticism and self-criticism of/by filmmakers? The cinema, in short, has been caught in an unimaginative rhetorical universe, an either/or situation where films are said to fulfill their highest function if they are "faithful reflections of reality." The popular cinema has deeply internalized the "other" of its practice, resulting in self-denigration or self-congratulation, but seldom in self-analysis. And so with its critics. In their eyes, the entertainment film enjoys the status of an alien destroying the moral fiber of society. Dire statements of the "evil effects" of the cinema are always with us. Indian cinema, like the nation whose recent history it parallels, evokes, and personifies, has thus always been "in crisis."

As a product of British colonialism, the cinema was nurtured in a chronic state of underdevelopment. This statement might seem to be at obvious odds with empirical fact, since India has been producing more films than any other country in the world for many years. However, its growth has been haphazard and subject to random and, in general, repressive legislation (very high rates of taxation, strict and unimaginative censorship). Accounts of the early years invariably show the pioneers struggling against "heavy odds," particularly in terms of securing finance. This condition has persisted, and filmmakers themselves almost uniformly consider their own position as shaky, fear-ridden, and vulnerable. The discourse of the economy governs their self-representation and their legitimation of the motivation to "give the public what it wants." Without prestige, they, for the most part, tend to be marginal culturally; their early influence in capturing the minds and hearts of large segments of the population and their growing influence in the field of politics since the seventies make them very much part of the mainstream. It is in negotiating this dual positionality that the commercial industry shapes its identity. Both its colonial history and its postcolonial development have made it secure in a kind of liminality, a rhetoric of struggle infused in the very texture of its products that capture, construct, and ultimately contain collective desires, hopes, and fears.

The Indian film industry is as old as Hollywood, with as complex a history. It is certainly no accident that the presidency towns of Bombay, Calcutta, and, soon, Madras, busy port cities active in the culture of commerce and bearing the deep imprint of British influence, should have developed into major film-producing centers. Bombay, in particular, had in the last quarter of the nineteenth century developed an industrial base, and its mixed population gave it a cosmopolitan atmosphere. Thus the influx of Western visual technologies, first photography and then film, found congenial soil and a commercially successful class which could adopt and exploit these technologies for profit. Just as Indian photographers and studios proliferated soon after the introduction of the camera in India in 1840,[17] so the arrival of the motion picture attracted a large number of businesspeople, artists, and craftspeople into film production and exhibition.

The agents of the Lumière Brothers held the first film screening on July 7, 1896, at Watson's Hotel in Bombay. The day's program started with the film *Entry of Cinematographe*, introducing the new medium, followed by other films such as *Arrival of a Train, The Sea Bath, A Demolition, Workers Leaving the Factory*, and *Ladies and Soldiers on Wheels*. Soon other shorts were introduced, as well as music, as the city's elite enthusiastically received the new medium. Purchasing cameras, Indian photographers started filming shorts which were shown in tents, playgrounds, and public halls in Bombay, Calcutta, and Madras. Among them was Harishchandra S. Bhatvadekar, known as Save Dada, who shot India's first motion picture in 1896—a wrestling match—with a Lumière movie camera. (Bhatvadekar's family made a gift of this camera to the National Film Archive of India in 1970.) Others such as Hiralal Sen of Calcutta imported shorts from foreign countries and exhibited them for *zamindar*s (landowners) and rajas in eastern India on ceremonial occasions on commission. The business proved very lucrative and led to many such concerns. In Bombay, F. B. Thanawalla, a Muslim electrical engineer, turned from exhibition to production and shot local scenes, calling it *Splendid New Views of Bombay* (1900). However, the bulk of the films exhibited were by foreign operators for whom India was the subject of exotic footage. Some titles are *Cocoanut Fair, Our Indian Empire*, and *A Panorama of Indian Scenes*.

As is to be expected, almost all the shorts made by Indians between 1897 and 1912 were of topical interest. These included *Reception Given to Senior Wrangler Mr. R. P. Paranjpe* (1902), *Great Bengal Partition Movement and Procession* (1905), *Bal Gangadhar Tilak's Visit to Calcutta and Procession* (1906), *The Terrible Hyderabad Flood* (1908), *Delhi Durbar and Coronation* (1911), and *Cotton Fire at Bombay* (1912). Meanwhile Jamshedjee Madan started the Ephinstone Bioscope Company in Calcutta and got into all sectors of the film business—production, distribution, and exhibition. He built the first cinema house in India and would later own Madan Theatres, "the gigantic empire with a big production output and a chain of theatres."[18]

The first indigenously produced feature was R. G. Torney's *Pundalik*, based on the legend of a famous Maharashtrian saint and released on May 18, 1912, at the Coronation Cinematograph in Bombay. While most people credit D. G. Phalke with being the founder of the Indian cinema, film historian Firoze Rangoonwalla contends:

> It is obvious that *Pundalik* being based on a story, specially enacted for the camera by actors made up for their roles and taking up a half of the bill of fare was a feature film in every sense and has, therefore, to be acknowledged as India's first picture, preceding D. G. Phalke's *Raja Harishchandra* exactly by a year. It also means that Indians saw their own first feature film earlier than the Americans, who, according to the noted film historian Arthur Knight, saw the France-made *Queen Elizabeth* as their feature film only on July 12, 1912. The only limitation of *Pundalik* was that it was shot by an English cameraman and was clubbed together with a foreign story film, whereas Phalke's effort was completely indigenous.[19]

Phalke (1870–1944), a man of many talents (artist, engraver, painter, magician, photographer), is generally acknowledged as having laid the foundations for the Indian film industry. Phalke records that his first feature, *Raja Harishchandra* (*King Harishchandra*, 1913) was inspired by the *Life of Christ*, which he saw in 1911. Thereafter began his quest for all available equipment and know-how (including three trips to Europe) associated with the new medium for his own films based on Indian mythology. Ambitious and self-taught, Phalke launched his family business of filmmaking by attending to all aspects of the craft (writing, set and costume design, photography, editing, processing, distribution, and publicity) himself. In a theme that repeats itself all too often in the Indian film industry's subsequent history, Phalke's efforts were dogged by financial difficulties and lack of adequate backing for his ventures. Nevertheless, he produced a hundred feature films, of which, unfortunately, very few have survived. What remains of the footage is striking for its experimentation, technical skill, and fine camera work. For instance, in Phalke's *Lanka Dahan* (*The Burning of Lanka*, 1917), which is a significant episode from the *Rāmayana*, the god-monkey Hanuman devastates the golden city with his ignited tail. Producer-director J. B. H. Wadia calls the film a minor masterpiece of its time, saying that the "spectacle of Hanuman's figure becoming progressively diminutive as he flew higher and higher in the clouds and the burning of the city of Lanka in table-top photography were simply awe-inspiring."[20] Phalke's films were immensely popular, with devout villagers coming to the Bombay outskirts in large numbers in their bullock carts to have a *darshan* (sight) of Lord Rama on the screen. Most films made between 1913 and 1923, including Phalke's, were mythologicals and devotionals.

What is the significance of the turn to the genre of the mythological as a form of inscription of Indian cinema onto the map of world cinema— a genre, moreover, that is "feminized" (appealing mostly to women)? In what ways do the discourses of developed colonialism and nascent capitalism criss-cross the subjectivity of the folk artist that Phalke undoubtedly saw himself as? How does the spectacle of myth (the Indian past) upstage or displace history (the colonized present)? And what might be some orienting principles to keep in mind as we turn to the beginnings of Indian cinema that have come down to us filtered in the form of the "great men" approach to history? Can we detect, at the inception of the cinema itself, those signs of self-alienation that are at once the mark of and a conscious grappling with the internal and external structures of colonialism? It is tempting to believe that this is indeed the case. Phalke's writings are replete with the awareness of the simultaneous centrifugal and centripetal tendencies within the structure of feeling of the folk artist in the age of mechanical reproduction. Self-promoting to the point of immodesty, Phalke would yet seem to be stressing his individuality as manifest destiny *for the sake of* the social collectivity, the emergent Indian nation. An inveterate entrepreneur, he nevertheless distanced money as good object as a conscientious Brahmin would be expected to do. A technological wizard, he nevertheless saw himself as a folk figure, the traditional storyteller called upon to bring alive for his audiences familiar myths and legends. The visual medium of cinema becomes a mere instrument, just as Phalke saw himself as a divinely ordained vehicle, for the transmission of images and meanings already present in the culture and familiar to the people. But it is above all in negotiating an alternative "feminized" space carved out of the dominant semantic universe of Western technology as colonial imposition that Phalke accommodates and extends the mechanical power of the cinema to duplicate itself. If colonialism had succeeded in denigrating Hindu culture and the bulk of the Indian people as effeminate and weak, Phalke's privileging of the mythological as a completely indigenous form of signification that returns meaning to the feminine realm may be taken as a bold decolonizing gesture. In a spirit of "raiding" that has become a venerable tradition in the Bombay film industry, this "father figure" (who ascribed his tenacity and his business success to his wife, his "divine spirit" and "comforting angel") made of the cinema a transgressive medium representative of a new folk persona.

Phalke's writings provide interesting glimpses of his early success and the conditions of the fledgling Indian film industry.[21] "These films [*Raja Harishchandra, Mohini Bhasmasur* and *Savitri Satyavan*] whose single copy could bring an income worthy of a millionaire were produced only in eight months and that also with hand-driven machines, without a proper studio and by technicians who were so new and inexperienced that they were ignorant even of the spelling of the word 'cinema.'" Phalke's technical skills were praised in the London film magazine *Bioscope*, which noted, "Since one of the greatest and most valuable possibilities of the cinematography is the circulation throughout the world of plays dealing with national life and characteristics, acted by native players amidst local scenes, it is with no small interest that one awaits the appearance in this country of Mr. D. G. Phalke."

Journalistic evidence from the period also shows the importance attached to Phalke's work as a cultural-nationalist vehicle. One Marathi-language newspaper, *Kesari*, quotes a Mr. Donald saying that "Europeans have hardly any chance to see such instructive plays and films on Hindu mythology. It is not possible to acquire this knowledge through books as the Europeans do not know the Sanskrit language. Hence the work of Mr. Phalke is valuable to the Europeans." Phalke himself had been motivated to make films after seeing foreign efforts and thinking, "Could we, the sons of India, ever be able to see Indian images on the screen?" However, Phalke's writings also suggest the lack of empathy for his vision of an indigenous industry on the part of nationalist leaders. *Navyug*, another Marathi-language magazine, wrote in 1917, "When a rare person is born who tries to start a new industry we see how badly he is treated by his fellow countrymen and how the so-called leaders mislead the people." The outbreak of the First World War nearly destroyed Phalke's painstakingly built up enterprise as all loans and working capital were refused him. "Was it due to the righteousness of my food or unfailing perseverance or just plain good luck for India—a country which claimed fitness for Home Rule, that my employees who were looked down upon as mere outcast entertainers, girded up their loins and offered to work without salary from January, 1917," he writes. Phalke was also perhaps the first to link the Indian film industry to Indian politics and statehood. "But if this institution, which was founded in the expectation of support from my fellow citizens, is to perish due to their false promises and if due to financial incompetence this useful entertainment profession does not prosper, let us admit with regret that India is still unfit to claim Home Rule." It seems clear from Phalke's writings that he saw the cinema as a nationalist undertaking, the success or failure of which metonymically signified the state of Indian polity as a whole. Phalke was also the first of a long line of film artists in India who had to respond to the charge of the cinema's immorality. He categorically stated, "Those who are susceptible to depravity do not need cinema or theatre to mislead them. There are numerous other factors which lead to immorality." He also asserted the primary function of the cinema as being that of entertainment.

An interesting gloss on the ideas of disguise, masquerade, concealment, and tricks associated with the cinema is provided in one of Phalke's articles in *Navyug* through the metaphor of the curtain/screen. Introducing his comments on film acting through a traditional Marathi stage convention known as the "interlude," whereby the stage manager appeals to the audience to appreciate his work, Phalke devises the following exchange between his wife's persona and his own:

Wife: This curtain has created duality everywhere. There is curtain for women. There are double dealings in thoughts and conduct in case of men, in politics, patriotism, at home and outside too. In short, this curtain has helped to show one appearance from the inside and the other from the outside and also to conceal mysterious things, to cover up secrets, and to prevent them from being disclosed, and to conceal filthy sights from people's vision. Human nature is also becoming more and more skilled in concealing vile. I am fed up with all this. The more curtains you have, the greater the absence of straight dealings and innocence. . . .
Phalke: Let nobody blame this [art of] motion pictures which has firmly established itself by entertaining learned men continuously for twenty-four years.
Wife: But don't you require a screen even for your motion picture?
Phalke: No, this is your misconception. What you call a screen or curtain in cinema is the substratum which holds my visual illusion. Should a water surface be considered a curtain because it reflects? We see our reflection in the mirror—can we, therefore, call it a curtain or a screen? . . . Although the dramatic art on the screen is still

young, it has conquered the world by its charming and child-like purity of gestures.

Phalke's claims for the cinema are as much an answer to his critics as they are a plea for social acceptance of this new art form.

One further point is striking in Phalke's writings, and that concerns his emphasis on the physical appearance of actors, especially their bodies. Phalke wrote that he was approached only by "dark, ugly and emaciated persons for actors." He provides a half-humorous, half-cynical account of "ugly, lacklustre or deformed actors" who answered his advertisements to act in his films. Arguing for the connection between physical beauty and spiritual well-being, Phalke emphasizes the cinema's absolute dependence on "physical manifestation" for its appeal.[30] Perhaps Phalke meant to signify the low prestige of the cinema at this point, perhaps he betrays a caste and class prejudice, or perhaps he is reflecting on the tyranny of the visual medium. These statements are a frank if somewhat crude indication of the exigencies of filmmaking in India in the early years of this century. For competition was great, not only in Bombay but between similar enterprises in Bombay and Calcutta. In Calcutta, Madan's early shorts had been succeeded by filmed stage plays. Although after Phalke's first feature, *Raja Harishchandra*, no Indian film appears to have been produced for four years, Calcutta soon caught up with its own *Satyavadi Raja Harishchandra* (*Truthful King Harishchandra*, 1917). Other filmmakers entered the field, and by 1918 "the semblance of an industry came into being."[22]

The Studio Era

The scramble to gain a foothold in the movie business during the years following 1918 bears all the marks of capitalist development under conditions of political servitude and economic "backwardness." Many features, of course, are reminiscent of the development of Hollywood in its early years: standardization and differentiation of product, advertising, the rise of stars, the investment in technological innovations, the work of "pioneers" in advancing the language of cinema, followed by the emergence of distinct studio styles and genres. Yet there is much that is different as well. These differences arise from the social and economic conditions that grounded the practice of moviemaking in India and the prior cultural traditions on which filmmakers drew in order to appeal to a very wide public. They reveal a pattern of intranational relationships whereby specific regional centers emerge as the locus of a particular order of filmic practice. One can note the prominence of Parsees, Gujaratis, and Marwaris (Chandulal Shah, J. F. Madan, Ardeshir Irani, J. B. H. Wadia), traditionally business and internally migrant communities, in the film enterprise. But the professions (B. N. Sircar, Debaki Bose, Himansu Rai) are represented as well, and the two forces shaping urban India come together to set their stamp on the fledgling film industry.

The 1920s were a period of consolidation. Production rose from a mere 8 per year to 18 in 1920, 40 in 1921, 80 in 1925, and 172 by the end of the decade.[23] In Calcutta, *Bilet Pherat* (*England Returned*, 1921) started the romantic social comedy. In the same year, the Madans produced a social farce called *Tehmuras and Tehmuljee*. Set in a Parsee background and derived from a popular Gujarati play, the film introduced another perennial in Bombay filmmaking, an actor playing the dual role of twin brothers. J. B. H. Wadia writes: "When the Parsee Natak Mandli of Appoo Brothers had staged the play in Bombay at Victoria Theatre, the producers resorted to an ingenious interlude. They projected a film sequence on the legitimate stage in which both the characters were shown together in camera frames by means of what is known in the film trade as 'masked shots.' This was the first time, at least in Bombay, that the stage and the film had combined to provide entertainment to the audience."[24] Other firsts included *Noor Jehan* (*Light of the World*, 1923), the first historical film of the Mughal era to be a box-office success, and *Light of Asia* (1926), the first Indo-German co-production. The Imperial Film Company produced the first Indian talkie, *Alam Ara* (1931).

Prabhat Film Company, formed in 1929 by V. Shantaram, proved to be one of the majors and is known for such films as *Sant Tukaram* (*Saint Tukaram*, 1936), *Amrit Manthan* (*The Divine Churning*, 1934), and the wartime effort celebrating Indian pacifism and neighborliness, *Dr. Kotnis ki Amar Kahani* (*The Journey of Dr. Kotnis*, 1946). In 1930, the second of the three major studios was established—New Theatres of Calcutta, founded by Birendranath Sircar. From one local studio, Sircar helped create a forceful production system "with the power to retain the best talent in the country, secure the most sophisticated technology and above all to determine exactly what films its vast public should see."[25]

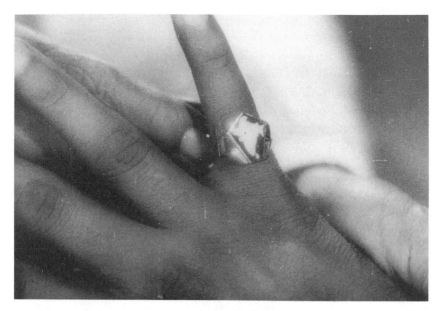

The nation as iconic sign in Dr. Kotnis ki Amar Kahani
(The Journey of Dr. Kotnis).

Through *Chitra*, a slick house magazine, New Theatres made the public film-conscious, explaining its views on filmmaking, story selection, and the persona of its stars. One of New Theatres' foremost "stars" (as director and actor) was P. C. Barua, best known for directing *Devdas* (1935), based on a famous novel by Sarat Chandra Chatterjee. The story of a young man who is unable to marry his childhood sweetheart and drinks himself to death, the Devdas syndrome has become synonymous with a failed romanticism. Barua's penchant for montage, editing for dramatic purposes and memorable images, and Hamletlike personality and early death through excessive drinking make him a charged icon of cinematic "genius" in film industry accounts. Barua's sensitivity made him alive to the duplicitous nature of filmic imagery; the cinema became to him a "very shoddy world of make-beliefs." Close to his death, he is said to have lamented, "*Devdas* was in me even before I was born, I created it every moment of my life much before I put it on the screen, and yet, once it was on the screen, it was no more than a mirage, a play of light and shade and sadder still, it ceased to exist after two hours. Now it's just a myth!"[26]

New Theatres is associated with a literary-based and socially conscious cinema, adapting works of Bengali fiction for the screen. Bombay Talkies was established in 1935 as a public limited company by Himansu Rai and Devika Rani. By that year, over eighty-five producing concerns had produced films in western India. Among them were Imperial Film Company, Ranjit Movietone, Sagar Film Company, Saroj Movietone, Prakash Pictures, Paramount Film Company, Wadia Movietone, Saraswati Cinetone, and Kolhapur Cinetone.[27] The studios came to be associated with specific genres: "While the pictures of Prabhat and New Theatres were noted for their dramatic appeal, Bombay Talkies established itself with light comedies, Minerva was unsurpassed in its historicals while Prabhat and Prakash scored their triumphs with outstanding mythologicals. Devika Rani gave a new status to the Indian artiste, while Mumtaz Ali provided a new type of light and popular dances through Bombay Talkies pictures."[28] In addition, the stunt films of Wadia Movietone were very popular, as was its *The Court Dancer* (1941), which tried to present Indian dances for the benefit of international audiences.

The outbreak of the Second World War, while bringing many British government—imposed restrictions (imports of raw film and equipment, length of films), had the unexpected result of stabilizing film production. An industry figure wrote: "Economically, this period was marked by increased returns at the box-office due to the influx of the population to urban areas and inflationary conditions which prevailed during the war period. Control on production and producers gave financial prosperity to those who had a record of production before 1943, since licenses were not generally issued to new-comers. Production was marked by stability the like of which has never been known in the Industry."[29] The same writer also remarks on the effects of the war on film audiences:

> During and after the war, a larger number of the working class patronized the cinema than at any time before. Their economic conditions and standard of living improved, while the conditions of the middle class did not alter for the better. To meet the altered weightage in the patronage of the working class, the production trend also underwent a change. The need for light entertainment was increasingly felt and this was reflected in the pictures produced after the war. The new censorship policy after the Independence of the country had also much to do with a change in the production trends.[30]

These perceptions, advanced in the mid-fifties, reflect a theme that has been persistent during the postindependence years; namely, that the

Devika Rani, star of Bombay Talkies, with Ashok Kumar in Achut Kanya
(Untouchable Girl). *The Museum of Modern Art/Film Stills Archive.*

middle class were/are the patrons of "serious" cinema, and that censorship in independent India has been more restrictive than in the time of
the British.

The war economy is generally acknowledged by film historians as responsible for the demise of the Indian studio system and changes in the

production system of the cinema in India. Barnouw and Krishnaswamy provide a detailed account of these changes, the primary one being the rise of the independent producer and the investment of illicit wartime profits in films. They write, "The new producer might be a complete outsider, or a star or a director who had found a backer. Many a studio owner, renting his studio to these new producers, gradually became dependent on them—and so helped to entrench the new system and destroy the old."[31]

Cinema in the Postindependence Era

Perhaps the most astounding development in Indian popular cinema since 1947 has been its size (800 films a year on average since the early eighties). Between 1971–72 and 1980–81, the number of films made rose from 396 to 742. While production of the Bombay-centered Hindi language film has gone down (182 films in 1988) to be overtaken by films in the four major South Indian languages (Tamil, Telegu, Malayalam, and Kannada), the former still sets the standards of star appeal, genre mutations, and overall popularity. Moreover, it was estimated in the early eighties that the Bombay industry commands nearly 75 percent of the Rs. 800 crore investment in films nationwide.[32] Bigger budgets and "multistarrers" cater to the ever-present need felt by Bombay filmmakers to attract a restless public. Big-budget "extravaganzas" were started with *Sholay* (*Flames*, 1975), to be followed by "blockbusters" like *Naseeb* (*Destiny*, 1981) and *Kranti* (*Revolution*, 1981), but by the mid-eighties the trend had waned and the star system seemed on its way out. The video cassette industry and television have made substantial inroads into the movie-going habits of Indians, along with other forms of popular culture such as *ghazal* singing and rock music.

The role of the national and state governments to promote an "art" cinema (discussed later in this book) meant that by the 1980s an infrastructure outside the dominant industry was in place. The Indian Film and Television Institute in Pune started functioning in 1960–61 to train people in all branches of film and television production, the Film Archive was set up in 1964 to construct India's film heritage, and the Film Finance Corporation (FFC) was instituted in 1960 to provide loans for low-budget films. Later the FFC merged with the Indian Motion Picture Export Corporation to become the National Film Development Corporation (NFDC), also incorporating the Directorate of Film Festivals responsible for the publicity of Indian cinema abroad. State governments, particularly in Kerala and Karnataka, have built theaters and film studios to encourage their own regional filmmaking practices.

Thus it is possible for journalists and critics to adopt either a very pessimistic tone (in relation to the "commercial mayhem" of the Bombay industry) or a guardedly optimistic tone (in relation to the "art" cinema) when commenting on the Indian film scene. In the early eighties, for instance, one commentator spoke of a "double life" and a "growing schizophrenia" pertaining to the film enterprise, including production and consumption. On the one hand, it stated, "rank commercialism has hit an all-time high with investment and production costs soaring, egomania and narcissism of the star system rocketing, and producers and distributors tightening their stranglehold on cinema networks. And on the other hand there is more scope for serious new directors to make a movie and get it shown than there was 10 years ago."[33]

But, looking back over Indian film history, one finds that the *rhetoric* of change has been a constant in describing the industry and the film business by insiders and outsiders alike. Ultimately, we ask, how explanatory is this rhetoric in terms of a broader understanding of film as a form of signification in contemporary India? True, statistical figures and on-the-scene accounts provide a sense of the parameters within which the movie business operates, but they still reveal little of the *relationship* between films and their viewers, or the notion of films as a cultural (not just an economic) system. The private industry/government-supported cinema or entertainment/art cinema dichotomies also foreground institutional structures or value judgments that can be limiting within a wider framework of understanding. For "change," after all, is a mediating concept and has to be worked *through* particular cultural forms. Moreover, "change" is *lived* or grasped as stasis, the moment held in the flux of time long enough for us to be able to mark its features. Film history is constituted in this dialectical process of "stop and go," arrest and movement, and films themselves allow us an alternate structure that holds in tension the mutations inherent in sociocultural processes.

Films, then, can be seen as punctuating moments in the sweep of history, caught up in their own contrapuntal movements of form and theme, meaning and sensibility. I have suggested such movements through the analytic construct of imperso-nation whereby change and metamorphosis in filmic texts suggest the larger dimension of experience in contemporary India, a form of "traffic" between historical period(s) and representational system. Specific debates over form, content, and policy matters are outlined in ensuing chapters of this study as these affect considerations of the Bombay film from the fifties to the eighties. Rather than anticipate them here, I would like to turn to the analysis of a specific film, *Guide* (1965), and to treat it as a paradigmatic instance of the theme of imperso-nation as it has been, and might be, played out in Indian popular cinema. *Guide* can be taken retrospectively as the emblem of the film industry's imaginary, a specific instance at a specific point in its history when the lure of the (successful and well-produced) artifact becomes a desired self-image. Enormously popular, imbued with high production values, drawing upon literary material, having an acclaimed musical score and choreography, *Guide* represents a checklist of the Bombay cinema's "success formula," the yearned-for right combination of elements only rarely actualized and validated at the box office. For the film analyst *Guide* is the overdetermined site of the ideological, institutional, economic, and aesthetic forces that represent the nationalist substratum codified in the very theme and structure of the filmic text. A veritable generic mélange of a unique sort (romance, melodrama, tragedy, satire), *Guide* is an extended commentary on the economic and sexual politics of performance and the performative dimensions of sainthood/philosophical humanism. It captures a particular ethos of the postindependence era in India, a kind of turning point in the sixties when the moral earnestness of the years immediately following the end of colonial rule has not evaporated into the national cynicism and artistic polarizations of the seventies and eighties. The fantasy of the cinema as the agency that would transport a celebrated national artistic tradition to the wider population (artists like Balasaraswati and Uday Shankar are mentioned), would blend art and commerce, would explore the national through the international (albeit in a Hollywood/American variant) makes *Guide* both a film of historical interest and a revealing instance of a particular mode of cinematic construction. Both promoting and undercutting the lure of the spectacle, the phenomenon of stardom, the contingency of human affairs, the film pits the modern sensibility against age-old belief and prejudice, desire against disillusionment, cynicism against redemption.

Guide was made under the banner of Navketan Productions, which was established in 1950 by Dev Anand. The Anand brothers—Chetan,

Dev, and Vijay—are perhaps more representative and iconic of the Indian film industry and popular cinema than any other group with the exception of the Kapoor family and the famous RK Studios. But while Raj Kapoor tried to purvey the image of the one-man industry, the Anand brothers, particularly Dev and Vijay, have been a directing-acting team over a major span of their careers. The first Navketan production was *Afsar* (*Officer*, 1950), directed by Chetan Anand and with Dev Anand in the lead role. Another Navketan production, *Baazi* (*Wager*, 1951), launched the directorial career of Guru Dutt, one of the best-known figures of the commercial cinema. These films were followed by *Aandhian* (*Storms*, 1952), *Humsafar* (*Companion*, 1953), *Taxi Driver* (1954), *House No. 44* (1955), and *Funtoosh* (*Clown*, 1956), most of them directed by Chetan Anand. With *Nau Do Gyarah* (*Nine and Two Is Eleven*, 1957), Vijay Anand moved into film direction as well, one of his early successes being *Kala Bazaar* (*Black Market*, 1960). Their record of roughly a film every year has remained fairly constant in an industry known for its volatility.

Navketan Productions are known for their music, some of the early films featuring music by the classical exponent Ali Akbar Khan and folk music specialist S. D. Burman. *Guide* was a big-budget, international co-production, and the English version of the film was made jointly with American author Pearl S. Buck and director Ted Danielowski. It was the first of many ambitious ventures launched by Dev Anand in the seventies and eighties (although few enjoyed the success, artistic and commercial, or the inspiration of *Guide*). The Hindi version, the one released in India, was directed by Vijay Anand. Waheeda Rehman won a best actress award for her performance in the film at the Chicago Film Festival. Adapted from a novel by the well-known Indian-English writer R. K. Narayan, the Anand brothers embellish Narayan's austere and simple tale not only by turning the film into a visual treat but by making the central consciousness of a tourist guide the intersection of the economic and social cross-currents sweeping postcolonial India. The metaphor of tourism simultaneously inscribes a condition of spatial mobility of the urban Indian and India's primal positioning vis-à-vis a global economy of desire. In contemporary India, it underscores the role of the city of Udaipur in Rajasthan, where the narrative is set, as tourist site in the national and local economy. The beauty of Udaipur's palaces and lakes, hills and mountains is presented for visual consumption through tracking and long shots, fluidity of camera movement, and vividly colorful East-mancolor photography. But one can also detect in this scenic extravagance an appeal to national pride, to space as nationally because visually shared, as both emblem and eraser of difference. Similarly, the "guide" of the film's title is not only a literal guide to the tourists flocking the princely kingdom who therefore occupies a pivotal niche in the local currency, real and symbolic, but also a practical guide and moral support to the heroine and a spiritual guide to thousands of miracle-seeking villagers. The figure of the guide allows the film to register the lower-middle-class milieu suggestive of the cinema-going audience, while Udaipur evokes the rural-urban, small town—big city compositional demographics of the time. But it is the hero's internalization of his role as guide that anchors the theme of illusion, masquerade, and impersonation that is central to *Guide*'s ideational system: illusions of love and faith, fame and power, human frailty and saintliness. While mocking the delicacy of illusions, the film also grants it pathos and a certain dignity.

The opening sequence foregrounds the motifs of travel and of impersonation, of chicanery and survival that are dealt with throughout the movie. In a shot reminiscent of many other films, we see a figure emerge from the iron gate of a jailhouse. The hero, Raju (Dev Anand), is about to return to society, but as he takes a jaunty step forward, his inner thoughts interrupt him. He wonders how he will be received by his old associates after his stint in prison, a series of quick images suggesting the life he has left behind. These images present the guide as a nonsectarian, all-India figure, even a cosmopolitan one, around whom briefly gather people from all over the world (the tourists) and who therefore is the locus of a global configuration. Raju is also shown addressing different regional groups of tourists in their own languages, switching from Hindi to Gujarati to Bengali to English to Punjabi—another obvious attempt at signifying national unity. As the flashes of memory end, Raju realizes there is no going back. Reluctantly, he sets out on a different road. The next series of shots indicate the passage of time as a progressively weary Raju covers thousands of miles in what is a metaphoric passage through India (reinforced by a song on the sound track by music director S. D. Burman). Finally, tired and hungry, his shoes worn out and clothes travel-stained, Raju takes shelter in a deserted village temple, where a mendicant covers him with his ochre shawl as he lies huddled and asleep. Soon he is mistaken for a holy man, fed and lauded

Raju (Dev Anand) poses as a holy man in Guide.

by the villagers. Raju tries to protest this deification, to reveal his true
identity, but finds himself succumbing to the commitments of the new
role thrust on him. The comic-ironic vision of R. K. Narayan perhaps
comes through best in these scenes.

Structurally, the film has two segments at the start and close of the
film that contain the "swami" episodes, with a long segment in between
devoted to the romance between Raju and Rosie (Waheeda Rehman),
their life together, and their gradual estrangement. In terms of diegetic
function, this structure of present-past-present is rather typical of the
Bombay film and serves to bring all the main characters together in the
end. The extended middle segment is initiated in flashback, with Rosie
narrating the events to Raju's mother when the two meet to look for Raju
after his release from prison. It is in this section that many of the familiar
themes of the popular cinema (and of Indian culture generally) are reworked, "estranged," and explored in philosophic-aesthetic terms. The
institutions of marriage and the family, the phenomena of prostitution
and social stigma, male-female relationships and dependence, the popularity of art, the price of stardom—all these concerns flesh out the central question of identity, change, metamorphosis. Moreover, change itself becomes a matter of seduction: the audience is drawn into the

narrative through the quick pacing of events, the emotional intensity of the drama, vicarious enjoyment of luxurious settings, and certainly the star appeal of the lead actors, Dev Anand and Waheeda Rehman.

The twin consciousness of their characters, Raju and Rosie, allows us to view both the joys and the perils of a sexual partnership. Their shared identity is the source of narrative tension and holds the promise of an incipient, though unfulfilled, feminism. The story of how their fortunes get intertwined is a complicated one. Rosie is the daughter of a *deva-dasi,* or temple dancer (a profession ambivalently located between spirituality or art and carnality or prostitution). In order to "save" her from a life of social disrespect, her mother arranges her marriage with a wealthy archaeologist, Marco. Marco is the caricature of the scholar-pedant, a man who is shown to be more interested in lifeless cave statuettes than the flesh-and-blood figure of his beautiful wife. There is a suggestion that Marco is sexually impotent and a misogynist. He forbids Rosie to practice dancing, an activity he associates with her background and basic "lowly" instincts. When Raju meets Rosie and Marco when they visit Udaipur, their marriage is already soured and Rosie desperately unhappy. She tries suicide and is saved by Raju, who also encourages her to abandon self-pity and her sense of helplessness and to take up dancing as a profession. Rosie leaves Marco and moves in with Raju. His mother and the neighbors are antagonized, but Raju sticks by Rosie and is instrumental in her training as a performer. As Rosie climbs the dizzying ladder of success and stardom, she and Raju lose emotional touch with each other. Raju drinks, gambles, loses Rosie's earnings, and once forges her signature, although not in order to embezzle her money. Nevertheless, he is found out and imprisoned for two years.

The theme of Rosie's rise and Raju's fall is conveyed in epistemological terms—as a question of the knowledge of self and of each other which eludes the central characters. Both adopt different roles (Rosie the dancer even has a public persona, Nalini, while Raju switches from guide to manager-agent for Rosie) but are unable to adjust to the circumstances that go with the roles. The irony to which *Guide* points is that Rosie attains her dreams of being an acclaimed dancer but is no longer able to feel emotion, while Raju attains the good life at the cost of Rosie herself, for whom he had assumed his new role to begin with.

The last segment of the film appears more contrived as the main characters, including Raju's Muslim associate and taxi driver, all assemble in the village and are united with Raju, the would-be saint. The villagers

The fast unto death: Raju keeps faith with the villagers in Guide.

are portrayed as gullible and trusting, eager for miracles and the agency of a spiritual guru. Raju had told the villagers the story of a holy man's fast in order to bring down the rains in a severe drought. This scenario is repeated here, and Raju is taken by the local people to have made a similar vow. Unable to disappoint them, Raju begins a fast, the film focusing on the validity of faith as a concept. The question is admittedly a difficult one to tackle under any circumstances, and *Guide* poses many versions of this problematic: the role of religion in the age of rationalism, faith in miracles and holy men, the nature of the soul, the mind-body dualism. Suggestively, some of these questions are put forth by an American woman journalist, and it is difficult to overlook the association being made with Gandhi, another mahatma given to fasting. Raju's consciousness also becomes a moral battleground; as he hallucinates, his image is split into representations of the baser and the nobler aspects of himself. Ultimately, Raju conquers desire, embraces the ethic of self-sacrifice, and takes refuge in the transcendental message of the Bhagavad Gita. As the rains come down at last to wet the parched earth, Raju dies peacefully.

Such an ending is at best ambiguous. It legitimizes faith in miracles and the dependence on one man as savior. The whole phenomenon of godhood is presented at face value, conflict reduced to an internalized realm rather than explored in social or class terms. The film's lack of a political vision and its sentimental and superficial portrayal of rural India are serious shortcomings. Moreover, the deeply Hindu cast given to the idea of faith, of illusion and reality, overturns the eclectic, nonsectarian tone established earlier in the film. Raju's deification, finally, effects a spurious resolution of the condition of masquerade into which he has been drawn.

Nevertheless, *Guide* remains a crucial text in the oeuvre of the Bombay cinema for its multiple allegories. In 1984, director Vijay Anand cited *Guide* as one of the two films in his entire career on which he had not "compromised." As an allegory of the cinema and of the life of the performer in general, it both exploits and undercuts the seductive power and the fragility of roles and the expectations they arouse. As a moral fable and source of philosophical debate, the question is whether faith and belief can indeed be the foundation of a collective grasp of social experience, an effective guide to the overcoming of self-doubt and apathy. While easy solutions are to be rejected, illusion has to be taken seriously. Finally, as a national allegory, *Guide* tries to juxtapose the discourses of both modernity and tradition without glorifying the former or underestimating the latter. In its ambitious conception as an international project, its thematic thrust across the boundaries of space and time, as well as its evocation of the power of impersonation, *Guide* may well serve as the Bombay cinema's ideal-typical scenario of self-reflexive desire. As a mid-sixties creation, it is both a throwback and a way out of the era of the fifties, to which we shall now turn.

part one
The Early Years of Nationhood

The Indian cinema is still held in its foreign leading strings and is totally unrelated to any tradition in Indian culture, old or new. In actual fact, what the Indian cinema is doing is to force Indian sensibilities into alien molds. Its disruptive effect is going to be, and already is, far-reaching among the common people. It is rapidly destroying their folk culture and converting them mentally into a typical town rabble, a disgusting plebs urbana *always crying for the circus.*
—Nirad Chaudhari, *"Is India a Cultural Vacuum?"*

Film production, even in the days of peace, is like going through a state of war, so increasingly heavy are the odds.
—B. N. Sircar, *film producer*

The Film Industry and the State

The Dynamics of Cultural Legitimation

Any discussion of the cinema and national identity has to be located in a notion of political economy, for, as we are all aware, films are big business. This is an aspect that Indian filmmakers obsessively harp upon, whether they perceive themselves as belonging to the "commercial" or the "art" camp or somewhere in between. As Satyajit Ray put it, "To spin the simplest yarn on celluloid the wheels of a large-scale, fully fledged industry ha[ve] to turn."[1] This fundamental union of the economic and the cultural, of the way they shape and determine one another, has of course long been recognized by critics, but it is the relationship between the two as a specific, context-driven, and ideologically inflected phenomenon that needs to be explored in each instance of a national cinema and its particular phases. As Bordwell, Staiger, and Thompson have shown in the case of the classical Hollywood cinema, a "mode of film practice" is supported within a "mode of film production—a characteristic ensemble of economic aims, a specific division of labor, and particular ways of conceiving and executing the work of filmmaking."[2] Other American and British scholars have also undertaken institutional analyses to illustrate and theorize the "inexorable interplay of . . . signifying practices with other social, economic, and technological practices."[3] Such detailed theoretical and archival work has yet to be conducted on the dominant Indian cinema and will take several years to develop, given the lack of the habit of preservation of documents, correspondence, and film scripts on the part of most commercial filmmakers and the fact that so much business is conducted orally in film studios and offices and on film sets. However, if the existing literature on "Third World" filmmaking is any indication, the art/industry, art/commerce nexus is a prime object of consideration for critics and filmmakers alike, even if in many instances the "industry" in question is Hollywood and its export apparatus.[4]

A key player in discussions of national cinemas in non-Western countries (one that has been irrelevant to the studies of Hollywood cited above) is the postcolonial state. Questions of film policy, of finance and government subsidies, of state censorship, taxation and licensing regulations, as well as of state-instituted awards and film festivals become crucial in determining the wider role of the cinema in society.[5] In the case of Indian cinema, the questions we need to raise are: What is the process of negotiation between the Indian film industry located in the private sector and the state apparatus, symbolizing the public sector? To what extent is the film industry the ideological arm of the Indian state, which is capitalist in its structure and functioning and socialist in its aims and rhetoric? How are competing definitions of a "national/popular culture" formulated and reconciled? In what ways does the cinema as a Western technological form become, in the hands of Indian filmmakers, a process of "reworking an earlier [mythical, feudal-traditional] language into one that moved into new and post-feudal uses," to quote film scholar Ashish Rajadhyaksha?[6]

The present chapter is informed by these larger questions, although it makes no pretense of engaging them in any depth. My more immediate concern is to present the primary research material garnered from popular journalism, government reports, and trade publications on which the rudiments of a political economy of the Bombay film of the fifties might be based. This empirical exercise and institutional (as opposed to textual) focus has its usefulness in that it illustrates the model of "complex causality" that has been proposed for the popular cinema, as for all cultural practices generally. Moreover, it allows me to anticipate and ground in a contextual framework the articulations of nationhood in popular filmic texts explored in later chapters. The present account is a reconstruction of a polyphonic discourse, a participational ritual, if you will, of fractious and contending voices of the nation directed at one another without the guarantee of being heard by the aggrieving party. The expression of the dominantly material-instrumental needs and interests of representatives of the film industry, the ideological-paternal voice of the state, the "voice in the wilderness" of novelists, poets, and screenplay writers, the popular (mostly English-language) press, the mediated presence of "the public": these are the discursively constituted entities through which Indian film culture of the 1950s takes shape. The combination of political economy and "period ethnography" attempted here allows us to reflect on the processes of film production and reception at a crucial time in the nation's history.

That the state in a newly independent nation establishes itself as a major actor need hardly be emphasized. Moreover, that the state is not an abstract entity but is itself the site of struggle of competing forces and interests is also an axiom of political theory. What needs to be clarified here is the nature of the power exercised by the Indian state vis-à-vis the Bombay film industry, the ostensible and proclaimed function of the state to represent all interests equally (particularly the weaker sections of the population), not just those of the film industry, and the impact of this struggle over issues of legitimation and control on filmmaking and on the overall sphere of cultural production. Since this sphere includes practitioners in the older artforms (novelists, classical singers, and dancers), people who felt the most displaced and robbed of audiences by the dominance and widespread leisure-time appeal of the popular cinema, they emerge as the indirect addressees of the cultural debate as well as articulators of the sense of cultural crisis that seems to pervade the fifties. As a decolonizing nation, India now felt threatened from within, victimized by the very forces of modernization it had rushed to embrace. What space would traditional culture (pre-British, premodern) occupy in the new milieu? How could the tide of film mania be stemmed? How could the "excesses" of the film industry be curbed? Who were the real guardians of the "public interest"? These were some of the questions that were repeatedly raised in official circles, by citizens' groups, by artists and critics.

For its part, the film industry's (producers, distributors, and exhibitors) overriding concern with money to run its operations emerges as the dominant theme from the sources available to us. Since banks did not loan producers money, they were dependent on distributor-financiers for loans at exorbitant interest rates to finance their ventures. Therefore, not only was there internal conflict in the industry among the three major groups responsible for the economic transactions underpinning the making and marketing of a film, but the industry as a whole (now including stars, technicians, and writers) would take on the government for its perceived "stepmotherly treatment" and "callous indifference" to their "plight." The control of the state over the film industry related to regulatory functions and granting of licenses to import technological hardware like cameras and editing machinery, raw film stock, and projection and sound equipment and to construct cinema houses out of scarce building materials such as cement and steel; it also centered on the issuing of censorship certificates. Taxation, another sore topic with filmmakers, was the province of the regional governments. Thus the conflicts ranged from those of "profit sharing" between the film industry and the capitalist state, to the more ideological and nebulous issues regarding the nature of the cinema (art, commerce, or entertainment), the cinema's social role and function, and the actual content of cinematic texts.

Two Detours

I shall approach the film industry—state—nation nexus in postindependence India by way of two related but tangential points of reference. Both carry us to an earlier period and to activities that can be taken to encompass the two ideological poles of discourse within which questions of art and industry were posed in the fifties (and have been ever since). The first relates to a favored genre of filmmaking of the thirties (the stunt film); the second to the role of writers in Indian society prior to independence and subsequently, especially in the context of the growing popularity of the cinema. The stunt film might be considered "entertainment" in its most obvious form, while writing or literature is the most "serious" of undertakings. Both were severely affected by changing political and economic conditions, and both conjure up certain intellectual and aesthetic norms and models. What can they tell us about India's postindependence decade?

As an analyst of films, one finds significant the fact that certain kinds of moviemaking get eclipsed at certain periods, to be replaced by other kinds. The reasons for this are many: the demise of a studio, the shifting tastes of the public, a reigning ideology, changing technologies. The fifties in India was not only the nation-building decade but also the decade which followed the monumental changes that had hit the film industry during the Second World War years, primarily the folding of the major studios. However, it is to *official policy* that a commentator attributes the disappearance of magical elements in cinema associated most strongly with the stunt films of Wadia Movietone. In the *Silver Jubilee Souvenir*, a 1956 publication, a writer mentions that the major film genres up to 1942 were social dramas, mythologicals, historicals, and stunts, then goes on to say, "After Independence and the new censorship policy of the Government of Bombay, which did not look favourably on magic and fighting scenes, production of 'stunts' of the type popular in the silent days and the early days of the Talkie, virtually ceased."[7] Such a construction puts a particular ideological twist to the material and economic conditions that no doubt played a part in the disappearance of stunt films from India's screens.

Stunt films enjoyed their heyday in the 1930s and depicted the struggle between good and evil through the magical agency of a well-executed rescue. The stunt film had been the vehicle for "Fearless Nadia," a Bombay actress born of a Greek mother and a Welsh father who appeared in roles of male action and disguise. She was woman-masquerading-as-man whose big physique lent credibility to the stunts she performed. In the 1980s, in his own rehabilitation of the genre, film actor–director Girish Karnad wrote, "The single most memorable sound of my childhood is the clarion call of 'Hey-y-y-y-y-' as Fearless Nadia, regal on her horse, her hand raised defiantly in the air, rode down upon the bad guys. To us school kids of the mid-'40s Fearless Nadia meant courage, strength, idealism."[8]

"Fearless Nadia," the stunt queen, in Hunterwali (Girl with the Whip).

The narrative followed an unvarying pattern:

The good king was imprisoned by the scheming minister. The righteous among the subjects were tortured or locked up. The helpless princess, driven to despair, unable to find succour finally decided to act on her own and set things right. And in a moment, the large fair woman, whose discomfort seemed to arise more from the sari she was wrapped in than from the political situation, transformed herself into a masked woman, in tight black costume, who could ride, swim, fight, wrestle, fence and take a reverse jump from ground to balcony.[9]

To a people still under colonial rule, such fantasies of power and action must have provided intense psychological satisfaction, particularly since the stunts were performed by a woman. The stunt film also built upon the fascination with modern technology. Many of Nadia's stunts were performed on top of moving trains, and trains figure in the titles of many stunt films: *Toofan Mail* (1932), *Miss Frontier Mail* (1936), *Hurricane Hansa* (1937), *Toofan Express* (1938), *Flying Ranee* (1939), *Punjab Mail* (1939), *Hurricane Special* (1939), and *Son of Toofan Mail* (1947). Stunts were again revived in the sixties, primarily with the rise of actor Shammi Kapoor, and reached their apotheosis with Amitabh Bachchan movies. Stunts posit an externality of action and tend to encourage cross-over states, transforming the ordinary mortal into the heroic individual. From the point of view of this study, the postindependence retreat of the stunt film is suggestive of a kind of literalness that governs the notion of self-representation and the cultivation of an officially sanctioned self-image. The fifties' emphasis on "authenticity" and the location of action to the internal and psychological plane may account for the low esteem in which the stunt film was held.

My second detour is through the terrain of writers, their political commitments, their economic situation, and their relationship to the film industry. Here again the 1930s were a crucial decade, particularly in terms of a generation of Hindi-Urdu writers who also wrote for films. The Progressive Writers' Movement had been formed in 1936 by two men, Sajjad Zaheer and Mulk Raj Anand, and included others such as Munshi Premchand, Sadat Hasan Manto, Rajinder Singh Bedi, and Ismat Chugtai. The group espoused the formation of a literature which took as its themes the downtrodden masses of India, social reform, and anti-British sentiment. Many of these writers could not make their living through literary writing alone and turned to the film industry for more lucrative assignments (film scripts and screenplays) which then allowed them to continue writing. This situation could be expected to make them highly ambivalent toward the film business, to which they owed both their livelihood and their marginality in terms of their true vocation. Despite the shortcomings of the Progressive Writers' Movement (it identified too closely with Moscow and Stalin's dictate of socialist realism, according to Rajinder Singh Bedi),[10] these writers did have a sense of accomplishment and no animosity toward the film industry. As Bedi stated later, "The language of films conforms to Urdu more than to any other language, even Hindi. The language of films is definitely Urdu, or if you don't like by that name [sic], call it Hindustani. It is the spoken language of the majority of people of the subcontinent."[11]

The Writer and Artist in Postindependence India

In 1956 the Indian film industry celebrated the completion of twenty-five years of the talkie with festivities, a seminar the previous year sponsored by the newly constituted Sangeet Natak Academi (Academy of Dance, Drama and Music), and the publication of a volume called *Indian Talkie, 1931–56: Silver Jubilee Souvenir*. This volume, consisting of short pieces by numerous people associated with the industry in different capacities, has become a source book of information of the period. The essays became opportunities for filmland to voice its grievances against government policies, national and regional, and for different groups (producers, actors, technicians, for instance) to describe the limitations of the film production scene as a whole from their own points of view. From the few glimpses available of the status of artists and writers in the industry and the society at large, we learn that while writers were generally hired, there was insufficient use for them. Noted screenplay writer K. A. Abbas wrote:

> The Indian film producer, too, suffers from some handicap which makes him nervous in the selection of his stories. For one thing, while in other countries successful stage plays and best-selling novels can always be confidently filmed because they have already been tested on the touch-stone of popularity, in India neither the stage nor the book trade is sufficiently developed to provide the same test of public approval. The Indian producer, therefore, is tempted to take the line of least resistance by re-making or adapting or plagiarising successful films from other languages. [12]

The point of view of the writer struggling outside the film business is indicated most forcefully by Nirad Chaudhari in the pages of a nationally circulated weekly:

There is indeed a depression in India whose existence is revealed by the inrush of strong cultural winds of a new type from abroad. The strongest of these is the cinematographic cyclone. If I were asked what human activity is most widely appreciated and easily understood as cultural expression in India today, I would not have a moment's hesitation in replying, it is the cinema. It is not simply that when you speak of being a writer or artist, your visitor takes you to be somebody in the cinema industry; actually almost all literary and artistic vocations are becoming harnessed to the bandwagon of that industry to an extent that has no parallel in the West. I know from personal experience how many promising Bengali writers have survived only by attaching themselves to the cinema, when they are starving by sticking to pure literature. Even when literary persons are found to be unaffiliated to the cinema, it is mostly through failure to be grafted rather than through principle. [13]

Chaudhari soon migrated to England and remained an acerbic critic of India in the style of V. S. Naipaul.

The efforts of the national government to step in as the patron of the traditional arts may have been the natural response of the postcolonial state, but not everyone looked upon these efforts favorably. A hierarchy in the cultural sphere was inevitable, according to political scientist Donald Smith. Taking a comprehensive view of culture that includes religion, social organization, law, customs, traditions, architecture, sculpture, literature, music, and dance, Smith points out that, as a newly independent state, India had to make some very basic decisions.[14] The matter of which language was to become the official one, the question of religious education in the schools, the responsibility of restoring "the greatness of the past" by taking charge of all historical monuments and of becoming the chief patron of the arts because of the elimination of the old patrons—all were taken over by the state. Three national academies were established by the government in 1953 and 1954 in order to promote the arts and, through them, the cultural unification of the country. The Sangeet Natak Akademi (Academy of Dance, Drama, and Music), the Sahitya Akademi (National Academy of Letters), and the Lalit Kala Akademi (National Academy of Art and Architecture) encouraged the study of the various arts and under the auspices of the Ministry of Scientific Research and Cultural Affairs, established in 1958, organized exhibitions, sent delegates abroad, and instituted awards for artists. Although the three national academies and the Indian Council of Cultural Relations were set up as quasi-autonomous bodies, a certain bureaucratization of culture was inevitable, and by the end of the fifties many writers and artists were quite cynical about the official patronage of culture. Well-known novelist R. K. Narayan even berated newspapers for publishing reports of literary events only when some cabinet minister or bureaucrat branded them officially as cultural activity, "the author himself [being] of no account unless he can serve as a peg for a dignitary's speech."[15] Another writer remarked more generally on the conditions on the cultural scene:

We in this country have a peculiar way of facing a cultural challenge. We try to convince ourselves that it does not exist. We dig up our heritage and try to find in it something that corresponds to the culture that challenges our way of life. We refuse to pose for ourselves in sharp logical terms the issues raised by the conflict of cultures. We just live with the challenge in the hope that time will soften it and that it will be lost in the vast multiplicity of our civilization. This is how we responded to the challenge of Islam, and this is how we hope to digest Western culture. [16]

Government attempts to sponsor cultural activities also included elements of "folk" culture such as the dances and music of the rural areas which became part of the Republic Day celebrations in New Delhi.

The Cinema: Art, Commerce, Neither?

Official recognition of the need to revive the traditional arts and to support "high culture" did not include the cinema in either category. Here, it was felt, colonization had not had the same effects of stifling or relegating to a precarious existence its performers and producers. The government's perception was that the Indian film industry was thriving economically, the number of films produced each year had been steadily increasing, and the years of the Second World War had created a boom in terms of the money (much of it illegally acquired) flowing into film production. The industry needed policing rather than nurturing, so the thinking went in official circles. What we witness during the fifties is a scenario of struggle, primarily over profits earned through entertainment, but also in the very definition of how business was to be conducted by the industry, what the social duties were of filmmakers and their obligations to the various governmental bodies and agencies.

Perhaps it is appropriate here to describe some structural features of filmmaking during the fifties. There were three kinds of studios: producing studios, or those which produced motion pictures exclusively for themselves; producing-cum-hiring studios, or those which, in addition to utilizing the facilities themselves, hired them to other producers; and hiring studios, which were meant exclusively for renting to independent producers. In western India, the majority of studios were hiring studios, a situation brought on by the great expansion in the movie business during the war years (1941 to 1945). For a brief period, government control on the distribution of raw film stock and shortage of equipment slowed production, only to be resumed at a phenomenal pace when controls were lifted. "Undercutting in studio rent and soliciting independent producers with credit facilities, supply of raw film etc. became the order of the day." [17] One source cited the extreme competition among hiring studios, a government ban on the construction of new cinema houses that gave exhibitors a free hand, and a tax increase as contributing to the poor production conditions in the industry.[18] Producers also deplored the Factories Act, which prevented them from working in unconventional time shifts (to accommodate busy actors, for instance), particularly as the electricity was cut off in the evenings in some parts of the city and could nullify an entire day's labor by making reshooting of scenes impossible.

However, the major problem cited remained that of securing the finances needed to make a film. With bank loans unavailable (since most producers had no property to put up as collateral), the producer turned to the distributor for money advances. Since the entire country was divided into five regional distribution circuits, the producer often dealt with several distributors. Three methods were in operation: (1) the commission system; (2) the minimum guarantee system; and (3) outright purchase. The first system meant that the distributor received a percentage of the collections at the box office as commission and had nothing else to do with the film. In the second system, the most popular of the three, the producer tried to safeguard his costs by taking a minimum guarantee and sharing profits with the distributors after the latter had recovered their investment. In the third system, the producer would sell negative rights or prints to the distributors.[19] The distributor, in turn, made contracts with the exhibitor in which he received about 55 percent of the revenue at the box office in the first week, with a reduction of 5 percent each following week. Thus a horizontal chain had been established by the early fifties in which each link in the chain resented the power of the other. Several articles in the popular press testify to this internal conflict in which producers, distributors, and exhibitors complained about one another's unethical practices, producers in particular feeling harassed by both the high rates of interest (30 to 50 percent) charged by financing distributors and the high rentals charged by exhibitors. Despite the rise in film attendance, increased grosses mainly benefited the exhibitors.

The high costs of production, lack of adequate returns on investment, and an unstable financial situation led some producers to call for government regulation, even nationalization, of the film industry. One representative called for a film licensing board that would grant licenses only to those producers who had a record of producing at least three pictures in the past three years. License holders would be under the strict discipline of a trade association whose rules and bylaws for self-regulation would be approved by the government. In short, a combination of government supervision and self-regulation was sought.

The postcolonial Indian state did not see itself as a protector of the film industry, from itself or from outside forces. For the professed emphasis on the nation's economic development, and the consequent focus on large-scale industrial projects such as power plants and factories, left the nation's political leaders with very little time or interest in the problems of the film industry. For various reasons, the film industry was not integrated into the mainstream of production relations and the mainframe of nationalist planning. As a business, it did not produce an essential commodity, and as a culture industry, its products did not enhance or embody the prestige of the new nation. Nevertheless, the wide popularity of the cinema made its position somewhat exceptional, and after the "unhealthy growth" and extreme competitiveness of the war years, the repeated demands from producers in particular for some form of government intervention to regulate business practices led to the setting up of the Film Enquiry Committee in 1950. The committee had three stated aims: first, to enquire into the film industry's organization and growth and to indicate the lines for further development; second, to examine what measures should be adopted to "enable films in India to develop into an effective instrument for the promotion of national culture, education and healthy entertainment"; and finally, to look into the possibility of manufacturing raw film and film equipment within the country and to suggest standards for the import of raw film and equipment.[20]

The committee's report corroborated many of the points put forward by people both within and outside the industry. It stated that the industry had an annual attendance of 60 crores (600 million) of people, represented a capital investment of Rs. 32 crores (approximately $64 million) in fixed assets and Rs. 9 crores (approximately $18 million) in working capital, and earned a revenue of about Rs. 20 crores (approximately $40 million). However, it asserted that despite this expansion, "the Indian film industry as a whole has not yet fully achieved the 'efficient organization and businesslike management' that the Indian Cinematograph Committee found lacking in 1928. The 'statistical and other material dealing with the industry, which is so necessary for a proper understanding of the real position of the trade and the best methods for improving it' are still absent."[21]

The Masks of the "Public"

When all is said and done, it is the viewing public that becomes the final court of appeal and prosecutor's stand for filmmakers in their search for social power and financial gain. Lacking both, some producers blamed the public for the ills the industry suffered. In the first eight months of 1952, sixty out of sixty-eight releases flopped at the box office. (A movie was considered a success if it had a continuous run of one hundred days in a major theater.) A general climate of fault finding and criticism prevailed in relation to the Bombay cinema. In response, V. Shantaram, an established filmmaker and co-founder of Prabhat Studios in the 1930s, remarked acidly: "Our films reflect the lethargy and purposelessness that characterize our nation today. Like the masses in our country, the filmmakers too are groping in the darkness. . . . Every country gets the films it deserves and before people criticize the filmmakers, let them look upon their own lives and find how much of inefficiency, lethargy and corruption flourishes around them. . . . Indian film today is at the cross-roads."[22] A few years later, we have a statement from the president of the Indian Motion Picture Producers Association:

An analysis of the economic situation will reveal that these ills [the star system, escapist films, etc.] were the direct outcome of the selective processes of the untutored masses suddenly becoming powerful enough to violently assert themselves against the intelligent and discriminating middle class which has become ineffective in our social and economic fabric.

These are largely the results of the economic policies pursued under the National Plan. Of every rupee of the Plan expenditure, about six annas [three-eighths of one rupee] go to the labour sector. This is reflected in its purchasing power. For films, it accounts for about 1 per cent of the Plan expenditure, which works out at an average increase of Rs. 10 crores [approximately $20 million] per year. The Plan has ignored the normal trade channels and is worked directly under executive control. This explains the absence of middle-class influence in any sphere of national planning. Increased taxation and intensified labour welfare are necessitated under a socialistic pattern of society, which has further accentuated the difference between the middle and labour classes.[23]

Appearing in the popular film magazine *Filmfare,* which catered to the educated middle class, the producer's complaint was probably calculated to hit a raw nerve. Although widespread strikes, lockouts, and protracted labor-management disputes were to come later, the middle classes were apprehensive and uncertain, feeling squeezed between the effects of black-marketeering and business expansion on the one hand and of price rises, sales tax and house rent increases, and the like on the other.

And then there is the half-cynical, half-serious comment on "audience reaction" to films made by popular producer-director-actor Raj Kapoor, who thus describes the "ingredients" of the successful film:

> All that is necessary is to adhere to the time-proven formula. The love between the hero and heroine must be quickly established. That is imperative. Romance sets the stage at once. Then there must be a few elderly characters, fathers and mothers, uncles and aunts, whose main business is to mouth vast quantities of sententious dialogue calculated to make the public applaud. There must be plenty of melodramatic situations and appealing songs. The villain must suffer in the end, and virtue triumph. [24]

That such a formula was tried often enough is true. Yet the very small number of box-office successes proved how difficult in actual practice it was to forecast audience preferences.

The Role of Popular Journalism

Despite gloomy prognostications, the growing appeal of the movies to the urban population, the huge number of people employed (close to 100,000) in the film industry, and rising production all belie the impression of an industry in deep trouble. Moreover, subsidiary industries fed off the cinema, circulating images of screen idols, screen classics, and a screen mythology. Of these, the role of the press in legitimating and promoting the status of the cinema was (and has traditionally been in modern societies) the most important. Since the 1930s, when the film industry formed various associations to represent itself (the Motion Picture Society of India was formed in 1932, the Bengal Motion Picture Association was established in Calcutta in 1936, the Indian Motion Picture Producers Association was formed in Bombay in 1937), trade publications, fan magazines, and film periodicals had come into existence.

They also had a high mortality rate, like production companies. However, with the launching of *Filmfare* in 1952 by the important Bombay-based newspaper company the *Times of India*, a new note was introduced in cinema coverage. As an English-language film magazine with a pan-Indian readership, it offered a challenge to the other major magazine in English, *Film India*, whose editor, Baburao Patel, used the magazine quite overtly as an organ for his politically partisan views. Although in its early days *Filmfare* carried, among other kinds of commentary, "exposés" of the condition of film extras, who were underpaid and exploited by unscrupulous producers and "suppliers," soon the focus shifted to glamor and the dominant figures of the industry.

Indeed, *Filmfare* strove for a sophisticated image, and its "serious" tone tried to lend prestige to the cinema by covering a broad spectrum of topics of interest to educated readers. In addition to carrying the usual news items of new releases and projects in filmland and attractive pictures of the stars and their activities, there were articles on the art of the various branches of filmmaking by practitioners and critics, Indian as well as foreign. There were frequent accounts of the growth of the German or Japanese or Italian cinemas, often by visiting representatives of those countries. Moreover, readers and filmgoers were invited to be actively involved through opinion columns, essay competitions, and the selection of awards for various categories of filmmaking. In 1953 *Filmfare* held an essay contest on the topic "My favorite actress and why" and received 334 entries (considered a fair response in view of the fact that questionnaires invariably go unanswered in India). The editorial claimed that all the essay entries were good. The rationale for the contest is revealing: "The purpose of the competition was not to discover the best or even the most popular actress. It was to induce filmgoers to name their choice and to support it with apt phrase and convincing argument."[25] The readers were also invited to submit their nominations for the various prize-winning categories when in 1953 the magazine instituted the annual *Filmfare* awards, along the lines of the Academy Awards of Hollywood. The aim was to declare that the awards indicated audience preferences and not those of the representatives of the industry or members of journalistic/critical circles. Respondents to *Filmfare*'s call for nominations for these awards voted for *Do Bigha Zamin* (*Two Acres of Land*) as the best film of 1953, and since it was also the film that had won international honors that year, the editors concluded happily that Indian film buffs had cultivated tastes.

The role of film stars as cultural figures also served to legitimize the cinema. Stars set the standards in fashion but also projected themselves as models of hard work and dedication to their profession. Indian film stars built upon what film scholar John Ellis has called "the oscillation between the ordinariness and the extraordinariness of the star."[26] Indian film stars projected themselves as average people capable, at the same time, of taking great risks for their profession. They also combined within themselves the personal and the public. The stars served as cultural ambassadors to foreign countries, and visits to the Soviet Union, the United States, Japan, and Ceylon, all at the invitation of the respective governments, are described. Nargis, one of the foremost stars of the era, on returning from a trip to the United States and the Soviet Union, said that between the two antagonistic First and Second Worlds was a "third world," the world of films and film people who worked for the peace and happiness of all. Nargis and many others took their role as national icons very seriously and tried to hold up to the public images of service and sacrifice. The days when the movies signified a disreputable profession in the popular imagination were apparently over. During the fifties, many people entering (or already in) the film business had college degrees, came from well-to-do families, and aspired to artistic and technical vocations in the cinema.

The Role of the Government

The prestige of film in the international arena also contributed to efforts made by the Indian film industry to improve its self-image. Film festivals had long been features of several major countries, and in 1952 the Indian government held the first International Film Festival of India, one of a series of efforts to carve out its place in international life. This event enabled filmmakers and the public at large to view for the first time films made outside of Hollywood. It also attracted foreign filmmakers to the Indian locale as a backdrop for films, an example of which was Renoir's *The River* (1951). The industry welcomed the opportunity for foreign collaboration, seeing the greater financial resources of foreign companies as a means to better standards in Indian films, higher technical levels of Indian filmmaking, and easier distribution and recognition abroad for Indian cinema.[27] In the fifties there was a spurt of foreign investments and collaborations in Indian cinema: for instance, *Last Judgment*, directed by Henry Decoin, was made in English, French, and

Hindi; *Jhansi ki Rani* (*Queen of Jhansi*, 1953), a costly Technicolor film by Sohrab Modi, had British collaboration; *Pardesi* (*The Traveller*, 1957) by K. A. Abbas was co-produced with Mosfilm of the U.S.S.R., to name just a few.

Apart from film festivals and film awards instituted in 1954, relations between governments (national and regional) and the film industry hinged on two issues: censorship (within the purview of the national government) and taxation (the domain of state governments). In addition, one can cite "cultural preservation" as an ongoing discourse of struggle between the two sides. With regard to film censorship, the Indian government simply took over the machinery instituted by the British, apart from purely administrative changes, while the industry argued for self-censorship along the lines of Hollywood. However, not only were there powerful groups which favored censorship, such as older and conservative politicians, high culture advocates, and various educational groups, but the government had assumed a significant role for itself as a constraining factor on business and as a guardian of public morality and order. In discussing such constraints, Raymond Williams's notion of "asymmetry" may help us. It is a condition that he finds particularly acute in the development of cultural institutions centering on the modern media in capitalist states.

Although Williams has in mind the advanced capitalist states of the Western world, it is interesting to note how similar conditions are reproduced in the so-called Third World. Williams describes asymmetry as "a deepseated contradiction between the reproduction of market relations (both directly, within the market, and indirectly, within state and educational functions) and the consequences of such reproduction in certain sensitive and perhaps crucial areas of public morality, respect for authority and actual crime."[28] Williams locates asymmetry in three major areas of tension, conflict, and struggle:

These areas are (i) the organization of licensing, censorship and other similar forms of control, and the struggle against these; (ii) the organization of the market, both in its aspect as a trading area whose purposes, in expansion and profit, may often be in conflict with otherwise dominant political and cultural authorities, and its aspect as a mechanism for commodities in this especially sensitive field, where inherent calculations of profit and scale may impose tensions with other conceptions of art and, at a different level, impose its own new forms of commercial controls; and (iii) the uneven and changing relations between a received and always to some extent recuperated "popular" (largely oral) culture and the new forms of standardized and increasingly centralized production and reproduction.

In India, the postcolonial state, while against censorship in art and literature, saw film as a separate case altogether, primarily because of its wide reach and potential influence. The power to censor films was an official weapon the national government thought fit to retain. Film censorship, first imposed through the Cinematograph Act of 1918 and operating through four regional censor boards, was now centralized. The Cinematograph Act of 1952 gave the Union government the authority to constitute a Central Board of Film Censors (CBFC) with a chairperson (a full-time paid member) and nine other members. The CBFC would operate from Bombay, with regional boards under it functioning in Calcutta and Madras. On April 29, 1953, a move was announced that would precensor all stories and scripts before they even reached the sets so that an "unlikely" story would not be passed by the precensor board. Then on March 1, 1954, new advisory panels of the CBFC were appointed. A *Filmfare* editorial stated: "What government is proposing is to strangle the industry by choking its freedom and destroying its initiative, and to replace it with a totalitarian machine which will turn out films trimmed to an official pattern."[29] And the *Illustrated Weekly of India* noted: "Every other day comes news of some picture being banned or cut drastically. Often those pictures suffer in which producers had tried to break new ground with subjects dealing with current social problems and matters of national import."[30]

The regime of "don'ts" created numerous instances of dispute between the censoring authorities and filmmakers over "objectionable" footage in films and provided the film industry with an incentive to band together and oppose the government. A *Filmfare* editorial conveyed this response: "Characteristically Mr. Vasan [Madras film producer and then president of the Film Federation of India] has lost no time. In his very first speech as President he called upon the industry to put its house in order and gird up its loins to fight for its place in the sunlight of official countenance and support as an enterprise of national value and importance, and made a trenchant appeal to the government for recognition in that behalf and alteration of its present policy."[31] There is little doubt that the censorship of films was rigid, unimaginative, and prudish. Indeed, the cinema was conceived in the very black-and-white terms that the guardians of public morality accused the producers of instituting in their films. Indian cinema was called upon to unequivocally portray virtue triumphant over vice, good over evil. Interestingly, the model for emulation in this regard was again none other than the Hollywood cinema (since the censorship rules were basically a copy of the Hollywood Production Code). One K. Sharma, press attaché and languages assistant to the prime minister from 1946 to 1951, quoted an American congressman (a Mr. Hoffman) as saying that the American public liked their pictures "clean and wholesome." Mr. Hoffman (it was quoted) looked forward to the day when in each city and town there would be a cinema house in which "clean pictures, modest actions were portrayed . . . where the rewards went to the decent, the honest."[32] Here we see the norms of an ideologically dominant cinema internalized even by those who wished to do things their own way.

Official views on how the Indian cinema affected public morals did not exhaust the issue, for certain sections of society were equally concerned about it. In 1954, 13,000 women of Delhi signed a petition to the prime minister asking him to curb the evil influence of the cinema as it made their children play truant from school, acquire precocious sex habits, indulge in misdemeanors, and the like.[33] The move added fire to the already vexed question of censorship and ranged opposing viewpoints held by the public against one another. One reader of *Filmfare* wrote:

With a censorship that is methodless in its madness, with anything that has a trace of romance, sex or crime deleted forthwith without a thought given to the context and meaning of scenes, it is inconceivable that Indian films can ever incite the youth of the country to undesirable habits.

The censors see vulgarity where there is none, and with sex, in any form or context, completely taboo in our films, it is more likely that the younger generation is in danger of growing up to be narrow-minded bigots to whom sex will signify something that lurks in dark corners and only to be talked about in horrified whispers.

If children steal money for pictures, as the women of Delhi claim, it only points to a woeful lack of ethics in the education imparted to them at home and in school. If they see too many films, it is only because there is no other form of entertainment or pastime to which they can turn.[34]

Such controversies not only signify the highly emotional reactions that the cinema elicited from different groups in society but the way in which these groups tried to influence policy in matters of culture. Indeed, the question of how film was to be perceived—as entertainment, as many filmmakers contended, or as education, which characterization government officials tended to favor—could never be resolved by those who debated it, revealing the confusion that pertained on the topic. That the cinema was placed in the Ministry of Information and Broadcasting rather than in that of Cultural Affairs certainly points one way.

Taxation was perhaps even more bitterly resented by the film industry than censorship. Its jurisdiction was with the states, some of which received a fair part of their revenue from entertainment taxes. Since India had adopted a federal structure, each state government could levy its own taxes to meet its expenditures. The entertainment tax on film had been introduced by the British, with most provinces charging 12 percent. When the Indian government came to power, taxes went up dramatically, the states charging between 25 and 75 percent in a variety of taxes and levies. One producer calculated that out of every 100 rupees spent by the public on film entertainment, 33 rupees went to the government as entertainment tax, 33 rupees were pocketed by the exhibitor, 15 rupees went to the distributor, 4 to the financier, and 15 to the producer, "out of which he has to pay his creditors who comprise the artistes, technicians, publicity agents, newspaper and magazine publishers, and others contributing to the production and showing of the film."[35] It was estimated that various forms of taxes—state entertainment tax on the price of tickets, entertainment tax levied by municipalities, octroi duties for transporting a film from one city to another, sales tax on cinema equipment, and heavy import duties on raw film—amounted to no less than 60 percent of box-office revenue.[36]

In order to represent its case to the state and local governments, the industry appointed an executive to be spokesman for the Film Federation of India (1951). He would also act as the industry's liaison officer with the public, "which needs to be educated not only in regard to its own right in the matter of securing the right kind of films for viewing, but also in regard to its no less real responsibility to protect the industry against the tyrannies of the government."[37] Also, the Indian Motion Picture Producers Association (IMPPA) made a move to set up a financing corporation which would provide funds to genuine producers at a reasonable rate of interest. Among the conditions it placed was that no artist concerned in the venture should have more than three contracts simultaneously, and a minimum of nine days of work per month per contract was essential.

If the government bodies could not shake off their antipathy to the cinema in the postindependence era, the same cannot be said of traditional artists whom they were anxious to safeguard from the cinema's dubious influence. Artists with training in the classical traditions of dance and music were not averse to trying the medium of cinema, even if their efforts did not bring big box-office returns. Uday Shankar, a world-famous dancer, made *Kalpana* (*Imagination*, 1948), using fragments from his various dances to form a surrealist collage. Many figures of the radical theater, like Shambhu Mitra, also directed films; others acted in them. No doubt the prospect of earning money if the films succeeded, as well as the ability to reach much wider audiences, were major incentives, but it is obvious that these artists did not perceive the rigid polarizations between the cinema and the older arts as many public officials did. More important, the artists realized that the earlier bonds directly attaching a musician or a dancer to a specific audience or patron were broken forever. New bonds via the cinema had to be created, but they would inevitably be different, for the majority of the viewing audience were not familiar with the classical traditions.

It is often said that music and dance are of the very essence of Indian social and cultural life, and while this may be true as a general statement, what are considered the established Indian traditions of music, dance, and drama are based on such sophisticated and elaborate techniques and theories as to be "accessible" only to a knowledgeable few. The famous quality of improvisation in Indian music cannot take place except through a thorough grasp of the underlying rhythms and patterns that guide it. The traditional mode of musical training was through the guilds of hereditary musicians, where a teacher orally imparted musical themes to a disciple who learned the craft over several years. Moreover, the cultivation of music, particularly in North India, had occurred in courts and under royal protection so that a musician had little contact with a lay public. Folk traditions developed among the rural people, and it was the popular cinema which first tried a major blend of the two traditions. Political as well as socioeconomic changes after independence meant not only the end of princely patronage for classical musicians but also the phenomenon of urbanization and a consequent cutting off of large numbers of people from the cultural forms to which they were accustomed. (In fact, the need to explore better economic prospects as well as the search for new audiences led many classically trained artists such as Pandit Ravi Shankar, Sitara Devi, and Ali Akbar Khan to take up occasional film assignments suited to their talents.) Classical performers made their own adjustments to the new conditions in order to survive as artists.

Following independence, one finds in the cultural sphere what political psychologist Ashis Nandy has described in another context as "the dialectic between the classical, the pure and the high status on the one hand, and the folksy, hybrid and the low-brow on the other."[38] Much of the debate over classical versus hybrid culture centered around film music and dance, for in the view of many purists, nowhere was the "bastardization" of the classical arts more apparent than in the realm of film music and dance compositions. One move to curb this trend and "educate" the people in the purer traditions of Indian music came in 1952, when Dr. B. V. Keskar became minister of information and broadcasting with responsibility for various government media agencies, including All India Radio, or AIR. Keskar thoroughly disapproved of filmsongs, and in July 1952 AIR cut down the time allotted to broadcast filmsongs; he also ended the practice of giving the song's film title, which he regarded as advertising, and only the singer's name was announced. This enraged the film producers, who were the copyright owners of the songs, and they ended the performing licenses by which AIR had been broadcasting the filmsongs. Hence there was a sudden disappearance of filmsongs on radio and a preponderance of classical programs. Fifty percent of all broadcast music was classical at this time. However, Radio Ceylon began broadcasting Indian filmsongs on its new commercial shortwave service, and apparently Radio Ceylon "dominated the airwaves" at peak listening times in India. AIR lost its audience and Keskar's plan failed, so in 1957 the producers renewed AIR's performance licenses and it began to broadcast popular music again to win back the Indian public.[39] Here one sees the relationship of film to other discourses, in particular to popular music.

The attacks that film music directors were subjected to by the patrons and exponents of classical music drew various responses from them.

Madan Mohan wrote, "Film music is the first really national music we ever had" and suggested that no music director could hope to succeed unless he had a thorough grasp of the classical ragas from which the best film music was derived.[40] Another music director, Salil Chowdhury, addressed the question of certain musical instruments such as the harmonium, used by most classical singers as accompaniment, being "taboo" for AIR because it was considered "foreign." Chowdhury wrote: "A living culture is not afraid of foreign influences. Sometimes there is an excess of imitation which the indigenous culture automatically rejects and progresses towards a harmonious synthesis." He argued that every age not only interpreted the existing music in its own fashion but created new music. Thus from the Dhrupad came the Khayal, from the Khayal the Thumri and the other lighter patterns, but "of all these the mother is the same—the folk music of India." Chowdhury traced the developments of modern songs to the freedom of expression which became evident at the end of the nineteenth century, helping to break the shackles of rigid grammar and make possible the introduction of new instruments for accompaniment—the violin, the clarinet, the harmonium, the piano, and the organ.

> We must realise that the modern Indian composer has around him a way of life, sights and sounds, aims and ideals entirely different from what his ancestors had. He tries to express in his music these new values and ideals. Exploring the entire range of ancient Indian music—the scale pattern and form—it is possible he may find it inadequate to express his feelings.
>
> Art has always changed according to its own needs, and the grammarian has to follow them and change the laws accordingly.[41]

Chowdhury went on to say that the songs for the masses composed during the freedom movement in India and also the music composed during and for the "terrorist movement" in Bengal, like marching tunes of Western music, could be sung by people marching in procession. The critics of film music accepted these innovations, he charged, as based on Indian ragas: "our raga classification is so vast that almost any melody from any part of the world can be classified as a raga or misra-raga," he said. "It is not the notes but the style—the form and expression—that matters."[42] Thus film music directors, without dissociating themselves from the classical traditions, argued for their right to innovate and extend the possibilities of Indian music in accordance with public mood and demand. On the question of dance, too, charges of the corruption of the pure forms, of hybridization, and of sexual vulgarity were often made, and filmmakers were exhorted to use the film medium to disseminate knowledge of classical dance to the lay public. Such debates through the press or on formal occasions took place throughout the 1950s between film professionals and practitioners and their critics, whether members of government or representatives of particular groups with particular attitudes toward films and filmmaking. Typically, it was the needs or wishes of the public that got cited as the justification for certain emphases or practices.

There were other ways in which the importance of the cinema as an economic and cultural institution was coming to be acknowledged. In 1957 a pilot survey of audience reaction to films was sponsored by the Central Board of Film Censors, assisted by the prestigious Tata Institute of Social Sciences in Bombay. Although the area covered was Greater Bombay only and the investigators did "not claim complete accuracy of their conclusions," the evidence showed that "cinema has become a part of the life of the people of Greater Bombay and a vital agency for entertainment and education."[43] In another direction, the central government made a move in 1958 to set up an Export Promotion Council for films so that they could be marketed properly abroad. It was hoped that hitherto virgin territory for Indian films such as the United States and the United Kingdom would provide opportunities for export. But in both the matters of taxation and censorship there was virtually no change throughout the 1950s and well into the late 1960s.

The relationship between art and industry is, to state the obvious, an extremely complicated one. Moreover, as I have tried to indicate above, this relationship constitutes a discursive field which various groups— producers, distributors, exhibitors, artists and technicians, state officials, representatives of the press, and the public—turn into an arena of struggle over problems of meaning and value. But we are still left with the question of economic determination. Three modes of interpretation have usually been available to critics of the Bombay cinema. The first considers the economic organization of the Bombay film industry as directly controlling the shape and form of its cultural products; in this view, the films are totally commodities, escapist entertainment, purely contingent. No differentiation of films can be made (on the basis of genre, style, or whatever) since they all emerge out of a system of assembly-line production, that is, a formula. The second mode considers the economic level as an unfortunate evil which only a few promising producer-directors of the Bombay cinema have succeeded in resisting in order to produce works of art. They emerge as artists struggling for expression in an atmosphere where they are misfits and lonely fighters. The third mode, which is the one I have tried to indicate and exemplify in this chapter, treats the economic as imbricated and expressed in a variety of intersecting and competing discourses. Money or finance, ideologically speaking, is a means to an end for filmmakers, audiences, and the state alike. In other words, no group is naive enough to think that good films can be made without adequate resources, or that money alone stands between quality and dross. In fact, it is the way in which money as a material sign is circulated in postindependence India that has been of interest here. Thus, rather than designate an implacably hierarchical arrangement in which the organization of the film industry occurs prior to the organization of the film text (the work of subsequent chapters of this book), I propose a linkage of contiguity (itself a historical-national and hence changeable arrangement) in which the economic affects, and is in turn affected by, other domains of signifying practice.

Two conclusions may be drawn from this stance regarding filmmaking practices. One is that neither filmmakers nor film texts can be ranged alongside a divide separating "committed" from "commercial." In the deeply competitive environment of commercial filmmaking in which the variables are potentially infinite, a wholly commercial outlook (filmmaking as an exclusively business proposition) has translated, at least in the Bombay setup, to the one-film or fly-by-night producer. All others, for whom filmmaking is the primary mode of activity, can then be regarded as "committed" insofar as they have chosen to make the filmmaking enterprise their primary occupation. How they then decide to manage their resources, intellectual and practical, in the actual organization of film texts will depend on specific situations. A maker of "realistic" cinema will turn to a thriller to generate some profits to finance his next venture. (Here, too, it is a *perception* that a thriller will make money; in actuality, it might not.) Following from the first, we can then say that even in the Bombay cinema, there is no way to "read off" the economic from the surface of a film text, no matter how trivial the latter may appear to be. Any form of widely disseminated culture is an interface of history and politics, contingency and compromise, implicitly held and stubbornly contested views and values. This chapter has attempted to chart that process.

*Can a serious filmmaker, working in India, afford to shut his
eyes to the reality around him, the reality that is so poignant,
and so urgently in need of interpretation in terms of the cinema?
I do not think so. For the truly serious, socially conscious film
maker . . . must face the challenge of contemporary reality,
examine the facts, probe them, sift them and select from them
the material to be transformed into the stuff of cinema.*
—Satyajit Ray, Our Films, Their Films

3

National Identity and the Realist Aesthetic

Of all the terms used by critics to characterize mainstream
Indian cinema, realism defined in the negative or as a systematic absence has undoubtedly had the most currency. Conversely, the achievement of realism in a film becomes a mark of value, a sign of sincerity
and truthfulness on the part of the filmmaker and of "authenticity" of the
material presented. This was particularly true during the postindependence period, when such qualities crystallized the hopes of a nation in

search of its "true" identity and trying to assign meaning to the complex process of change. As the medium with the potential power to bring India symbolically face-to-face with its own image(s), the cinema found itself implicated in paradoxical ways in the whole cultural response to nationhood. For realism not only seemed to deny established film practices but also Indian literary, dramatic, and philosophical traditions. Moreover, the call for realism meant that the cinema should project not images of what Indian society was but what it *should be*. This "idealist" thread is what shapes the specific contours of realism as it evolved in Indian popular cinema, even as it tried to both articulate and diffuse the ambivalence of social attitudes to change. Realism is the masquerading moral conscience of the Indian intelligentsia in their assumed (though not uncontested) role of national leadership during the fifties. The debate on realism, therefore, has implications for the politics of self-representation.

Realism as elaborated here intersects with the idea of impersonation in important ways: as the "other" of impersonation, it gives shape to the social/national imaginary, the ideal of wholeness of perception and unity of common experience. It can thus be seen as a historical phenomenon, not new to the fifties but privileged in that period as a nation-building tool. As the aesthetic rallying cry emanating from the educated middle class, whose intellectual vanguardism conflicts with their economic decline, realism registers the ambivalence toward technology and progress and a general "Westernization." The intelligentsia's gloss on realism as coincident with morality and sincerity of purpose rather than a strict adherence to the principle of impartial observation of social phenomena subverts realism itself as empiricist doctrine. (The Ray statements quoted above exemplify the contradictory pull of this tendency, with their use of words like "serious," "poignant," and "interpretation" alongside the social scientific jargon of process: "examine," "probe," "sift," "select." Although addressing the situation in Bengal in 1958, Ray is concerned with commercial filmmaking.) The appeal of realism in popular culture invariably rests on a heightened emotionalism, the call to an empathic identification with the underprivileged. Finally, as a set of conventions in the Bombay cinema, the genre of realism self-consciously points to itself as superior (narratively coherent, carefully crafted) and yet refuses radical differentiation from the average commercial product by incorporating its range of pleasures (particularly stars, songs, and dances). All these factors have to be taken into account in order for us to be able to grasp realism as ideology, worldview, and genre in Indian popular cinema.

Toward an Archaeology of Indianized Realism

Before we can consider the particular inflections of imperso-nation in films that represent the turn to realism during the fifties, we need to trace the idea of realism through a number of discourses and practices in Indian culture and society. Generally, several problems arise in such an analytic endeavor. For while realism has a specific place in Western philosophy, with a history (as an artistic and literary movement) and a critical tradition (it is the subject of endless debate), its status in the Indian philosophical and classical aesthetic traditions has been marginal. It is not possible here (nor is it strictly necessary) to do a comparative analysis of the occidental and Indian epistemological systems that form the basis of arguments for and against realism as the desired norm for artistic products.[1] One can only make the general observation that the Hindu worldview (similar to the Platonic worldview) posits material reality as an aspect of spiritual or transcendent Reality, and so what we see is "the reflection of reality in the mirror of illusion."[2] Scholars of Indian aesthetics have stressed its nonmimetic view of art, which posits an essentially autonomous artistic world and an elaborate *rasasutra* (theory of aesthetic enjoyment) of depersonalized emotions.[3] It is not surprising, therefore, that in India standards of realism are evoked in relation to the novel and cinema, the two "borrowed" or "imported" art forms. Yet, as the critic Meenakshi Mukherjee shows us in her study of the novel in India, conventions of realism were slow to take hold, and details of surface reality never achieved a high place in the Indian literary tradition. "In almost every major novel of the nineteenth century, behind the obvious European influences can be found the bedrock of a different narrative structure and value systems."[4] Nevertheless, the conscious attempt of many nineteenth-century Indian novelists was to achieve realism in the manner of the Victorian writers they were familiar with, and this meant a preoccupation with the depiction of (often oppressive) contemporary social conditions such as the subordinate status of women, caste prejudices, joint family problems, and the like. The authors tried to render faithfully the details of the social milieu to which their characters belonged, reproduced patterns of speech in everyday conversation, and were concerned with ordinary life. Mukerjee points out the high place accorded to English education by these writers which contributed, paradoxically, to their own self-definition: "English education becomes closely associated with the process of achieving a new social and individual identity."[5] The reason is presented as follows:

A part of the power of the British in India was technological superiority. This has always been the basis of colonial domination (one recalls the magical power of gunpowder in *Robinson Crusoe*, an early paradigm of colonial experience) and in *Indulekha* [1888] Kesavan Nambudiri is awed by the thread factory in Calicut where the wheels move "as if they heard the word of command." He speculates on the power of the smoke that comes out of the factory and the dark sacrifices that must be made to generate this power. Kesavan Nambudiri's confusion is between two systems—the rational and the magical, or the natural and the supernatural (factory smoke—sacrificial fire). His wife knows that English education is the only means of demystification. Indulekha is not awed by anything because she can even explain "the principles on which the railway is driven."[6]

What appears now as naive technological optimism was, in the nineteenth century, an unbounded belief in scientific progress, both in the West and, by extension, in the colonies. (More than half a century later, Satyajit Ray used the railway as the beckoning symbol of modernity in his classic realist film *Pather Panchali* [*Song of the Little Road*, 1955].) Faith in science, one of the cardinal elements behind the European realist movement, was also a factor that drove Indian authors to strive for credibility and realism in their works.

Yet, what Raymond Williams has characterized as the scientific *attitude* implicit in Western realism—arising out of a host of specific historico-cultural factors such as the industrial revolution and secularism—could not easily be implanted on Indian soil, despite Macaulay's "Minute on Indian Education" (1835), which envisaged "a class of persons, Indian in blood and color, but English in taste, in opinions, in morals and in intellect." Strong ideas about individualism, democracy, linear time, and material progress go against the grain of Indian philosophical speculations and experiential value systems; however, the educated middle class was affected by Western ideas, and "realism" as a representational strategy in fiction was one way of coping with the processes of industrialization and modernity. Popular Indian novels of the late nineteenth and twentieth centuries have combined richness of detail in the description of a social milieu with some of the conventions of Indian oral narratives and openness of form rather than closure in the Western fictional mode.[7]

In postindependence India, the emphasis on "realism," particularly in the context of Hindi literature (and, as we shall see, in film), has taken on a force that has complex, indeed contradictory, associations with questions of individual and national identity. While Indian writing has maintained cultural continuity with the *past*, the perceived need of the writer to come to terms with the *present* and to locate him/herself within a *world* context has been, perhaps, greater. One interesting result of this phenomenon was that, in the fifties, stories were discussed as much or more than they were written.[8] In other words, interest in evolving a modern critical tradition, shaped by the particular literary and extraliterary (historical, linguistic, social) problems faced by the writers, is evident. Moreover, as scholar Gordon Roadarmel writes, "Justifications for literary forms and trends have been sought in a more universal framework, comparing the fiction of each new generation with that of the previous generation, with that of writers in other Indian languages, and with that of writers in other world languages." Roadarmel goes on to say that "criteria related to newness, realism, authenticity and the reflection of a 'modern consciousness' are most highly valued" by Hindi critics and writers.[9] These were used as synonymous terms, so that the ideal of realism signified at once being attuned to one's own time and place and working within a broader international tradition. The soul searching that writers went through regarding the urban/rural dilemma or their ability to give authentic portrayals of village life (the "true" India) in view of their urban backgrounds was one instance of the broader cultural question of identity. Of course, the conception of what constitutes realism changed from that of Premchand and others (writing in the 1920s, 1930s, and 1940s) who used realistic settings and characters to promote a social or political view to a less direct, nondidactic mode of writing which would only communicate the complexity of contemporary experience. There was even the extreme position, such as that of the writer Nirmal Verma, who held that a writer could not even identify reality, much less express it: "For one who is truly a realist, reality is always hidden in the bush."[10]

Although conducted on a less sophisticated or sustained level, the discussion about realism in Indian cinema is no less complex for the purposes of critical analysis. First, the demand for mimetic cinema may itself represent the attitude of a limited, though still important, section of the movie-going public, namely, the city-bred, middle-class person, often English-educated and conscious of "world standards" in the cinema. In the absence of proper ethnographic studies of audiences and in the face of the box-office popularity of different kinds of films, not just realistic ones, it is difficult to push the argument for realism as manifesting itself in *all* classes of the movie-going public.[11] The conventions of realism are generally absent from India's oral storytelling traditions (which the Bombay cinema partly draws upon) with their digressions, asides, stories within stories, interposed political, social, or philosophical commentary, and the like. As Salman Rushdie pointed out in a television interview some years ago, this style of storytelling is actually quite sophisticated when placed beside any straightforward notion of naturalism or illusionism in art. The latter, then, might be the expression of a predominantly middle-class sensibility, and this might explain why certain "landmark" Bombay films espousing realism such as *Dharti ke Lal* (*Children of the Earth*, 1946), *Do Bigha Zamin* (*Two Acres of Land*, 1953), and *Jagte Raho* (*Keep Awake!*, 1956) were acclaimed by film reviewers and award panels but did quite poorly at the box office.

Nevertheless, there is evidence to suggest that a general mood supporting realistic cinema prevailed in the postindependence era and that it was linked to the intelligentsia's feelings of being alien in their own environment and of their search for the "real" India. Edward Shils has dwelt on this in his book *The Intellectual between Tradition and Modernity*, finding on the basis of interviews he conducted a deep sense of guilt among city-bred, English-educated people over being cut off from their roots and not being able to communicate with the "authentic" Indian, the villager.[12] Even as late as 1983, Girish Karnad, Oxford-educated filmmaker, playwright, and scholar, said, "If you want to know the real India, you cannot get it from an Indian who lives in the city. It is the village Indian who is the real Indian."[13] Since this is also the average Westerner's perception of India, it is interesting that in the very act of self-assertion and self-knowledge, the Indian urban intellectual should "objectify" him/herself. And so one of the anomalies contained in the demand for realism in cinema is that the concept itself is alien to Indian philosophic and aesthetic traditions (not to speak of Bombay filmmaking practices generally) and certainly owed some of its impetus to the international climate favoring neorealism, but it was taken as a transparent means whereby "Indian reality" could be revealed. In other words, the West provided the frame whereby Indians could view themselves. I do not wish to imply by this a disingenuous attempt on the part of Indian intellectuals to know themselves as Indians or any conscious aping of Western views and ideas. Rather, what is evident is the very complex nature of the notion of national identity, particularly in instances where a society contends with its colonial past, at the same time feeding upon it. It is in this sense that the urge to find verisimilitude in commercial entertainment takes on meaning, although on the face of it the tendencies that the two represented, particularly in the Indian context, would seem incompatible.

As suggested in the previous chapter, the participants in the struggle over the question of "legitimate" culture were joined in the perception of realism in narrative and storytelling (with Indian settings) as the antidote to a host of ills plaguing films, including their low social and international prestige. As the government sought to revive *Indian* cultural forms and traditions, Indian filmmakers and popular figures in the industry such as actors renewed their calls for moral integrity, sincerity of purpose, and realism in their own efforts to revitalize their products. In this regard, the Indian film establishment did not only look to the experiments of other countries but invoked a realistic "tradition" from within the indigenous cinema. Film reviewers and filmmakers harked back to the "golden age" of the 1930s, when the stability of the studio era had allowed filmmakers to portray contemporary social evils as they appeared. "Realism" also meant a popularization of Indian literary classics, the works of Tagore, Bankim Chandra, Sarat Chandra, Premchand, Banbhatta, and Kalidasa, which constitute India's literary heritage. It involved choosing "the beautiful national forms of our song, dance and music, so long and widely neglected in our films."[14] Further, the important commercial filmmakers whose names were familiar to audiences and whose films earned awards, notably Bimal Roy, Zia Sarhady, V. Shantaram, Nitin Bose, and Mehboob, not to mention Satyajit Ray, working independently and outside Bombay, all issued statements or made claims regarding their realist intentions. Sometimes all these emphases were present in the official view that perhaps provided the lead in this demand for films communicating an "authentic" national consciousness. We have as an example the view expressed by a public figure (R. R. Diwakar, then governor of the state of Bihar), on the occasion of the silver jubilee celebrations of the Bombay film industry: "Some of the things necessary [to reach higher standards in the cinema] seem to be: diving into the very soul of India, deep study of the all-sided as well as varied culture of this great land, attempt at originality and the boldness to depict India as India, venturing out of the studios into the tumult and bustle of life, full utilization of colour and poetry that is profuse and inherent in the India scene, developing technical skill on all fronts and, above all, high idealism."[15] As one can sense from this quotation, the burden placed on the cinema was indeed great.

Expectations of the Bombay film, then, ranged from straightforward notions of verisimilitude such as representation of the surface details of dress, decor, and social environment, to more totalizing and ambitious views such as the one expressed above. More important than these film-as-reflection views, however, is the effort by some film directors and writers to incorporate within the notion of realism a view of visual art rooted in Indian philosophy. We have, on the one hand, the Aristotelian claim for art as a mirror of life and, on the other, a claim for art that elevates and improves the mind through the agency of character types, patterned emotions, and a delicately balanced moral universe. This "duality" is apparent in a statement entitled "Realism as I understand it" made by Bimal Roy, described as the "high priest of cinema realism" in the Bombay film world. We find a hint of familiarity with the Bazinian idea of the camera as uniquely suited to capture reality: "The very nature of photographic art invites belief in the actuality of what is recorded. As a result, the film developed most consistently and successfully in the direction of realism, that is, reconstruction of life in such a way as to give its environment and psychology the effect of complete authenticity."[16] However, Roy makes it clear that the goal of realism is not the scientific understanding of the human condition at a particular time and place but a knowledge of self (*atmanam biddhi*), not interpretation but the creation of a mood, "realism which becomes 'rasa.'" The camera only *enhances* and concretizes the viewer's enjoyment and understanding of the play of forces of good and evil in the world, it does not radically alter them.

Thus the new technological art of cinema is *incorporated* into the basic Hindu religious and aesthetic traditions. This incorporation is further articulated by scriptwriter Nabendu Ghosh, who explains that according to Bharata Muni's *Natya Shastra*, "our conception of right and wrong is based on religious books such as the *Dharmashastras*, the Vedas and the *Mahabharata* which enjoin upon the Hindu a code of ethical conduct. But in order to explain the seeds of truth, illustrations must be drawn from men and women's lives. That is the purpose of art as expressed in the *Natya Shastra:* to show how people react in various situations, how they decide between right and wrong."[17] Ghosh goes on to say that the cinema can magnify emotions, as in a closeup, thus providing what gives a human being the greatest pleasure: to see. The Sanskrit word *darshan* (from the verbal root *drsh*), which means "to see," is also the word for philosophy. The primacy of the visual sense implied by this comparison stems from the all-inclusive meaning of seeing as integral vision, apprehension, understanding to be found in the earliest Hindu scriptures, while the notion of pleasure here would mean spiritual pleasure in "seeing" the Truth. Ghosh's testimony is one instance of the sanction and inspiration that people seek for contemporary linguistic and cultural forms and practices from the past.

The Neorealist Window of Opportunity

In 1952, India held its first international film festival. The occasion is regarded in the film industry as something of a milestone as people in the country had a chance to see contemporary European and other "foreign" films for the first time. Previously, Hollywood films had provided the model for commercial filmmaking in India, but now the works of the Italian neorealists were also available as the "other cinema" attracting the more seriously inclined Bombay filmmakers such as K. A. Abbas, Bimal Roy, Nitin Bose, B. R. Chopra, and a few others. Abbas and Chopra had been journalists before they started making films, Bimal Roy and Nitin Bose had migrated to Bombay after initially being employed and trained by New Theatres of Calcutta with its tradition of "socially conscious" cinema. They thus aligned themselves with progressive causes and the representation of contemporary Indian reality without necessarily renouncing the more pleasurable aspects of the commercial cinema such as songs and dances. In the polarized world of Indian film criticism, the realist impulse informing certain films is therefore seen as "contaminated" by nonorganic and extraneous elements.[18] While Bimal Roy's name, for instance, is associated with film realism, he has not gained admittance into the ranks of the "greats" because he mixed modes which are perceived as fundamentally at odds with one another (realistic mise-en-scène with songs and dances).[19] Needless to say, attempts at hierarchization are beside the point in trying to understand why certain filmmakers were accepted as "realistic" by audiences as well as the specific version of realism their films sought to project.

Realism and Nationalism: Bridging the Gap

In discussions of Hindi film realism, three films made in the late forties and early fifties are invariably mentioned by critics and industry representatives: Chetan Anand's *Neecha Nagar* (*World Down Below*, 1946), K. A. Abbas's *Dharti ke Lal*, and Bimal Roy's *Do Bigha Zamin*. Although award winners, all three films did poorly at the box office. In them we have some of the dominant themes and oppositions of the realistic mode: the struggle between the haves and the have-nots, the country and the city, the tenant/peasant and the landlord or moneylender. These themes had found earlier expression in Bimal Roy's enormously popular Bengali film made for New Theatres, *Udayer Pathe* (*Awakening*, 1944), soon remade in Hindi as *Humrahi* (*Fellow Travellers*, 1945). Satyajit Ray comments that the Bengali version "was widely regarded in its time as a milestone in Indian cinema. Timely in its theme, bold in its use of unknown amateurs in leading roles, and admirable in its moral stance, it was a step in the right direction, though not a big one."[20]

Udayer Pathe is an overtly nationalist film and a socially conscious one, traditions already well established in Indian cinema, as S. T. Baskaran and others have pointed out. Why then did *Udayer Pathe* have such an impact? I shall suggest that, within the parameters of a very conventional narrative (poor boy meets rich girl), we have a realist idiom struggling to break through, an idiom that draws upon the cadence and patterns of everyday speech for moral effect. The film sought to apprehend the contemporary mood and moment through the evolution in language, literalizing the rise of subaltern (working-class and colonized) consciousness in the power of common speech. But by a further crossover, the power of common speech reposes in an urban intellectual, not in the representative of a village. In fact, the film is rare in the history of Indian cinema in that it presents the intellectual as hero and heroism as the ability to articulate class-consciousness.

Made at the height of the freedom movement, the film makes obvious use of symbols such as the national anthem, the Bengali literary and social reform tradition (photographs of Shri Aurobindo, Tagore, Vivekananda), as well as references to an international socialist tradition

(Bernard Shaw) to create the intellectual milieu of its protagonist, Anup Lekhak (literally meaning "Anup the Writer"). The story presents the polarized social worlds of the rich (the industrialists) and the poor (workers and wage-earners), with the former as exploiters (also identified with the British through their dress and life-style), the latter the exploited class (identified with the nationalists). The dice are fairly heavily loaded against the former, the dramatic tension arising out of such situations as Anup's sister being accused of stealing a necklace in her rich friend Gopa's house, and Anup's writing being plagiarized by Gopa's brother. Countering these class conflicts and personal rivalries is the developing romance between the poor Anup and the rich Gopa herself, his sister's friend and an industrialist's daughter. Gopa's contact with Anup results in her moral education about the lived conditions of poverty and deprivation and leads to her growing alienation from her own class. Gopa now dresses more simply, reads progressive literature (a novel written by Anup), and visits the tenements of the workers that are located in the shadows of her father's factory. As matters come to a head in the conflict between workers and management, Gopa leaves home and meets Anup, afraid that she has left the glamor of her existence behind. Assuring her that her destiny lies ahead, not behind her, Anup walks with her toward a symbolic dawn.

The film's frank populism and social idealism, its stereotypical representations of the rich and the poor, and its message of hope at the end suggest a moral parable overlaying the ideology of social realism in cinema. One way in which morality meets realism in cinema is that the rich-poor dichotomy translates into the appearance-essence problematic. Realist cinema usually relies on dress and life-style representations to signify social status. Film researcher Stanley Corkin cites clothing as a resonant aspect of characterization in certain late nineteenth- and early twentieth-century American novels. He writes, "In a world of mass production and commodified goods and experiences, the material elements that garb a character have a meaning that suffices for the entire notion of a character's humanity."[21] Clothing is, of course, a major signifier of social status as well as a vehicle of fantasy in the visual medium of the cinema. In *Udayer Pathe/Humrahi*, the world of mass production and a commodified life-style is also the villainized world of the rich, the arrogant preserve of the powerful. The heroine's humanization and proletarianization cannot come about until she willingly abandons her finery and embraces a plain, unadorned appearance. The code of clothing partakes of realism (the poor cannot afford fancy clothes) as well as metaphor. But it also suggests simplistically that class positioning is a matter of the externals of dress and jewelry which Gopa can abandon to signify her empathy with the poor.

Ultimately, it is not change in their material conditions but a moral victory that the workers and their spokesman, Anup, garner. The film's heady message of change becomes absorbed in the pacifist dream of interclass alliances and togetherness to fight oppression. Nevertheless, its portrayal of the intellectual as activist and its popularization of a nationalist intellectual tradition makes it a provocative instance of translation and transposition of a Bengali ethos and sensibility to the all-India level. Today, *Udayer Pathe/Humrahi* is interesting to us as a "realist" film embodying preindependence moral passion and visionary zeal, and also for the implications that a film made in two languages has as a national-historical allegory. For here it is not a filmic character but film itself that assumes the garb of interchangeability to partake of a national identity. The question of language has always been very crucial in India, and the efforts of some filmmakers to make some films in two languages (even if ostensibly for marketing purposes) is not without its significance.

Neecha Nagar is very similar to *Udayer Pathe* in its plot, symbolic structure, thematic concerns, and social message. Winner of the Grand Prix at the Cannes Film Festival of 1946, it too dramatizes class conflict through anticolonial and nationalist images and motifs. The central image is that of water, the source of life, contaminated by big industry and turned into a life-threatening hazard for the poor. The pollution of water is both the effect and the analog of bourgeois oppression of the working class. The world depicted in this film is separated into *ooncha nagar* (upper town/area) and *neecha nagar* (lower town/area) inhabited by the very rich and the struggling poor, respectively. The source of conflict between these groups is a dirty stream that a rich industrialist known as Sarkarji ("Your Lordship") is diverting to pass through the poor section of town so that new houses can be constructed in the cleaned-up upper section. His daughter, Maya, objects to this decision but to no avail. The poor are represented by Balraj, who had attended college with Maya. Much of the film establishes the dynamics between the two opposing groups, including the activities of those who sell out to the factory owner. Balraj's negotiations, meanwhile, fall through. As the dirty water works its way through the poorer section of town, an epidemic breaks out and many people die, including Balraj's sister, Rupa. The people band together and march toward the Sarkar's house, demanding justice. Cornered, and faced with the prospect of huge debts and bad investments, as well as a threat to his life, the Sarkar collapses on the floor, dead. Maya and Balraj are united in the end.

Neecha Nagar uses certain props to convey the bourgeoisie as a sinister power, the most prominent being a sculptured demon against which the industrialist is often framed. The film also juxtaposes a benign and becalmed natural world at the beginning of the narrative and images of the poor singing and happy, unlike the shadowy and cavernous interior spaces (home, office) associated with high living. It thus projects a romantic image of poverty, although that image gives way to more complex dynamics as the film progresses. Weighted with symbolism, including that of the central character, a Gandhian activist professing nonviolence, *Neecha Nagar* evokes worker power within an overall framework of the nationalist struggle.

Neecha Nagar is, strictly speaking, an expressionist rather than a realist film. In fact, director Chetan Anand called his film "pretentious" in a retrospective glance.[22] The film is shot in high key lighting and is heavily symbolic in its use of props. The scenes of the people marching with torches glowing in the night, chanting freedom slogans, the momentum of the rising force of the oppressed, and the images of decay associated with the colonizing power translate the contemporary situation into cinema in a curious mixture of Gandhian and Marxist ideologies. Also, the heroine here, as in *Udayer Pathe*, serves as the link between the opposing classes and the mode of reconciliation rather than class hatred and mutual destruction.

Dharti ke Lal is an attempt to bring to all-India awareness the tragedy of the Bengal famine of 1943–44 in which five million peasants died. It was produced by the Indian People's Theatre Association (IPTA), of which Abbas, the film's director, was a founding member (as was Chetan Anand, the director of *Neecha Nagar*). This group of progressive writers, artists, musicians, and activists, born in the politically tumultuous days of the early forties, sought to enact consciousness-raising themes of contemporary relevance that would involve the people in street and neighborhood performances. At its inaugural conference in Bombay on May 25, 1943, the call went out: "Come writer and artist, come actor and playwright, come all who work by hand or by brain, and dedicate yourself to the task of building a brave new world of freedom and social justice. And let us all remember, if we wish for a motto, that the workers are the salt of the earth and to be part of their destiny is the greatest adventure of our time."[23] Khwaja Ahmad Abbas wrote and produced a number of plays for IPTA, such as *Yeh Amrit Hai* (*This Is Immortality*) and *Zubeida*, the latter a very popular play. "At certain open-air performances, there were as many as ten thousand spectators. It is of some historical importance that many of the spectators of *Zubeida* included women who had never seen a play in their lives."[24] *Dharti ke Lal* was based on another IPTA play, *Nabanna* (*New Harvest*), by Bijon Bhattacharya, and a Hindi story, *Annadata* (*Foodgiver*), by Krishen Chander. The film was a cooperative venture by IPTA members under egalitarian working conditions and distribution of labor.

About the historical circumstances leading to the Bengal famine, drama critic Rustom Bharucha writes:

> It is now widely acknowledged that the Bengal famine was not a natural disaster but a man-made one. The terrible irony about the famine is that it was not caused by any significant shortage of food. On the contrary, the per capita availability of food supply was 9 percent higher in 1943 than in 1941, which was not a famine year. The problem was that this food was not made available to the peasants and laborers in the rural areas of Bengal. Instead, it was exported by the British to feed its armed forces fighting in Europe and Japan.[25]

Abbas's film concentrates on the human dimension of this tragedy. As is usual in the Hindi film, the British do not enter the picture, and the agents of oppression are their Indian counterparts—the landlord, the moneylender, the grain dealer. Abbas presents images of tranquillity and quotidian village life in the beginning of the film that are gradually replaced by both stark city images of human destitution and (occasionally) stylized evocations of suffering.

The action centers on a peasant extended family in a Bengal village: the old parents and their two sons—one has a wife and the other is about to wed. The family harvest will pay for the wedding feast but the big landlord and the grain dealer from the city refuse to pay a fair price for it. The villagers get poorer though Niranjan, the older son, tries to hold out against the exploiting city bosses. Ramu, the younger brother, finds no rice to offer to the gods when his son is born. Several natural calamities force the villagers to migrate to Calcutta in search of a better life. But a worse fate awaits them there. Ramu and his wife are separated, he reduced to begging and she to prostitution. The old father dies, urging them to go back to the land. Niranjan and his wife return, along with some of the other villagers. Together they work hard to create a new harvest, benefiting from their sense of solidarity. Only Ramu and his wife remain outside, too alien now to go back to the simple rural life.

Dharti ke Lal tries to create a documentary look, particularly in its presentation of masses of starving and dying people. The hunger march into the city, shot with the help of the Kisan Sabha (Farmers Union) in Dhulia district, is a memorable scene. Film critic Kobita Sarkar writes, "Two and a half decades later, it is easy to criticize the stiffness of the fabricated backgrounds, the stilted quality of some of the acting, the note of semi-hysteria that prevails at times and some of the contrived situations, for which the original form of the film, as a play, is at least partly responsible."[26] The film celebrates some of the symbols of rural life such as the cow, the land, and rice, using them to suggest the villagers' ties to nature; the city, by contrast, is a cruel and ugly place, a camp for refugees. The film conveys messages of communal harmony, Hindu-Muslim unity, and patriotism. Director Abbas explains the film's poor reception at the box office as resulting from its badly timed release which coincided with the outbreak of the communal riots during partition.[27]

Do Bigha Zamin

Bimal Roy's *Do Bigha Zamin* is perhaps Indian cinema's most-cited film after *Pather Panchali*. The reasons are many: its "contemporary" (that is, fifties) tone and texture, its exemplification of "serious" intent within the popular commercial format, its Janus-faced view of Indian development. Like *Dharti ke Lal*, it deals with the harshness of village existence, an exodus, a symbolic return to loss and emotional devastation. Made after Indian independence, *Do Bigha Zamin* registers the ambivalence of the fifties toward the large-scale industrialization supported by the state. A contemporary review of the film remarked on its deep pessimism, saying that "it is very odd that, at this early moment of Indian independence, any Indian director should make so savagely pessimistic a film. . . . Not only is it a harsh film but, in the manner of Italian neo-realism, it gives an extraordinarily vivid picture of the living conditions in a great Indian city, where neon lights, occidental commodities in smart shops, and men and oxen sleeping in the streets are all part of the higgledy-piggledy scene."[28] The film opens and closes

Shambhu (Balraj Sahni) and Paro (Nirupa Roy) are reduced to poverty in
Do Bigha Zamin (Two Acres of Land). *Courtesy Bimal Roy Productions. The*
Museum of Modern Art/Film Stills Archive.

with two stark images, the first of parched and cracked earth and the last
of wire fence separating the main characters from their two acres of land.
But the two images highlight a contrast: while the parched earth can
become green and smiling again with the arrival of the monsoons, the
farmer's land, once lost, is gone irrevocably. This is the concern voiced
in *Do Bigha Zamin*—the destruction of the age-old Indian village by
the forces of modernization allied to capital. The film's claim to realism
rests in its double vision: showing the village through the perspective of
city people and the city through the eyes of its villager-protagonists. In
one shot early on in the film, a car stops at the edge of the fields and
four strange men occupy the foreground of the frame, with the villagers
in the middle ground and a cow in the background, a symbolic hierarchization that upsets the village structure. For developers, the village
only signifies land to be bought and turned to profitable use.

The village/city divide, like the good peasant/evil moneylender divide, is of course an old theme in literature and cinema. Roy is not quite

able to transcend the burden of this inheritance in the interests of realism so as to allow both to emerge as complex entities. The early segments, for instance, focusing on village life, show the protagonists Shambhu (Balraj Sahni) and Paro (Nirupa Roy) as a hardworking and devoted couple and peasant life as one of simple, communally shared pleasures. (The only thorn in the side of this rural paradise is the archetypal figure of the moneylender, who, for all practical purposes, is an outsider.) The city, on the other hand, is a ruthless jungle where it is easy to become dishonest and where the poor are trampled upon, women are molested, children are exploited. Shambhu's struggle to earn the necessary cash to extricate his two acres of land serving as collateral for the money he owes the village loan shark is elemental. As the overworked rickshaw puller, he becomes labor personified, an urban work-horse, a representative of the forgotten rural masses. The film seeks to nudge the moral conscience of the urban intelligentsia. Balraj Sahni admits as much when he notes in his autobiography how he had spent time with some rickshaw pullers in Calcutta in order to make his performance credible and his actions believable. Referring to a reviewer's observation that his acting in *Do Bigha* had a touch of genius, Sahni wrote, "I owed this 'touch' to that middle-aged ricksha-wallah."[29]

Sahni also wrote that the character of Shambhu had two major flaws: one, he is never shown to stand up to the injustice and oppression he is subjected to, and two, he shuns the company of friends and colleagues.[30] Sahni seems to have put his finger on the tension at the heart of *Do Bigha Zamin* and in Indian sensibilities regarding realism: the manifest need to present at once an individualized consciousness *and* a prototype, an agent *and* a victim. The filmmaker seems unable to resolve the contradictory pulls of inherited conventions on the one hand and political concerns on the other. To make matters more complicated, these do not divide neatly into art versus politics or (Bombay cinema) convention versus (Western cinema) innovation. For a political concern can make for conventional characterization, whereas realism as an artistic creed adopted from neorealism would still have to be adapted and contextualized to suit Indian social reality and its moral-emotional core. It is these correlations and cross-linkages that the film is not quite able to negotiate.

Why, then, is *Do Bigha* cited by Indian cineasts as a landmark realist film? I believe that the triumph of *Do Bigha* lies in turning land into a

contested symbol, a good-bad commodity, for what signifies independence and dignity for the farmer (and, by extension, the mass of the
population) is also, taken on a massive scale, the source of capitalist
and landlord power and rural exploitation. Earlier films in this genre
either did not show peasants as owning any land or simply did not treat
the land as an object of emotional and psychic investment. *Do Bigha* is
able to evoke the anxiety that we feel about property as a mark of material well-being and livelihood (the realm of necessity) and property as
privilege (the realm not, spiritually speaking, of freedom but of class
division). This anxiety, moreover, was inscribed in the very profile of
India's nationalist ideologies and resulted in its peculiarly divided aims
and policies. As a film that was able to capture and give shape to these
ambivalences, *Do Bigha* remains a document of its time and an instance
of popular cinema's moral realism.

The "Figurable" Nation: "Morbid" Realism

If the above films reveal a deeply felt engagement with contemporary
Indian life on the level of content and directorial purpose, what of style?
Here we observe the characteristic turning to Hollywood as a model, for
within the Bombay production mode, no radical stylistic departures
could be or were proposed in the demand for realism. The question was
of the cinema maintaining the illusion of reflection or representation
within the fictional mode—that is, in the Hollywood style of smooth
storytelling and invisible enunciation rather than in the cinema verité
mode or in open rebellion against studio conventions, as in Italian neorealism. The star system was firmly entrenched in the Bombay industry
and, as Fredric Jameson has said, "the star system is fundamentally,
structurally, irreconcilable with neo-realism."[31] Most self-styled realist
film directors operating out of Bombay worked with big stars but introduced the convention of deglamorizing them, of trying to write over the
sign "star" another sign which would read "average man/woman." Other
conventions of the Hindi film, notably song and dance, did not necessarily interfere with the proposed realist stance, so long as the songs
were few in number and appeared to be "motivated" by the narrative.
This does not suggest a naïveté on the part of filmmakers and viewers
but rather a pragmatic acceptance of the basic ground rules of Bombay
commercial cinema and modifications within its framework. Thus the

lead performers in a film might burst into song at several key points, but if the story was set in Assam, for instance, the music director would feel obliged to provide Assamese rhythms and tunes and be congratulated for being realistic.

Filmmakers, then, brought this highly context- and culture-specific view of realism to bear on films. Nationhood provided the particular moment for the popularization of this view. The question we have raised is how the cinema actually incorporated concerns about realism and nationhood in its storytelling practices, narrative structure, and character motivation. But did the ethic of realism, however narrowly or broadly conceived, conflict with the notion of a *national* identity? How does one establish the "truth" of social reality *as well as* allegorical representations of the nation? Three dilemmas may be pointed to. The first relates to how emphatic identification with character (Hollywood's classical realism) can be reconciled with the notion of objective observation, also aspired to by filmmakers. The second relates to the problem of how dramatic conflict, the core of fictional entertainment, can then be turned around to suggest the sense of a collectivity integral to nation building. And third, the desire to reflect the diversity and difference within Indian social life, its oppressions and prejudices, perhaps coming closest to the aims and intentions of realist filmmakers, is then faced with the gap between the "local" and the "global" within the Indian context. The question is of evolving a language of realism uniquely responsive to Indian needs. (As I point out in Chapter 7, one reason for the obvious lack of success and decline of India's parallel cinema movement, in addition to the very material difficulties of finance and distribution, is its inability to forge a national idiom of cinema which could truly contest the Bombay film on its own terrain.) These dilemmas reveal, as Janice Radway points out, "the thorny question of how culture and ideology are embodied in the content of mass-produced entertainment and how that entertainment affects the behavior of its consumers."[32]

We can turn to Fredric Jameson's notion of "figurability" as a way out of a theoretical bind. In his article "Class and Allegory in Contemporary Mass Culture: *Dog Day Afternoon* as a Political Film," Jameson contends that to be figurable is for something to be accessible to our imaginations, to become *representable* in tangible form. Through narrative figurability, films can help us detect changes in the underlying forces shaping social reality, "since social reality and the stereotypes of our experience of everyday social reality are the raw material with which commercial film and television are inevitably forced to work."[33] In certain Indian films of the postindependence period, though by no means in all, "nationhood" assumes figurability—that is, it can be sensed "through the tangible medium of daily life in vivid and experiential ways."[34] The visceral quality of the experience of nationhood, quite apart from the abstract notion of it, is signaled in the films by changes in the narrative structure. The conventional "happy ending" of the typical Bombay film, for instance, is replaced by an open-endedness that is unusual in that particular context of production. Moreover, the terms in which the central narrative conflict is delineated in the films implicate the broader social world outside the film in pointed referentiality. I shall concentrate on this dual process and its meanings in my discussion of some films in which the vision of realism itself becomes an issue.

As mentioned earlier, in postindependence India a major source of tension affecting the social and national consciousness was (and continues to be) the problem of holding on to established norms and value systems while the nation made the challenging and vaunted transition from feudalism to industrialism, from colonialism to democracy, from economic backwardness to material advancement. The impetus for the change was particularly strong right after independence, but while the leadership of the society was certain of the goals to be pursued the question of how to make the transition smooth or gradual was less often considered. Since the Indian sensibility tends to view complex issues as manifestations of moral choices, popular culture represented the felt experience of social change in terms of individual morality, of right and wrong, and "resolved" them in various ways. Realist cinema could then explore the mixture of technological optimism (faith in the camera to reflect reality) and cultural pessimism, the idealization of village and community life in the face of mounting migrations to the city, material deprivation and the promise of easy wealth, widening class, regional, and communal divisions eclipsing the vision of an unfractured *national* identity. The "truth" that the cinema was expected to "capture" on the screen was not only the truth of social and psychological experience but the "truth" of the right solution to moral dilemmas for the edification and satisfaction of the audience, in keeping with narrative traditions that Indian audiences were accustomed to. One way in which the Hindi film of the fifties sought to respond both to the cultural anxieties and the narrative expectations of its viewing public was through the problematization of the notion of poverty and the delineation of character progression along a trajectory that moves from a state of economic and social deprivation to material wealth to a deliberate return to poverty. The eschewing of definitive narrative closure (the "happy ending" where the hero is at peace with, and part of, society) takes on significance in this regard. The closing frames of a film, for instance, might bring the stars of the film together, but only in the iconography of the marginalized or rejects of society. Before turning to the films in more detail, I would like to point out the cultural meanings attached to the deliberate embracing of poverty as signified in filmic and other discourses of the fifties.

The idea of poverty has a special significance in India. ("Poverty" here is only an approximate term. The word "poverty" in its everyday sense denotes a material condition signified by lack of economic resources and consequent difficulty in maintaining a decent standard of living. I want to use it in this descriptive sense but without the wholly negative connotations and with the added dimension that makes it coextensive with spiritual gain.) While most religio-cultural beliefs and value systems embody some variation of the idea of material wealth as corrupting, in the Hindu religious and philosophical tradition the concept of poverty or nonattachment to material things has the status of an elaborated ethic. Apart from the fact that the essential thrust is toward the attainment of spiritual knowledge, there is the concept of the four stages of life on earth through which every Hindu passes—*brahmacharya* (that of a student learning the *shastras*, or holy books), *garhastha* (that of the householder fulfilling his or her social obligations), *vanaprastha* (that of a hermit, gradually withdrawing from society for meditation in the forest), and *sanyasa* (complete renunciation of worldly ties and desires). While the first half of a person's life is given over to his duties and responsibilities in the world, in the later years one is to concentrate more and more upon the spiritual and upon the search for liberation. The final stage of renunciation and withdrawal, therefore, marks the culmination and highest point of human achievement and is embodied in the image of the wandering mendicant who does not even care where his next meal is going to come from. This state of material poverty is a positive and willed condition, necessary for a person's self-realization, and one can think of numerous historical figures (Buddha, Shri Ramakrishna, Shri Aurobindo, among them) who chose to traverse this path.

In the twentieth century Gandhi sought and enjoyed an identification with this image of poverty and deliberate renunciation, thereby earning the title of mahatma, or "great soul."

A view of money as tainted and of poverty as sublime is thus part of the Indian psyche. But it is the act of *becoming* poor, not the state of being already poor, that attracts the Indian imagination. For poverty as degradation, breeding suffering, squalor, and death, has long been a harsh reality of the Indian landscape. In the postindependence era this poverty came to be called by its social scientific name of "economic backwardness" and stood in the way of India's self-image of progress and equality with other nations. Economic backwardness was a condition that could be eliminated, our leaders fervently believed, by industrialization, science, and technology. The model of the affluent Western nations was there for all to see. But it was not a model that India wanted to import wholesale, that is, it could do without the materialistic attitude of the West, its worship of money. Rather, in the nature of a transaction, India could offer to the (Western) world its spiritual traditions, its sense of ethical values, community, and compassion. Nehru's doctrine of Panchsheel, or the "five principles" of mutual respect, nonaggression, nonintervention, equality, and peaceful co-existence, was cast in this optimistic and mediatory mode. This idea of the spiritual East complementing (or counterposed against, depending on the political winds blowing at the time the comparison is drawn) the materialistic West was not new in the Nehru era. It has been subscribed to by both Westerners and Easterners, finding its most creative expression in India in the mid- to late nineteenth century and having known various types of modifications and vulgarizations over the years. India's fragile sense of identity as a nation during the early years of independence (with the ambivalent view of "poverty" as one of its symptoms) created both a moral and an intellectual dilemma. As Richard Lannoy states:

> The idea of national identity—the self-awareness of the nation, its self-image, and its values—springs from a desire for fixed points of reference in the enlarged world of today. The self-image of India is tentative in character and has evolved from the way it perceives its history from ancient times through many centuries of decline and foreign domination to the decades of its recently achieved status as an independent sovereign state. The difficulties in forming a contempo-

rary national self-image may be more clearly appreciated when it is realized that while India is now building a modern, secular state, its traditions are permeated by a sophisticated religious sensibility.[35]

An impediment to the creation of a self-image that India could proudly embrace was indeed the excessive poverty in which half the population lived. But there were dangers in the dominant ideology endorsing too strongly what was its opposite, namely, money or material affluence. Not only did affluence have negative connotations in the folk imagination, but a too eager pursuit of money could unleash the undesirable social traits of cupidity, fraud, theft, and the like. Since implicit in the creation of a new society is some vision of utopia, an idea of what type of society is desirable and what sort of citizens should inhabit it, forms of mass culture can become instrumental in embodying the tension that results between the utopian ideal and the bedrock of practical considerations to which it must be linked. Richard Dyer has suggested, "Entertainment offers the image of 'something better' to escape into, or something we want deeply that our day-to-day lives don't provide. Alternatives, hopes, wishes—these are the stuff of utopia, the sense that things could be better, that something other than what is can be imagined and maybe realised."[36] Moreover, Dyer asserts that entertainment responds to real needs created by society and that the utopian sensibility "has to take off from the real experiences of the audience."[37] Much of the realistic cinema of postindependence India can be seen in this "utopian" vein. Broadly speaking, the utopian sensibility was linked to a strong moral stance vis-à-vis fetishized images of money. Indian mass culture translated the allure of money (with its materialistic and unethical connotations) into an instrumental view of money. In other words, filmmakers could provide what seemed a naturalistic portrayal of social reality, the world of "dirty" business, black money, corruption, and greed, while at the same time imply through point-of-view shots and sympathetic and morally upright characters the availability of the utopian solution. The ethical code suggested that money earned through honest hard work was a desired social virtue, but excessive accumulation of it or an obsession to acquire it could create a social world that was the opposite of utopian. At its simplest we have in films the national stereotypes of the poor but happy peasant, the hard-working and honest laborer, the idealistic schoolteacher, the philanthropic doctor. These figures were touched but not corrupted by the social environment created by the momentum of a fast-growing economy supporting capital accumulation, the struggle for higher wages, illicit profits, and the like. But the utopian sensibility may also be generally absent in some films, to be replaced by a deliberate exploration of negative modes of feeling like anxiety, pessimism, fear, and resignation. *Hum Log, Andhian, Footpath* (1953), *Shri 420 (The Gentleman Cheat,* 1955), *Jagte Raho (Keep Awake!,* 1956), *Pyaasa (The Thirsty One,* 1957), and *Kala Bazaar (Black Market,* 1960) were a few of these films.

Such films work with the raw materials of the contemporary experience of the lower middle class and the laboring classes of urban Indians (the target audience of the Bombay cinema) and may be said to present the city as the microcosm of the nation. This is apparent in terms of formal structure and the use of narrative space. In the typical Hindi film (and in commercial entertainment generally) the central conflict engaging the characters allows for a division of the fictional space available to them, so that they can retreat to the part of it that represents refuge, harmony, and happiness. The home, the village, scenic natural surroundings provide this kind of privatized fictional space. In some of the well-known postindependence films, however, particularly in *Jagte Raho, Pyaasa, Shri 420, Deedar (Sight,* 1951) but also in others like *Mr. Sampat* (1952), space is alien and threatening, allowing the central character no escape outside it. This space is the big city, a closed urban milieu impressionistically rendered, with an atmosphere that is claustrophobic, evil, corrupt. Divided between a naturalist (focusing on objects to define character) and a realist (focusing on the individual) impulse, these films create a morbid realism. Filmic space provides the testing ground for the character's moral sense, but moral victory can only result in withdrawal to a nonexistent space, to nowhere, a space that the films do not indicate visually at any point in the narrative.

A few examples should make this clear. In *Jagte Raho* the opening shots present a deserted city street at night where the "hero" finds himself wandering, lost and alone. The iconography of dress and makeup suggests that he is a villager but we are never told where he belongs, no flashbacks connect him to the place he has left, and at the end of the film when he walks away from the apartment building where he was trapped as in a maze he only gets as far as beyond the gates of the building. In *Shri 420,* similarly, the hero's arrival in and departure from the big city mark the beginning and end of the narrative. Urban space engulfs him, symbolizing the closed world of the city dweller who is

Textual ambivalence in Boot Polish: *a kindly bootlegger (David) befriends slum children. Courtesy National Film Archive of India.*

The clash of discourses: "Mother India" and Kala Bazaar (Black Market). *Courtesy National Film Archive of India.*

forced to confront pain and temptation. Vidya (meaning "knowledge"), the heroine of the film and its moral center, is a poor schoolteacher. In *Pyaasa*, the alienated hero is not from the village but is city-bred, educated but expendable in terms of the operative values of urban society. He is a poet and therefore unemployable, important to society only in death, shunned and institutionalized in an insane asylum when alive. He has a family but no home and can only leave at the end of the film for an unknown destination with a similar marginal figure, a one-time prostitute. In *Mr. Sampat*, based on an R. K. Narayan novel, the hero as antihero is also without family or attachments, but unlike the central characters in the other films, he embodies that rare phenomenon in the Bombay film, the corrupt hero who is thoroughly immersed in the fraudulent city milieu and remains a liar and opportunist till the end of the film. He is the man of the world incarnate, turning every occasion to his benefit and someone else's loss. But he is no more corrupt than a host of other social types who inhabit that fictional world—tall-talking politicians, unethical businessmen, heartless journalists, get-rich-quick merchants, scheming philanthropists—and may even elicit grudging admiration from the audience for being able to live by his wits.

Within this all-encompassing urban world "poverty" and "wealth" as signifiers act on two levels. In terms of contemporary experience they point to economic and social divisions within society and of the fantasies of the poor to get rich and of the rich to get richer. But they also embody the stock opposition between the "traditional" moral values of honesty, hard work, and fellowship and "modern" urban culture breeding hatred, suspicion, greed, and loneliness. The two worlds are poised against each other, and seldom do the films explore the possibility of infusing the values of the one in the culture of the other. The result in terms of dramatic movement is a circular one; the hero returns to his initial state and to a space outside urban society, which is nevertheless denied a palpable existence in visual or narrative codes. The return involves a conscious and deliberate rejection of the values associated with city life that stem from the possession or the pursuit of wealth. For instance, in *Deedar*, childhood as an idyllic condition where class divisions do not count is juxtaposed with the adult world of social hierarchy and distance. The narrative charts the hero's spatial and temporal movement from childhood and "inside" society to adulthood and "outside" it in terms of his loss, recovery, and then self-inflicted loss of vision, the final act of

Signifying value-systems: the Indianized "good" woman, Vidya (Nargis) . . .

self-directed violence signaling his disenchantment by a departure from the depicted social world.

The central characters of *Do Bigha Zamin* return to their village after a sojourn to the city only to find that they have no place to live. In *Jagte Raho* the outsider-hero can only quench the thirst that has driven him

. . . and the Westernized vamp (Nadira) in Shri 420 *(The Gentleman Cheat).*
The Museum of Modern Art/Film Stills Archive (photos, pp. 106–107).

to the city by stepping outside its stultifying and corrupt confines and symbolically retracing his steps back to the village. The narrative agent of *Shri 420* follows a similar circular trajectory after having nearly lost his integrity (*imam*) among the city sharks. In *Pyaasa* the poet-hero's fortunes involve a tortuous succession of "worldly" success and failure through which he can only liberate himself by willfully choosing the anonymity from which he had started out to escape. What is interesting here is that contestation of the dominant generic conventions of the Bombay film at the level of narrative paradigm can be offset by the assertion of traditional moral values at the level of the image. In each of these films wealth serves also as an object of desire at the level of the subtext, revealed on the visual track by an excess of images of money—paper currency, bank notes, gold coins—gratifying the viewer's eye and imagination by means of close-ups, superimpositions, and other cinematic techniques. The conflict itself is inscribed within the *dharmic* code (signifying the law) that Vijay Mishra talks about in an article on the Bombay cinema. Poverty and wealth, then, are associated in the texts with *dharma* and renunciation on the one hand and *adharma* and worldliness on the other. As Mishra tells us, "The opposition between *nivritti* ('re-

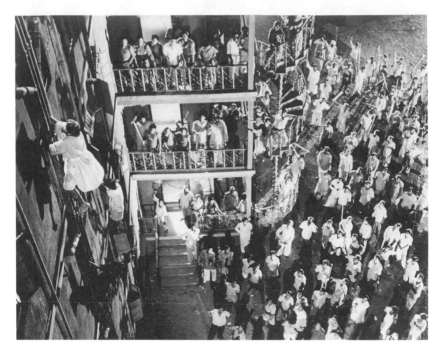

The villager trapped and hounded in the city: Raj Kapoor in Jagte Raho (Keep Awake!). *The Museum of Modern Art/Film Stills Archive.*

nunciation') and *pravritti* ('worldliness') constitutes a major epistemological shift in Hindu thought which survives, in its various forms, to this day. Needless to say, its ramifications in the Bombay film too are considerable."[38] Most Bombay films rework this opposition and work toward a mediation through the agency of the hero. How then are we to read the act of renunciation in the films under review? Does it offer a genuine alternative, either on the real or the symbolic/representational level? I have suggested above that the renunciation that the films espouse has only an emotional force (it does not appear as a concrete possibility), and I find this as evidence of the enlarged national context that the films allegorically represent. In these texts the mediation operates on another level. The films accommodate the demands of verisimilitude and those of ideology by representing the human costs of economic growth and social Darwinism, but they prescribe a strict moral code and "legitimize" renunciation of the ways of the unscrupulous. So while renunciation is negated, since it is the opposite of involvement, the required and desired state for citizens of the new nation, it is also

The lonely poet-hero: Guru Dutt in Pyaasa (The Thirsty One). *The Museum of Modern Art/Film Stills Archive.*

proposed as a fitting rejection of the social evils of cupidity, fraud, and competitiveness.

Bimal Roy's *Parakh (Test,* 1960) brings these themes together through the medium of social satire. With story and music by Salil Chowdhury, a long-term member of the Bimal Roy production team, *Parakh* is a thinly veiled attack on the nation's politicians, particularly those with vested interests who manipulate the common people for personal gain and power. The action is set in a small village with its ensemble of representative characters: the postmaster; the schoolteacher; the *pundit,* or professional prayergiver; the *zamindar,* or landlord; the moneylender; the village doctor; the astrologer; and the politician, who is a union board president. The film introduces each of these characters, all of whom, with the exception of the postmaster and the schoolteacher, Rajat (Vasant Chowdhury), are satirized as embodiments of the negative traits of meanness, greed, fraudulence, pomposity, and pretense. Mostly Bombay film comedians (some often cast as villains as well) were chosen for these roles, so as to build on prior associations, a practice common in the Hindi cinema. The eye of the camera catches, as it were, each man revealing his own negative trait as he goes about his activity in the village. Only the postmaster (Nasir Hussein) is decent and honest, as is Rajat, the hero, who is in love with the postmaster's charming and child-like daughter, Seema (Sadhana).

The plot in *Parakh* involves an enigma and an impersonation: a lame postman, Haradhan (Motilal), delivers a letter to the postmaster from a wealthy beneficiary named Jagdish Chandra Ray, whose identity is not known. The letter says that a reward of Rs. 5 lakhs (roughly $50,000) will be given to the person in the village with the best record of social service. When the letter is read out in the presence of all the village notables, their expressions are captured through freeze frames: mouths fall open, swallowing motions are seen, the *zamindar* stops smoking. Rajat suggests that a vote be taken, and the elections are set for the first day of the following month. Then starts a veritable scramble for the good will of the people as the candidates vie with one another to reverse their habitual mean or greedy attitudes: the doctor gives free treatment, the *zamindar* forgives his debtors, the *pundit* fakes a miracle. Processions, banners, and loudspeakers proclaim the virtues of different candidates, and fights between rival factions break out. Only the postmaster remains aloof and is on the verge of losing his home because he cannot pay the mortgage. Rajat also withdraws from the election. But the people find none of the candidates worthy of the award and declare the postmaster the winner. The identity of the benefactor is also revealed: he is Sir J. C. Roy, a rich and powerful man masquerading as the lame postman and studying the dynamics of the village. The villagers rejoice with the surprised postmaster as honesty and goodness are rewarded in the end. Haradhan's fantasy over, he regretfully leaves the village.

This parable of political corruption and chicanery in postcolonial India is explored through the "victimized" space of the village (where politicians routinely make their appearance before an election) in which moral order and disorder can be presented in fairly clear-cut tones. In keeping too with the conventions of the Bombay film, the saree-clad and innocent village belle is contrasted with a Westernized and spoilt city-bred woman, the sister-in-law of the *zamindar*. Through the medium of satire, traditional and new-found authority is challenged. But the vision of change offered by the film is a paternalist one. Fantasies of escape into a romanticized "averageness" are only available to the very rich, who can afford to pass on some of their wealth to the poor provided the latter are good and honest. The upper-class, aristocratic benefactor masquerading in the village and upsetting its routines preserves the broader social hierarchies even as he holds himself beyond them through his superior knowledge and wisdom.

Sujata

Parakh is a crossover from "morbid" realism to moral realism. That is, it is anxious to morally frame the social evil it depicts, to present contemporary life in the form of a fable. *Sujata* (*The Well-Born*, 1959), on the other hand, is much more gentle in its approach, the camera more objective, the characters psychologically rounded. It may be considered a condensation of many of the elements we have discussed as constituting realism in Bombay cinema: a Bengali-Hindi combination (the film was based on a Bengali novel by that name written by Subodh Ghosh), a nationalist purpose (Bimal Roy, the director, responded to a call for a film to be made on untouchability), a highlighting of emotions through subtle editing and camerawork, naturalistic mise-en-scène, and a morally elevated tone. *Sujata*'s theme of stability and change seems to reproduce its maker's own transitional state. By the time Bimal Roy produced *Sujata*, he was a prominent and esteemed commercial filmmaker. An emgiré from East Bengal, he had started his career in the mid-thirties as a cameraman, first with the pioneering director P. C. Barua, then with Nitin Bose of New Theatres in Calcutta. He was forced to move to Bombay when the Calcutta market suffered a serious setback with the Second World War and impending partition, bringing his own group of unit members (Hrishikesh Mukerjee, cameraman, Nabendu Ghosh, writer, Asit Sen, actor, and Paul Mahendra, dialogue writer) with him. He was later joined by Salil Choudhary, Kamal Bose, Sudhendhu Roy, Nazir Hussain, and others. He set up Bimal Roy Productions in 1953 and made many films under his own banner. Although exposed to all the commercial pressures of the Bombay industry, he tried to continue the tradition of "social realism" of New Theatres, also running his company in the old studio manner of the big extended family. The influence of the Bengali "sentimental" novelistic tradition of Sarat Chandra Chatterjee is evident in his films, which usually have a strong story-line, psychological characterization, and ennobling sentiments. His films bear the stamp of the sensibility of the middle-class intelligentsia, who shared the idealism of the national reconstruction phase and subscribed to broadly socialist values. *Sujata* is invariably included in the official retrospectives of Indian films at international film festivals and enjoys the status of a classic. Its mechanisms of pleasure, blend of realism and idealism, and the humanitarian vision that it embodies denote a powerful, if fading, current in the fifties' symbolic universe.

In *Sujata*, many of the oppositions discussed earlier—between poverty and wealth, renunciation and worldliness, *dharma* and *adharma*, desire and law—are worked out in terms of the family as nation/nation as family idea. This is the culmination of the utopian vision, for it integrates within the construct of the nation the self-sufficiency implicit in the image of the modern bourgeois family (by extension the modern bourgeois state) and the ties of blood and genealogy that characterize traditional Indian notions of family. The story concerns the adoption of an untouchable baby girl by a Brahmin family and the problems that then arise. The child is not so much adopted as allowed to stay on because a suitable home cannot be found for her, her parents having died in an epidemic. She is named Sujata and grows up with the family's own daughter, Rama. When a relative with orthodox religious views visits, matters get complicated and Sujata (Nutan) learns of her low-caste origins. Her adoptive mother wants Rama to marry Adhir (Sunil Dutt), a highly educated and accomplished Brahmin boy who, however, falls in love with Sujata. Enraged, her "mother" insults Sujata and has an accident that leaves her in need of a blood transfusion. Only Sujata's blood matches her own and Sujata is thus able to save her life. The family is reunited and Sujata and Adhir are married.

The narrative is structured by posing the toughest problem of all in class and genealogical terms: the "pollution" of blood and the "mingling" of blood. The film is openly didactic in that it stresses the correct moral position with respect to caste distinctions, operating at both the discursive and emotional levels. At various points in the narrative the opposing views regarding untouchability are counterposed in dramatic conflict, while the viewer's empathy for and identification with the central character, Sujata, is assured by every means available to the entertainment cinema: star quality, cinematic techniques of the close-up, point-of-view shots and framing, the narrative pleasures of romance, suspense, and a happy ending. Illusionism is maintained by projecting the fictional world as co-extensive with the real world, with common reference points and shared (Gandhian) values, as also by "natural" acting, dress, and speech and the use of outdoor sets. The film is ideological in the sense that it presents the possibility of the ideal society in the here and now under the spirit of Gandhi, who is a sort of patron saint to Sujata, saving her once from suicide and unfailingly offering comfort, strength, and hope in her darkest moments. (In fact, the very idea of the narrative situation, that of an untouchable being "adopted" by an upper-caste family, is taken from Gandhi's teachings: Gandhi advocated that Hindus should adopt Muslim children and vice versa to promote communal harmony.) Moreover, the film is firmly grounded in a middle-class, upper-caste ethos, for it is Sujata who is "elevated" in the caste hierarchy by her induction into a Brahmin family rather than the other way around, and time and time again in the narrative the essential nobility of spirit of the major Brahmin characters becomes evident, including the two caste-conscious women characters in the film, Sujata's "foster mother" and Adhir's grandmother, who experience a change of heart at the end of the film. On the other hand, the few portraits of people belonging to Sujata's own caste are decidedly unflattering, fulfilling the stereotypes of the drunken, physically unattractive lower castes.

Against this background, it is Sujata's character which becomes a poignant instance of impersonation: she is "Brahmin" among the untouchables and "untouchable" among the Brahmins. She, and we, the audience, are always conscious of her split identity. The fact that Sujata is an untouchable by birth is almost incidental, though it has a crucial importance in the unfolding of the narrative. Sujata's associations are with nature, and some of the most beautiful shots in the film show her in close proximity with flowers, against rain-laden clouds, in the garden among rare and delicate species of plants. (The visual and symbolic "distance" of Sujata from the condition of untouchability is underscored by the fact that one of the foremost stars of the period, Nutan, plays this role with great finesse.) Sujata is a floating signifier; her natural parents are dead at the beginning of the film and her entry into the dominant social order must be initiated through a reconstruction of genealogy and connections of blood. In spatial terms, she must move from outside society to inside it, from a "natural" state to marriage and domestication, from poverty and dependence to wealth and social position. Membership in the family/nation, in other words, leads to upward mobility along several axes. We will examine each of these coordinates as they affect the notion of utopia in the film.

At first glance it would seem that the film makes an unproblematical statement about the insiders of society, the wealthy and upper caste, versus those like the poor and lower castes, who have to suffer the status of outsiders and have to be incorporated. But the distinctions are not always so clear. Upendra Chowdhury is not rooted to place and community, the fact that is taken as the mark of identity of the twice-born Hindus. In a sense he has lost his caste, since he has a job (as an engineer) that takes him to remote places, remote from his own kind, that is. His taking in and then harboring an untouchable is to some extent possible because of these circumstances. Moreover, he is a man of science and therefore rational, enlightened, free from outmoded ideas of caste. It is in such apparently incidental details (the film does not draw attention to Upendra's job although it does to his enlightened thinking) that *Sujata* has a contemporary resonance and is "realistic." It directs its message to those whose lives were changing as a result of the nation's industrialization and development projects, forcing them to travel outside their regions and thereby loosening, to some extent, the hold of caste taboos on them. Yet even here the film is at best cautious. Upendra and his wife, Charu, are always conscious of Sujata's "difference" and never fail to underscore it—particularly Charu, whose verbal distinction between her own child and the adoptive child ("my daughter" and "like my daughter") runs as a motif through the film and is an index of Sujata's emotional and familial isolation. It is only when Sujata "proves" herself through the biggest test of all, the giving of her own blood to save Charu's life, that she is finally accepted into the caste identity and social milieu of Upendra's family. Sujata must transcend the conditions of her birth before she can truly "belong," and the agent of her upliftment is not something she does but something that *is:* her blood type happens to match that of the dying Charu. The film, while making the point that caste is not a matter of polluted blood, nevertheless ossifies caste by making the breaking of caste barriers dependent upon accident.

The conflict of values represented by the opposition of "poverty" and "wealth" that is central to the films we talked about earlier is here less overt, but the question of inheritance does occupy a key place in the narrative. We (the audience for the film) sense, although there is no specific sign, that one reason for Charu's anxiety in safeguarding the prospects of her daughter, Rama, in securing Adhir's affections and her perception of Sujata as a threat in this regard is that Adhir is the sole heir to his grandmother's wealth. Only such an unspoken hope can explain the viciousness with which she turns on Sujata when she hears that

Sujata has "usurped" Adhir's love, accusing her of being a serpent in their midst. Sujata has done the ultimate wrong that a foster child can perpetrate: she has tried to take the place of the natural child and, in a sense, disinherit her. The question of property and inheritance, then, plays an unobtrusive but forceful role in the motivation of character and plot. Wealth is obviously part of the utopian vision and the hero, Adhir, has enough of it. But he does not possess it directly and is apparently uncaring about it, for he likes to be immersed in books (the "displaced" source of wealth) and even spurns his grandmother's legacy when she opposes his marriage with Sujata. Since one of the points that the film wishes to make is that modern education is true wealth, the means of dispelling ignorance, superstition, and prejudice, inherited wealth, which goes with social class, is an attribute of the upholders of prejudice in the film such as Adhir's grandmother, who probably inherited *her* property. But by making Adhir and Sujata ultimately come into a lot of money, the film maintains both sides of the contradiction: money operating as class and caste barrier and money as ascension into a higher class and caste. In a country where a major social division is perpetuated as a result of inherited wealth (and status), inherited wealth can only be justified as a source of philanthropy. Inherited wealth is morally justifiable when it is instrumental in bringing about social upliftment. The film, however, does not propose any radical change in the basic economic divisions in society. If we then pursue our family-as-nation metaphor, the lower castes and untouchables can be incorporated into the larger body of society by a symbolic purification of blood and the sharing of inheritance.

Just as deliverance from a lower-caste identity can come through integration into a higher-caste family, deliverance from a subordinate sexual identity must come through marriage. Sujata's subjectivity is defined by the two characters emotionally closest to her, both of whom are male: Upendra, her substitute father, and Adhir, her wooer and prospective husband. As mentioned earlier, one of the projects that the film sets itself is to confer on Sujata an identity in social and familial terms. This involves, among other things, the process of naming. Early in the film, Upendra names the foundling "Sujata," meaning "of good birth," in a symbolic reversal of her true origins that is to continue throughout the film. With Adhir's arrival on the scene, this task is taken over by him. A particular sequence, quite movingly and beautifully presented, makes this clear. Rama's birthday party is being celebrated, as it is every year,

Privilege confers the power of naming: Adhir (Sunil Dutt) and Sujata (Nutan) in Sujata *(The Well-Born). Courtesy Bimal Roy Productions. The Museum of Modern Art/Film Stills Archive.*

and Charu has just hurt Sujata's feelings once again by identifying her to one of the guests as *beti jaisi* ("*like* my daughter"). Sujata leaves the enclosed space of the room where the party is being held and, as is her wont, seeks refuge in the open air of the night. Adhir has noticed her pained embarrassment and quietly follows her. In the course of their conversation, he asks her when her birthday is and she replies that it is lost in the darkness of oblivion. Adhir then points to the sky and "names" her birthday by saying that on that day too the stars were shining as brightly and they were witness to the event of Sujata's birth. In reply to his question of what gift she would like for her birthday, she replies that he had given her the greatest gift of all: recognition as a human being to one whose birthday was unknown and who was therefore without any sort of identity.

The film thus poses Sujata's dual identity, as daughter (to Upendra) and wife (to Adhir), as problematic and sets about clearing the obstacles to its establishment. Marriage to Adhir is considered, by Sujata and by all others in her social world, as the ultimate good fortune, and the film offers Sujata no options to make it on her own. She has had no formal education and no chance to prove herself except in domestic matters, as an "elevated" and very efficient servant. Marriage to Adhir is also linked to her financial independence: Adhir's grandmother, in a gracious gesture of defeat, leaves Sujata the money that she had set aside as a gift for Adhir's bride. A woman's social and individual identities are therefore both conferred by marriage, for without it Sujata is simply an appendage, and often an embarrassment, in the Chowdhury household. While part of this has a dramatic function, to highlight Sujata's plight as an untouchable, the overall traditional attitude to women remains in place. The fact that the men in the film are open-minded and progressive while the women are superstitious and rigid in their thinking (with a change of heart in the end) can be seen as an extension of this attitude. In terms of the utopian vision, then, an upper-middle-class, male-dominated culture remains in place, but it is a culture infused with the ideals of liberal education, scientific thinking, and class and caste mobility.

From *Sujata*, to Bimal Roy, to fifties moral realism in cinema, to realism as the metaphoric site of displaced intellectual anxiety in postindependence India, we can retrace our mental steps in order to apprehend "realism" as a historical process of cultural consensus building in which, briefly, the cinema saw itself as a dominant player. Each of these discursive constructs has served as a nodal point in the preceding analysis to illustrate the convergence of ideological purpose, social and economic change, artistic endeavor, and traditional values. In other words, nationalist goals as envisioned and articulated by political leaders were widely shared by all influential sectors of the population and the general public more than in any subsequent period of the nation's history. Vast projects of industrialization unleashed conditions of social flux that found in realism a stabilizing discourse. The influence of Western narrative models, both literary and cinematic, meant the striving after the "truth" of lived experience and social reality, the minimizing of the gap between the fictional world and the referential world. And, finally, the valorization in cultural texts of traditional values of duty, renunciation, and poverty was meant to offset the greed, selfishness, and individualism associated with Western-style progress. Realism, then, is that which crosses over, binds, and translates one domain of social experience and capitalist development with, and for, another.

But I have also tried to present realism as an impersonating discourse. By this my impulse has not been toward constructing a hierarchy of "realisms" within the Indian cinema (regional and all-India) in which the commercial Hindi film can be reconfirmed to hold the lowermost space. Whose realism is more real is not a question that concerns me in this study (although I do not deny that there might be a context for raising such issues of aesthetic differentiation). Rather, it is the *adoption* of realism as a guiding principle that has been of interest here. Moreover, in keeping with the idea of impersonation elaborated so far in this book, I have tried to show the co-presence of contradictory, even opposed forces and tendencies that makes *this* realism a uniquely Indian phenomenon; that is, a social and psychic investment at a given place and time. Thus "realism" has been a code word for "moralism"; an aesthetic yardstick to gauge commercial filmmaking practices; a mode of juxtaposition of the intellectual with the working poor (as in the actor Balraj Sahni's comments regarding his "education" at the hands of a rickshaw-puller prior to the shooting of *Do Bigha Zamin*); an ethic of deglamorization of stars and of cinematic production generally, within the generic frameworks already in place; and a mode of national self-examination, self-reflection, and self-representation, again within the parameters of "idealist" conventions, in which pain, humiliation, and agony as contemporary conditions can only have meaning as the masquerading forms of the eternal verities of truth and beauty. Realism, in other words, allows Indian popular cinema to will itself as an (ambivalent) participant in a worldwide hegemonic formation (the "modernization" formula), seeking to disclose from within the bases of technological power and bourgeois capital technology's human face.

August in Bombay: a month of festivals, the month of Krishna's
birthday and Coconut Day; and this year [1947] . . . there was
an extra festival on the calendar, a new myth to celebrate,
because a nation which had never previously existed was about
to win its freedom, catapulting us into a world which, although
it had invented the game of chess and traded with Middle
Kingdom Egypt, was nevertheless quite imaginary; into a
mythical land, a country which would never exist except by the
efforts of a phenomenal collective will—except in a dream we all
agreed to dream; it was a mass fantasy shared in varying
degrees by Bengali and Punjabi, Madrasi and Jat, and would
periodically need the sanctification and renewal which can only
be provided by rituals of blood. India, the new myth—a
collective fiction in which anything was possible, a fable rivaled
only by the two other mighty fantasies: money and God.
—Salman Rushdie, Midnight's Children

4

New Uses of the Romantic-Mythic Tradition

Realism and myth represent a dialectical tension: the pull
of the everyday, the normal, the contemporary against that of the imaginative, the unexpected, the timeless. Each contains the other, for realism as a particular set of conventions points always to the larger traditions and belief systems within which those conventions are embedded,
while a mythic structure or image often embodies the most "real" though
indirect expression of the ways of seeing and believing of a society and

its culture, what film critic Parker Tyler has called "imaginative truth." Insofar as this is so, they are both impersonating phenomena, not only in the sense that they appear in different garbs and assume different forms in specific social-symbolic contexts, but also in that they are both ultimately constituted in language (verbal and imagistic) and hence are premised on a basic instability. This instability is evidenced in the range of meanings that each of these terms evokes and the fact that they endlessly explore and re-explore (indeed, seek to lock into place) the relationship of the human world to the concrete and the "natural" one.

That "realism" and "myth" generally function as antithetical terms is significant, suggesting their mobilization for modes of thought and artistic approach that are considered appropriate at certain times and in certain conditions. In cinema, strategies of realism and myth are meant to evoke different responses in audiences, to codify, channelize, and diversify the felt needs of people. If the stated purpose of realism is to stay close to "life," the purpose of myth is to go beyond it, to incorporate the unfamiliar and the abstract, to allow the *dreams* of a collectivity to take shape. "Myths," says Mark Schorer, "are the instruments by which we continually struggle to make our experience intelligible to ourselves."[1]

In this chapter, I explore how myth and its related term, romance, function as narrative and structural forms in the Bombay cinema for the construction of the nation myth. Primarily, my focus is on the construction of mythic figures of authority who represent a unifying force in social life. The mythic design has to do with sacrificial death whereby evil is averted or nullified and the social body healed. Moreover, mythic resolution comes through the reconciliation of state authority with more traditional centers of allegiance such as the family, caste, or romantic partner. Indeed, it is the *transformation* of parental figures to impersonal, threatening, even sinister forces of power that at once represents the repressive apparatus of authority and sanctions it by aligning it with the personal. Drawing somewhat heavily on psychoanalyst Sudhir Kakar's work to connect notions of self and other, individuation and kinship affiliation, eroticism and sublimation, I argue that the commercial films discussed below perform the ideological function of investing with libidinal energy the new collective myth of the fifties: the secular myth of the nation. The films reflect a dominant concern of the period to inculcate the values of citizenship and obedience to a legal code that must be posed as impersonal, impartial, infallible. Such a symptomatic reading alone can help us see how often the drama of the courtroom is played out in the Bombay film and how the subjectivity of the central characters is split between contrary allegiances. Often, the use of the double underscores this split in the films whereby the potential for subversion is recuperated by the mythic-ideological framework.

But posing the "problem" of reading in these terms may seem to elide the more "positive" notions of myth: what the Peruvian José Carlos Mariátegui called "a need for the infinite," a need for transcendence on the part of the masses of people of a nation, or what Gramsci saw as a utopian mythical language that produces images of desired connections.[2] At a time when we are skeptical of all visual forms of commercial culture, it is indeed difficult to envisage what such a mythical language would look like unless one could locate it in certain forms of hybridity itself as the hallmark of a process of definition of the new national subject. The task would then be to see how such forms are mapped onto possibilities of social change in the concrete circumstances of an unfolding history.

It should then be clear that this book does not have much use for those meanings of the word "myth" that associate it entirely with lies and falsehood, or romance with "escapism." Just as "impersonation" in this study does not signify "deceit" but rather the mutual "contamination," juxtaposition, and jostling of categories, myth here suggests a dynamic textual process where meanings are inherently unstable. In other words, the conservative pull of myth is contested by the enervating playfulness of romance; the repressiveness of state authority is undermined by the quirky twists of fate; the masquerade of the goddess Kāli as Mother India is also the face of a lonely, struggling woman and a passionately fond mother. These scenarios from some of the films discussed below point to the centrifugal and centripetal forces at work in the popular cinema, even if, on balance, the tendency of mythic narratives, as French anthropologist Claude Lévi-Strauss asserted, is toward closure and the resolution of social contradictions.

It is necessary to introduce a caveat here. There are no ready-made mechanisms whereby the mythic narrative in cinema may be set apart a priori from the nonmythic one, and therefore my choice of films for analysis is meant to be suggestive and exploratory rather than representative or exclusionary. Outside the range of those Bombay films which deal directly with the classical myths, distinctions between the mythic and the realistic become a matter of emphasis, stylization, thematic preoccupations, and the structuration of dominant motifs. Just as the

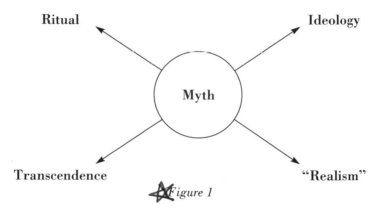

Ritual   Ideology

Myth

Transcendence   "Realism"

Figure 1

most realistic film strains toward allegory, so the mythic idea in cinema is tied to the imagery of the physical world. Moreover, much of contemporary criticism has relegated the whole of secular bourgeois culture to the realm of myth and falsehood, reserving progressive utopian tendencies for the avant-garde. Indeed, it is the enormous fecundity of myth criticism that renders this term amorphous, a fecundity that informs its range of semantic fields as represented in Figure 1. These are the constituent elements that must go into a theory of myth as a composite, context-bound structure. My interest here is in understanding not only how these are mobilized in particular texts, but how the idea of myth itself is used in postindependence India to yoke together the traditional and the modern, the sacred and the profane.

Indeed, the tradition of the companionate opposite inhering in Indian mythic thought and intellectual inquiry goes back many centuries. D. D. Kosambi, the Indian classical scholar and historian, provides us with a powerful image of contrast when he poses the rhetorical question in his *Myth and Reality*, "Why should anyone ignore the beautiful lily of Indian philosophy in order to concentrate upon the dismal swamp of popular superstition?"[3] Kosambi answers that "it takes a considerable scientific effort to discover the physiological process whereby the lily grew out of the mud and filth," an effort that he then proceeds to make in a series of masterly analyses. While the details of his archaeological investigations cannot detain us here, a few points of interest may be appropriated for our own purposes. Kosambi tries to relate ancient Indian myths to their social substratum—to the forces and relations of production in ancient and feudal times. His effort is not only to counter the rarefied philosophical abstractions of ancient Indian scholars (and their modern counterparts) but to propose a view of myth, popular religion, and ritual as a "palimpsest" history. "This is not too difficult in a country where contemporary society is composed of elements that preserve the indelible marks of almost every historical stage." Kosambi writes:

> The religious observances of the various human groups in India, particularly those that are lowest in the social, cultural and economic scale, show roughly the order in which the particular groups were enrolled into a greater, productive society. In a general way, this is true of many higher strata as well. The fossilized and stratified remnants of primitive observances, combined with caste and religion, holds a particular group together. The observances also located the coherent group relatively to others within a highly composite society.[4]

As we can see, mythography here is transformed into the scientific mode and ethnographic history.

Kosambi's history-from-below shows us the material basis of cultural fusion. In a somewhat different vein, and echoing Roland Barthes, myth is "a second-order semiological system" connecting and enlarging upon prior meanings.[5] Other researchers have also pointed out the parallel development in India of a high tradition and a popular tradition, mostly separate but often merging. If we turn to the nation myth, it is clear that it is both continuous and discontinuous with the high and popular traditions in a transverse way. That is, insofar as it is a manifestation of a system of power and privilege at the heart of society, it partakes of the elite/classical/high tradition and not of the popular tradition; however, insofar as the myth bears the psychic force of a common existence, of practices and values widely shared by the disenfranchised, it comes closer to reflecting the popular tradition. Predictably, the Bombay film, anxious to belong neither to the one nor to the other, points to the ruptures in both modes of discourse, ruptures that must then be healed in one way or another. It takes elements from one level of national experience or consciousness (the political or civil) and overlays them on a more primary or fundamental level of experience, and vice versa. Thus myth in commercial popular cinema partakes of all the elements captured in the following definition by media scholar Roger Silverstone:

> Myth occupies a particular space in culture, mediating between the sacred and the profane, the world of everyday commonsense and the arcane, the individual and the social. Myth is a form of speech, distinct in its character, marked by definable narratives, familiar, ac-

ceptable, reassuring to their host culture. Myths are stories. Some are heroic. Most are formulaic. They are the public dreams, the product of an oral culture musing about itself. Myths shade into folktales, more secular, more literal, more narratively predictable or coherent, not asking to be believed in quite the same way, nor marking so insistently the cultural heartland of a society. Myths are associated with ritual, as beliefs to action, both together defining a transcendent and liminal space and time for a people in their otherwise mundane reality. Myths are logical; they are emotional. Myths are traditional. Myths persist, though often in a diluted form, and, like some good wines, do not always travel well without at least changing some part of their character.[6]

While lacking the evocative power of myth, "romance" as used here refers both to the ordinary sense of a love story and to the way it has functioned as a genre in fiction, having larger-than-life characters and lush settings. In her excellent article "Irresistible Romance: The Foundational Fictions of Latin America," Doris Sommer calls the romance "more boldly allegorical than the novel."[7] She shows how nation building in Latin American countries was inscribed as a project in romances which were "inevitably stories of star-crossed lovers who represent particular regions, races, parties, or economic interests which should naturally come together." In India, where a large proportion of the population was nonliterate, such a mission was taken over by the cinema.

The association of the cinema with myth is not new, nor are mythic forms such as the Hollywood western or the Japanese samurai film recent trends. Indian cinema's own genre of "mythologicals" reiterates Hindu ideals and norms of conduct. In fact, so inextricable is the notion of "Indianness" with India's huge abundance of mythological tales, the epics, the Jatakas, and classical literature that in the early years after independence, Indian intellectuals urged filmmakers to turn to these sources for their subject matter (a parallel to Satyajit Ray's injunction to commercial filmmakers to reflect contemporary reality in their movies). Film critic Chidananda Dasgupta, representing the Fanonian second stage of decolonization, wrote in 1957:

The [Indian] myths are so great that they are capable of countless interpretations. . . . In India, mythology often borders on history, social history at any rate. . . . Hence, the renewed material consciousness of today can find inspiration in the mythological tales. There are examples of folk dancing and singing, such as the Gambhira in West Bengal, which feature contemporary problems within the framework of mythology. One basic idea in the present resurgence of India is that it is the re-assertion of an ancient civilization, reoriented to the problems of the present. The most "progressive" Indian is today engaged in a rediscovery of his own country, on which he had once turned his back under the influence of his Western education. The deeper the Western education has been, the stronger is now the urge for this rediscovery.[8]

Dasgupta felt that because of this urge and the impetus to understand the self through a search in the past, the mythological tales were acquiring a new meaning, their origins and intentions were beginning to be understood. Thus in his view "the epics and myths of the country would seem to present the most widely acceptable base for the artistic development of the Indian cinema."[9]

The Nation Myth and Rituals of Blood

The Bombay cinema was busily creating a mythic tradition of its own, with a secular impulse and arising out of contemporary concerns. Its myth-making effort involved rites of passage into responsible roles of citizenship and occasionally involved "rituals of blood." An early effort in this direction was *Jagriti (Awakening, 1954)*. Directed by Satyen Bose, the film deals with children and their gradual awakening into a sense of collective identity through the guidance of a dedicated teacher. Set in a boys' school, the film is literally and metaphorically about education, primarily in the love of country and of one's fellow beings. It is an overtly "nation-building" film, liberally strewn with references to the teachings of Gandhi, Nehru, Subhash Bose, and other public figures, heavily laden with the iconography and emblems of a glorified national tradition which it also helps construct, primarily through its songs, which were very popular. The story revolves around Ajay, a young boy who is always "up to mischief" and is generally misunderstood at home. Unable to discipline him, his parents decide to send him to live in a hostel, where, it is hoped, he will learn to obey rules. At school, Ajay and Shakti, a boy with only one leg, become friends. Shakti's mother struggles to keep them going and the two share an idealized closeness in a heavily sentimental rendition of the mother-son dyad.

The language of "realism" to denote the quotidian features of school life is laced with a caricatural stance toward various marginal authority figures. A space is thereby created for the installation of the mythic figure, Shekhar (Abhi Bhattacharya), the new school superintendent. (The film seems to draw upon various versions of the morally uplifting tale: the eighteenth-century British novel of instruction, the twentieth-century style of Soviet socialist realism, the mode of the Indian government newsreel presenting images of reconstruction of the national heritage) One might also note the influence on the film's mood and texture of a Bengali, New Theatres' tradition of an unadorned visual style to connote simplicity, honesty, integrity. Shekhar arrives at the school with the avowed purpose of instituting a new program of internal reform. The disciplinary space of the school is to be transformed into an experimental workshop for the production of "normalized" citizens-in-the-making. As the iconic modern Indian, Shekhar is always dressed in native attire. He helps the students perform many new tasks and wins over their confidence and affection. He even accompanies the boys on a trip to the country's famous historical sites and monuments in a sequence which suggests the documentary as mythic mode as well.

Only Ajay still persists in his unruly ways, and the other teachers talk of throwing him out. As Ajay packs up and goes out into the street, his friend Shakti follows him and is hit by a car. He dies in the hospital, and the loss of his friend "reforms" Ajay. He now turns into a model student, poring over his books. It has taken his friend's death, and much persuasion by his mentor, to make Ajay conscious of his obligations to society. The schoolteacher's project complete, with the problem character having been reintegrated into the social mainstream, Shekhar is transferred to another institution. Bidding farewell to his colleagues and students, he urges them to carry on the work he has initiated. Arriving out of nowhere and leaving for the diegetic unknown, with no love interest to render him more human, Shekhar's presence takes on mythic overtones as he exhibits the charisma of the "authoritarian" personality.

As a film that pitched its appeal to children, *Jagriti* raises interesting questions about the disciplinary mechanisms of the nation-building project as inscribed in the popular cinema. In a dual reinforcement of education as "awakening," the potentialities of the film medium as educational tool are explored. Its address is simultaneously turned inward and outward, to the Bombay industry itself in its self-policing mode and to the young spectator who might be tempted to consider the movies as purely an entertainment medium. The film seems entirely unselfconscious about the attitudes to individuality and "deviance" that it demonstrates, perhaps reflecting the widespread support for the middle-class reformist ethos of the fifties. The taming or channeling of rebellious energies for utilitarian ends (upward social mobility, reconciliation with family) is presented as the mark of superior moral purpose.

Jagriti uses the film medium and particularly film songs to reinforce a sense of continuous struggle and service for the motherland. The opening lines of the last song, when Shekhar is leaving, translate as follows: "We have steered the boat safely through the storm/Take care of this nation, O my children!" Another song expresses the fantasy of passage to the realm of dreams that Shakti, the lame boy, often sings to his mother: "Let us go, mother, to the village of dreams/Away from strife and thorns, in the shade of flowers." Shakti tells his mother that when he grows up, she will not have to work so hard to support them. The mother here also represents the motherland, which sacrifices for its children. All these images associate the nation with vital familial bonds and nature—both the storm (the past) and flowers (the future). Thus the film connects to very ancient sentiments associated with the motherland. For as Mircea Eliade has shown,[10] the idea of the "mother land" (earth mother), particularly of a symbolic integration with it stemming from a sense of rootedness to place, is ancient. It survives in folklore and popular traditions and is seen in the desire to be interred in the native soil. "Creep back to the earth thy mother!" says the *Rig Veda* (X, 18, 10). "Thou, who art earth, I put thee into the Earth!" is written in the *Atharva Veda* (XVIII, 4, 48).[11] These are articulated with more recent mythic invocations to the motherland which go back to the mid-1800s.

This more recent history moves from regional to national, from books to the cinema. It first arose in its "regional" forms through the interest revived in the history and culture of the different regions of India during the early years of the nineteenth century. Fostered though not created by the efforts of some European oriental scholars and missionaries to develop the study of regional languages and local histories, this interest started much cultural ferment and sparked incipient nationalist sentiments.[12] The collection of manuscripts on south India, Bengal, Maharashtra, and other regions and their organization and cataloging were at first actively promoted by the British authorities. Poems, stories, historical works, epics, religious discourses, treatises on medicine and astrology, erotic manuals, plays, and children's tales were unearthed, giving the nationalists of the later nineteenth century ample cause for pride in the ancient glories of the motherland. Christopher Baker tells us that the search for indigenous sources of cultural inspiration throughout the period of nationalist struggle went hand in hand with "re-creative" use of the new technologies of communication imported by the imperial rulers: "the printed books, the newspaper, the photograph, the sound recording, the broadcast, the cinematograph—and with them the cultural forms of the novel, European classical drama, journalist editorial, perspective painting and moving picture."[13] Bengal's literary renaissance is perhaps the best-known instance of cultural revival during the nineteenth century, and a key figure of that movement, Bankim Chandra Chatterjee (1838–1894), first introduced the theme of the great mother into Indian nationalism. In Bankim Chandra's famous poem "Bande Mataram," contained in his novel *Anandamath*, one of the characters invokes the goddess Kāli as both deity and motherland:

> Mother, to thee I bow.
> Who hath said thou art weak in thy lands,
> When the swords flash out in twice
> Seventy million hands,
> And seventy million voices roar
> Thy dreadful name from shore to shore.[14]

The mythography of India as a powerful mother (Sakti) inspired many subsequent nationalists and was drawn upon by many filmmakers, including Mehboob Khan in the cult classic *Mother India*.

In *Jagriti*, the sentimental and morally uplifting text is undermined, however, by its more sinister subtext. The weak are sacrificed so that the strong can survive and realize their potential. Shakti is not only lame but poor and presented as an object of pity. Teased by the other boys for his physical disability, he is portrayed as gentle and morally upright, the film's vehicle for the articulation of noble sentiments through a child. But he has to die (in the cause of friendship) in order for the myth to take shape, the myth of a people united.

Not all films were so "preachy," however; not all of them invoked the nation directly. A very popular film which mythicized the Indian concept of love, belonging, and togetherness through ghostly fantasy and mirage was *Madhumati* (1958). Directed by Bimal Roy from a story by Ritwik Ghatak, the film is a visual and musical delight which communicates on various levels. Shot mostly outdoors, "the rolling mists on the terraced

landscape, the brooding monsoon in the hills, the silent death of a decadent age and a joyous primitive culture, and the haunting girl, all come
together in the form of a unique vision of the past."[15]

Past and present commingle in this narrative of reincarnated love.
Devendra (Dilip Kumar) is an engineer who is driving with his friend
down a hilly road on a stormy night to pick up his wife and child at the
railway station. Unable to proceed because of a landslide, they take
shelter in an old mansion off the road. Inside, Devendra has the uncanny
sense of déjà vu, that he has been here before. A portrait on a wall which
he recognizes, as well as strange noises in the house, bring more flashes
of memory of the past. He recalls these images in the form of a life story
told to his friend and the old caretaker of the mansion. We see Anand
(also Dilip Kumar), the new manager of a timber estate in Shyamnagar,
a beautiful hilly region. Anand sketches in his spare time and meets
Madhumati (Vyjayantimala) as she sings and dances in the hills, the
very embodiment of tribal freedom and innocence. They fall in love,
although her father is initially distrustful of Anand. The father had been
the former tribal king of the area but was displaced by the timber estate
owner. When Anand meets the estate owner, Ugranarayan (Pran), they
dislike each other instantly. (Pran, of course, is easily identifiable as
"the villain" from his previous film roles.) In a key sequence, Ugranarayan, a womanizer and libertine, has Madhumati kidnapped and presumably rapes her. She is never seen again, although Anand looks
everywhere, is beaten up by the villain's hirelings, and starts halluci-
nating. He sees Madhumati in other women, notably in Madhavi, who
resembles her. With her help, they restage the crime, and the ghost of
Madhumati herself appears, to lure Anand to his death and an after-life
reunion with her. Then the flashback ends and Devendra declares that
Madhumati is his wife in this life. As the friends rush to the station on
hearing of a train accident, we wonder for an instant if Devendra will
lose his wife again. But she is safe, and she is a spitting image of the
dead Madhumati.

Madhumati's deft evocation of tribal scenes and rituals and their association with supernatural power and passion offset their actual exploitation by land developers and business interests. The tribals as uninte-
grated pockets of ancient cultural vestiges have a peculiarly anomalous
and marginal status in Indian society. They function in *Madhumati* as
symbols of exploitation, culminating in the self-destruction of the pursued heroine, as well as represent a resilience of spirit and a continuity

with a primal past. But if tribal culture is marginal and tragically beautiful and the mainstream culture is literally and figuratively violating it, Ugranarayan and Anand are both culpable. Ugranarayan (whose name refers to the mythical story of the divine Narayan in the form of the half lion half man *avatar*) is the vicious face of the exploiting dominant culture, Anand its softer face. For Anand is as much an outsider to the tribal community as is Ugranarayan, and together they represent the forces of capitalist rationality and the myth of progress. The whole story can be read as a parable of the assimilation of the tribals into mainstream culture—through love, not through violence. There is a basic assumption in the film that assimilation is inevitable, but that it should be achieved through romance and mutual surrender.

It is here that the fantasy or fairy-tale dimension of the story connects with its material substratum, in the Kosambi model cited earlier. Moreover, through the framework of immortal romance, India's little traditions can be treated as flowing into the dominant cultural tradition. The film merges past and present through the merging of two transmigrating "souls" united across time, space, life cycles. Sudhir Kakar informs us that this is a romantic-mythic ideal in Indian culture to be found recurrently in all artistic forms. He writes that the ideal of perfectibility inheres not in individual self-consciousness but perfect (spiritual) union through a merging of the self with another:

> Man [*sic*], not as a discrete presence but absorbed in his surroundings; ego, not in opposition to the id but merged with it; individual, not separate but existing in all his myriad connections: these versions of human experience provided the main thematic content of Indian art. In Sanskrit drama and verse, this is expressed in a marked preference for the theme of union (and separation). In Kalidas's *Meghduta* ('The Cloud Messenger') the drama is in the forlorn state of the lover exiled from his home and separated from his wife; in Bhavabhuti's *Uttara-rama-charita* ('Rama's Later History') it is in the desertion of Sita; while in the best known play of them all, Kalidas's *Shakuntalam*, replete with the reunion symbolism of water—tranquil pools and turbulent streams, rushing rivers and deep lakes—this central theme of union attains its highest poetic expression. [16]

Kakar goes on to say that it is the same in the graphic and plastic arts: "the figures of the Ajanta frescoes appear to retreat and then 'emerge from a mysterious, undifferentiated continuum,' the temple sculptures are an 'all-encompassing labyrinth flux of the animal, human and divine . . . visions of life in the flesh, all jumbled together . . . suffering and enjoying in a thousand shapes, teeming, devouring, turning into one another.'"[17] In most forms of popular culture in India today, such as folk festivals, many religious rites, communal *kirtans* (devotional songs) sung in the temples and in the riotous celebrations of *holi* (the festival of color), what Kakar calls the "unitary vision of *soma* and psyche, individual and community, self and world, me and not-me" is present. Kakar notes:

> Nor does this vision of communion rule out its opposite, the expression of loss and separation and a nostalgic longing for reunion with a beloved "Other," the divine or the mortal lover. This theme characterizes renowned Hindu poetry like Tagore's as well as the widely popular devotional *bhajans*. When it comes to Indian light classical music, the *ghazals*, *thumris*, and *dadras* of northern India, pathos is everything; and the sentimental delight of the audience leaves little doubt about the main criterion of aesthetic merit. The presence or absence of these sentiments of pathos and longing differentiates even the much-maligned and ubiquitous film-songs into the spiritually elevating or the merely pleasing.[18]

Madhumati's enduring popularity may be a further reinforcement of this thesis. Its combination of nostalgia, pathos, and hope of return and renewal forms the ingredients of the Indian myth. Giving up a fragmented identity for a more whole and bigger identity which found expression in the love story could easily be fitted into the nationalist project. Other examples are provided by Mehboob's *Andaz* (*Gesture*, 1949), Raj Kapoor's *Barsaat* (*Rain*, 1949), and Ramanand Sagar's *Ghunghat* (*The Bride's Veil*, 1960), in which the ideals of constancy in love leading to union here and hereafter persist amid changing life-styles and apparently modern settings.

Merging Patriarchy and Judicial Law

A particular myth formation in the Bombay cinema of the fifties centered on the law. Films like Raj Kapoor's *Awaara* (*The Vagabond*, 1951), Mehboob's *Mother India* (1957), Shantaram's *Do Ankhen Barah Haath* (*Two Eyes, Twelve Hands*, 1957), K. A. Abbas's *Anhonee* (*The Impossible*, 1951), B. R. Chopra's *Kanoon* (*Law*, 1960) fall into this category.

As we have seen, in the postindependence era, a new dimension was added to India as (timeless) mythic entity—India as a political entity existing in (modern) time, a secular state, the source of not moral but judicial law. The intimate and generally benign images evoked by the ideas of *matri bhumi, vande mataram, bharat mata* (all denoting the motherland) had to be integrated with the often stern and impersonal face of the nation-state as signified by its laws. As Ashis Nandy remarks, "A civilization constantly needs to generate new concepts, symbols and structures of authority and to renegotiate terms with its older gods."[19] In order to function as a collectivity (in a sense that would transcend the lived experience of class and group struggles) Indian cinema devised myths that would give meaning to the conduct of national life and citizenship, break down older configurations of loyalty, and create new ones.

Put crudely, the ideological imperative might be phrased thus: how to establish the claim upon the individual's allegiance by a secular source of authority, the state, to supersede the traditional sources of authority residing in religious and parental figures. In other words, how could people be made to feel part of one nation when their primary loyalties were to family and caste groups? In the political climate of the postindependence years, when differences in language, religion, caste, and subculture that had been suppressed by the general feeling of unity during the independence struggle surfaced, the need for new myths was strongly felt. One way was to construct narratives of the human/familial face of the law. *Awaara, Do Ankhen Barah Haath, Mother India*, and *Kanoon* attempt a mythic fusion of the law of the parent with the law of the state, the personal with the impersonal, which dual authority is then ranged against the protagonist. The search for communion embodied in interdependent social relations is shown to be in conflict with the values of independent action and individual accountability that characterize the modern ideal. Myths of birth and rites of passage are the structural forms that highlight such conflict. And yet the films maintain a contradiction: the model of individual action is affirmed even as authority is posed as inevitable and hence not to be seriously challenged.

These films draw upon the vast store of Indian myths relating to parents and children, "good" and "bad" parent figures and "good" and "bad" children. The theme of crime and punishment, a key preoccupation of many films of the fifties, explores in these cases the bounds of family loyalties and the extent to which these conflict with obligations to the larger social group. (A variant of the parent-judge versus child-offender relationship has become a staple of the Bombay cinema: two brothers on opposite sides of the law, one a policeman and the other a criminal, the films invariably ending with the triumph of the former.) Sudhir Kakar argues that family ties are central to the conduct and maintenance of social relations in India and that identity formation involves a specific relationship to authority.[20] How then does one explain that the pivot of attention in the Hindi cinema has been the fragmented Indian?

The answer may lie in the changed composition of the audiences that patronized films in the post-1947 years, "an uprooted population [that] came to the cities as a consequence of Partition and the devastation of the countryside. This population had the qualities that characterized the next phase of our cinema: both anger at being torn from its roots, and a great sentimentality for the family."[21] The Bombay film had to construct its nation myth out of the elements it had at hand—the urban populace of the big cities. As London-based media person Farrukh Dhondy has written, film "came to a colonized India and developed its nationalist instincts against the colonizers. It continued through a 'free' India looking for a national personality that transcended the histories—separate and distinct—of regions, castes, religions. It found its mass audience in an India in which a settled way of life is giving way to a new settlement, in which a peasantry is being dragged into the influences of urbanization and the ways of the modern world."[22] Using the romance of the gangster figure, the social outlaw, the Bombay cinema constructs some popular heroes of those years who appear as members of the lumpenproletariat caught in the shady underworld life of the big city and in search of the security and identity provided by family ties (Raj Kapoor, Dev Anand, and Guru Dutt all portrayed such characters). We know that the Second World War boom in industries had also contributed to large migrations to cities like Bombay and Calcutta and that more people were flocking to the movies than ever.

These mass audiences for Hindi films also constituted the new citizens of India and as such faced the problems of developing some notions of social responsibility, of building community and solidarity that went beyond the "traditional" loyalties to family and caste groups. In a new "impersonal" context, they had to find ways of seeing in the harsh conditions of their existence the promise of change and renewal, with the old certitudes brought back via the new agencies of state power and authority. Since no institution better symbolizes state power, particularly in the popular consciousness, than judicial law, it becomes a means whereby questions regarding a person's role vis-à-vis the state can be explored and suitably dramatized.

Perhaps the most conscious attempt in the popular cinema to present such a national personality as mass culture hero was Raj Kapoor's *Awaara* which portrays a seductively rebellious, law-breaking youth who is both daring and vulnerable, charming and reckless. Raj Kapoor projected himself as the Indian Charlie Chaplin, the "little man" at odds with a world in which he survives by his wits and hides the pain in his heart behind a smiling face. He copied Chaplin's gestures, facial expressions, and movements and created a screen persona that was a reflection both of himself and of the average Indian that he sought to construct, matching his "Raju" to Chaplin's "Charlie." *Awaara*'s huge commercial success, not only in India but abroad, is now part of Bombay film folklore: "Raj Kapoor's 'Awara' swept through Iran, Iraq, Syria, Egypt, Turkey, and the Soviet Union like an uncontrollable brush fire. Raj Kapoor and Nargis became virtual folk heroes; the film's songs were translated into a dozen different languages and were sung on the streets of cities and small towns thousands of miles away from India."[23]

Awaara is a romance straining toward myth. Ostensibly concerned with the plight of an individual caught in the heredity-versus-environment debate, it asks: Can a highly placed, well-born man, guardian of the law of the land, produce an offspring who is a vagabond and a criminal? Which is the greater influence—that of family antecedents or that of the social circumstances in which one finds oneself? While the film tries to resolve this contemporary debate by coming down on the side of environment as the determining factor in a person's life, it builds on some "mythical" overtones: sacrifice and atonement, guilt and punishment, the redemptive power of love, the glamor of the outlaw.

Awaara's play on recognition and misrecognition literalizes family relationships: Judge Raghunath, the father of the hero, Raj, is also the real-life father of the actor Raj Kapoor. The early sequences deal with this stern upholder of the law who is incapable of dispensing justice in his own life. He disowns his wife and throws her out of the house because she had been kidnapped by a band of robbers and spent four days in their custody. Since her reputation as the wife of a judge has been compromised, she cannot retain her former status, although she pleads that she is as pure as the divine Sita. Soon to become a mother, she is picked up and given refuge by the same robber, Jagga, who had kidnapped her, having planned it as a vendetta against the judge for a

Fusing patriarchy and the law: Judge Raghunath (Prithviraj Kapoor) in
Awaara (The Vagabond). *The Museum of Modern Art/Film Stills Archive.*

The social outcast redeemed by love: Nargis and Raj Kapoor in Awaara. *The Museum of Modern Art/Film Stills Archive.*

previous wrong conviction. Since the judge had presumed Jagga guilty simply because he was the son of a criminal, Jagga wanted to prove that the son of a judge could also be a criminal in the "right" environment. Raj grows up on the streets, a vagabond and petty thief under the tutelage of Jagga. One day he meets Rita while trying to snatch her purse. They get to know each other and fall in love, and Raj decides to turn over a new leaf. But Jagga resents this, and Raj kills him in self-defense. He is put in jail, Rita defends him in court, and the judge is none other than his natural father. Events unfold so that the judge is reminded of his earlier error (Raj's mother has died, meanwhile) and finally accepts Raj as his son. Raj has to serve a three-year sentence, but the movie ends on a note of hope as Rita promises to wait for Raj.

The narrative unfolds by means of flashbacks. The diegetic space is the courtroom, and what takes place there is essentially a rite of passage. The events of the film cover a period of twenty-four years, and the flashbacks show the different stages of the hero's life from childhood innocence to a confused adolescence to youth given over to petty crime. The sequences negotiate dual identities for each of the principal characters, whose relationships are built on presence/absence, recognition/nonre-cognition, losing/finding. Raghunath refuses to recognize his son in the dishevelled, poorly dressed man in the dock; yet the audience is prompted toward making the connection since Raj Kapoor and his fa-ther, Prithviraj Kapoor, are actually acting. Raj only "finds" his father when he loses his mother (she makes the revelation regarding his true paternity just before she dies). Raj has killed his surrogate father (Jagga); Rita tries to "challenge" hers (Judge Raghunath) as she defends Raj against him. She is also responsible for ultimately bringing father and son together. As a practicing lawyer she goes against the judge, also her adoptive father, but is actually on his side since she too wishes to rehabilitate the criminal. So the impersonal workings of the law become a family affair. Everything is connected to everything else. Even Rita, whom Raj meets as an adult, turns out to be his long-lost childhood friend and classmate. The interplay of the personal and the social is reinforced through visual contrasts. The heavy studio atmosphere casts an air of unreality on the unfolding drama, which contrasts with the exuberance and verve of the acting of the protagonists and the eroticism of the romantic sequences. How, then, should one interpret the "mythic" workings of this film, its process of conflict resolution through fusion?

Here it is necessary to digress to Raj Kapoor's own history as a con-venient symbolic construction of the enfant terrible of the Bombay cinema. In statements made by him during that period, it is evident that he makes use of his own myth for self-promotion. He splits himself into two people, the neutral observer and the adored film hero, the former explaining the latter. Kapoor comments that in India, the cinegoing pub-lic, after years of seeing films and admiring film stars, had built up an unconscious expectancy and identification.

Every star stands for something in the collective mind. . . . The public has a very definite conception of each star, and knows before entering the theatre what it wants of them on the screen. Thus it was with the Raj Kapoor of "Barsaat," "Awaara" and "Shree 420" (and before that, of "Sargam" and "Dastan"). They gave him rousing cheers. But "Aah" fared badly. After all, Raj's zest for life is inexpressible, inimitable. He laughs and makes you laugh. He speaks and you respond. His is not the stuff of which tubercular heroes are made.[24]

With the release of *Awaara* and *Shri 420* in the Middle Eastern coun-tries and Russia, Kapoor says he saw vivid demonstrations of the public's conception of him as a universal figure. In Russia they called him Tavarish Brodigya (Comrade Awaara); in Iran, Agha Raj Kapoora. He asks, "Why did these two films appeal so immensely even to foreigners? . . . The young people of those countries . . . saw in the films their own sufferings, the revolt of modern youth and the striving to achieve basic values, and in the ultimate triumph they saw their own triumph over a world in chaos." Youth, optimism about life, revolt against authority, and the return to a more primary level of experience and feeling—these were the promising components with which Raj Kapoor tried to shape the myth of the fifties hero. By extension, he embodied the nation myth. Yet often, what seemed like rebellion may actually have reinforced the old. This dynamic is present in many films.

Part of the success of *Awaara* and subsequent Raj Kapoor films undoubtedly owes to an intertextual system that the producer-director-actor built up over the years. The appearance of the same hero (and often the same heroine, Nargis) in film after film provided both visual continuity and a sense of progression for the audience. The films evoked viewer engagement by presenting the "little man" as the protagonist, one who straddles some of the great divides in the Indian folk imagination: village and city, poverty and wealth, naïveté or innocence and cleverness or pseudo-sophistication. Around Raju and through him are ranged the forces of good and evil, and in the elemental struggle that ensues, it is the purity of the heart's affections that ultimately triumphs, with the hero expounding the same message at the end of each film, that of peace, harmony, brotherhood, honesty, and hard work. Intertextuality is also patterned through music. A tune used as a background score in one film is provided with lyrics to become a song in a later film, or a very popular and familiar tune from an earlier film is played in a later one. This was possible because the same team of music directors, Shankar-Jaikishen, provided the music for Kapoor's films. Through this intricate self-referential system, as much as through elaborately designed sets, catchy tunes, and smooth narration, the Raj Kapoor films bore a distinctive trademark.

In every sense *Awaara* is larger than life, a self-conscious mythic undertaking. This is evident in all the accounts of the production of the film, including critiques of it advanced by some of Kapoor's contemporaries. There is an extravagance in it—of emotion, of dramatic movement, of sets and sequences—that seeks to overwhelm and enthrall the viewer. Even the dynamics of the burgeoning romance between Raju

(Raj Kapoor) and Rita (Nargis) is a marked departure from the established Bombay film tradition. A cynical comment was provided on this by a contemporary filmmaker, Kidar Sharma. In an article in *Filmfare* called "Cupid Directs the Film," he talks about three different conceptions that directors hold of the female lover in films. The first kind of director copies Western films, the second draws upon Indian tradition for the characterization of "the principal woman," and

> the third and last category, and one representing the latest trend in screen love-making, can very accurately be described as the director with the Cave Man conception of love. This is the technique made vivid on the Indian screen mostly by Raj Kapoor and other film artistes graduating from the Prithvi Theatres. Fortunately or unfortunately it has become a craze with the younger generation of artistes and directors. To a certain extent, it is a different approach to love. Here love is symbolised by a series of acrobatics causing physical pain to the "principal woman." This group of people believes that tears of love can be made to flow from a woman's eyes if she is manhandled. . . . The Cave Man lover would drag her by her hair, make her kiss his feet, dash her against the floor of the room, if not the ceiling, and thus kindle love in her heart. This is an approach to love that is essentially the approach of virile, manly youth.[25]

There is also the famous "dream sequence" in *Awaara*, the dramatization (or "picturization" as it is called in the Bombay film world) which reveals that something new was being tried. The dream sequence is an elaborate and lengthy piece of surrealism to denote the tortured state of mind of the hero, Raj, who has traversed the path of petty crime since childhood but, under the influence of the woman he loves, would like to change his ways and become a respectable, law-abiding person. The dream sequence had not originally been planned, as the music directors explain:

> Nobody had thought of a dream sequence for this film. The situation required two songs, "Tere bina aag ye chandni" [Without you this moonlight is like fire] and "Ghar aaya mera pardesi" [My traveler has come home], each of which was composed independently of the other. One day we were sitting in Raj Kapoor's office—we had no separate music-room in those days. It was a friendly gathering. Suddenly we began making "ghost sounds" for sheer fun—shrill screams, yells and weird cries! Now an idea struck Raj.

"Why not make it a part of the music?" Raj Kapoor exclaimed. There and then we decided to have a dream sequence, and link the two songs by a third one.

"There will be three songs," Raj said. "A girl calling her lover, the boy caught in the grip of evil, and the final song of reunion."[26]

These sounds, high key lighting, and expressionist decor conjure up visions of heaven and hell, and the moral dimensions of the hero's dilemma are underscored as the dream annuls the difference between "life" and imagination.

Awaara's expert cinematography, seductive images of the heroine, and polarized worlds of the rich and the poor, youth and age, rebellion and authority give it a ritualized form. But what of the central conflict between husband and wife, father and son? In this myth of birth and origins and the enactment of a rite of passage, what do the central relationships articulate? Here it is useful to turn for a moment to a consideration of the position of the family in Indian society in order to see how the film evokes the tensions and integrates the patterns of family relationships for its larger end of signifying the law of the nation. Sociologists, anthropologists, and social psychologists have written about the centrality of the family and of family ties in the social life of India. Not only is enormous emotional investment made in the observation of duties and obligations to family members (and, by extension, to the *jati*, or caste group), but other obligations are subordinated to the primary familial one. A problem in modern free India has been the pervasive corruption and nepotism that have marred political and administrative functioning. Sudhir Kakar explains that among those Indians closely identified with the process of modernization, the well-educated urban elite who hold positions of power in modern institutions, the psychohistorical fact of the primacy of relationships, of family loyalties, of *jati* connections is often a source of considerable emotional stress. For although intellectually the Indian professional or bureaucrat may agree with his Western counterpart that, for example, the criterion for appointment or promotion to a particular job must be objective, decisions based solely on the demands of the task and "merits of the case," he cannot root out the cultural conviction that his *relationship* to the individual under consideration is the single most important factor in his decision. This conflict between the rational criteria of specific tasks and institutional goals rooted in Western societal values and his own deeply held belief (however ambivalent) in the importance of honoring family and *jati* bonds is typical among highly educated and prominently employed Indians.

And among the vast majority of tradition-minded countrymen—whether it be a *bania* bending the law to facilitate the business transaction of a fellow *jati* member, or a *marwari* industrialist employing an insufficently qualified but distantly related job applicant as a manager, or the clerk accepting bribes in order to put an orphaned niece through school—dishonesty, nepotism and corruption as they are understood in the West are merely abstract concepts. . . . Guilt and its attendant inner anxiety are aroused only when individual actions go against the principle of the primacy of relationships, not when foreign ethical standards of justice and efficiency are breached.[27]

Yet it was precisely these standards of justice and efficiency that had to be enforced and maintained if India was to function as a modern nation. But in order to give a concrete shape and presence to "the nation" (in order, that is, to make it a myth), the Bombay film invested the law, representative of the nation, with the moral authority that inheres in a parent. Raj in *Awaara* is not only allowed to play out his Oedipal fantasies of killing the father (or making an attempt, at any rate) but is also incorporated into the symbolic order of the father and thus of the state, thereby gaining the chance of a new ("mature") existence. Nor does the father-son confrontation provide the means for Raj's redemption alone. In dispensing justice against his own son, the judge learns the lessons of humility and open-mindedness, qualities that are required in the socially and economically privileged.

As a figure in revolt against state authority, Raj typifies the perception of filmmakers regarding the popular hero of the fifties. The Devdas character—upper-class, weak, vacillating, and adored by the public in 1935—no longer captivated the popular imagination in Bimal Roy's remake of the film in 1955. The certitudes of that era were gone, and so were the primarily middle-class audiences. The cohesiveness of social and family units was being affected by work mobility, and in the absence of familiar authority figures, the temptation to break the law, to strike out on one's own, must have loomed large in many minds. But the very circumstances of their lives as citizens made the acceptance of impersonal authority imperative, just as the ideology of modernization and mobility reinforced the nostalgia for the family. Perhaps a film like

Awaara sought to resolve tensions in society regarding the acceptance of norms that threatened commitment to personal loyalties. Through its dramatized and embellished sequences, its attractive but wayward hero, its double-edged portrait of authority, it brought to the surface people's unconscious hostility toward the state as lawmaker. It tried to convince its audiences of the inevitability of submission to the law by showing that "justice must take its course" (Raj is behind bars in the final shots of the film), but the submission is an extension of the hero's moral duty to his parent rather than a punishment, since the judicial establishment has been incorporated within the orbit of the family. With this sleight-of-hand, *Awaara* passes off the impersonal as the personal.

The theme of judgment involving parents and children reappears that same year (1951) in *Anhonee*. The film plays upon the submerged fears of people about the failure of authority and the resulting chaos, but here the authority in question is moral rather than legal. Like *Awaara*, *Anhonee* (written by the same screenwriter, Khwaja Ahmad Abbas) presents the nature versus nurture controversy, but it embeds the argument in a sinister plot of guilt, punishment, and expiation motivated by the stark oppositions of good and evil. With the help of folktale elements such as children exchanged at birth, the good sister and the bad sister, mistaken identities, impersonations, and the like, the film explores the dark underside of authority in libidinal terms. (While the father, the symbol of authority, is not a repository of state law, the film foregrounds the issue of legitimacy and the giving and taking of rights through the conflict between the good and the bad sister. Moreover, the legal dimension appears before the audience as a sustained metaphor throughout the film through the person of the hero, who is a lawyer.) However, it is the father, Thakur Harnam Singh, who is invested with all the accoutrements of power: wealth, social prestige, family background, the respect of friends and associates. The "law" of the father is central to the narrative, extending beyond the grave, since he dies fairly early on in the film but continues to dominate through his pictures, which serve as both a visual icon and a plot device. It is significant that while the moral force that the father represents for his "legitimate" daughter, Roop (Nargis), is tempered or problematized by the revelation of his secret past and the existence of an illegitimate daughter, his authority does not diminish, and most of the film is taken up with the fulfillment of obligations that he has left behind.

Anhonee is concerned with blurring the boundaries between public and private, between a public persona embodying virtue and honesty and a private life involving libidinal impulses, and it does this, predictably, through the medium of family relationships and commitments. The Thakur ("Lord") considers himself unworthy to occupy a public role, that of municipal chairman, because of his dark past, which nevertheless comes to haunt his offspring. The two sisters may be said to embody the public and private aspects of one personality: Roop, the bright and beautiful one, is exemplary in character and conduct, manages her father's financial affairs, is conscious of her social role and status; Mohini (whose name means seductiveness) can be taken as a projection of his hidden and negative side, as the anima, with her obtrusive sexuality and her desire for revenge. The public-social is inflected by the personal-moral or immoral; that is, the socially respected good sister is also morally chaste, kind, and noble, while the disreputable, socially deprived sister is a prostitute whose thoughts and actions are evil. The film noir photography indicates the latter's corruption, while bright lighting is reserved for Roop. Thus the family, that "ideal" institution in Indian social life and popular belief, is here a confining web of false identities and destructive passions. Why, then, is the father built up as a god by both sisters? Why does the film reveal an obsessive anxiety to rehabilitate him? Here again, one might note the desire for reconciliation of opposing forces through their containment within one body. The mythic becomes concretized in the secular-mundane. Roop and Mohini, who look alike (Nargis plays a double role) but are as different as night and day, are brought together under the same roof through circumstances that reveal to them their common paternity. To suggest claustrophobia, the major part of the narrative takes place indoors; the camera usually pins figures against objects, and tight compositions are the norm.

Caught between the two forces is Raj (Raj Kapoor), the male protagonist in the film who inadvertently brings the sisters together and has to suffer the consequences. He is the deglamorized fifties film hero who works hard at his job as a lawyer and is honest and outspoken, making the obligatory remarks against the ways of the rich. But if the model for heroism in the fifties invoked the virtues of self-sacrifice, dutifulness, and respectability, then Roop rather than Raj might more appropriately be regarded as the "hero" of the film. And so, while we see much of the action through Raj's eyes, Roop is meant to engage our sympathies. Not only does she readily admit the claims of her half-sister to their father's property, but she makes the supreme sacrifice of her love for Raj by arranging the marriage between him and Mohini. Throughout the film, contrasts are self-consciously drawn between her manners, deportment, tastes, and virtues and those of her sister. But Roop cannot be separated from Mohini, her alter ego, since they look alike and are often mistaken for each other. Mohini's "criminal" tendencies represent not only the suppressed impulses of the id (her identity as a nautch-girl [singing-dancing prostitute] is carefully hidden from others when her sister is trying to "civilize" her, but it constantly threatens to erupt) but also provide the challenge to the authority figure (the father) that has to be destroyed. While the father's "failing" does not in any way take away from his (social) power and prestige, since both are carefully guarded by the good daughter even after his death, the "bad" daughter, presenting as she does the threat of plunging *Anhonee*'s diegetic world into chaos, is driven by her own passions to a violent death. Normalcy is restored, Raj and Roop are reunited, and the film ends with Roop, dutiful as ever, apologizing to her father's memory for not being able to make the impossible (*anhonee*) possible.

Interestingly, the lawyer remains a pawn in the film, essentially denied any moral choice in the "conflict" between the two sisters. They decide among themselves who will have him, and only on his wedding night does Raj find out that he has married the wrong sister. His revulsion toward Mohini may mask the film's subtext of fascination (and accompanying guilt) with the prostitute figure that Bombay cinema and Indian culture in general has always harbored. (I explore this fascination in a later chapter.) *Anhonee*'s duplicitous treatment of the theme of normalcy is evident in its contradictory tone: while nurture rather than nature makes the individual, the social outcast (particularly in the form of woman) is burdened with every vice imaginable—not just the "bad habits" of drinking and smoking, but of lying, cheating, and being a nymphomaniac. Such aberrant behavior is punishable only by death. Raj, on the other hand, is a lower-middle-class hero who needs to be integrated into the propertied classes. It is the triumph of property that the socialist Abbas "unwittingly" endorses in *Anhonee*.

In V. Shantaram's *Do Ankhen Barah Haath*, the theme of crime and its relationship to authority is even more overt, the zeal of social reformism and the recourse to myth quite evident. For if, as Mircea Eliade holds, one of the chief characteristics of myth is the creation of exemplary models for a whole society, the hero of this film is such a model. We read in the opening text that *Do Ankhen* is based on the real experiences of an "idealist" from a small state in India who tried a bold experiment: to turn "beasts" into men. This man was branded a "lunatic" because of his unusual ideas but he remained "undaunted" and pursued his goal with great faith. It is interesting that this exemplary character is a jailor whose experiment involves taking a group of dangerous criminals out of the prison and teaching them to become useful and law-abiding members of society again. But this heroic figure is himself at odds with the received or accepted norms of his peers, for he challenges his superior officer in insisting on proving his "experiment" a success. As a jailor who leads a group of convicted killers out of prison, he is himself subverting the law and, in a sense, pays the price for it by getting killed at the end of the film. The film resolves this ambivalence by a recourse to myth. It isolates the hero both visually and thematically, for he generally appears alone in the frame while the experimentees invariably appear together. His looks too set him unmistakably apart: he is slender in body and has a soft voice and a pleasing appearance, while the ex-prisoners fulfill all the stereotypes of "brutes," having heavy bodies, bushy eyebrows, unkempt hair, loud voices, and uncouth manners. The aura of uniqueness and difference that surrounds the jailor is reinforced by the distance he keeps from the others, a distance that increases symbolically as the film progresses and enlarges upon the myth. More and more the watchful eyes of the hero occupy the screen, serving to represent the moral force of truth, faithfulness to duty, and integrity to the ex-prisoners. At one point they compare the look in his eyes to that of a local deity in a temple, preventing them from leaving the farm and spoiling the experiment. The jailor's "martyrdom" at the end (he dies protecting his wards against the attack of a bull let loose in their fields by a rival farmer) completes the process of deification. His eyes appear to look down from the clouds, and their tears form raindrops that rejuvenate the ravaged earth.

As an authority figure the jailor plays the role of an austere though kind father. In fact, the fusion of the jailor's authority and demeanor with that of a father is quite systematic in the film. He is called "Babuji" by the six men in his charge, a term by which a father is often addressed in India. His role is to teach them how to live in the outside world again, and one of the first things he does is to (re-)create for them their social identities by calling them by their names. The father-children relationship is also conveyed through mode of acting. While the jailor is usually calm and poised as an authority figure is supposed to be, his wards dance, frown, shout, throw tantrums, and get into scrapes. They are of course dangerous "children" who can decide to slit their captor's throat if he does not gratify their wishes. As the ex-prisoners learn to channel their energies to socially useful ends, like farming, digging wells, and the like, they become more rather than less dependent on the jailor to keep them on the straight and narrow path of right conduct. When they slip, they are repentant, saying that a father must forgive his errant children. In fact, the jailor is acknowledged as both father and mother, as an androgynous figure and hence truly heroic, for in Hindu culture, androgyny rather than masculinity or femininity is a mark of the saintly. The model for this portrayal is of course Gandhi—the jailor's martyrdom, his experimental farm (recalling Sabarmati Ashram), his favorite hymn stressing truth and nonviolence, his moral victory over the "dark forces" in the minds of the killers all suggest Gandhi the folk hero. The jailor considers that the six men in his charge have passed their greatest moral test and established their courage when they suffer terrible blows at the hands of some ruffians without retaliating. Yet the "children" remain children at the end of the film, for they refuse to leave the farm even when the government pardons them. They are afraid that without the unseen gaze of their Babuji on them their animal natures will reassert themselves.

Regarding the idealization of authority figures and the search for charismatic leaders in India, Sudhir Kakar has written:

> Indian men tend to search for external figures to provide that approval and leadership not forthcoming from their own insufficiently idealized superegos. Relatively unintegrated into a weak superego, the narcissistic configuration of the *idealised parental imago* operates throughout life with much of its original intensity and many of its archaic aims. This results in a state of affairs in which the individual is perpetually looking for authority figures he can idealize whose "perfection" and omnipotence he can then adopt as his own.[28]

The hero of *Do Ankhen* is a reflection of this idealized parental image superimposed upon the image of impersonal state authority. While the overt message of the film is that criminals can be rehabilitated in society and contribute to social gain, the treatment of the narrative and its finale reinforce the charisma of powerful authority figures and the need for dependence on them.

Another very popular film which mediates impersonal law through personal relationships by fusing the roles of a father and a judge is B. R. Chopra's *Kanoon*. The film belongs to the crime thriller genre, in which a murder has taken place and must be solved, the criminal brought to trial. According to the director, a one-time journalist who turned to commercial filmmaking and became enormously successful, his concern in the film was to question the nature of evidence in court proceedings and its role in deciding cases. How reliable is the testimony presented in courts, since both human evidence and human judgment are fallible? What if a person is accused and convicted on the basis of false evidence? Chopra says that with the country's independence, filmmakers were thinking of such issues for the first time and presenting them for consideration to the public. When *Kanoon* was first released, it was widely publicized as a Hindi film without songs and dances, a move toward serious consideration of a serious subject. The film's pragmatic concerns, however, provide the stuff for high drama and tension as the level of the impersonal is articulated with the personal. Much of the action proceeds through courtroom scenes, and this serves two simultaneous functions. While the courtroom, besides being a staple feature of the commercial cinema because of its promise of dramatic revelations, provides a modern setting and established procedures in the life of a nation, its ritualized norms and proceedings are also conducive to the reenactments of primal events. Questions of life and death are settled there, dark secrets revealed, feeling and passion find utterance. The film integrates the public and the private realms for mutual reinforcement.

Kanoon presents a murder, that of an unscrupulous moneylender, for which a petty thief has been caught and accused. But the suspicion is deflected (for the viewer) on the most unlikely person in terms of his position and social prestige—Judge Badri Prasad, a distinguished man of the law. And the suspicion is harbored by none other than the protagonist, Kailash Khanna, whose relationship to the judge is that of a prospective son-in-law. Moreover, the judge functions as the *"idealised parental imago"* for the young protagonist, who is also a lawyer and hence would like to model his career on that of his senior colleague. In fact the judge is a surrogate father to Kailash, having raised him (we gather that the hero has no family of his own) and then trained and guided him in legal practice. In one courtroom sequence, when Kailash puts up a good performance in cross-examining a witness, other lawyers praise him by saying that he will bring honor to his "father's" name, and Kailash himself addresses the judge as "Papa" in an emotionally

Kailash (Rajendra Kumar) points to Ashok Kumar (off-screen) as the murderer in Kanoon (Law).

charged scene. Moreover, the close filial bond between the two is underscored by negativizing the relationship between the judge and his biological son, the latter fulfilling all the Bombay film stereotypes of a distinguished man's son being a buffoon. In *Kanoon*, therefore, the whole gamut of legal and moral questions that are raised, such as the controversy over the death penalty, wrong convictions, the element of human error in evidence, personal bias, and the like, becomes a vehicle for the working out of family relationships. But the fusion of the professional with the personal, the law of the father with that of the state, nullifies what would be the conflicting demands of personal and civic responsibilities. Through the cinematic/mythic means of their "transcendence," new relationships, new understanding, and knowledge are only possible through vindication of the law of the father.

The enigma that *Kanoon* poses (what is the "true" identity of the judge, is he or is he not the killer?), which the protagonist sets about to solve, is also the source of an intense moral crisis for a prospective son-in-law forced to apprehend a parent figure. As keepers of the law, both Badri Prasad and Kailash must rise above personal considerations and loyalties, but the film does not minimize the agonies involved in doing so. They must pass the acid test that membership at the bar requires—to facilitate justice and be above censure. For the judge this means that he cannot be tainted with the suspicion of having committed a crime, and for the public prosecutor (Kailash) it means thinking of his public responsibilities at the expense of family ties. The film dramatizes the fears and fantasies of the average citizen that lead to distrust of those in authority and allays those fears by showing both men of the law to be above blame. The enigma of the judge's identity and thereby of the killer's is resolved by means of another mythic device: that of "splitting." Just as the image of the "good" parent is separated from that of his "bad" side, here the apparently criminal judge is proved innocent when it is discovered that the real murderer is a look-alike, a man who resembles (and perhaps impersonates) the judge but is quite separate from him. Thus the legitimate suspicions that people might harbor about the integrity of judges is projected on to an "other" who is a murderer, while the representative of the law remains what he always was—a good judge as well as a good parent.

While *Kanoon* is concerned with the reestablishment of faith in the state and its legal institutions (personified by its representatives), it seems to be fascinated with the alternate scenario of a challenge to authority. As in *Do Ankhen*, the protagonist proves himself exemplary through such a challenge; namely, the charge of murder that he lays at the judge's door. In lengthy courtroom sequences, Kailash appears as a rebel with a cause, as the man to whom the inner voice (*zameer*) has spoken and aroused to action. Through his arguments, legal questions are turned into moral ones, and his challenge of one source of authority is carried out for the sake of adherence to greater sources of authority: truth and justice. It is ironic that his challenge is based on mistaken premises, legally, but that does not take away from his moral victory, for which he is rewarded in the end by "getting back" his erstwhile family— the judge and the judge's daughter. Thus the film reintegrates the individual with his personal obligations and connections via his obligations to the state.

If the films discussed above embody, however obliquely, the mythic tendencies at work in depicting concerns about authority in the new nation, Mehboob Khan's *Mother India* (1957) evokes the myth of the powerful nation through its central metaphor. *Mother India* is perhaps the best-known film of the fifties and a landmark of the Indian commercial cinema in general. Being one of the three greatest box-office hits of all time in Indian cinema history, it has drawn considerable attention from diverse film critics, much of it contradictory. E. H. Johnson sums up reactions to the film as follows:

> Without a doubt, Mehboob's greatest triumph was *Mother India* if only because of the place it occupies in Indian popular culture. Screenings of the film still produce "House Full" signs every time it plays anywhere in India; the appearance of the actress Nargis on the screen produces the kind of idolatry which Garbo evokes in the West. Basically a reworking of *Aurat*, it undercuts social comment with a poetical use of the mise-en-scène. The story is once again the plight of the poor, snatching at happiness during respite from the ceaseless toil, marriages and festivals are brief occasions when oppression is momentarily lifted. Yet in this oppression comes spiritual solace and strength, which is where it has been accused of being ultimately reactionary in the message it preaches. But the way the plot has been constructed, suggests the film deserves a closer look than a superficial dismissal. The ending appears negative but is actually open-ended leaving the audience to decide for itself the solutions to social problems.[29]

Perhaps the enduring popularity of *Mother India* has to do with the way it shapes a fundamental level of the Indian experience of suffering into the stuff of myth, investing the everyday with the heroic, allowing its audiences to renew their most cherished cultural assumptions. These pertain to the conduct of woman, to her mythic strength and endurance, to her ability to provide stability and continuity in Indian social life. In a patriarchal culture, man's anxieties about and expectations of the harnessing of female sexuality for nurturance and the guardianship of communal norms and values have become embodied in idealizations of woman. Mehboob himself encapsulated these troubled and troubling tendencies in his statements about the making of *Aurat* and *Mother India*:

> I had studied village life in Kashipura in Baroda State, my mother's home town, and I have always had the most profound respect for Indian womanhood. The story of *Aurat*, as visualised by me and developed by Babubhai Mehta, was centred round the fact that the true Indian woman enters her husband's home when she marries and leaves it only when she dies, that she will never sell her chastity for any price on earth.

The archetypal peasant woman as mother: Sardar Akhtar in Aurat (Woman).
Courtesy National Film Archive of India.

Now that times have changed and life is different, I thought of re-making *Aurat* in the context of the changing world. But the main character has not changed: the Indian woman who is one with the land she works on.[30]

The celebration of woman's role as wife and mother, to offset the fear of the destructive and vengeful woman and the prostituting woman, finds expression in myth and folklore. Mehboob drew upon this source of popular consciousness for his message of service and devotion to the (mother)land. The chronicle of one woman's struggle against the oppressions of both man and nature becomes an unconscious encapsulation of India's long history of domination by foreign powers and its struggle to maintain the integrity of its soil. On the diegetic and imagistic level, the film embodies an idealization of the Indian peasant's will to survive against overwhelming odds.

The association of the idea of India as nation with the idea of rootedness to *place* was made by many patriots during the independence struggle. And since the vast majority of India's population has been (and continues to be) a rural population, working on the land and identifying with it, the idealization of the earth and the peasant finds deep resonance in evocations of the motherland.[31]

The idea of "Mother India," as we have seen earlier, borrowed much of its symbolism from the cult of the mother goddess that enjoys a wide following in certain parts of India. While the mother goddess is part of the mythology of all cultures, as Erich Neumann has shown, its imagery permeates Indian religious and folk beliefs and practices to an extraordinary degree.[32] Scholar E. O. Cousins is of the opinion that "the apotheosis of the mother has reached a greater height in India than anywhere else. No other religion of the present time worships goddesses, no other looks on the Mother as Divine."[33] The ritual glorification of women does not of course preclude concrete social debasement, and pedestalization and oppression exist side by side. But woman as mother is able to rise significantly above woman as mere woman.

Both in popular tradition and in social life, then, the celebration of woman as mother is a key element. It is not surprising that this should provide an important symbolic force in national life as well. (After the Bangladesh war in 1971 Indira Gandhi was cheered all over the country as Bharat Mata, an association she herself encouraged.)[34] In *Mother India*, which sought to articulate for mass consumption the values that should guide this national life, woman mediates tensions and oppositions, is life-giving as well as life-destroying, is pitiable and yet terrifying. Mehboob weaves into his ambitious project (*Mother India* was three years in the making with three hundred shooting days) elements from mythology, cult worship, social tradition, and custom in order to elaborate codes of behavior in contemporary India.

Mother India takes as its narrative form the archetypal life experiences of the rural woman whose "adult" life begins with a childhood marriage, to be followed by childbirth and child-rearing, and then on to maturity and old age. Portraying the vicissitudes of fortune that mark each stage, the film moves from the individual to the social, the personal to the communal. That the move is deliberate is evident from a brief comparison of *Mother India* with the earlier film, *Aurat*. While the outlines of the story remain the same in the later version, the conflicts portrayed and the major characterizations have acquired more "representativeness." In *Aurat*, Radha is the long-suffering village woman and mother whose lifetime is spent in fulfilling her duties and obligations, first to her husband, then to her sons, and finally to her community.

The nation-building project: Radha (Nargis) and her sons in Mother India. *The Museum of Modern Art/Film Stills Archive.*

Except in the final scenes of the film when she shoots and kills her "bad" son, Birju, she is a simple, hard-working victim of circumstances harried by poverty and desperation. At one point after her son has taken to crime and started terrorizing the villagers, she appears utterly alone and vulnerable, teased and laughed at by the village children as a crazed old woman, and people even throw stones at her. The Radha of *Mother India*, on the other hand, has already become the mother of the whole community at the beginning of the film. Heavily garlanded, with the aura of distance conferred by "greatness," she is persuaded by her "good" son, Ramu, to inaugurate a dam built for the mechanized irrigation of their fields. The era of technology that independence is ushering in (symbolized by shots of tractors, machines, and dams no doubt very familiar to the viewers from public announcements, newspapers, and state-produced newsreels) promises relief and a new era in village life as well. What better figure to mark the transition from the old to the new than the culture's feminine principle incarnate? As the village celebrates, Radha's life unfolds in flashback, but she has already been identified as a special figure, and every aspect of her life and character shows her to be exemplary. As a bride, her beauty and her virtues are the talk of the village, as a wife her devotion to her husband is the envy of other males, as a woman she fulfills her biological and social role by repeatedly giving birth to *sons*, as a mother she fiercely protects and supports her offspring, and as a peasant she battles fire and flood to make the earth yield a rich harvest.

Other characters and situations are correspondingly enlarged upon in *Mother India*. Whereas in *Aurat* Birju as the son who has taken to evil ways selects his targets at random, here he nurses a lifelong vendetta against his mother's tormentor, the village moneylender. The forces of good and evil in village society are more clearly opposed, and Radha's "sacrifice" of her son is doubly meaningful because Birju is the agent of deliverance for the village. The actors chosen to play Birju in the two films represent quite different physical types. The Birju of *Aurat* is heavy, bald, and unattractive, but in *Mother India* he suggests dark passion and mystery by appearing in dark makeup (resembling the folk hero and god Krishna, as the name Birju also suggests), has a brooding look, and teases the village maidens (again like Krishna). Even Radha's husband, Shamu, who has a minor role in both films, merely abandons his family in *Aurat* when the burden of poverty and debt becomes insupportable for him. But in *Mother India* he undergoes a symbolic castration: as he works in the fields one day, both his arms are crushed under a huge rock and have to be amputated. His "castration" confers greater authority on the female figure, releasing her from her conjugal obligations so that she can assume her all-powerful role as mother.

This role shifts from the individual to the communal plane in terms of Radha's deteriorating relationship to her younger son, Birju. As Radha triumphs over her difficulties and becomes more and more conscious of her duties toward her fellow villagers, she is confronted with the greatest challenge to her authority in the form of her own son. One of the images of Birju's truancy and deviance that the film repeatedly provides is that of him teasing the village women, breaking the mud vessels that they carry on their heads to fetch water from the pond. On one level, Birju is merely playing out his Krishna role. But Erich Neumann tells us that the uterus in mythology is a vessel that is "broken" at birth, pouring forth water like the earth.[35] In protecting the women from the actions of her son, Radha may in fact be protecting motherhood, the source of authority and fertility.

As she sides in Birju's eyes with the forces of order symbolized by the older son, Ramu, she is metamorphosed into the "bad" or phallic mother (Sudhir Kakar), that image of an aggressive, treacherous, annihilating mother who haunts the fantasy life of Indian males. It might be said that Birju, who takes to gambling, thieving, and ultimately to highway robbery, is actually indulging in a form of self-aggression to protest what he sees as a withdrawal of his mother's affections. His nostalgia for her softer and nurturing side, as also his oedipal longings, is expressed by his obsessive attachment to her bracelets. They are of course also the signifiers of her married status. (It might be mentioned here that while the shooting of *Mother India* was going on, Sunil Dutt [the actor who plays Birju] and Nargis [the star who plays the mother's role] became romantically involved and were married soon after.) The film "sublimates" Birju's incestuous longings for the mother by presenting the motivation for Birju's actions as anger that his mother's bracelets have been pawned to the moneylender. But the plot is highly layered: the father has abandoned the family, the bracelets are pawned, the moneylender has designs on Radha. Birju steals the bracelets for her once, and it is the reason for which he murders the unscrupulous moneylender and tries to kidnap his daughter. While it is a crime (the "crime" of desire for his lost mother?) for which he must forfeit his life, Birju's portrayal as a criminal is decidedly ambiguous, for he is, as pointed out earlier, an erotic and a redemptive figure. To the audiences of the fifties, he perhaps expressed the temptations to disregard the impersonal codes of law by which they were bound in urban and national life, even as he provided the channel for the expiation of the guilt that such temptations might give rise to. And by subjecting him to the judgment of "the ultimate authority," which "in the Indian mind has always been feminine," as Ashis Nandy has convincingly argued, the film brings to bear upon the theme of punishment the cumulative force of ancient belief and practice.[36]

One question which arises in relation to *Mother India*'s use of myth is whether it is regressive and to what extent. It is said that the cult of the mother ultimately projects an authoritarian regime and supports the status quo. Radha does not allow her son to change the basic power structure in village society. She repeatedly exhorts him not to take the law into his own hands, and hence the film's message is that the peasants must continue to suffer stoically and rely on inadequate government relief measures and nominal land reform. Mehboob, the director, was himself unsure of his political leanings, being a devout Muslim and professing vaguely socialistic ideals. The logo for Mehboob Productions reflected this contradiction: the visual image was of a hammer and sickle while a voice-over proclaimed a very familiar Urdu saying, "No matter what evils your enemies wish for you, it is of no consequence. Only that can happen which is God's will." *Mother India* no doubt is a patriarchal and dominant view of woman's experience and responsibility in society. Moreover, it relies on many stock situations and conventions of the Bombay film. But to the degree that its use of them is at least partly ambivalent, that its characterizations are quite powerful, and that it associates the mythic with the oppressed, it touches a deep responsive chord in the mind of the average Indian viewer.

Wendy O'Flaherty has remarked, "A myth is like a palimpsest on which generation after generation has engraved its own layer of messages, and we must decipher each layer with a different code book."[37] The commercial cinema has long been considered a site of mythic elaboration, a site where the archaic layers of myth as utopian or unifying force are given a modern resonance through the creation of the nation myth. But the investing of mythic status in individuals as authority figures contains the potential of the mobilization of myth toward privileged seats of power rather than for national-popular ends. This is a dilemma that the films discussed above are unable to solve or even address. Indian political culture's dependence on the mystique of individual leaders since independence suggests that this remains a problem. In the movies, the resolution through romance of class and status differences reveals the fragility and the "urgent" appeal of the nation myth.

Memory has a texture which is both social and historic: it
exists in the world rather than in people's heads, finding its basis
in conversations, cultural forms, personal relations, the structure
and appearance of places and . . . in relation to ideologies
which work to establish a consensus view of both the past and
the forms of personal experience which are significant and
memorable.
—Michael Bommes and Patrick Wright in
   Johnson, Making Histories

The Recuperation of History and Memory

      The historical genre in Bombay filmmaking, which goes
back to the earliest days of the cinema, has all but disappeared over the
last decade. Although historicals were always far outnumbered by other
genres, perhaps because of the costs involved in presenting lavish spectacles on the screen, their decline is suggestive of the "proletarianization" of the Hindi film in the postcolonial era. From 1947 to 1967, historicals averaged roughly three a year. Since the late sixties, however,

their number has fallen further, with several years producing no historical films at all. In recent years, television has become the new site for the reconstruction of history: "Tippu Sultan," "Mirza Ghalib," "Tamas," and "Bharat ek Khoj" ("The discovery of India") have been popular series.

The issue of historical representation is perhaps the most contentious in the annals of moviemaking. History and cinema are both institutions, forms of narration, and sites of ideological struggle. As such, the cinema of a particular nation selects historical events that either glorify the past or help to throw light on the present. The commercial Bombay cinema has sought to stay clear of controversy by converting history into pageantry and spectacle and developing a repertoire of characters, mostly from Maratha and Mughal history, who are presented over and over again in forms firmly lodged in the popular memory. Shivaji and the queen of Jhansi are popular heroic subjects from the nationalist phase, Akbar and Jehangir symbols of Mughal imperial grandeur. Of the old studios, Minerva Movietone specialized in historicals, with *Pukar* (*Call*, 1939) and *Sikander* (*Alexander*, 1941) two of its well-known and popular products. Its *Mirza Ghalib* (*Ghalib*, 1954) was awarded the President's Gold Medal for the best film of that year. In these and other films, colorful characters from the past reinforce themes of patriotism, and their actions are woven into narratives of romance, intrigue, or conflict. Notions of historical accuracy or attention to detail are subordinated to the larger imaginative sweep of legend and heroic sentiment.

This tendency would seem to bear out the contention, in relation to film history, of theorists like Stephen Heath, Keith Tribe, and Colin MacCabe, who all point to the inability of the cinematic apparatus to present anything other than repetitions of its own structures of fiction. Heath argues for the recognition of a basic duality in the historical film: past/present, construction/reconstruction. As a genre with impersonation built into its very identity and codes, the historical film provides a rich source of knowledge into the way a society constructs its self-image by projecting onto the past the imperatives of the present and vice versa. But it also reveals a particular attitude to the past and the kinds of relationships to be established between past and present. The historical film addresses the spectator in a particular way, establishing both (temporal) connection and disruption, identity and difference, autonomy and dependence.

Because Western film criticism has had little to say about the treatment of history in the cinemas of the colonized non-West, our starting point has to be a notion of alternative histories and alternatives to "history." Philip Rosen has pointed out the coincidence of the birth of the motion pictures with a crisis in Western historiographic thought, its questioning of the security of historical knowledge.[2] But what if "the security of historical knowledge" is doubted to begin with, as it is in one dominant strand of the Indian cultural tradition? What if history is inseparable from myth and myth from narrativity, art, and representation? Would not such a situation require its own conception of film-critical historiography and analysis? And what if the history of colonialism enables "the natives" to rewrite themselves as objects-turned-subjects of history? The camera, "the machine for ideal looking" (Rosen), can then accommodate two modes of seeing, a double vision, as it were, which is also a double bind. That is, the cinema spectator both accepts and denies the capacity of the camera to "secure" the historical.

It is at this point that film-critical concerns with "national cinemas" as particular forms of mediated history intersect with the notion of the historical genre in film. The "national" as mode of knowledge and identification stakes out its territory in the space between prior knowledge or belief systems and new knowledge appropriated from the colonizer-colonized relationship. "Myth" meets "history" across the textual body of the historical film. In other words, in order to negotiate its dual identity as history and film, indigenous and Western, the historical film may be considered, as Thomas Elsaesser suggests in another context, as the site of ambivalence and as an "Edisonian imaginary."[3] The choice of representing history on the screen is also a choice made by the filmmaker to articulate a "new" language of desire vis-à-vis the cinematic apparatus itself. The historical film, in short, makes a distinct break with normative expectations of realism and the transparency of the text and strains toward the grand, the opulent, the classical. The "Edisonian imaginary" merges with a "Third World" imaginary, the triumph through technology over scarce resources and means. In the context of the Bombay cinema, the decision to make a historical film on the part of a filmmaker becomes a signifier of "difference," an invitation to visual pleasure resulting from high production values, the expansive sweep of a historical narrative, the scope for stylistic excess. In foregrounding construction (elaborate sets and props), defamiliarization (costumed actors), impersonation (stars as historical personages), distanciation (the past as completed event), the historical film tells us that it is not history but only the shadow-play of history. In approaching the historical film, then, as an object of study, our task is not simply to note what is history and what is not or to treat history as a mere subtext, but to see why a film engages history in the first place and what are its formal mechanisms for doing so. We have to keep these considerations in mind as we turn to the specific cultural and ideological context into which the Bombay historical genre inserts itself.

To begin with, imperso-nation in the Bombay historical film takes the particular and culturally privileged form of syncretism, history being an amalgam of mythical tales, legends, and folk knowledge rather than a search for the "truth" of past events and personages. Filmic constructions of history therefore extend an ancient and venerable tradition in Indian historiography in which history is not separable from myth, legend, and drama. This tradition both undertakes and reveals a process of cultural syncretism which is associated with India's survival from ancient times to the present. Terms like "unity in diversity," "synaesthesia," "synthesis," originally used by the Orientalist scholars, try to capture what is essentially a very complex process of cultural adaptation and adjustment. It is easy to see how these "positive" depictions lend themselves to a reversal into their negative equivalents—"timeless," "ahistorical," "devoid of history"—which a certain Western mind-set has found difficult to wholly shake off in relation to India.[4]

Indian historian Romila Thapar tells us that interest in India's past was initiated by the European Orientalists beginning in the late eighteenth century. The officers of the East India Company could ensure a securer base for trade and exploitation if they learned the history and customs of the people they were dominating. Thapar writes, "For the Orientalists, the most significant discovery was that of the relationship between Sanskrit and certain European languages, which led to subsequent work on the common Indo-European heritage. The ancient Indian past was seen almost as a lost wing of early European culture, and the Aryans of India were regarded as the nearest intellectual relatives of the Europeans."[5] In 1817, James Mill published his *History of British India,* in which he maintained that Indian society had remained substantially unchanged from the time of its beginnings, the coming of the Aryans, until the arrival of the British. Other influential theories, such as those of Oriental despotism and the Asiatic mode of production, were later discredited or substantially modified by Indian historians. Meenakshi Mukherjee writes about the unprecedented interest in history in the late nineteenth century, the writing of historical fiction, and the starting of historical journals aimed at discovering regional history—*Banga:darshan* (1872) and *Aitiha:sik Chitra* (1898) in Bengali, *Kavyetiha:s Sāṅgrahā* (1878) in Marathi.[6] Artist-intellectuals like Rabindranath Tagore looked to the epics and scriptures "to understand our identity both in space and time, as a unified and great nation."[7]

However, etymological and traditional ideas about time do not reveal a strong historical sense in terms of a linear chronology. The Indian word for time is *ka:l* (from the root *kal*, meaning "to calculate") and may signify either the past or the future. In other words, both "yesterday" and "tomorrow" have the single equivalent *kal*. Romila Thapar tells us, "In early India the concept of time according to some was in the form of a circle and according to others in a series of waves. The Hindu tradition as recorded in the *Purāṇas* (literally meaning "old") saw time as moving in a cycle—the Mahāyuga—the great cycle which lasts for 4,320,000 years."[8] And Sudhir Kakar writes that "not only is the meaning of the word *Kal* . . . derived from the syntax and context of the sentence, it also depends upon the inflection of the voice which conveys the speaker's mood. *Kal* can mean tomorrow or yesterday, a moment or an age; it may refer to an event which just happened, or to a future likelihood (as in the Spanish *mañana*)."[9] The past and the present are connected through memory, which, as Mircea Eliade points out, has a high place in the Indian philosophical system. Memory is regarded as the preeminent form of knowledge, and "one frees oneself from the work of Time by recollection, by anamnesis."[10] Eliade writes: "Indian literature uses images of binding, chaining and captivity interchangeably with those of forgetting, unknowing, and sleep to signify the human condition; contrariwise, images of being freed from bonds and the tearing of a veil (or the removal of a bandage from the eyes), of memory, remembering, being awakened, the waking state, express abolishing (or transcending) the human condition, freedom, deliverance (moksa, mukti, nirvana, etc.)."[11] Through the agency of memory, the (Hindu) individual connects with the heterogeneity of past lives to a prior state of collectivity or oneness with all Being.

Time, memory, and history tend to have a circular movement. In ancient India, on the other hand, "the Hindu cycle concept is essentially a cosmological concept . . . [which] emphasized continual change. Thus there was an implicit rejection of the idea that history repeats itself."[12] The ancients showed a lack of concern for authorship or chronology, and "some of the most famous names to which history attributes certain philosophical doctrines or systems are now admitted to be legendary."[13] Romila Thapar tells us that in some of the ancient texts, for instance in the genealogies provided in the Puranas, the dynastic lists appear in the form of a prophecy, using the future tense.[14] Moreover, they were often fabricated, so that "traditional genealogies are rarely faithful records of times past."[15]

Itihāsa, the nearest equivalent term for history used in Sanskrit literature, means "thus it was" or "so it has been." But the word did not denote the factual in the strict sense and came to refer to legend, history, and accounts of past events. The purpose of *itihāsa* was to refer to the events of the past in such a manner as would relate them to the goals and purposes of the Hindu tradition. The historical tradition grew out of a variety of literary forms current during the Vedic period, the most significant being the *gathās* (songs), *nārasamsi* (eulogies of heroes), *akhyāna* (dramatic narratives), and *purāna* (ancient lore). The forms of historical writing produced in India, such as the historical biographies of royalty written in the period from A.D. 600 to 1200, testify to the dominance of literary conventions. The authors were sophisticated court poets who did not hesitate on occasion to sacrifice historical veracity to an elegant turn of phrase or to dramatic analogies. "The link with the *itihāsa* and *purāna* tradition was maintained both indirectly when the court poets used these earlier texts as source material and more directly by associating the subject of the biography with the earlier heroes and legends."[16] Mythology, genealogy, and historical narrative are now regarded as the three main constituents of the Indian historical tradition. In Sanskrit poetics, *itihāsa* is considered a genre of composition, like *kāvya* (poetry), or *nātya* (drama). While the word *itihāsa* was meant to stand for history, the "presentation of facts was never accorded a high premium in *itihāsa* compositions."[17] It has been pointed out that though in English commentary both the *Rāmayana* and the *Mahābhārata* are referred to as epics, in Sanskrit a clear distinction was made between the two works, the first being *kāvya* and the second *itihāsa*. Such a conception of *itihāsa* dominated both the historical novel of the nineteenth century and the historical film of the twentieth.

During the nationalist movement in the nineteenth century, when the intellectuals felt most acutely the tremendous divisions of caste, creed, and race that had to be overcome to create a sense of national identity, efforts at synthesis drew diverse texts together. In "A Vision of India's

History," Tagore presents the epic *Mahābhārata* as a historical document of the Aryan period.

> Another task undertaken by this age was the gathering and arranging of historical material. In this process, spread over a long period of time, all the scattered myths and legends were assimilated, along with all the beliefs and discussions which lingered in the racial memory. This literary image of old Aryan India was called the Mahabharata—the great Bharata. Even the name shows an awakened consciousness of unity in a people struggling to find expression in a permanent record.[18]

The *Mahābhārata* thus becomes a historical record, a work of "creative synthesis." Tagore attributes the "glories" of Indian civilization to the success of the Aryans in assimilating non-Aryan features, its failures to the presence of unassimilable elements. He then voices his faith in India's capacity again to "find her truth, her harmony, and her oneness, not only among her own people, but with the world."[19] The reverberations of an East-West synthesis were strong. Yet, as Kalyan Chatterjee writes, "he alternated sharply between his impulse to embrace the world and his urge to go native. Between a past in which imagination had freedom and a present in which colonialism constrained action, Tagore's mind was a crucible of his nation."[20]

Indian cinema, with its history of drawing upon diverse indigenous cultural and narrative traditions, as well as those of Hollywood, its spectacles of the "grand historical" and "romanticized legend," its biographies of celebrated saints, heroes, and freedom fighters: how did this cinema inflect the realities of postindependence India through historical portrayal? What particular forms did imperso-nation take in the historical film? For if, as Vijay Mishra has argued, Indian historical consciousness is nothing but a "black hole," does that relegate the Indian historical film to a bottomless pit?[21] Unfortunately, such a view of Indian history advances its own brand of Orientalism and a rather uncomplicated view of historiography. For whereas historians like Hayden White have now quite convincingly demonstrated the fictional or narrative form of all history writing,[22] to hold to a positivist notion of history seems to me regrettable and to add nothing to our cross-cultural understanding of the historical film. Just as "realism" is a matter of representation, so is "history." If, however, we are concerned, as I believe Mishra to be, with the theoretical dilemma of how to hold the popular film accountable for its obligation to depict actual social events, the answer lies not in constructing a set of (essentialized rather than discursive) oppositions—realism versus romance, artistic versus commercial, or metatext versus history. Such an approach is a version of reinventing the wheel in the case of the popular cinema, to pose ignorance of the vast literature on genre, conventions, textuality, mode of production, and the like available to students of film. Rather, we might do worse than turn to "*histoire/discours*" (a glaring omission in Mishra's text), for here the actual processes of *translation* and *enunciation* are foregrounded.[23] We can then start out from the premise, to use Stephen Heath's words, that "no film is not a document of itself and of its actual situation in respect of the cinematic institution."[24]

Historical representation is, indeed, a question of the present impersonating as the past. For the purposes of film analysis, we have to ask: What are the mediations between history (past events) and power, memory, and desire (configurations in the present of the actual filmmaking)? In the context of the Bombay cinema, keeping in mind its cultural definition of history and its context of production (industrial and national), our questions become: How does ideology masquerade as history? What elements of synthesis, of syncretism, are built into the structure of the narratives? How do the films deal with historical and cultural contradictions? My aim in this chapter is to ground these questions in the discussion of two films of the postindependence period which were both critical and commercial successes: K. Asif's *Mughal-e-Azam* (*The Great Mughal*, 1960) and Guru Dutt's *Sahib Bibi aur Ghulam* (*King, Queen, and Knave*, 1962). They deal with two separate "moments" in Indian history which any ideal or ideology of synthesis could not incorporate: Hindu-Muslim antagonism, here displaced onto a nostalgic image of Mughal grandeur, and the excesses of feudalism (the divisions of "race" and class, respectively). Both these realms of experience might be said to have engaged strong, if often confused, feelings for many Indians, for they had been modified as a result of Indian independence. With the memory of Indian liberation from British rule were mixed those of the unimaginable horrors of partition. Independence had also brought about the abolition of the *zamindari*, or feudal land ownership system (although not of the smaller landlords), and the extinction of a whole way of life. *Mughal-e-Azam* and *Sahib Bibi aur Ghulam* are nostalgic evocations of selected pasts, but they may also be seen as texts of motivated excess, stretching genre expectations, in the one case of "legend," in the other of "social melodrama." The films follow a structure of heightened emotional orchestration, where the past becomes the means of resolving tensions in the present. Imperial justice and order in *Mughal-e-Azam* and sexuality in *Sahib* threaten to get out of control in the narrative and have to be deliberately harnessed. These texts illustrate that the impulse toward synthesis becomes a means of exploring ideological and psychic disturbances pertaining to the group in question that then get resolved through emotional drama. *(love story - seems to be the theme so far)*

Fredric Jameson identifies three concentric frameworks or three "horizons" of interpretation whereby a particular text must be read: the first is that of "political history, in the narrow sense of punctual event and a chroniclelike sequence of happenings in time," the second that of society or the struggle between social classes, and the third of history in its broadest sense as a succession of modes of production.[25] Approaching *Mughal-e-Azam* with this methodological schema in mind, it might be observed that the historical film, which elaborates itself along the first level, makes the past the symbolic realm in which the social and historical contradictions of the present are resolved. Here the "punctual event," the "glory" of the emperor Akbar and his power struggle with his son, Prince Salim, opens out to the conditions of social life in India for Hindus and Muslims in relation to each other and to history and its reversals. Moreover, in addition to the successive outward movement of analysis suggested by Jameson, the historically motivated text encourages a split or double vision, the past as always already encased in the present, history as allegory.

The Bombay film has not so much addressed the Hindu-Muslim relationship as sublimated it by displacing it onto the canvas of history. A film like V. Shantaram's *Padosi* (*Neighbour*, 1941), with its social message of Hindu-Muslim amity, its wooden characterization of intersubjective communal harmony submerged and sacrificed in a (literal) sea of hostility, did of course address the issue through the genre of "the social," while countless Bombay films have a Muslim character to fill out their demographic view of India's social universe. But the historical film has been the privileged site of elaboration of the Muslim sensibility, particularly by directors like Ezra Mir, Sohrab Modi, Mehboob (with *Humayun*, 1945), and K. Asif, some of them Muslims (although non-Muslims have also made historical films based on the Mughal period).[26] Apart from the scope for spectacle and romance, the appeal of the

Mughal period for these directors might have meant the assertion of identity through identification. Moreover, the nationalist ideology of historical synthesis found an effective though hardly unproblematic milieu in the Mughal period.

The need to address the issue of Muslim identity within Hindu-dominated India that one perceives in *Mughal-e-Azam* is masked but undoubtedly there. K. A. Abbas has described in his autobiography the atmosphere of tremendous animosity, fear, and tension during the partition years prevailing in many areas of Bombay among people belonging to the two communities who had lived side by side for years but felt they could no longer trust one another. Others have recorded similar experiences. Because the film took fifteen years to make, *Mughal-e-Azam*'s makers no doubt experienced the trauma, although it is not known to what degree they were directly affected by the events of the time. Other "happenings" that were direct or indirect responses to partition relate to policies of control on the one hand and a self-induced loss of memory on the part of writers on the other. Not only did the threat of censorship deter filmmakers from attempting communal subjects, but perhaps the events were too close in time and therefore painful to confront. (It was not until 1975, with *Garm Hawa* [*Hot Winds*], discussed in a later chapter, that an Indian filmmaker could take up the subject.) Refuge in the distant past was one solution.

Throughout the fifties and sixties, historians debated the proper mode in which the Muslim "intervention" in Indian history might be explained. They accused one another of distorting the facts, of bending to ideological and bureaucratic pressures in assessing the Muslim role in India's history. R. C. Majumdar, for instance, charged that during the period of the freedom struggle, there was a conscious attempt, in writing about medieval India, to "rewrite the whole chapter of the bigotry and intolerance of the Muslim rulers towards the Hindu religion. This was prompted by the political motive of bringing together the Hindus and Mussalmans in a common fight against the British."[27] He adds that during the postindependence period, Indian historians sacrificed historical accuracy in order to please those in power:

> The evil is enhanced by the fact that the Government, directly or indirectly, seeks to utilize history to buttress some definite ideas, such as the Gandhian philosophy of non-violence, the artificial conception of fraternal relations between the two great communities of India sedu-

lously propagated by him, and several popular slogans evoked by the exigencies of the struggle for freedom. These have been accepted as a rich legacy by the Government, even though it practically means in many cases the sacrifice of truth, the greatest legacy which Gandhi meant to bequeath to mankind.[28]

Romila Thapar, on the other hand, has argued against the projection onto history of narrow prejudices and divisions. In a more recent essay entitled "Communalism and the Writing of Indian History," she points out the distortions of colonialist historiography, particularly James Mill's periodization of the history of India into Hindu civilization, Muslim civilization, and British civilization. This periodization was adopted by nationalist historians and intensified with the demand for Muslim separatism from the 1920s onward. It was argued that the Muslim period saw the evolution of the two "nations," Hindu and Muslim, whose logical outcome in terms of modern nation-states could only be the partition of the subcontinent. Thapar writes:

> That religious groups in themselves do not constitute a nation was an argument which was not given serious consideration.
>
> The term "Hindu" is not found in pre-Islamic sources relating to India. . . . Similarly the term "Muslim" was rarely used until the 13th century in the sources, which do not use a religious terminology but refer to the Arabs, Turks and Persians in a purely political manner.
>
> Historical interpretation is integrally related to a people's notion of its culture and its nationality. This in itself makes historical writing one of the most sensitive intellectual areas with wide repercussions on popular nationalism and political beliefs.[29]

If there was no consensus among historians as to the true nature of the Hindu-Muslim interaction, writers and musicians in the Bombay film world were at pains to stress the theme of unity and communal harmony. Alison Arnold has found, in her study of Hindi film music, that music directors employed both "overt" and "covert" means of musical fusion. Of the former, she lists the following: (1) the mixture of a recognizable Hindu or Muslim musical form with contrasting, that is, Muslim or Hindu, lyrics and/or screen characters; (2) the combination of recognizable Hindu and Islamic musical features within one film song; (3) lyrics that openly express Hindu-Muslim brotherhood and amity. The covert means of musical fusion include the adoption of existing Hindu or Muslim tunes for film songs of contrasting character and the combination of Indian ragas with other Indian musical elements for songs in Muslim social and historical film.[30] *Mughal-e-Azam* presents instances of such musical fusion in a richly composed musical score. The motivation was no doubt also commercial, meant to maximize audiences.

Indian historical films tend to be retellings of the same episodes, legends, heroic deeds, and characters. Since they are cast partly in the *itihāsa* tradition outlined earlier and partly in the conventions of the Parsee theater, which incorporated Persian influences of the romantic tale, legend and historical fact are freely mingled. The thin line between history and legend becomes evident in the case of Anarkali herself, the heroine of *Mughal-e-Azam* and *Anarkali* (1952), both of which Firoze Rangoonwalla classifies generically as "legendary." Yet at least two texts assert her historical identity. A dictionary of Indian history describes Anarkali as "a lady with whom Prince Salim, later Emperor Jehangir (1605–27) was in secret love. The Emperor built a beautiful marble tomb on her grave in Lahore in 1615 and inscribed on it a couplet expressing his passionate love for her."[31] Edward Balfour's *The Cyclopaedia of India* also mentions Anarkali's tomb and says, "He [*sic*] was a favorite of Jahangir, but was seen to smile to one of the zenana, and was bricked up in a cell."[32]

If legend merges with history in the Hindi cinema, history provides embellishment to legend. As a historical setting for romance and spectacle, the Mughal period (1526–1707) and particularly the reign of its greatest monarch, Akbar (1556–1605), has been extremely popular with Bombay moviemakers. Through the figure of Akbar, known for his religious tolerance and for encouraging Hindu artists in court, filmmakers could convey messages of Hindu-Muslim brotherhood. Biographical films on the lives and careers of famous musicians of Akbar's court of reign, such as Tansen (*Sangeet Samrat Tansen*, 1962) and Baiju (*Baiju Bawra*, 1952), were made, these being characters who embodied a blending of Hindu and Muslim cultural influences. Yet even within the conventions of this genre of "historical" or "legend," where historical accuracy is seldom at issue, filmmakers would find it necessary sometimes to assert or deny a film's claim to historical truth. Thus *Anarkali* flatly refuses any connection with history by beginning and ending the film with a disclaimer, "The picture *Anarkali* is based on the legendary love between Prince Salim and Anarkali and has no foundation whatsoever in history," even though all the major characters in the film are "real." Perhaps it points to the situation of film reception in the early fifties, when any sort of historical portrayal relating to Muslims could stir up a controversy.

Mughal-e-Azam, in contrast to *Anarkali*, is interesting precisely because of its dual address: it claims both the authority of history and the license of legend and inscribes its dual focus in an oedipal conflict. History and legend no longer blend smoothly and casually (as in the *itihāsa* tradition) but appear in a hierarchical relationship. In choosing to call his film *Mughal-e-Azam*, the filmmaker makes Akbar as much a protagonist as Salim, who has the romantic lead. Part of the motivation is apparently to signify the grandeur, wealth, and power of the Mughal dynasty. We learn of the very ambitiousness of the project from film historian Firoze Rangoonwalla:

> For more than fifteen years under production . . . and finally completed at a reported cost of more than a crore [Rs. 10 million, roughly equivalent to $1 million]. . . . Everything about the film was in grand style. It had a star cast led by Dilip Kumar, Madhubala and Prithviraj in the three pivotal roles, four renowned writers contributing its rich Urdu dialogue, huge sets like the glass palace (Sheesh Mahal), sweeping battle scenes and some highly appealing songs penned by Shakeel and tuned by Naushad. It had also English and Tamil versions, the latter being called "Akbar" and a few of its sequences were in color.[33]

The opening shot of the film inscribes Mughal history within the visual frame of the Indian nation. The sonorous tones of a voice-over narrator are heard on the sound track while a map of India slowly moves upward in the frame, as though India is arising from its present state of fractured identity for Hindus and Muslims to a former state of elevated glory. As the image is held for a few seconds, the voice can be "recognized" as the voice of India because it speaks in the first person. It speaks of being bound in chains (a dual reference perhaps both to British colonialism and to the chains of hatred fomented by the British to break up Hindu-Muslim ties) by the naive (those suffering from illusions of power?). But, it says, "those who cared for me taught people to love one another and so forever took me into their hearts." The composite voice-image invites collective spectator identification, for each individual viewer to recognize him/herself as a national subject or citizen in relation to the map. The idea of history-geography as constitutive of a national discourse, "of implanting and inculcating the civic and patriotic spirit," has briefly

been dealt with by Foucault. He sees it as having the effect of constituting a personal identity "because it's my hypothesis that the individual is
not a pre-given entity . . . but the product of a relation of power exercised over bodies, multiplicities, movements, desires, forces."[34] The
map as instrumental of power/knowledge has a long history in the Western world, and one might consider its usefulness as visual allegory in
the context of Indian national subjectivity. Certainly the Hindi cinema
from its earliest days used the image of the map in interpellating viewers
in all their diversity as unified national subjects. Also, here the map is
a geographical rather than a political one. The features of physical geography are allied to nature, the natural and organic; India, the image
tells us, has always been the same, in the sixteenth century as in the
twentieth, through all the vicissitudes of history. Political lines are
drawn to separate people, but nature/land knows no such differences.

The voice-over continues its rumination, and the flashback device is
used to signify India reliving its memories. The camera slowly pans and
takes in a high-angle view of the Mughal legacy—architectural monuments of Delhi and Agra, the places which had been the seat of Mughal
power. These spatial configurations signify solidity, permanence, immobility. They also embody the highest cultural synthesis of Hindu and
Islamic artistic and philosophical styles. Akbar and his grandson Shah
Jehan (1628–1658), the builder of the Taj Mahal, were patrons of architecture, the buildings now symbolizing Mughal rule at its best. These
buildings are aids to historical memory and almost have a life of their
own. The camera's panning movement shows the magnificent and deserted Fatehpur Sikri, the city that Akbar built near Agra and where he
held court from 1569 to 1585. First the coordinates of space and then of
time are established as the narrator begins his story, "Three hundred
and eighty years ago . . ." and presents a monarch known not only for
his love of India but for his piety as well. The narrative initially follows
an episodic structure, presenting the circumstances that led to Salim's
birth and a few scenes of his childhood.

This shift to the domestic scene would seem to bear out Stephen
Heath's assertion that "the constant force of the narrative of history given
is familial and family history" so that history is provided with the per-
fection of a story.[35] The "absence" of history is the "presence" and
"present" of film in the sense that film or any other narrative form tries
to grasp and render history in each telling. Moreover, in the Indian
narrative tradition, family history is not strictly demarcated from social

history but opens onto the latter. The most obvious examples are provided by the two great epics which many believe have a historical basis: in the *Mahabharata,* the battle between the Kauravas and the Pandavas, two branches of the same family, engages vast social, political, and cosmic forces, all of which are then sought to be compressed within a single philosophical framework; in the *Ramayana,* Rama's relationship with Sita is largely determined by his obligation to his people and his social dharma.

It would not be too far-fetched to claim that *Mughal-e-Azam* draws upon this frame of reference in making the central conflict in the film one between family affection and social role. For Salim, the answer to Akbar's prayers at the tomb of Salim Chisti (although the *Memoirs* of Jehangir state that Akbar made the trip *after* Salim's birth) is not above the law. Whatever the actual historical reasons for Salim's rebellion against his father, the film makes romance the cause of it. Thus for both Akbar and Salim love and duty become irreconcilable options.

The film associates history with the exercise of power, its heights and its limits. All of the major characters—Akbar, his Hindu queen Joda Bai (Durga Khote), Salim (Dilip Kumar), and Anarkali (Madhubala)— are trying to reconcile conflicting identities and roles. Akbar is a powerful monarch but unable to control his own son, Joda Bai is a fond mother called upon to be a proud queen, Salim is a prince in love with a maidservant, Anarkali is a commoner who dares to dream of the palace. The film explores the characters' vulnerabilities, their temporary lapses but ultimate triumph, for which history remembers them. Although there is conflict between private passion or feeling and public duty, the two realms cannot be separated. This is evident in the handling of romance and spectacle. Film researcher Leger Grindon has noted these as the recurring generic figures of the historical fiction film, where "the romance dramatizes the personal experience, the spectacle the public life." He adds that the romance and the spectacle have corresponding formal tendencies. "The romance favors characterization in interior space and invites two-shots, shot-counter-shot structures, and the close-up. The spectacle, on the other hand, solicits broader expression in the *mise-en-scène,* favoring group compositions and mass movements that suggest the long shot and the pan in expansive exterior landscapes."[36] But in *Mughal-e-Azam,* it is the romance that provides the spectacle, the public dimension of the private domain being reinforced continually.

When Anarkali is first introduced, she appears in the form of a statue presented in Akbar's court to celebrate Salim's return home after a long absence. Amid the assembled crowd, Salim drops the veil that covers the "statue" by shooting an arrow at it. Anarkali's doubling as a statue has many meanings: it is an early hint at Anarkali's "impudence" in falling in love with the great Akbar's son, thus exceeding her lowly status; it recalls her tragic end when she is buried alive, a condition of death-in-life; and finally it is an homage to the actress Madhubala's statuesque beauty. The "statue" moves and speaks, and the distant Salim is mildly interested. Thus begins the great romance in a very public way. In several other sequences, the romance develops as much through spectacles that present Anarkali performing dances or singing in front of the king and his courtiers as through intimate love scenes. The visual highlight of the film is the famous *shi:sh mahal* (glass palace) dance, which is shot in color in a black-and-white film and creates an effect of both fragility and brilliance. The romance has been forbidden by the emperor, and Anarkali is seemingly repentant and hence commanded to perform in court again. But Anarkali's dance and song convey to Salim that she still loves him, and she openly defiés Akbar. As she dances, Anarkali's sparkling image is replicated in this hall of mirrors, reinforcing the notion of (slave) woman as spectacle. Other scenes are also mediated through other gazes. In a sequence where the lovers secretly meet in a garden, to the strains of classical music to denote almost spiritual ecstasy, the presence of an eye watching them is a sinister reminder of the invasion of privacy.

As a historical romance, *Mughal-e-Azam* is reminiscent of other texts lodged in the cultural memory. Like Rāma, Salim returns home from battle after fourteen years; like the heroes of Kalidasa'a plays, Salim is caught between desire and duty, which is aesthetically manifest in the relation of the erotic sentiment to the heroic. No doubt other texts from the Muslim tradition found their way into the thematic and visual elements of this film. Indeed, the reference to art is more than accidental or unconscious. Hints of the darker side of Akbar's famed power and prestige are given through the character of the sculptor who had provided Anarkali's "disguise." He is sometimes shown at work and portrayed as fearless and morally strong. A representative of the worker-artist, his function is that of the chorus, commenting on the action and creating works of art which speak of injustice, violence, and the emptiness of pride. He can defy the emperor (refusing to marry Anarkali just to have

Akbar rid of her), spurning fame and money to follow his own vision. His look and speech align him with the "common man": he is dark and unattractive and speaks in less florid language than the others. Toward the end of the film, when Akbar orders Salim's death, the sculptor's song saves the prince's life, Salim now being associated with rebellion against oppressive authority, broad democratic sympathies, and freedom of choice. The artist is the life-giver, the social commentator, and one who, being above class and creed, can shape the course of history.

Mughal-e-Azam sees the artist as the mediator between opposite forces in society and "greatness," effective through justice, as immortal, as having conquered time. Guru Dutt's *Sahib Bibi aur Ghulam* positions the *ghulam* ("slave") as the narrator-chronicler of a decaying feudal society. The two films differ greatly in their visual style, narrative handling, characterization, and mood. Nevertheless they both use memory as a structuring device and associate the past with glamor, pageantry, and fascination.

Sahib is based on a very popular Bengali novel of the same name written by Bimal Mitra and published in 1953. The Hindi film was preceded by a Bengali screen version which had also been very successful commercially. *Sahib* spans the late nineteenth and early twentieth centuries and charts the process of decline of the Bengal *zamindari*, or land ownership system, and its distinctive way of life. It tries to capture the fading away of one social class and the emergence of another. Whereas *Mughal-e-Azam* actively seeks connections with history by incorporating some "facts," the author of *Sahib* would like to deny the status of history to his work. It is instructive to turn for a moment to the novel, not only to find out what the film leaves out, but also to get a clearer picture of the context of the choice and motivation of historical portrayal. What is immediately striking is the disavowal of the role of historian on the part of the novelist. In the preface to his novel Mitra writes:

> I am primarily a storyteller, not a historian. For the sake of storytelling, sometimes history, science or social studies become important. That is what has happened in this case. For the story I have used material from Calcutta's social and cultural history, and only because such use was indispensable for the story, not because I had anything new to say about history. Here the story is primary, history or anything else secondary. But if my story is embellished by riding upon the

wings of history, I have been ever watchful that history should not be embellished by its involvement with the story. Constantly I have kept myself tied to truth. For the story I have used portions of history, it is true, but I have not tried to falsify history.[37]

Bimal Mitra wishes to retain the liberty of the writer to create fictions and promotes an instrumental use of history. One is reminded of the *itihāsa* tradition, which can blend history with legend or mix fiction with "fact." Nevertheless the opening pages of the novel contain an absolutely fascinating and masterly, if compressed, account of the history of Calcutta, that most visceral of modern Indian cities. Here one finds a brilliant image of syncretism, of a city whose history is one of seemingly endless absorption. The narrator is almost a combination of bard, storyteller, and grandfather who roots his description to very local landmarks, to names of streets and shops and families as his memory ranges over past and present for the benefit of an uninformed younger generation. Rumor mingles with fact, certainty with conjecture. The relaxed tone of the narration and its leisurely pace suggest that memory supplies what formal histories cannot—the lived experience of change.

What motivates this effort at recuperation of Calcutta history? It is the image of destruction brought on by the force of postindependence industrialism and "improvement." Old buildings are being demolished under the orders of the Calcutta Improvement Trust, buildings bursting with memories and sole reminders of the city's tumultuous past. As the buildings go, so will the memories. Here again we have a sense of buildings as spatial metaphors for permanence against the impermanence of time.

Snippets of history become available. Calcutta, or rather Bengal, is referred to as a country (*desh*) with its own history, its own past of almost three centuries. Even the Ganges had a different name then (in 1738); it was merely a thin stream. Calcutta's origin is associated with the Portuguese, the East India Company, and various other trading groups. Calcutta, earlier called Shutanuti, was founded by Job Charnock, a company officer who married a Brahmin woman: "One day came the Portuguese. Now you can see them in Murgihata. Half-English, half-Portuguese. They were called Phiringees. They were the first generation of Company clerks. Later they became the Englishmen's servants, cooks and their women the Memsahibs' ayahs. Also came the Armenians. . . . With them came the Greeks, the Jews, the Hindus and Muslims— everybody. Thus was established Calcutta. All this happened in

1690."[38] It is apparent that the novelist regrets the general population's ignorance of this history of Calcutta and wants to make it available to a wide readership. The decline of Bengal from its heyday in the nineteenth century disturbed Bengali intellectuals as the center of power and leadership shifted to Delhi. Bengal's regional identity, always strong, has co-existed uneasily with an identity conceived in national terms. The film dispenses with this outer historical framework and concentrates on the main narrative, although it stays quite close to the events and characters of the novel.

The novel and the film foreground decay, dissolution, death. The epigraph of the novel, taken from Kipling, suggests this powerfully:

Thus the midday halt of Charnock—
more's the pity
grew a city.
As the fungus sprouts chaotic from its bed
So it spread—
Chance-directed chance-erected, laid and
built
On the silt—
Palace, byre, hovel, poverty and pride
Side by side;
And, above the packed and pestilential town
Death looked down.

The opening sequence of the film presents high-angle long shots of the ruins of a building and workers engaged in the job of demolition. The camera dollies forward to a man in middle age who is apparently supervising the work, then again cuts to shots of broken pillars and walls, cobwebs, and other signs of decay. Suddenly there is music, the man looks around, then hurries toward the sound as though summoned by the ghosts of the past. We see a woman's image in superimposition over the ruins, her voice calling, "Bhootnath." The flashback starts at this point and continues till the end, except for a few last scenes.

The story, at first reckoning, seems to fulfill the classic Marxist paradigm of the decay of the old feudal aristocracy and the rise of the new bourgeois class. Bhootnath, an architect and overseer, is the agent of change entrusted with the job of demolishing the huge imposing mansion of the *zamindar* family. Bhootnath relives the memory of his association with this household, in particular with the *choti bahu* (the youngest

Bhootnath (Guru Dutt) approaches the feudal mansion in Sahib Bibi aur Ghulam (King, Queen and Knave). *Courtesy National Film Archive of India.*

daughter-in-law), who remains nameless in the film. Bhootnath befriends her, and the two share a deep, though sublimated, attachment. As in so many other films of the fifties, the hero is a young villager who has come to the big city in search of a job. He stays with his brother-in-law, a tutor in the *zamindar* household, and from his vantage point he is able to observe the dissolute life-style of the male members of the Chaudhari family while the women folk while away their time in ritual observances or preoccupation with finery. *Choti bahu* is deeply unhappy because she barely sees 'ier husband, who spends most of his time in the company of his favorite nautch-girl. Lonely and childless, she tries desperate measures to please her husband, even taking to drinking as he wishes. For a while, *choti bahu* succeeds in getting her husband's attention, but soon he goes back to his former pleasures. At a brawl he is beaten up so severely that his health declines and he remains confined to his bed.

Meanwhile, the family fortunes decline as a new class of developers and creditors aligns itself with the managers of the *zamindari* estates to rid the feudal lords of their possessions. *Choti bahu,* by now an alcoholic but still the devoted wife, decides to shake off her addiction and go on a short pilgrimage to help her husband recover. She leaves in the company of Bhootnath, but the older Chaudhari has her murdered for breaking the codes of the house. Here the flashback ends. In the last sequence Bhootnath finds *choti bahu*'s skeleton in the ruins of the mansion, identifying it by the bracelet around her wrist bone.

Interwoven with the main plot is a subplot which serves as a spatial, temporal, and historical counterpoint to the narrative focus on the *zamindars*. To the nocturnal life in the feudal mansion, the harsh unnatural lighting used to depict it, and the lack of meaningful activity are juxtaposed the airy dwelling of Subinay, the light of day and the bustle of productive labor that it produces, and the luminous beauty of Subinay's daughter, Jaba. Subinay is the owner of a *sindoor* (red powder used in the hair by married women) factory, a business he inherited from his father, but his interests lie in nationalist politics (the time frame in the film is of the early decades of this century, when India's independence struggle was in its "terrorist" phase). As members of the Brahmo Samaj, the influential nineteenth-century movement of Hindu religious reform, Subinay and Jaba represent the progressive element of the upcoming bourgeoisie. Bhootnath is our link between the two worlds, for he is employed by Subinay in his factory, and the film anchors its love-interest in the interaction between a naïve Bhootnath and a lively, quick-tempered Jaba. Unfolding events reveal that Bhootnath and Jaba had been married as children, and the last scene shows them leaving the scene of the ruins in a carriage. In the novel, Bhootnath does not reveal his identity as Jaba's husband but encourages her to marry the man her father had chosen for her.

Sahib Bibi aur Ghulam uses individual memory as the structuring consciousness that shapes, orders, and reveals a historical past. Bhootnath's memories propel him to more than thirty years in the past, to a time in which it seems that the world (for him) was whole, alive, brilliant. The ruins among which he sits and remembers get transformed through a fade-in into an imposing mansion which serves as an index for power, beauty, and pride. Bhootnath is suffused with guilt as he realizes his own role in demolishing the very structure whose walls had provided him with shelter and nurture. He is still the servant who is afraid of having bitten the hand that fed him. Bhootnath's class origins, therefore, shape his thinking, and although he has risen in status from his humble beginnings while the feudal class has in effect disappeared, he still

The virginal woman: Waheeda Rehman as Jaba in Sahib Bibi aur Ghulam.
Courtesy National Film Archive of India.

clings to a notion of class difference. Bhootnath's position would then seem to be undermining class mobility as at least to some degree pretentious. The world which Bhootnath has known and nostalgically recalls was rigidly hierarchical, but everything had its place. The *zamindari*, Bhootnath seems to say, was not *all* bad.

Bhootnath's historical role as chronicler of a vanished past almost seems to exceed his social and intellectual endowments. This is visually communicated in the shot where Bhootnath has his first glimpse of the "big house" (*baṛa ghar*), as the mansion was called. Fresh from the village, in villager's garb, he is framed in the gateway in extreme foreground, his back to the camera, while the house, white, with huge tall pillars and a fountain with a statue, appears in frontal view. Against it, Bhootnath is a small and vulnerable figure. The house becomes a character in its own right, and some magnificent effects of lighting suggest its moods, its dark secrets, its seeming power. The house is emblematic of the very *zamindari* existence, and as Bhootnath moves through its immense spaces, different aspects of life there are revealed.

The *zamindars*, who dominated Bengal's social life to a greater extent than *zamindars* of other parts of India, are shown to live in a self-enclosed world, governed by its own rules, given over to its own pleasures and pursuits—and its own brutalities. Some of the typical habits and propensities of this idle, rich class that elicit immediate recognition are presented in the film. It is a structure that is imposed by what is already historically available as common (popular) knowledge. The *zamindars* were known for their patronage of music and dance performed by a special professional class of singer-prostitutes. Several song and dance sequences, with wine flowing freely, signify *zamindari* decadence as well as a colorful life-style. *Choti bahu*'s husband, known as *chote babu* (literally meaning "younger lord"), first appears in such a sequence, signaling his state of total abandon to sensual pleasures. The opulent and wasteful habits of the *zamindars* is also signified by a pigeon fight conducted by the *majhle babu* (literally, "second lord") and his cronies and the wedding of his favorite cat. While the tenants starved, the *zamindars* indulged in frivolities. In one sequence, an emaciated villager is shown shouting at the *zamindars* for robbing him of the land that was rightly his. Suddenly the *majhle babu* appears on the balcony (in a low angle signifying his power) and barely nods to his henchmen; they advance toward the villager, seize him, and strike him down. As the subjective camera shows the sky spinning, there is a fade in to fireworks, wedding bands, and a procession. The bride, all decked out, is feline, the smug host for the wedding is the second lord. The situation of exploitation is starkly juxtaposed.

Such are the pursuits of the *zamindar* men; the women of the mansion are the widowed elder *bahu* ("daughter-in-law"), *majhli bahu*, and *choti bahu*, not including their serving maids. A wry humor and pathos accompany Bhootnath's first glimpse of the senior *bahu*. She is obsessively ritualistic and goes for a dip in the Ganges enclosed in a tentlike purdah. In another shot, she sits frozen with her hands held high, having washed them sixty-five times. The fear of pollution of Brahmin widows is pathetically evoked. The second *bahu*, shown only once, lives by the rules of the *zamindari* code for women, indulging herself with jewelry and rich clothes and chiding *choti bahu* for not accepting that it is the privilege of her husband, long established by tradition, to spend his nights whoring.

It is *choti bahu* who engages viewer sympathy and identification, for she is simultaneously inside and outside, belonging to a poor family but married to a *zamindar*, willing wife and unwilling whore (to him), having a *devi* (goddess) image and yet slave to her desires. The contradictions

Choti bahu (Meena Kumari), seen through the eyes of an adoring Bhootnath:
Sahib Bibi aur Ghulam. *Courtesy National Film Archive of India.*

of her situation and her personality provide the narrative movement and
the emotional intensity of the film. When Bhootnath first meets her, she
is framed like the image of the goddess Lakshmi, seated in a chair and
smiling as she looks down benevolently at him. The light is evenly on
her face while the rest of her room is in shadow. As *choti bahu* progressively succumbs to her passion for her uncaring husband, losing herself
in it and in drink, the lighting casts deep shadows which envelop her
and only partially reveal her face. She appears mostly lying down, hair
dishevelled, out of control. But through her transformation and her anguish, *choti bahu* is conscious of her difference from other women, both
within the *zamindar* family and outside. She is different in her desire to
change the conditions of her life, to please and thus attain her husband even if it means breaking one of the sternest taboos on the Hindu
woman (that of drink), different ultimately in her very capacity for self-
immolation. Sober or drunk, she is fond of asserting proudly, "I am not
like other women."

Arun Khopkar has written that the representations of the two women
in the film, *choti bahu* and Jaba, complement each other and together

present a composite picture of Indian womanhood.[39] *Choti bahu* is photographed in dark or somber tones, usually within the closed space of her room or in the half-darkened passageways of the mansion. She always appears in a lot of jewelry and in richly brocaded sarees which shine, as does her hair. Her whole being is sensuous, her beauty, as it were, in full bloom. Jaba, on the other hand, is almost austere in her simplicity, her sarees are white, she appears in the open air, with bright and even lighting. *Choti bahu* represents the death wish, Jaba the forces of life. As such they signify the forces of history at a particular juncture, that of the decay of the feudal class and rise of the enterprising bourgeoisie.

The perspective on the different characters of the film is provided by the hero. In fact, *Sahib* tends to valorize vision. Through skillful use of editing and point-of-view shots, perception is foregrounded. It is through Bhootnath that the absent (vanished) world of the *zamindars* is made present for the viewer. (His) memory is equivalent to (our) vision. But vision is privileged in another way: Bhootnath's look is voyeuristic, for *we* see *him* looking, constantly looking, and then the camera cuts to what he sees, in the classical point-of-view shot structure. Vision is problematized, for while Bhootnath, as the bearer of the look, has control over what he sees, his gaze is drawn outwards and repeatedly held in fascination by what he sees. This would seem to render him captive and immobile. The "action" and excitement are all out there, in comparison with which his own (class) position is dull and uneventful. Although Bhootnath has a job and is shown working, the film undermines this dimension through its focus on the activities and obsessions of the *zamindars*. Bhootnath's feelings of helplessness and low self-esteem are narratively reinforced when, in the sequence where he learns that the *sindoor* he had taken to *choti bahu* had been ineffective, he experiences a strong, almost violent emotional outburst which is the only one we see from him, and he views himself as a total failure. Yet the function of the servants (with whom Bhootnath is narratively and visually allied, at least in the first half of the film) to look at and comment on the upper classes gives them more power than those who are objects of their gaze. Thus the structures of the film show the protagonist as both disavowing and identifying with class difference.

What is ultimately perhaps the most important and problematical question in the present context is the relationship between memory and desire in *Sahib*. How are we to interpret the film's investment in memory and perception? How does desire—Bhootnath's for *choti bahu*, the spectator's for pleasurable experience in the cinema, the social subject's for mastery and control—operate in relation to what is seen or the ability to see? Much has been written about the cinema and visual pleasure, memory and desire. Yet the relationship between these and their relationship to history, whether that of a national group or of a particular type of cinema, remain vague. As Thomas Elsaesser has suggested:

> Pleasure, as it is bound up with signification, representation, meaning, perception and memory, is therefore perforce implicated in history as the shifting and fixing of the relationships between desire and representation, which can be specified even if the question of how these relationships are articulated in the cinema via aural and visual perception is extremely complex. Perhaps the issue we are concerned with is what in the cinema fixes (under the regime of repetition) meaning, perception and subjectivity—all of which have their own distinct and different historical momentums—and whether it is this fixing process we call pleasure. If cinema is historical, so is pleasure. If cinema is ideological, so is pleasure.[40]

Elsaesser uses the case of Germany's Weimar cinema to see how historical accounts of this cinema have used notions of pleasure, desire, and memory to posit its connection with a "national psyche" or "national character." He critiques these models of reflection theory, suggesting instead a kind of archaeological investigation that takes account of specific mediations of this cinema, such as market considerations, cultural debates, and filmmakers' practices. However, the questions that he raises about the historical and psychoanalytic dimensions of spectatorship, vision, and narrative may be useful in the present context.

Here what is undoubtedly of importance is the way in which invariably (male) images of female sexuality are sublimated onto a spiritual plane. Visual iconography and popular literature are both steeped in the lover-goddess image. Moreover, "the historical nature of human perception, visual decoding, attention span and memory" explains how urbanization and industrialism have affected the reception of female images by the urban Indian. There is little doubt, for instance, that the publicity posters and huge billboards of stars and new film releases in all major Indian cities must have operated as powerful visual stimuli upon the dislocated mass audiences of the postindependence era. One way of interpreting the relationship of memory and desire in *Sahib* (bearing in mind that a single text can only serve as a test case) is to see the fascination with images of unbridled sexuality in *choti bahu* (here displaced as alcoholism) as connecting through memory with a process of atonement. In Hindu culture, memory is a disciplinary mechanism, associated with the cultivation of yogic powers, entailed in which is the harnessing of (sexual) energy for spiritual ends. Bhootnath suffers intensely as he relives his memories. The power of the cinematic apparatus lies in making of that suffering the stuff of the spectator's empathy and enjoyment.

The historical film raises many complex issues for the student of cinema: the question of history as a mode of knowledge, of historical accuracy, of memory and desire, of generic hybridity, of modes of address that seek to be both culturally specific and universalized. More than other genres, the historical film evokes a sense of the "grand," the visually enthralling, the huge canvas to portray the sweep of events that the past as completed action allows in contrast to the incompleteness and in-the-making quality of the present. The commercial Bombay film has usually represented past epochs of Indian history through some central and well-known historical figures: kings and queens, patriots, saints, and singers. During the fifties, the historical film, a rare phenomenon due to the costs involved, looked back at the past with a mixture of nostalgia and sympathy, pride and awe. Recreating history became a labor of love even as the past receded as irrevocably separate from the present. New social identities, new historical configurations, embodied in the artist-worker of *Mughal-e-Azam* and the rising bourgeoisie signified by Bhootnath in *Sahib Bibi aur Ghulam*, would not sustain for long a preoccupation with royalty and aristocracy.

During the seventies and eighties, India's colonial history, generally absent from films, found its way onto celluloid. Satyajit Ray's *Shatranj ke Khilari* (*The Chess Players*, 1977) and Richard Attenborough's *Gandhi* (1983) are considered here because they allow us to raise new questions about the historical film in the context of India's postcolonial identity. The questions of power and agency, the dialectical pull of historical detail against a conception of historical vision, always key to an understanding of the historical film, are particularly pertinent here. Although the names of neither Attenborough nor Ray are associated with the Bombay film industry, both films were made with the help of people working in it and raise significant issues about the representation of history via fiction or fictionalized renderings of actual events. Catering to an international audience, the films examine different phases of the Indo-British encounter and construct their versions of India through selective appropriations of the past. It is these appropriations that need to be examined.

Shatranj ke Khilari

For Ray, the making of *Shatranj* marked a significant departure from his usual practice, for he had never before worked outside his native Bengal. Using Hindi/Urdu as the linguistic medium, popular film stars (Shabana Azmi, Sanjeev Kumar, Amjad Khan, and the voice of Amitabh Bachchan) and other creative talent from Bombay, as well as expensive sets, Ray's foray into historical drama resulted in what Andrew Robinson has called "the first adult film about the British Raj in India."[41]

Based on a short story by Munshi Premchand that had been published in the mid-1920s, *Shatranj* is set in the year 1856 and depicts the political event of the annexation of the kingdom of Oudh by the British East India Company. Alongside this historical narrative is the story of two rich landowners in Lucknow, the capital of Oudh, who are addicted to chess and battle each other over the chessboard, oblivious of the political upheaval around them. Through the activities of its Muslim and native characters, the film creates the ambience of luxury and decadence that Premchand had evoked in the beginning of his story:

> It was the age of Nawab Wajid Ali Shah, and his capital, Lucknow, was steeped in subtle shades of decadence and bliss. Affluent and poor, young and old, everyone was in the mood to celebrate and enjoy themselves. Some held delightful parties while others sought ecstasy in the opium pipe. All of life was charged with a kind of inebriated madness. Politics, poetry and literature, craft and industry, trade and exchange, all were tinged with an unabashed self-indulgence. State officials drank wine (a practice forbidden to Muslims). . . . In fact, the whole kingdom was shackled to sensuality.[42]

The opening shot of the film presents a closeup of chessboard and hands moving pieces before the camera pulls back to show Mirza and Mir, the two landowners, playing a game. That the game is symbolic as well as real is soon evident as a narrative voice-over ironically suggests the "bloodless" nature of this battle, an early enactment of Wajid Ali Shah's loss of his kingdom without a fight. The narrator proceeds to present the viewers with background information via images of Lucknow life in Wajid Ali's time as well as a capsule history of one hundred years of Oudh-British relations. Ray wrote later, "According to all available evidence, this was marked throughout, right from Shuja down to Wajid, by an anxiety on the part of the Nawabs to maintain friendly relations with the Company, in spite of the fact that treaty after treaty progressively stripped them of their territory and their autonomy."[43] In the film, the seven-minute prologue humorously evokes past events and the present machinations of Lord Dalhousie, the governor-general of the company, through a series of animated cartoons. Ray selects the metaphor of the cherry to denote the Indian states that are gobbled up by the East India Company: Punjab, Burma, Nagpur, Satara, Jhansi. Other gastronomical images suggest the greed of the British, who extracted large sums of money from the nawabs of Oudh whenever they waged their diverse campaigns. Now Lord Dalhousie writes of Oudh, "That is a cherry which will drop into our mouths one day." Dalhousie's instrument for this coup is General Outram, the British resident of Lucknow who bears a severe dislike for Nawab Wajid. The film's diegesis weaves fiction and history through the twin stories of Mirza and Mir on the one hand and Wajid Ali and Outram on the other.

Shatranj spans a period of one week, ending on the day of the annexation. Mirza and Mir's singular obsession with chess is symbolic of the many factors that bind them together; they are invariably framed together in the film. They are similar in appearance, background, and temperament, although subtle shades of difference are humorously revealed as the narrative progresses. Lazy and self-indulgent, Mir is also naïve and cowardly. As the two men keep playing, Kurshid, Mirza's wife, tries different tricks to lure her husband away from the drawing-room and into her bed, but to no avail. Mir's wife, Nafeesa, more vivacious and jovial, enjoys a love affair with her cousin in the absence of her husband.

In the meanwhile, Outram has made his maneuvers to carry out Lord Dalhousie's directive. Citing misrule, the company asks King Wajid to abdicate and leave Oudh, with compensation from the company. The news is brought to Wajid by his prime minister, Ali Naqi Khan, in the midst of a *kathak* dance recital, one of the many song and dance festivities that the king indulges in. Wajid refuses to abdicate, and Outram goes to see the queen mother the next day, asking her to advise her son to sign the new treaty. She refuses and plans to petition Queen Victoria herself. But Wajid has already reconciled himself to the new situation

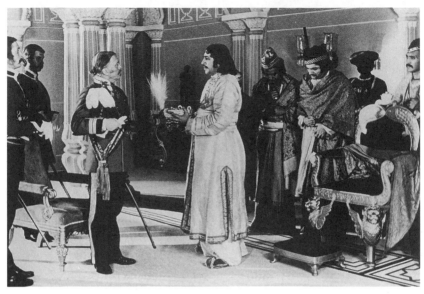

Wajid Ali Shah (Amjad Khan) surrenders his crown to General Outram (Richard Attenborough) in Shatranj ke Khilari (The Chess Players). *The Museum of Modern Art/Film Stills Archive.*

and orders his men to disarm when Outram comes to see him. In a gesture of magnanimous self-defeat, he hands over his crown to an abashed though determined resident.

As news reaches the friends Mir and Mirza of political rumblings and British armies marching on the outskirts of Lucknow, they run away to a remote village area to pursue their game without disturbance. They find a local boy, Kalloo, who ministers to their needs of the hookah and food. As Mir and Mirza settle down to play, Mirza becomes progressively annoyed that he is losing. He then insults Mir and taunts him for being cuckolded. A confrontation takes place and Mir accidentally fires a gun. Mirza escapes narrowly but is shaken and sits down brooding. Kalloo brings the news of the king's abdication. Mirza's anger evaporates and he calls to Mir to share the lunch. Mir reflects sadly, "If we cannot cope with our wives, how can we cope with the British army?" The next moment, however, the two friends turn to their chessboard and start another game.

Ray deviates from Premchand's ending, in which the two men kill each other, saying that the idea was abandoned "because I felt it might be taken to symbolize the end of decadence. In fact, Nawabi and all that goes with it did not end with the British takeover. The U.P. noblemen kept up their way till well into the present century. Hence the decision to show Mir and Mirza continuing with their game. That they decide to play according to British rules can be seen as a symbol of the acceptance of British domination by Indians.[44] Ray also stated that Premchand took wild liberties with history in depicting a captive Wajid being led away by the British on the day of his abdication, whereas in reality Wajid left of his own accord and well after the annexation. Ray was himself sharply criticized for falsifying history in his portrayal of Wajid Ali Shah as "effete and effeminate," his characters being "lifeless dummies in an empty shadowplay."[45] In response Ray detailed fifteen sources that he had consulted and the careful planning and research that had gone into the film. "What emerged from all this research is there in the film, which is *not* a full-fledged biography of Wajid as Rajbans [the critic] seems to assume, but an attempt at juxtaposing a story (based on Premchand) about two chess playing jagirdars in Wajid's Lucknow, with the historical event of the Annexation where the protagonists are Wajid and Outram."[46]

Structurally the film balances these two strands of story and history, which remain essentially separate, the passing of Oudh from the hands of Wajid to those of the British having little ostensible effect on the lifestyle or habits of Mir and Mirza. The statement by Mir at the end of the film, quoted above, is finally meant to bring the two strands together, albeit superficially. And yet the central metaphor of the game of chess reminds us ceaselessly of what is at stake and provides the terms and context for an assessment of the historical dimensions of the film. As the sequences involving the two pairs of characters alternate with a sort of scrupulous regularity, itself reminiscent of the turn taking and the intellectual rhythm of chess playing, we are led to ask: What does this rhythm signify? What is the nature of the confrontation being laid out here between the British and the Indians? What are its aesthetic terms? What is at stake here in the depiction of a period and a culture? How is the viewer's relationship to a reconstructed past constituted? These questions arise and need to be considered if we are to take Indian critical response to the film seriously without conceding the charges of historical inaccuracy made against it.

As a postcolonial film, *Shatranj* is engaged in (re)creating "the past" as object of knowledge and representation in the present. The film seeks to enhance the viewer's knowledge of the actual nature of the relationship between the nawabs—"effete and ineffectual"—and the British—"vigorous and malignant."[47] To convey this intellectual content, chess, famed as an intellectual game (Ray conceded that it was not inherently dramatic on screen),[48] may be taken as an appropriate metaphor. The association of chess with the intellect and the rigors of a rule-bound system has been made by other thinkers. As Teresa de Lauretis notes in another context, the textual metaphor of the game of chess appealed to the fathers of structuralism, Ferdinand de Saussure and Claude Lévi-Strauss, who used it to illustrate the concept of system, Saussure's *langue*, and Lévi-Strauss's structure.[49] In *Shatranj*, the British authorities' cold and calculating moves toward colonizing the whole of India is part of the intellectual lesson for postcolonial Indians (and international viewers of the film) that the film's history provides or reiterates (the other part being Nawabi decadence). The political/intellectual mode may therefore be considered the mode that informs one strand of this two-stranded narrative—that involving Outram and Wajid. Mirza and Mir's story, on the other hand, is meant to provide the "emotional" ingredients of viewer identification and is infused with humor, passion, and action. The film effects a series of complex transmutations and shifts on this basic pattern. By their metonymic association with chess, Mir and Mirza become objects of the viewer's intellectual curiosity. The characters of Mir and Mirza are mediated through their intellectual preoccupation with chess: they are shown almost wholly in visual or rhetorical connection to it even so far that it represses their sexual or libidinal impulse. We apprehend history, on the other hand, through the affective prism of song, dance, and poetry. Because Wajid is presented as a symbol of the famed "Lucknowi culture," he does not emerge as a convincing historical character in his own right. His cultural preoccupations, his colorful and changing attire, his poetic diction, his vaporous eyes are all ornaments that effectively evoke surface rather than depth. Ultimately, "history" and "culture" remain separate rather than inform one another. "History," appropriated by Outram, becomes the province of the strong, "culture" the domain of the weak.

Ray has recorded his aversion to the character of Wajid which was eventually overcome because of the king's poetical and musical talents. "The fact that the King was a great patron of music was one redeeming feature about him. But that came after long months of study, of the nawabs, of Lucknow and everything."[50] In the prologue of the film, Wajid appears in four successive shots. "In the first he plays Lord Krishna in his raas; in the second he leads a Mohurrum (commemorating the Prophet's death) procession; in the third he is shown in his harem with half-a-dozen concubines. The fourth shot shows Wajid at a durbar." This composite introductory portrait condenses the major known facts about King Wajid which are then somewhat fleshed out in the main text of the film. As the sequences alternate between story and history, the vocabulary of chess (presumably unfamiliar to most viewers) mediates our response to the fictional protagonists, while the language of Urdu poetry, music, and dance in the historical segments serves to aestheticize politics. When we first encounter General Outram in scene two in his study, the dialogue which takes place between him and his aide-de-camp, Weston, is not about mundane state matters but about the culture of the "natives" and their king. Outram even gets Weston to recite in the original a four-line poem written by Wajid, though its contents leave him unmoved. In fact, the portrayal of Outram is unmistakably patriarchal, reinforced by the phallic cigar protruding from his lips. Wajid emerges from their discussion as effeminate and of unstable identity. When Weston informs his superior that the king dances, in addition to versifying and composing, Outram replies, "Yes, so I understand. With bells on his feet, like nautch-girls. Also dresses up as a Hindu god, I am told." Most of the sequence is taken up with an enumeration of Wajid's cultural pastimes/idiosyncracies, and only toward the end of it does the business at hand get addressed. "Eunuchs, fiddlers, nautch-girls and 'muta' wives and God knows what else. He can't rule, he has no wish to rule, and therefore he has no business to rule." While this exchange is meant to underscore the great gulf that separates the colonizing culture from that of the natives, despite the efforts of enthusiasts such as Weston, we are ultimately led to identify with Outram's point of view and to feel alienated from Wajid. Because he is presented as an orchestrated amalgam of exotic cultural traits and habits, he does not emerge as a convincing character.

The first sequence to be entirely devoted to Wajid comes at sequence five (scene five in the screenplay), roughly the mid-point of the film, and it is primarily devoted to a *kathak* dance performance taking place before the king for his entertainment. This demonstration of the classical dance heritage of India, performed through artists of high caliber and authenticity (Birju Maharaj, the famous dance exponent, accompanies the young female dancer's movements with song), is the visual, aural, and narrative crux of the film, the last because here Wajid's prime minister is reduced to tears at the end of the recital when he blurts out, "Your Majesty, you shall no longer wear the crown." The haunting beauty of the song, the camerawork that renders the pyrotechnics of the dance, and the graceful movements of this art form are certainly assertions of cultural/national pride in the face of the humiliation of colonization. It is the supreme moment of the aestheticization of history.

In the third long scene containing Wajid, Ray writes, "This is virtually a scene of monologue where Wajid passes through a wide range of moods. He is remorseful one moment, resigned the next, and seething with righteous indignation as the scene ends."[51] The emotional instability portrayed here, as Wajid reprimands his officials, reflects on his own kingship, and boasts of his people's love for him and his poetry, serves to undercut the serious nature of the situation and the monarch's essential helplessness in the face of a predetermined colonial agenda.

It is Munshi Nandlal, a friend of Mirza who makes his appearance in the fictional part of the film, who represents the voice of reason and caution, perhaps the "objective" stance of the filmmaker himself. A deglamorized character in a film whose stunning visual effects derived from expensive sets and colorful costumes for all the major characters (a recent filmography categorizes *Shatranj* in the "costume" genre), Nandlal is the first one to report to the unheeding *jagirdars* that the East India Company plans to take over Oudh. He also imparts the information that chess is an Indian invention taken over by the British. Nandlal, a Hindu character, was not there in the Premchand story but was introduced in Ray's film "to establish the important historical fact that friendly relations existed between the two religious groups in Oudh in Wajid's time."[52] Thus the enigma of *Shatranj ke Khilari* may lie in its structural ambiguity, its tendency to present history/politics as an emotional/aesthetic experience for the viewer and fiction/entertainment as an intellectual landscape. Masquerade in Indian cinema and culture involves many substitutions.

Gandhi

Like *Shatranj ke Khilari*, the popular Academy awards–winning biography of Mahatma Gandhi, directed by Richard Attenborough, raises many complex issues of form and function, nation and narration that pertain to historical representation. Its inclusion in the context of the

Bombay cinema may seem anomalous since it uses many Anglo-American actors and has a British director and screenplay writer. Nevertheless, the historical figure of Gandhi, the film's central character, and the Indian independence struggle, its ostensible subject, may be cited as reasons for its claim to our attention in this study, not to mention the fact that it was partly financed by the National Film Development Corporation and was entirely shot in India with the assistance of a sizeable technical crew from the Bombay film industry. *Gandhi* (1983) is a cosmopolitan hybrid, drawing upon the "venerable" traditions of Hollywood filmmaking as well as some deeply seductive strains of Indian cultural and collective memory, primarily through shots of landscape and the use of music (provided by Ravi Shankar). But hybridity comes in many shapes and forms and here risks being dangerously superficial. For *Gandhi* constantly balances the needs and expectations of its two perceived audiences—the people of India and a non-Indian global, though primarily Western, public. Familiarity and knowledge of context must continually be offset by trivia and exotica. The "double billing" of historical narrative in the guise of a suspense thriller is one way in which different constituencies are accommodated, different agendas met. Indeed, the play upon structures of historical knowledge and cultural-epistemological distance or ignorance is orchestrated without any fundamental damage to either. For the majority of Indians, Gandhi is a hallowed (but largely remote) figure and remains so in the film; for the average Western viewer, Gandhi and, by extension, India are "reconfirmed" as the purveyors of spiritual enlightenment and moral values (truth and nonviolence). Gandhi's "difference," therefore, remains an inviolate space, despite the energy and fervor brought into the characterization by Ben Kingsley in the lead role. As a historico-biographical film, *Gandhi*'s insertion into the discourse of Indian national identity may be read through its structural play upon the mechanisms of identification and alienation.

The opening sequence, with its solemnity and grandeur, captures this dual process quite neatly. In fact, it contains all the motifs—visual, narrative, ideological—that pervade the film. The sequence contains a murder and is therefore an immediate "hook" for a curious but by no means committed audience. Indian viewers presumably are drawn into the scene of a chilly winter morning, women and men in shawls and waistcoats hurrying across a lawn against the mist-covered buildings of official Delhi. Then the aged Gandhi appears and is soon shot by a man in the crowd. By starting the film with Gandhi's assassination, this empirical fact of history "seals" the account, as it were, forecloses the parameters of knowledge and expectation that one brings to the film-viewing experience. As the garlanded martyr is shown on his last journey, Western reporters eulogize the political achievements of the man through his moral greatness. Gandhi is thus "packaged" for Western consumption, a tactic used repeatedly in the film, sometimes with farcical exaggeration. But this particular framing of the Gandhian story is also calculated to arouse in Indian viewers a temporary relief from nagging feelings of inferiority vis-à-vis "the West." Witness the following comment made by one M. Bhaktavatsala that appeared in the *Illustrated Weekly of India:*

> Yes, for many of us, and those of the older generation, *Gandhi* will be a memorable experience. For we will sit there not as critics but as Indians; the Indians of the Gandhian era, eager to identify with the Indianness of the man. With Sir John Gielgud, Trevor Howard, John Mills and many other absolutely typecast faces of British and American films whose names we will never know, the film is something to feel proud of. In this, probably, is the poetic justice of an Englishman making a film on the life of an Indian who was responsible for kicking the British out of India.[53]

We can turn for a moment to some glimpses of behind-the-scenes "financial wheeling and dealing" prior to the making of *Gandhi* provided by M. Bhaktavatsala which reenact Sarojini Naidu's affectionate though caustic remark that it was costing the Congress a lot to keep the Mahatma in poverty. Bhaktavatsala, one of the persons called upon to advise the Ministry of Information and Broadcasting on the feasibility of the *Gandhi* project, writes that Attenborough outlined a project worth $20 million, with the choice put to the Indian government to produce the film by footing the entire cost or to invest as partners in the rupee expenditure of the project. What he wanted was moral commitment, "and what was better than money to concretise morals?" The Indian government's willingness to support Attenborough's project was motivated by the desire to get into the international film market:

> The overriding consideration in handling a project of this kind was that it was truly international. The fact that actors like Sir John Gielgud, John Mills, Trevor Howard, Martin Sheen, Edward Fox and

Candice Bergen offered to work for less than their normal remuneration was precisely because this was such a film. If India (or any country) wanted to get into the international market, this, clearly, was the way to go. A film on Gandhi made either by Ray or Benegal with an all-India cast and crew would, at best, run at the art cinema houses like the Academy in London—rather like Ray's *The Chess Players*.

The costs incurred by the film team in the preshooting period were in the order of Rs. 7 lakhs in fourteen days. M. Bhaktavatsala notes:

> The scale of payments was staggering by Indian standards. Among the Indians engaged were a Production Manager at Rs. 3,000 a week, the Delhi Liaison at Rs. 1,800 a week, a continuity girl at Rs. 1,500 a week, a camera operator at Rs. 3,000 a week, a projectionist at Rs. 1,500 a week, a hairdresser at Rs. 1,000 a week, the set decorator at Rs. 1,900 a week—all expenses founded. In fact, the Bombay film industry, with its taste for opulence, was the biggest beneficiary of Project Gandhi. One-and-a-half years after the completion of the project, it has still to recover from the euphoria.

Bhaktavatsala further comments that "all the food, including water, for the crew was frozen and shifted from England to India in kitchen vans, complete with chefs and butchers."

To the cynical, such a sanitized approach might suggest something about the filmmaker's attitude to his subject. However, I do not want to minimize the difficulties, practical and directorial, attending upon a project of the scale of *Gandhi*. The subject of Gandhi the man as well as the political leader is a highly controversial and "sensitive" one. Books on Gandhi's life, activities, and philosophy are too numerous and the Gandhi legend too vast for a definitive biographical treatment within the popular-commercial mode adopted by the filmmaker. Thus I feel it is somewhat beside the point to harp on omissions or wooden characterizations of other personalities in the film, although they do serve a valuable critical function. Here, however, it is that mode itself that I wish to critique, the broader point being that intentions alone do not an anti-colonial film make. For even if one were to grant Attenborough's self-proclaimed dedication to the project, our concern is with the portrayal of Gandhi and of Indian politics and society that emerges from the film.

How does the film *Gandhi* structure its thematics of history, biography, and national struggle? I shall make three points in this regard.

The first is that because the emphasis is on history as action, and "Third World" action is associated with violence, the generic expectations of the thriller are fulfilled through the periodic recurrence of violent scenes. (The opening scenes are meaningful in this regard as well.) The thematic focus on Gandhi's creed of nonviolence is ironically legitimated through textual epiphanies of violence. While much of the violence is perpetrated by the colonial powers (and their native underlings), the visual impact of these repeated scenarios is a negation of the colonized body, a body-mind dichotomy that informs a colonialist perspective. It is a new version of the "noble savage." Gandhi the character is himself both inside and outside this definition, for he is an ethereal version of the spirit made flesh. He is often framed alone, in close-ups, in mid-shots, or in profile, marking his proximity to yet difference from "the people."

My second point relates to the role of Western journalism in the historical reconstruction of the Gandhian legacy. *Gandhi* is literally crawling with Western reporters, some of whom are also Hollywood stars (Martin Sheen, Candice Bergen). Since history and journalism are both forms of narrative, it seems natural to see them deployed together. And yet, in *Gandhi*, the use of Western reporters, of first-hand Western vision, is meant to authenticate Indian history and to legitimize its claim upon the attention of Western audiences. Gandhi's own substantial journalistic writings are not used.

My third point concerns the relationship of the national-popular to the persona of Gandhi himself. In a sense, Gandhi had been all things to all people, simple with the peasants, crafty with the politicians, manipulative with the business community. Perhaps Gandhi's historical significance as a cultural "text" lies in the fact that he seems to emerge as a different person with each new interpretation. He was modern India's greatest impersonator, a man who cannot be separated from the masks he adopted. But the question is: Should he be? Attenborough's characterization reduced Gandhi to a set of moral attributes in order to fulfill the film's own goal of colonist appropriation: to "salvage" the "message" of nonviolence for the world, but particularly for disenfranchised peoples. Gandhi's too neatly conceived character finds its counterpart in the figures of the British officials—they are bumbling fools, but essentially well-meaning and Christian at heart. Thus neither the interests of history nor of myth are served in the portrayal of Gandhi, and the national-popular needs both. This despite Ben Kingsley's masterly performance as Gandhi, which film critic David Denby calls "one of the most astounding impersonations in movie history" and which was no doubt responsible for the film's box-office success.[54]

The issue of historical representation, and of historiography generally, has become an object of much theoretical work and discussion in recent years. For our purposes history communicates, to borrow Timothy Brennan's phrase, "the national longing for form."[55] In an era given to passionate assertions of identity and the painful lessons of decolonization, the forays into history in Indian commercial entertainment provide us with potent avenues into the processes of our own subjectivity. The historical film reworks the past by simultaneously distancing us from the pageantry it works to provide and by allowing us the intimacy of visual access to past events unfolding in the (diegetic) present. In this contrariness, does the Indian historical film allow for a contestation of the conceptual with the visual, an epistemological critique of the past in terms of its effects on the present? Can the packaged drama of the historical film, with its smothering layers of visual tapestry, bear the scrutiny of the postcolonial gaze? Of the films discussed above, *Shatranj ke Khilari* and *Sahib Bibi aur Ghulam* may be taken as instances of the postcolonial sensibility at work in the historical genre. They take both a critical and a lyrical view of the past and hence adopt a postcolonial perspective. An acceptance of a flawed past is accompanied by the need to move on with the business of restructuring the present. It is significant that the last shot in both films is one of movement, signaling a new stage in the passage of time.

part two

The Sixties and Beyond

The body is not a static phenomenon, but a mode of intentionality, a directional force and mode of desire. As a condition of access to the world, a body is being comported beyond itself, sustaining a necessary reference to the world and, thus, never a self-identical natural entity. The body is lived and experienced as the context and medium for all human strivings. . . . the body is always involved in the quest to realize possibilities.

—*Judith Butler, "Sex and Gender"*

The National-Heroic Image

Masculinity and Masquerade

In an article on Latin American fiction written some years ago, critic Jean Franco describes how its discourse of nationalism constructs images of the male as active and of the female as passive and private. If the feminine is associated with immobility and hence "territoriality," masculine creativity becomes the agency whereby heterogeneous elements in Latin American culture are valorized as a sign of carnivalesque pluralism.[1] A similar though historically and culturally distinct effort at in-corporating heterogeneity and reveling in it is evident in Indian commercial cinema in terms of the male body as the interface of multiple regional, class, and religious identities and texts. The male hero as the center and source of narrative meaning is "resemanticized" into a mode of instability and the dispersion of meaning. Forms of disguise, impersonation, and masquerade are the visual means that serve to render this move from the natural to the acculturated body, allowing the spectator means of recognition of his/her social world within the world of the film through the hero's "play" with the signifiers of dress, accent, and gesture. This distinct tendency within the Bombay film to both identify and nullify marks of (intercultural) difference in a wide variety of textual situations allows national identity to surface as so many styles of the flesh.

Whether as a dominant theme played out through the use of the double and/or various forms of disguise, as in *Hum Dono* (*The Two of Us*, 1961), *Mera Naam Joker* (*My Name Is Joker*, 1967), *Naya Din Nayi Raat* (*New Day New Night*, 1974), *Chinatown* (1962), and *Johnny Mera Naam* (*My Name is Johnny*, 1970), or as a visual motif in particular sequences, as in *An Evening in Paris* (1967), *Love in Tokyo* (1966), *Amar Akbar Anthony* (1977), and *Desh Premee* (*Patriot*, 1982), or as a narrative element in romantic comedy, such as *Padosan* (*Neighbour*, 1968), or *Chupke Chupke* (*Quietly, Quietly*, 1975), or *Victoria No. 203* (1972), the Bombay film has been obsessively concerned with the "enigma" of (male) subjectivity and the need for the disavowal of fixed notions of identity. In a society where the social markers of identity are so well-defined, where caste, creed, region, and education all translate into distinctive visual emblems (the Brahmin's mark on the forehead and sacred thread, the Bengali versus the Gujarati woman's style of wearing a saree, the Sikh's turban—the list goes on), where to give one's name is (usually) also to reveal one's caste and regional background, it is small wonder that the popular film engages with the question of identity at various levels of articulation. Critics have usually pointed out one or other of several tendencies whereby the Bombay film "fails" to identify its characters. Thus Ashis Nandy tells us that the Hindi film hero "will simply be Mr. Rakesh or Mr. Raj or Mr. Ashok—surnameless and, thus, regionless, casteless, ethnically non-identifiable and ultimately ahistorical. He is in this sense an archetype, a representation of cultural concerns which, if given a specific historical setting, would become less forceful, less black-and-white, and thus less communicative."[2] While this observation is generally true, the film text is usually less unambiguous than such a view suggests, and visual codes function to "situate" the hero, at least broadly as either Hindu or Muslim, upper class or poor, educated or not, Westernized or not. Also, Vijay Mishra, Peter Jeffery, and Brian Shoesmith's notion of "the actor as parallel text," of "the actor as text in his own right," addresses the issue of stardom and how star quality and presence working *within* films construct processes of identification and continuity of spectatorial response.[3] One might add that this continuity of recognition and response hinges on the notion of authenticity, on how filmic transformations metonymically evoke the actor's "real" personality and conduct. Amitabh Bachchan and Rekha's off-screen romance, for instance, affects our reading of their on-screen performance, creating textual gaps or openings through extratextual awareness. Along the same lines, although Amitabh Bachchan has been cast in every working-class role imaginable (in addition to portraying a Hindu, Muslim, and Christian), one does not forget his actual class and caste affiliation. Rather, this knowledge is used to judge how he measured up to the expected behavior patterns associated with each group that are themselves textually constructed and lodged in the popular mind through repetition.

How, then, can one reconcile these contradictory impulses within the average Bombay film? In particular, how do recurrent uses of disguise and masquerade define masculinity and heroism in Indian mass culture? How are particular scenarios constructed that mediate between private longings (of romance and family life) and public social roles? What are the possibilities of male imperso-nation? Psychoanalytically informed accounts of the masquerade have stressed its relationship to femininity.[4] Marjorie Garber's recent book, *Vested Interests*, also a study of forms of masquerade and cross-dressing in popular culture, sees them primarily as expressions of the blurring of gender boundaries.[5] In film criticism as well, attention has been focused on how women spectators are positioned in relation to the screen.[6] The masquerade's carnivalesque possibilities and the significance of the *male* body as it presents itself as a social-semiotic field have been less systematically studied. But as James Naremore, in his book *Acting in the Cinema*, writes, "Clearly films depend on a form of communication whereby meanings are *acted out;* the experience of watching them involves not only a pleasure in storytelling but also a delight in bodies and expressive movement, an enjoyment of familiar performing skills, and an interest in players as 'real persons.'"[7] Naremore's excellent study of the rhetoric of screen acting, his emphasis on the visual aspects of film performances, is important for our purposes, since so much of the effectivity of the performative codes of the Bombay cinema depends on the audience's complicity with the multiple roles adopted (and gaily abandoned) by the actor.

Nevertheless, it is worth stressing that the notion of disguise and masquerade in relation to the cinema is rarely discussed. In a sense, this is understandable, since "acting" denotes a kind of artifice, and disguise, when used in the cinema, is generally taken as a plot device or as an embellishment of the mise-en-scène. Charles Affron's view may be cited here as representative: "Coated with layers of makeup that obliterate blemish and dissymmetry, modeled by a miraculous array of lights, located and relocated by the giddy succession of frames, the stars capriciously play with life and subject it to a range of fictions from preposterous to profound."[8] Contrarily, when masks are studied as social and cultural myths and artifacts, as in Joseph Campbell's *The Hero with a Thousand Faces*[9] or David Napier's book[10] on the facial mask, attention is devoted solely to its traditions of use in drama and in ritual events, but no mention is made of film. The latter's technological base and naturalistic conventions would seem to render it "alien" to the essentially symbolic function of masks and masquerades in traditional forms of representation and validation of group existence. However, as Robert Ezra Park, in the context of symbolic interactionism, reminds us, there is a more fundamental aspect to masking:

> It is probably no mere historical accident that the word person, in its first meaning, is a mask. It is rather a recognition of the fact that everyone is always and everywhere, more or less consciously, playing a role . . . It is in these roles that we know each other; it is in these roles that we know ourselves. . . .
>
> In a sense, and in so far as the mask represents the conception we have formed of ourselves—the role we are striving to live up to—this mask is our truer self, the self we would like to be.[11]

The mask is here the very condition of subjectivity, of interacting with the world, of defining oneself in relation to others. It is also a mode of idealization and of a projected narcissism. It might be said that screen performances, particularly of stars, narrativize this tendency by foregrounding a repertoire of roles. The transition from one role to another across individual film texts is at once a sign of the actor's talents and evidence of the "emptiness" of the actor-as-sign. It is this emptiness that allows a star to become a popular cultural icon, a receptacle, like a wax mold, into which may be poured the social collectivity's needs and desires of the moment. Roland Barthes's classic reading of "the face of Garbo" speaks of a time in the history of cinema "when one literally lost oneself in a human image as one would in a philtre."[12] Likening Garbo's face to a mask in its mystical promise of transcendence, Barthes suggests a kind of interaction between the face and the mask that leaves this star's beauty suspended, so to speak, between two incompatible states. Although facial masks, even of the kind described here, are not common in the cinema, masquerading the body, "arranging" it in various ways so as to invite new combinations of meaning, so as to assert the body as acculturated, an absence known only through its significations, has remained a recurring feature in the cinema.

In the Bombay film, it has been the male star whose body has lent itself most consistently to various forms of masquerade. In this chapter we shall explore how conceptions of the hero, coalesced around certain star personas, have rendered the discourse of nationhood as "creative geography," to appropriate Kuleshov's evocative phrase. The romantic hero as man of action can extend himself in myriad ways to transform and transcend his social conditions of existence and reconcile the irreconcilable. As his body at once orchestrates and absorbs difference, racial and cultural, dress, makeup, and behavior patterns serve to anchor recognition and invite misrecognition. Pastiche and parody are the hallmarks of identities which valorize fragmentation and yet seek wholeness.

The incorporation of several (transnational) identities by a single hero, expressed both visually and rhetorically (through song), was invested with an early and enduring appeal in Raj Kapoor's *Shri 420* (*The Gentleman Cheat*, 1955). The lyrics, roughly translated, mean:

> The shoes I'm wearing are made in Japan
> My trousers fashioned in England
> The red cap on my head is Russian
> In spite of it all my heart is Indian.[13]

This was the Nehru era and being national also meant, in some sense, to declare oneself to be international. The use of the body is as a particular nexus of culture and choice, a field of possibilities susceptible to infinite rearrangements. The irony, of course, is that the vagabond and rolling stone who is singing this song is laughing at himself because his assortment of clothing is also a signifier of his impoverished state and a reflection on the society of which he is a part. His nationalist message puts India at the center of a randomized global accumulation of accessories, seeking to put a distance between the core (heart, sentiment) and the periphery (limbs, outward appearance). India itself was simultaneously core and periphery: at once ancient and young, civilizationally advanced and "Third World." Suggesting transcendence, the body of the hero becomes a map on which nations can appear to coexist in harmonious yet distinctly separate spheres. Indian identity would have it both ways: to be a composite and yet claim a prior and more significant status. By transforming the social marginality of the filmic hero into the centrality of the Indian citizen, material needs are displaced onto a more intangible (emotional) level of experience.

The fifties hero also reveals another valorized feature of Indian culture which gradually disappears in films of the postsixties era: androgyny.[14] However, androgyny in a patriarchal society was only acceptable in evoking new and marginal states of being and consciousness. The desire to evolve or represent new forms of urban experience, particularly the fact of close proximity to different types and classes of people, found expression in the kind and gentle hero—Balraj Sahni in Amiya Chakravarty's *Seema* (1955), Dilip Kumar in Kidar Sharma's *Jogan* (*Ascetic*, 1950), Raj Kapoor in *Aag* (*Fire*, 1948) and *Barsaat* (*Rain*, 1949), Dev Anand in *Aandhian* (*Storms*, 1952), Sunil Dutt in *Ek Hi Raasta* (*One Path Alone*, 1956) are some examples—often dressed in the traditional *dhoti* and *kurta*, with the villain or buffoon adopting Western attire; for example, Johnny Walker in *Naya Daur* (*New Race*, 1957). Side by side, however, there was emerging the early noir hero with links to the Bombay underworld. Dev Anand in *Baazi* (*Wager*, 1951), *Kala Bazaar* (*Black Market*, 1960), and *Taxi Driver* (1954) epitomized this new type: cigarette dangling from the mouth, eyes slanted to look off-screen, a tone of daring, a posture of risk taking. This type was to reappear in the seventies and eighties.

A combination of factors is responsible for the emergence of the new film hero in the early sixties. The introduction of color, the perpetual search for new acting talent in the film industry, the death of acclaimed and popular filmmakers like Guru Dutt, Bimal Roy, and Mehboob Khan with their distinctive styles, perhaps even the passing of the Nehru era

Satirizing technology: Comedian Johnny Walker (at left) in
Naya Daur (New Race).

and the immediate concerns of nationhood all changed the film scene. *Junglee* (*Savage*, 1960) signaled the change from the deglamorized heroism of Raj Kapoor's Indianized Chaplin to the more cosmopolitan, rambunctious personality of the sixties hero. Psychoanalyst Sudhir Kakar creates a typology of screen heroes, distinguishing between the Majnun-lover of the fifties and earlier from the Krishna-lover of the sixties (his third type is the good-bad hero of the seventies and eighties). Dilip Kumar in *Devdas* (1955) and Guru Dutt in *Pyaasa* (*The Thirsty One*, 1957) are the ideal Majnun-lovers, passive, poetic, and childlike. In contrast, the romantic hero of the sixties is the Krishna-lover:

> He is phallus incarnate, with distinct elements of the "flasher" who needs constant reassurance by the woman of his power, intactness, and especially his magical qualities that can transform a cool Amazon into a hot, lusting female. The fantasy is of the phallus—Shammi Kapoor in his films used his whole body as one—humbling the pride of the unapproachable woman, melting her indifference and unconcern into submission and longing. The fantasy is of the spirited and

The lure of the big city in Taxi Driver. *Courtesy National Film Archive of India.*

androgynous virgin awakened to her sexuality and thereafter reduced to a groveling being, full of a moral masochism wherein she revels in her "stickiness" to the hero.[15]

It is now generally acknowledged that from the sixties to the late eighties, Indian popular cinema has been increasingly male-oriented. From Shammi Kapoor to Rajendra Kumar to Rajesh Khanna to Amitabh Bachchan, an escalating trend of male stardom seemed to evolve. (By a curious shift, the "new cinema" projected itself as a woman's cinema and provided the histrionic grounds for the emergence of the two foremost actresses of the postsixties era, Shabana Azmi and Smita Patil.) Recently, fifties star and highly regarded actress Waheeda Rehman explained her "semiretirement" from the Bombay film scene thus:

I got fed up with the repetitive roles I was being offered. It was invariably the same story: that of the father being murdered and then the children growing up to avenge him and the widowed mother steering them through all kinds of hardships. It all seemed very stale and mechanical. Also, our films, male-oriented as they are, find little use

Baazi (Wager): *the fifties'* noir *hero (Dev Anand) and the* femme fatale *(Geeta Bali). Courtesy National Film Archive of India.*

for actresses; the story revolves around the men. Besides, after a certain age actresses are not readily accepted as heroines.[16]

These comments highlight both the entry into the big-budget or "multistarrer" era of Bombay filmmaking and the industry's perennial demand for new faces.

The Heroics of Natural Identity

The first male star to break out of the mold of the fifties hero as champion and prototype of the underclass was Shammi Kapoor. As the younger brother of the very popular Raj Kapoor, Shammi sought to invest his screen image with a totally different appeal, one that was predicated on the lure of the all-powerful, all-enveloping presence of the romantic hero. Lacking Raj Kapoor's (and younger brother Shashi Kapoor's) more sensitive and chiseled features and smaller frame, Shammi could boast of a powerful physique, which he used to signal brute strength. Quite appropriately, his first film was entitled *Junglee* (*Savage*, 1960). This "retreat" into a more "natural" state is a distinct departure from the socially and culturally embroiled heroes of the films of earlier decades. Their stance of commitment to progressive social change and to the values of film realism finds no place in this more vigorous narcissistic male persona. Social markers of class and region (urban or rural) are replaced by a more free-floating and individualized universe of rapid change and frantic movement. The boundaries between the external and the internal, so cherished by the fifties hero (and encapsulated by the song stanza quoted above), collapse in the new heroic image. All is surface; surface is all. The sixties hero is most comfortable straddling—and thereby eliminating—the distinctions between different social and national worlds. He moves effortlessly between the palace and the hut, not as an intermediary but as one to whom these distinctions are no longer significant or worth signifying. In *Junglee*, the polarities of wealth and poverty, endemic to the structure of the Bombay film, are mapped onto different forms of "naturalness": the Shammi Kapoor persona belongs to a very rich family but is basically an innocent with raw emotions and manners in need of taming; the heroine (Saira Banu) is outside (urban) civilization, symbolizing the beauty and playfulness of one used to the openness of natural surroundings. But it would be a mistake to read *Junglee* as merely one more Rousseauist parable, rather than as a deconstruction and reconstruction of a film hero. This is signaled by the parodic opening sequence, in which a voice-over presents an isolated protagonist-hero—a creature who does *not* invite identification because he is lacking in any semblance of human grace. Shammi Kapoor's exaggerated mock-serious acting (his eyes appearing cold and angry, his brow knitted, nostrils flaring, cheeks sucked into a pout) is a facade because generic expectations promise romance later on. Seated alone inside an airplane, a convenient phallic symbol, we are told that this symbol of masculinity gone awry is returning from England and America armed with the latest business training to take the Indian business world by storm. The association is deliberate, and yet the film, soon after, reveals the real reason for Shekhar's strangeness: a strict upbringing in accordance with rigid patriarchal-familial norms transferred through another parodied figure, his mother (Lalita Pawar). The scene is gradually set for the hero's transformation into an independent and likeable personality through the process of falling in love with a beautiful and fun-loving girl, Raj (Saira Banu).

Saira Banu is the quintessential new heroine (childish, unsophisticated, naïve) who complements the new film hero, and together they conquer the Bombay film's most exotic colony—Kashmir. The strategic importance of Kashmir as the eroticized landscape of the mind in the social imaginary of Indians (paralleling perhaps its political importance in configurations of the integrity and unity of 'he Indian nation-state) can hardly be overstated. Kashmir as the place for honeymoons and lovers, arising no doubt from its scenic beauty (it is known as the "Switzerland of India"), has been translated by the Bombay film into a symbol of purity and unspoiled nature and as visual therapy for audiences coping with life in overcrowded cities and towns. Kashmir, over which India has fought several wars with Pakistan, serves as the limit-text of what it means to be Indian: its geographical location at India's apex, its captured facial imprint of the Aryan inheritance, its demographic admixture of Hindus and Muslims, perhaps its ambivalent status as at once virgin ("no compromise on Kashmir," say the politicians) and coquette (eternally coveted by neighboring states)—all these serve to render Kashmir as both site of fantasy and national projection of overarching identity and connectedness.[17] Kashmir can therefore effect the transformation of the *junglee*-as-uncivilized, lacking social graces or emotions, to the *junglee*-as-naturally-exuberant.

The therapeutic nature of his experience of awakening love for an "unspoiled" girl-woman enables this new film hero not only to transcend the boundaries of social class (he is wealthy, she is not) but those between the human and animal worlds as well. In Indian culture, where ideals of manhood incorporate some attributes of femininity, the valorization of Shammi Kapoor's masculinity necessitates an association with the nonhuman or prior-human. He is the wild one, a visual anarchy, a body in frenetic movement: head jerking, arms flailing, shoulders and hips seemingly moving independently of each other. *Junglee* inaugurates the cinema of indulgence: spectacular shots of landscape, particularly of virgin snow and majestic mountain ranges, provide the playground for desire and fantasy where the possibility of physical union between the romantic couple is a palpable one. Rolling in the snow, the hero proclaims the joy of existence by inviting, rather than resisting, associations with an animallike state. The "Yahoo" song, which became as much Shammi Kapoor's insignia as "Awaara Hoon" (I am a vagabond) was Raj Kapoor's, is the animal mask which signifies a rite of passage. It also suggests the ambiguity of this transformational state.

For "real life" must be resumed in the big city. Shekhar returns home, a different man, eager to socialize with his employees where formerly he barked orders at them. The animal is humanized, and after a series of plot complications, he is able to convince his mother of the error of her "high-and-mighty" ways. As Raj and her father arrive, bringing with them a taste of the mountains, the pretensions of the rich crumble. All ends well, as youth and wealth are aligned in the obligatory happy ending.

An Evening in Paris

The Bombay film hero of the sixties negotiates sociocultural and spatial mobility through creative uses of the masquerade. As the setting for romance shifts from national to international locations, the West is no longer an internalized presence/absence in the hero's psyche but becomes the purely and wholly Other, the exotic backdrop against which the Indian hero and heroine can act out their fantasies of unhampered courtship and romance. Many big-budget films at this time seek the spectacle of Western sights and sounds, among them *Sangam* (*Confluence*, 1964), *Love in Tokyo* (1966), *An Evening in Paris* (1967), *Around the World* (1967), *Purab aur Paschim* (*East and West*, 1970), and *Hare Rāma Hare Krishna* (1971). Although occasionally, as in *Purab aur Paschim*, the West is stereotypically the scene of spiritual degradation or somnolescence, of violence and material craving, in most of the other films spectacle overwhelms moralism as the audience is sped along from one world capital to another (Paris-London-Vienna-Rome-Switzerland is the usual beat). The "domestication" of the West during this period coincides with India's brain drain and official concern over the loss of scientific and technically trained people who were emigrating to North America. The Bombay film feeds this longing of the average Indian to travel abroad by locating its narratives partially outside India.

An Evening in Paris presents a set of globe-trotting characters and a hero who is no longer anxious to proclaim his "Indianness." The film draws attention to itself as entertainment and spectacle in its opening sequence, when the protagonist, Shammi Kapoor, looks directly at the camera as he gyrates and sings, "Aji, aisa mauka phir kahan milega?" (Folks, when will you get such an opportunity again?). The hero promises to be a tour guide for the audience and to take them sight-seeing in Paris. The "evening" of the title refers to the evening at the movie theater, and the song exhorts, "Dekho, dekho, dekho, dekho, dekho!" (See,

see, see, see, see!), an invitation to viewers to immerse themselves in visual and sensual enjoyment. This throwback to the promise of the earliest days of cinema, when the novelty of seeing distant lands and places was a major attraction, renews the process of "alienation" between the spectator and the cinematic apparatus, with the screen abolishing spatial distance and underscoring psychic distance simultaneously. Long-shots and tilted angles structure a sort of hierarchical arrangement between the world of the film and the world of the spectator, the first of which must forever be beyond the reach of the second. Yet the glamor of the West and of the rich (if not famous, on-screen) can lure the viewers to an entrancing evening.

An Evening in Paris brings together the attractive and chic Sharmila Tagore and, by now, the reigning sixties star, Shammi Kapoor, in a romantic drama that seeks to give a new twist to the age-old Bombay film themes of wealth-poverty, insider-outsider, heroism-villainy. Here we have both the hero and the heroine subject to different kinds of doubling and masquerade. The initial setting is Paris, where arrives Deepa (Sharmila Tagore), the beautiful daughter of a wealthy businessman, in search of true love. She wants to be loved for herself and not for the money she will inherit from her father. Paris, she is led to believe, will effect this miracle. Settling down in an apartment, Deepa initially tries to masquerade as her maid and is soon pursued by two men: Shekhar (Pran), her Paris guardian's son, and Sam (Shammi Kapoor), who passes himself off as a Frenchman who can speak Hindi. Both men frantically court her, trying to outwit each other in gaining her attention and affections. The lovers move from one foreign location to another, with Shekhar in tow, frolicking and romancing in extravagant and lavish settings.[18]

Then plot complications set in, and the romance turns into action drama. The villains are introduced so that the heroic side to the male protagonist's personality can be presented. Since nothing happens singly in the popular film and identities harbor subidentities, characters and events now reveal their sinister underside. It is soon clear to the audience that Shekhar, son of the honest caretaker/guardian of the heroine, is associated with a crime gang headed by Jaggu, whose name and iconicity evoke villainy through the accumulated force of repetition in countless previous films. The heroine, too, is metonymically associated with evil: Jaggu employs Suzie, a cabaret dancer who is the spitting image of Deepa and actually her long-lost twin sister. And the worlds of big business (represented by Deepa's father) and big crime (represented by Jaggu and his cohorts) come together when it is revealed that the disgruntled servant who had kidnapped Suzie-Rupa as a child is an associate of Jaggu. The centrifugal tendencies in the first half of the film are balanced by the plot's centripetal movement in the latter half as past and present, vendetta and retribution, lost innocence and sacrifice meet and do battle. Ironically, the hero alone is unburdened by a past and hence able to traverse contradictory states at will. He easily slips from playful Casanova to shrewd private eye, able to upstage the villains and rescue Deepa. A prolonged chase-and-fight sequence at the end of the film includes ostensibly hair-raising stunts over the Niagara Falls in Canada. As the wet and tired hero and heroine are rescued from a tiny ledge by a helicopter, they burst into song, one of the hit songs of the film.

A notable feature of the male-dominated romantic drama of the post-sixties era is that while the identity of the villain is fixed and self-evident, the proof of the hero's heroism is that he can change identities at will, if only temporarily and often playfully. The villain has no access to the masquerade (or his efforts to pass himself off as a good person are patently false and obvious); the hero, on the other hand, can literally become "the hero with the thousand faces." However, changing personas is a sign of ingenuity and sportiveness (Shammi Kapoor in one sequence masquerades as an Arab in flowing robes), rather than the eraser of cultural boundaries. All extranational identities are ultimately collapsible into a hypostasized Indianness, left suitably vague and no longer expressly articulated either through iconography or patriotic dialogue. (This condition changes again in the eighties, when both elements become strong markers of "Indianness.") Released from its moorings in history, tradition, or space, the concept of "Indianness" is naturalized through the mobile hero, an entitlement to a passport with the assurance of a return ticket. Like the hero's adopted name, "Sam," which can always be converted back to its original version, "Shyam" (another name for Krishna), the sixties hero inhabits several worlds at once, his identity always already recuperable.

Parody, Community, Fraternity

The palimpsest effect that results from the slippage between different personas available to the Bombay film hero is akin to what James Naremore[19] isolates as three elements of characterization that make up all star performances. First, there is the *role*, or that description of a character that is written down in a script, preconceived, or improvised during shooting. Second, we have the *actor*, a person whose body and performing skills bring other important traits to the role. "The actor is already a character in some sense, a 'subject' formed by various codes in the culture, whose stature, accent, physical abilities and performing habits imply a range of meanings and influence the way she or he will be cast." Finally, there is the *star image*, also a character that emerges as a product of the other two categories and is further "a complex, intertextual matter, owing not only to the actor and her or his previous roles, but to the filmic qualities of microphones, cameras, editing and projection; it derives as well from narratives written about the actor in publicity and biography and thus becomes a global category."

If the role and the star image seem to work at cross-purposes, the one promoting audience identification and the other dispelling it, the male actor's body in disguise in the Bombay film anchors these disparate tendencies. In the sequence from *An Evening* described above, the hero's parodic flaunting of foreign garb to gain access to the heroine is both a sign of his transcendence within the terms of his assigned role in the film and an instance of his recognizable brand of acting and self-presentation. It might be useful here to list some other masquerading instances of this nature dispersed along the entire spectrum of the Hindi film romance.

The use of parody to suggest the limits and limitations of fixed notions of identity is particularly evident in those sequences in romantic drama which involve intergenerational conflict between different regional groups within India. The hero will usually come to the service of a male friend who happens to be in love with a girl from another linguistic group. Stereotypes of that group are then parodied through the adoption of an "open" disguise, where the audience is aware of the purpose of the disguise and takes the whole situation as an assertion of freedom and the triumph of romance. In *Love in Tokyo*, for instance, the comedian Mehmood engages in a series of masquerades in order to deceive the irate father of the South Indian girl he loves. While his slippery moves are meant to evoke laughter, "South Indianness" itself is reduced to a set of external marks worn on the body. The same may be said for *Padosan* (Neighbor, 1968), in which Mehmood's parody of South Indians

(Madrasis) remains on the level of surface identity marks and accent. Similarly in *Coolie* (*Porter*), the hero, Amitabh Bachchan, and his friend Rishi Kapoor parody a Madrasi by adopting his dress and accent, usually shown as attributes of the older generation of parents opposed to the more open and flexible choices of their offspring. Not only are regional differences portrayed as entirely superficial, they are turned into occasions for comedy. The acting becomes one of "expressive incoherence" where there is a break with the naturalist tradition and a deliberate filmic intertextuality prevails. In other words, the actors draw attention to their acting, parodying former performances. In *Amar Akbar Anthony*, parody, spectacle, and masquerade combine to orchestrate an elaborate scenario suggesting intercommunal harmony. Here the heroic triptych of the film's title (three brothers separated in childhood and brought up in a Hindu, Muslim, and Christian family, respectively) appear in a climactic song sequence dressed up in costumes that extravagantly proclaim their religious affiliations while simultaneously erasing specificity through their shared camaraderie in the presence of danger. Their disguise is meant to serve the purpose of outwitting the villains from whose clutches their three girlfriends have to be freed. But it is worth noting that the idealistic transcendence of fixed social and psychological identities can only go so far. Each hero is in love with a woman from his "own" community, and there are no intercommunal romances suggested. (The reason usually given is that such scenarios would not get past the censors, who would see them as potential sources of disturbance.)

The parodic rendition of internal division and otherness in the national body-politic is mediated, then, through the male star. What implications could this have for theories of the gaze?[20] The specificity of address to either male or female spectators does not seem to apply here, given the Bombay film's generic instability and the economies of its production and reception. Moreover, parody in the service of utopian community is usually accomplished through the register of songs and dances, which are themselves utopian moments in the narrative, points of connection between the diegetic world and the larger film world generally, as well as between subjective and shared experience. Also, the crowded mise-en-scène, rapid camera movements, and editing of these song sequences invite fragmentation and multiple subject positions rather than the penetrating power of the gaze. The situation is further complicated by the motif of male bonding that serves as the metonym of national unity and amity. The male body in disguise, having recourse to everything from cross-cultural dressing to cross-dressing, would seem to structure a gaze that is neither simply male nor female but a "gaze-in-crisis," a differential gaze that the cinematic image simultaneously destabilizes and appropriates. I would like to suggest that the mode of parody to problematize difference charts new territory in notions of the gaze.

But if maleness makes possible the hero's ingenuity in playing with appearances and extending the signifying possibilities of his body, what of the heroine's double, as in the case of Deepa/Suzie in *An Evening in Paris*? The social/sexual divide falls along gender lines here: Suzie is not only Deepa's alter ego but her competitor as well. For Sam, she is a double who signifies danger, threat, evil, a voracious sexuality. She is also a "tragic" figure (like Nargis's double in *Anhonee*), for she has to die in order to redeem herself and pay the price for her "immorality." Woman, therefore, unlike man, cannot change herself at will, cannot adopt and discard identities to signify a wider social embrace. On the other hand, it is her fixity that allows the hero to narcissistically (dis)play his body.

Shammi Kapoor's personification of the brawny hero with his distinctive brand of acting spawned many imitators, notably Joy Mukerjee, Jeetendra, Shatrughan Sinha, Sanjay Khan, Biswajeet, and other less well known figures, although as with all imitation, their performances lacked the finesse and energy of the original. It is interesting that at the moment when the Bombay film hero was "releasing" himself from character types and models of behavior that might be identified as Indian (or had been constructed as such by the screen heroes of earlier decades) and when he imbibed a more "international" identity, he was helping to evolve a (body) language of the cinema that seemed totally nationally and culturally coded according to Western perceptions. The popular cinema of the sixties, unlike that of the fifties, is totally unknown in the West and does not get included in any festival packages. A kind of hedonism, a visual smorgasbord, is what the larger-than-life hero offers Indian audiences. This hero has also risen above his circumstances, outsmarts those around him, can be a romantic lover at one moment and an astute private eye the next. As Mishra, Jeffery, and Shoesmith have pointed out, the Hindi film actor has remarkably few "material" antecedents, and he is a process and a construct produced by the complex practices that make up Bombay cinema. "As complex signs embodying historical, cultural, and economic meanings (reconstructions), the stars are in themselves cultural interfaces and 'compromises' of bewildering complexity."[21] Shammi Kapoor is one such interface where the different discourses of the fifties and the sixties collide and clash; what emerges is the male body made powerful, playful, changeable.

Male Narcissism and Hysteria: *Sangam*

With Raj Kapoor's *Sangam* (*Confluence*, 1964) we come to a fractured text in which two heroes share screen space and the dynamics of male rivalry masquerading as male friendship are worked out. One of the early films to deal with the theme of male friendship and sacrifice, no film better exemplifies the hero as narcissist. Of course all the RK films were "about" Raj Kapoor, or "Raj," his screen persona. But as a director-actor who had risen to prominence and immense popularity in the fifties, both the director and the actor in him faced middle age and new developments in the cinema with the impulse to chart new directions without quite obliterating the memory of the Indianized tramp. The result is a mélange of various trends and scenarios of the sixties (location shooting abroad, national war service, male camaraderie, obsessive self-pity) and an analogue of Kapoor's reflection on his own screen career, a process he continued in *Mera Naam Joker*. *Sangam* seeks to combine the spectacle of Western backdrops with what might be called male psychological drama. It is the way these two impulses function here that is of interest, rather than the film's usually touted "historic" status within Raj Kapoor's oeuvre as the initiator of his reputation as "showman" of the Bombay industry.

Although *Sangam* does not present us with actual disguises or masquerades, the film's discourse of masculinity and heroism is predicated upon different forms of playacting and their psychological consequences. The dramatic tension of the narrative is then centered upon the ability of the protagonists to decode each other's playacting. The distance or discrepancy between inside and outside, what is displayed and what is kept hidden, how "true" is one's behavior—these become important moral issues within the narrative. Perhaps the challenge for the actors was to either overdo or underplay their roles, a phenomenon that marks this film. A triangular love story, *Sangam* involves three central characters: Sundar (Raj Kapoor), Gopal (Rajendra Kumar), and Radha

(Vyjayantimala), with the film spanning the period from their childhood to their adult lives. The metaphor of "confluence" is meant to suggest the ideal of an identity shared by not two but three people who have grown up together. The film wishes to problematize this notion of bonding when one of the friends is a woman. Thus jealousy and suspicion become the flip side of love and friendship. Sundar manages to marry Radha but cannot forget that Gopal had loved her first and she him.

The tortured workings of suspicion and their tragic consequences (Gopal magnanimously decides to remove himself through self-annihilation) form the thematic core of *Sangam*. The film offsets its grim subtext by the twin lures of visual pleasure and patriotism: Sundar transforms himself from child hero to responsible adult by serving in the Indian air force, and his honeymoon with Radha takes place in the affluent setting of western Europe. These sequences, however, also serve to underscore the developing relationship of the protagonists. Consciously or unconsciously, the hero's narcissism appears indistinguishable from the overt text of male bonding and friendship. The thrust of the narrative is toward the realization of the social, sexual, and moral aspirations of the protagonist, Sundar, whose blind egotism (indistinguishable from a childish callousness and self-absorption) destroys all in its path. By locating the viewer's interest in this central consciousness and by turning the other two characters into ciphers, the film becomes a vehicle for Raj Kapoor's self-contemplation of his own stardom from the perspective of impending middle age. Even the acting reveals a straining after effects achieved effortlessly in Kapoor's earlier films, particularly as there is a visible incongruity between a now somewhat puffy figure replaying the actions of his younger self. Raj as Sundar in *Sangam* is undergoing a metamorphosis, his pranks and laughter punctuated by sudden bursts of rage or jealousy, his childish naïveté undercut by sinister irony. In a party sequence celebrating the return of Gopal from London, Sundar's overt jollity is underlined by a more somber mood, especially as he senses Radha's moves toward Gopal. On a later occasion, when he sits at the piano in his house and sings, "Dost, dost, na rahaa, pyar pyar na rahaa!" (My friend is no more, our love and friendship are no more), he uses the musical instrument to convey his rage. The film extols male camaraderie and sacrifice at the expense of a ruthlessly exploitative male-female relationship wherein the woman's purpose is to gratify the hero's ego.

Indeed, Radha in *Sangam* would seem to be the classic sign of communication and exchange between men that anthropologist Lévi-Strauss

discovered in the articulated kinship systems of "primitive" societies. [22]
If, as Lévi-Strauss suggested, the exchange of women was a means to
integrate self and other, Raj Kapoor short-circuits the process, since
here no real *exchange* is involved: only one woman is to be fought over,
or shared, by the two men. Lévi-Strauss talks about "the synthetic nature
of the gift, that is, the agreed transfer of a valuable from one individual
to another makes these individuals into partners, and adds a new quality
to the valuable transferred." [23] However, "man still dreams of a time
when the law of exchange could be evaded, when one could 'gain without
losing, enjoy without sharing'" or imagine a future "eternally denied to
social man, of a world in which one might *keep to oneself.*" [24] *Sangam*
would seem to be operating on this level of wish-fulfillment, and hence
its scenario of an ideal world of male bonding, friendship, and sacrifice
is a masquerade for "selfish" longings and desires. By displacing fears
of male rivalry and fratricide onto woman, the film is able to maintain
the myth of the social control of meanings as the province of men.

It is interesting to see how "the West" is a player in the lines of force
drawn between the male protagonists and how it serves the process of
equalization between them. On a purely visual level, of course, *Sangam*
(like *An Evening in Paris*) uses the West as spectacular backdrop for its
tale of friendship and duplicity, passion and guilt, love and death. The
association of the West with erotic fantasy and fascination is more prominent here, for the shots taken in European capitals are diegetically
linked to the protagonists' honeymoon. As we saw with the scenario of
war, that of the West is used to lend glamor and an enhanced social
standing to the hero. Sundar, as a celebrated national hero, has the
world open to him, and it is now a simple matter for him to plan a
honeymoon visiting the beautiful scenes of the West. It is his courage
and dedication to a cause that now make him the social equal of his
friend and rival, Gopal, who had had the benefit of a Western education.
When they meet again on foreign terrain, however, Gopal and Sundar
are evidently not equals, for the latter has married Radha and is the
winner, Gopal reduced to being "the other." Radha recognizes this and
not the two men, who continue to live their lies by not accepting their
implicit rivalry. The beautiful nature shots of Switzerland take on a sinister aspect as Radha draws Gopal aside to warn him not to reappear in
her life. The beginning of the rift between the three characters emerges
here. The garden of Eden reveals its snake.

Transformation and Paradox in the War Romance

The war of romance in the assertion of masculinity in the Bombay film is complemented by the romance of war. The spectacle of war in the popular film has been the classic ideological site for the testing of heroism and male camaraderie. While *Sangam* uses war as an episode in the transition of the hero-as-buffoon to the hero-as-heroic, other films of the sixties present war in a more extended way to suggest the working out of duties and obligations in a visual rhetoric of transformation. The Bombay cinema, while not cashing in on the war genre to the same extent as Hollywood, responded to India's conflicts with its neighboring states (notably Pakistan and China) by putting some of them on the screen, with varying degrees of naturalistic detail and energized emotion. *Usne Kaha Tha* (*She Had Said*, 1960), *Hum Dono* (*The Two of Us*, 1961), *Aas ka Panchi* (*The Bird of Longing*, 1961), *Haqeeqat* (*Chance*, 1964), *Aradhana* (*Prayer*, 1969), and *Saat Hindustani* (*Seven Indians*, 1969) were some films which portrayed either war or the war hero as contested sites of patriotism and national duty on the one hand and domestic bliss or romance on the other. It is in keeping with the "apolitical" stance of the Bombay film that the actual circumstances of the particular war are rarely spelled out and that the enemy is often unspecified. *Haqeeqat* did identify the Chinese as the aggressors, and *Saat Hindustani* was a response to Goa's liberation struggle. In both these instances, however, the directors (Chetan Anand and K. A. Abbas) were avowedly leftist and socially conscious filmmakers, somewhat marginal in the Bombay industry. *Haqeeqat* explains, through the character of an army colonel (Iftekar), the reasons why India was so unprepared for the border attack by the Chinese and why it lost the war. India's pacifist stance under Nehru and its ideal of nonviolence are registered as superior cultural and moral traits shared by the Indian people, and hence the film claims for India a moral victory in this unexpected war (the hero and heroine die fighting). The idea is to extol the virtues of selfless duty to the nation and the opportunities offered by war for spiritual growth and fellowship.

Dev Anand's *Hum Dono* (*The Two of Us*) takes us back some fifteen years to the Second World War, when India, as a colony of the British, fought on the Allied side. While colonialism is not an issue here, war itself becomes the occasion for exploring issues of separation and reunion, loss and gain, not only through the body/mind dialectic but also

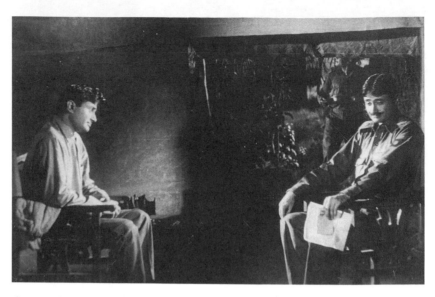

Captain Anand (Dev Anand) meets his double, Major Verma (Dev Anand) in Hum Dono (The Two of Us).

the self/nonself dialectic. Masquerade, the double role, and mistaken identity become the narrative and visual means of thematizing these relationships. (Here, as in *Aradhana* [*Prayer*, 1969], the gains rather than the losses stemming from war may be said to accrue through the extension of the self in another body that the double role makes possible.) *Hum Dono* treats war as the external analog of moral and spiritual crises, of the performance of dharma and national duty, and hence as a symbolic agent of change and transformation. Doubling is perhaps the pervasive metaphor of the film, starting from its title to the sets of complementarities that move it along. Certain questions may be posed to tease out the implications for spectatorship of this generic cross between a romance and a "male buddies" film. If the film is categorized as the latter, how do we respond to the fact that one buddy is a shadow, the result of trick photography? How does war highlight the ambiguities of presence and absence, of private romance and public duty? The radical disjunction from "normal" life that war brings is symbolized by the hero's moral crises, his forced abandonment of his obligations at home (to an aging parent, for instance) in order to do his job and become a man. War, as the "public" event that impinges on and disrupts private lives, is also the mode whereby privatized sentiments can be harnessed to public ends.

The opening scene beautifully encapsulates the play on the image that the film advances, its lure of presence/absence an analog of the cinema itself. The hero, Anand (Dev Anand), is sitting under a tree in a wooded area with a lake close by. His face cupped in one hand, he looks pensive and lonely, obviously waiting for someone. The camera moves to the left to show an inverted image of a woman reflected in the water. The image smiles and faintly beckons to the hero. He smiles back and tosses his cigarette stub into the water, dispelling the image in a succession of ripples over which the film credits appear. This gesture of masculine assertion, this signature over the body of woman, is somewhat startling in its abruptness and suggests perhaps a prefiguring of the suppression of the "softer" feminine values by dominant masculine ones in a war situation. Later in the film, the inverted image is used again, this time of Anand as he bends over the water, using it as a mirror to shave in a junglelike area that signifies Burma during combat. A naturalistic shot changes to reverie as Anand's memory recalls the image of his girlfriend, linked to the motif of a musical cigarette lighter she had presented to him. She appears beside him in his reflection in the water, only to be dismissed again as he starts another song, this time expressing his intention to take life as it comes.

The initial segments of the film are fairly typical of the Bombay film romance. Anand, poor and unemployed, is courting Meeta (Sadhana), the only daughter of a very rich businessman. In order to support himself and marry Meeta, he joins the army and immediately leaves for training camp, while his fiancée moves in with his widowed mother in order to take care of her. This is the first of a series of "class reconciliations" that service in the war brings about. The scene shifts to the war front and Anand's meeting with his double, a Major Verma (Dev Anand in makeup). A center hair parting and a moustache distinguish one man from the other. The two become friends, and Verma shows Anand pictures of his home, his wife, Ruma (Nanda), and mother, these being accompanied by flashbacks providing glimpses of a tender loving domestic existence. Anand, on the other hand, says nothing of his own background, a kind of class consciousness operating here. When during an enemy attack the major is wounded and captured by the enemy, Anand takes on the care of Verma's wife and mother, though not without being mistaken for the major himself. As he slips deeper into the masquerade, Anand finds himself misunderstood on all sides. His girlfriend, Meeta, breaks off their engagement, Ruma, a heart patient, complains of her "husband's" inattentiveness, Anand's own conscience badgers him unceasingly. Finally, a now lame Major Verma returns from enemy captivity and accuses Anand of role usurpation, deception, and depravity. As he throws himself at Anand to kill him, Anand pleads for the chance to prove his innocence. They all meet at the overdetermined site of a temple, symbol of purity, where past misunderstandings are cleared up and vows renewed. The original couples are reunited in the end, with brotherhood thrown in to boot.

The visual and narrative appeal of the masquerade in general lies in the fact that we know and yet suspend disbelief in the "deception" being practiced. David Napier's idea of a "perceptual paradox" is useful here, for what we have is

> the awareness of an ambiguity informing the simplest transitions. This awareness aids us in establishing a point of view and in evaluating phenomena that we may later view quite differently. The potential for *ambiguity*, therefore, remains fundamental to change despite any claims we might make about an inferred, innate, or even empirically perceived identity, and disguise is, in our ontological experience, the primary way of expressing this ambiguity. The use of disguise is thus conducive both to make-believe and to changes of state that are imputed to be real.[25]

The paradox inherent in the double role is that the presence of the "real" or prior role is always implied. In *Hum Dono*, double vision evokes both humor and pathos at the moment when the two characters meet one another. Anand is taken for a ghost by the major's orderly and by others in the camp. Also, the major is first introduced as absence: his wallet is discovered by Anand as he is driving by in his jeep, and it contains a picture of a woman (the major's wife). This evidence of vulnerability serves to undercut the machismo of the army officer. For the acting styles of the two Dev Anands is differentiated in such a way as to make the two characters complement each other: Captain Anand conveys the "presence" of the star in his normal film roles, and Major Verma appears in the pop-cultural guise of the back-slapping, cigar-puffing, hearty army officer. Toughness and softness become terms of negotiation in the film.

In addition to the potential for ambiguity that Napier speaks of above, the notion of closeness or sameness between an actor and his masquerading self as double is presented here. Usually in the Bombay cinema this takes the direction of the plot device of twins separated in childhood and brought up in different circumstances, one turning out as the hero, the other as the villain (until the moment in the end when the latter realizes the badness of his ways). The link between the two appearances of an actor is a negative one: a dichotomy is posed between the good persona and the bad persona, a kind of Dr. Jekyll and Mr. Hyde syndrome. In *Hum Dono*, however, the two characters are strangers to one another with no genealogical links. War service becomes the "parent" that provides the link of brotherhood and fellowship between them. Major Verma serves at once as the older brother and father figure that has been absent in Anand's life. Although the film does exploit the idea of oedipal rivalry and the "father's" symbolic death, cultural ideals of brotherhood win out and are played out in the relationship between the two men.

If the war film circulates a rhetoric of masculinity and turns man into the object of desire, the splitting of the male body into two may be seen as one way to achieve this goal. The maiming of the hero's buddy (in combat) puts this process in crisis. In fact, sexual abstention that is one result of being away on the field further problematizes the representation of masculinity in war conditions. Anand is away from his girlfriend, Meeta, for the bulk of the film, he lives with Ruma after his return but does not sleep with her, and the major comes home with only one leg and expresses fears about having lost his masculinity. The process of sexual sublimation is the film's answer to the libidinal anxiety that men may feel when they are away fighting wars. Thus the film not only uses the masquerade to signify rites of transition but to move the characters from one social and sexual state to another.

Sexual sublimation is also the lot of the women in the film. The women, confined to the domestic sphere, are tearful mothers and wives, etherealized icons of purity and self-sacrifice, waiting and longing for the return of their lovers and husbands. *Hum Dono* presents a polarized world in which men are identified with the public world of action and women with guarding the home front. When Anand leaves to join the army, Meeta preserves his home by fulfilling the duties of a daughter-in-law, although she is not actually married to Anand. Ruma, Major Verma's wife, has the larger role of maintaining harmonious relations in the community. She is portrayed as deeply religious (a complement to her husband, who is an unbeliever) and is shown leading the *bhajan* (song) in the temple. Her song (beautifully composed by Sahir Ludhianvi and set to music by Jaidev) addresses the one true God who is known as both Allah and Ishwar and asks for divine blessings for all. Both women are beautiful in a doll-like way, although Meeta also shows courage in leaving her home to live the life of the lower middle class. The women are rewarded for their faith and constancy by the return of their lovers in their "original" forms (having incorporated change).

The Performer-Clown and Universal Identity

Hum Dono, seen from the vantage point of the nineties, is vintage Dev Anand. The mannerisms of the star have not hardened to clichés, the lure of romance is not dissipated by aggressive constructions of masculinity, ambiguity and perceptual paradox allow viewers to negotiate meanings. We can now turn to two films which are "about" performance and hence constructed entirely around the idea of disguise and masquerade: Raj Kapoor's *Mera Naam Joker* (*My Name Is Joker*, 1967) and *Naya Din Nayi Raat* (*New Day New Night*, 1974). In these films, the notion of the hero as exceptional being is both promoted and undermined; the cinematic medium is used to translate other entertainment forms such as the circus and the theater. Both films seek to reclaim the heritage of mass entertainment in India by constructing a history of sorts. *Mera Naam Joker* is the more ambitious in this regard, for Raj Kapoor seeks to encapsulate the history of Indian popular cinema through the career of Raju the clown, a metaphoric construct for himself as "showman" of the Bombay film industry. *Naya Din Nayi Raat* presents the actor Sanjeev Kumar in nine different roles to signify the principles underpinning the Indian theatrical tradition.

One of Raj Kapoor's most extravagant films but a flop at the box office, *Mera Naam Joker* weaves an episodic plot around the central figure of a circus clown. The critics Dissanayake and Sahai attribute the failure to confused motives on the part of the film director, to the self-pitying tone and propagandistic nature of the film.[26] To this one might add the incongruity of the central character's function within the film. For in the circus the joker's presence ensures comic relief, and the clown only appears in the intervals between acts. His or her appeal lies in a certain repetiveness as well as the ability to disappear. Raj Kapoor, on the other hand,

The masquerade of universal love: Raju (Raj Kapoor) in Mera Naam Joker
(My Name Is Joker). *The Museum of Modern Art/Film Stills Archive.*

keeps the spotlight resolutely on himself. We are expected to adopt the clown's vision of the world, and while this is a valid claim, no distance is allowed between the surface manifestation of identity and its change-ability. The gap between different modes and levels of experience is closed that the disguise makes possible in the first place.

Appearing in a clown's makeup and his baggy clothes, Raj Kapoor would seem to be trying to deglamorize his image, to play the antihero. However, the clown also suggests continuum of the Raj Kapoor brand of screen hero, since from the persona of the tramp to that of the clown is but a short step. Kapoor takes back his screen name, Raj (temporarily abandoned in *Sangam*), to slip back to his habitual role of inhabiting the margins of mainstream society. The dynamics of inner and outer, sur-face and depth, inclusion and exclusion is played off the iconicity of the clown's smiling face hiding his sorrowing heart. But the sorrow is as much for a failed vision of masculinity as for the lack of appreciation of a fickle public for a performer. While Raj Kapoor seeks to hide the one behind the other, the fact that the clown's life history is presented in terms of failed romances suggests that masculinity is certainly an issue here.

The film opens with the aged clown Raju having sent invitations to the women he loved to witness his last performance in the circus. These women are Mary, his schoolteacher, Marina, a Russian trapeze artist, and Meena, a film star. The story unravels through extended episodes or chapters involving these women, who may be said to mark the major stages of Raju's life: adolescence, youth, and maturity. The opening se-quence is described thus by Dissanayake and Sahai:

> He (the Joker) floats down inside a huge red heart that splits down the centre, after which Raj slips out to be greeted with applause. He looks at David (Mary's husband) in the audience and makes the thumbs up sign, which David repeats. This sign is later explained as meaning, "God is the biggest joker ever." A team of doctors played by leading Indian comedians Om Prakash, Agha, and Rajendranath tell him that he is ill. His heart is big whereas the world is small; at this rate the heart will encompass the whole world, and thus it must be operated on. Raju asks the doctor to operate not on him but on the world. His face freezes into the Greek mask of tragedy. The operated heart keeps growing while Raju searches for it in mime and asks each of the women in his life whether she has found it. Having found it, he dances, holding it lovingly, and sings a song which says, "Heaven

and hell are both here (in this world). We have to live and die here. I will always be here and after me my song will be taken up by others." [27]

There are several points of interest here, all of which might be said to construct the mythology of the actor-as-joker. Three different strands feed into this mythology. The first is of the clown as a Christlike figure amidst the Last Supper kind of scenario constituted by the guests he has assembled. The body in disguise is here the body of the hero that embraces not only different nationalities but different beliefs as well. The names, Mary and David, of two of the characters suggest the association. Second, the clown-performer claims for himself a superior status and immortality. The third strand involves the heart as substitute (transcendental?) phallus which the clown-actor passes on to each of the women he has brought together. This latter point may be pursued a little further in terms of the visual motif of the clown doll that ties all the episodes of the film together.

In the first episode, an adolescent Raju is in love with Mary, the Christian schoolteacher. The episode is devoted to the unfolding of his sexual awareness and has been praised by critics for its convincing handling of the conflictual feelings of a sixteen-year-old boy. A key moment is when Raju offers a clown doll to Mary, a prototype of his adult "self," and asks her to keep it. This might be read as the hero's wish that the woman bear his child, a scenario that is repeated with the other two female characters. One is reminded of Gayle Rubin's contention that "The girl never gets the phallus. It passes through her, and in its passage is transformed into a child. When she 'recognizes her castration,' she accedes to the place of a woman in a phallic exchange network. She can 'get' the phallus—in intercourse, or as a child—but only as a gift from a man. She never gets to give it away." [28] The return of the clown doll in each instance suggests a crisis of paternity, the only resolution of which comes through the sublimation of the clown's erotic desires and the diffusion of the ideology of humanism.

Different models of masculinity are also presented in *Naya Din Nayi Raat*, a film that again reveals the range of options open to men in representation. Here one actor (Sanjeev Kumar) appears in nine different disguises, each of which embodies one *rasa*, or aesthetic mood or quality (surprise, fear, compassion, anger, devotion, hatred, love, bravery, and bliss). Together, the *rasas* are meant to encompass all of life's experiences, and the form befitting the exemplification of the *rasa*s is a string of episodes in the fairytale–adventure story variety. The film seeks to close the gap between some folk theatrical traditions and the romance framework of the Bombay cinema. The skeletal narrative structure involves the idea of the testing of true love. A young girl, Sushma (Jaya Bhaduri), and her college sweetheart, Anand (who is not shown till the very end of the film), are exemplary in their attachment to each other, so that when Sushma's father arranges her marriage elsewhere, she runs away from home. She heads for her lover's home, hoping they can elope and get married. However, she finds (mistakenly, as it turns out) that he is himself marrying some other girl to please his dying mother. Shattered, Sushma decides to commit suicide and runs toward a cliff. In the meantime, her father finds her missing and has the police looking for her. Pursued from within and without, Sushma encounters a series of characters as part of the experiences of her runaway life which form the substance of the film, and the characters she meets on her way (a forest officer, a drunkard, a doctor, a robber, a charlatan holy man, a leper, a folk drama actor, and a police officer) comprise her worldly education. The last impersonation is that of Anand, her boyfriend, who appears as Sanjeev Kumar without disguise. Here again the male body is turned into a complex field of representations, of linkages and connections— between the social and cosmic, the past and the present, the theatrical and the filmic, and appearance (man) and essence (woman). If this film presents an allegory of the world, it is a world peopled by men caught in actions and temptations to which woman's role is to bring stability.

Populism, Film History, and the Changing Semiotics of the Star Body

The latest manifestation of the changeable hero is undoubtedly Amitabh Bachchan, Bombay filmland's erstwhile superstar. Bachchan's body (his very tall frame and unusually long legs) might be considered a text in its own right, for no actor before him had his screen presence, nor did the evolution of an actor's career bear such a close affinity with a shifting conception of the body as character. In his early films, Bachchan's thinness and angularity connoted simplicity, idealism (as in *Anand* [*Bliss*, 1970]), and emotional vulnerability (*Mili* [*Found*, 1975]). These quali-

ties carried over into *Zanjeer* (*Chains*, 1973), in which, however, Bachchan's tall frame appeared to advantage in a police officer's uniform. The
rest, as we know, is history—Indian cultural history, at any rate. The
spectacular success of *Zanjeer* at the box office conferred stardom on
Bachchan and initiated the orchestration of his body in movement (primarily in fight and dance sequences, but also in his routine camera
presence) that was to be a staple in countless Bachchan movies. Many
sequences, particularly humorous ones, were constructed around the
distinctiveness of Bachchan's height: shorter comedians would be made
to pass between his legs, or he would rest his elbow on their heads, or
the funnyman would stand on a stool to be closer to Bachchan's eye
level. In revenge-fight sequences, low-angle shots were used to show
Bachchan's legs descending, in slow motion, onto his opponents, crush-
ing them with their power. As he lashed out with his arms and legs, the
audience cheered and knew that the villains didn't stand a chance
against this superhero.

In direct contrast to his body, however, are the semiotics of Bachchan's eyes. Heavy-lidded, slightly deep-set, with a bare suggestion of
a squint (his gaze seems a bit out of focus, like Bogart's), his eyes are
the most striking feature of his face. They have been used by the actor
to register a whole range of emotions, primarily the softer ones of ten-
derness, shyness, humility, all playing against a backdrop of pathos and
unspoken sadness. One of the common ways, therefore, to create a sense
of crisis and expectancy in a Bachchan film has been to show his eyes,
in close-up or in tight shots of his face, changing from a "normal" state
to one of rage and vengefulness. They become blood-shot and moist,
with the muscles around them working as knowledge of a deep wrong
dawns on the star-character and his body tenses, readying itself for an
assault. The eyes convey the transition of the hero from a state of innocence (regarding the ways of the world) to one of karma, or involvement
(resulting in the removal of evil). Thus the eyes serve to underscore the
moral dimension of the struggle, even as the patterned nature of the fight
scenes and their predictable outcome contain few surprises.

Coolie might be said to have signaled the (downward) turning point in
Bachchan's career, for it was on the sets of this film that he met with his
near-fatal accident. But until the late eighties, "the phenomenon"
reigned supreme, as attested to by the film magazines. To industry representatives and the public alike, it is perhaps fitting that the fall of the

Amitabh Bachchan as underworld boss in Deewaar (Wall).

big star signals no less than the "collapse" of the industry itself. In 1989, *Filmfare* eulogized:

> They called him the One Man Industry and for sixteen years he churned out hits with assembly-line regularity. *Zanjeer, Deewaar, Don, Amar Akbar Anthony, Muqaddar Ka Sikander, Trishul, Kasme Vaade, Kaala Patthar, Mr. Natwarlal, Laawaris, Kaalia, Naseeb, Namak Halaal, Andhaa Kaanoon, Coolie, Mard, Geraftaar* . . . It seemed as if the sun would never set on the reign of Blockbuster Bachchan. Never before had a star seen this kind of success, and for so long. The distance between him and his rivals was so vast that in the number game, they'd allotted the numbers 1 to 10 to him, the competition really took place way down there and it never affected the big man at the top.[29]

The anonymity and the all-inclusiveness of the "they," signifying at once the producers, the public, and the critics, is set against the concrete details of a career that had made of its star at once a historical and a godlike phenomenon. Characteristically, Bachchan himself did his best to promote an image of an enigmatic personality, at once polite and distant, friendly and inaccessible, humble and arrogant, maintaining a facade that interviewers could not pierce. The gap between his "real" self (the son of an eminent poet, the childhood friend of Rajiv and Sanjay Gandhi, the product of elite educational institutions and exuding "good breeding") and his screen roles could not be more striking. (It is interesting that the only film in which Bachchan appears as a "gentleman," in the romantic comedy *Chupke Chupke* [1975], he wears his education and breeding as a masquerade, appearing foppish and naïve in the role of a botany professor.)

Bachchan came to prominence as the "angry young man" of the Indian screen, the lower-middle- or working-class hero out to fight a corrupt and unjust system. As noted above, Bachchan's haunting and haunted eyes told it or hid it all. An icon of male sexuality, he yet appeared vulnerable, a sensitive soul adrift in a callous universe. The film *Sholay*, marking roughly the mid-point of Bachchan's extraordinary career, shows the paradox/transition at work. Here the Bachchan character is a petty thief who is in and out of jail, along with his buddy (Dharmendra). Called upon by circumstances to become unwilling heroes, protectors, and avengers of the law, the buddy-team elicit identification by undermining their adopted roles as they don masks of courage and authoritative action. As a romantic hero, however, Bachchan is shown as a loner and marked for tragedy, the text privileging the more popular romantic team of Dharmendra and Hema Malini. His eyes hunger from afar for glimpses of the young widow, daughter-in-law of the ex–police officer who is giving the jailbirds a chance to redeem themselves. His love for the unattainable woman is a sublimated desire for death or, perhaps, within the norms of the Bombay film, an intimation of death.

With each new film, a process of accretion or accumulation seemed to be at work, not only rendering Bachchan's films a collective text but each film a palimpsest of his various roles. *Coolie* seems particularly intertextual in this way, for its narrative recycles various by now very familiar scenarios of the Bachchan oeuvre: a disrupted family, a murderous villain, a working-class hero, a perky and upper-class heroine, a mother who has lost her voice, a friend who turns out to be a "brother" lost in childhood. Since it is the figure of Bachchan that connects all these strands together, it is as himself that he is presented. The impersonation in this film is that of Bachchan himself as cultural hero whose status is used in the film to incorporate the supernatural world itself into the world of railway porters, wicked businessmen, and dispersed families.

The Hindu-Muslim brotherhood theme is played out through various

The strong, silent hero: Amitabh Bachchan and Jaya Bhaduri in Sholay
(Flames). *The Museum of Modern Art/Film Stills Archive.*

motifs and symbols. The story centers on a Muslim family, consisting of a couple and their eight-year-old only son. A rejected lover of the woman, Salma (Waheeda Rehman), comes out of jail at the beginning of the film and virtually destroys the whole town where she lives by opening the floodgates of a dam where her husband works. The husband and wife appear to be drowned, while Iqbal, the son (Amitabh Bachchan), is saved by a Hindu family friend whose own wife and infant son are washed away. Later the villains try to kill Iqbal, but he is saved by his guardian and a pet eagle which seems to be modeled on Jatayu, the bird that tried to save Sita from Ravana in the *Rāmayana*. Iqbal and his "uncle" live at the side of the railway tracks, and when he grows up he too wears a porter's uniform, like his guardian. When trouble breaks out on a Bombay railway station through an encounter with the same villains, the porters go on strike, the credits appear, and the film proper begins.

The beginning of the narrative, therefore, positions the spectator in relation to a hero who is expected to play upon a more or less fixed repertoire of roles and to have them all coalesce in some sense; as champion and protector of the poor, as the romantic hero and entertainer, as a unifying cultural symbol. The plot goes through many tortuous twists and turns until all the characters originally introduced and then dispersed come together again and recognize themselves as part of an originary family. Justice is served, the villains are routed, and the show ends as it generally does in the Bombay film—happily and with the union of the working-class hero and the rich heroine. *Coolie* makes of its hero a near-divine phenomenon, or at least one who can easily mediate between the human and the supernatural world as between classes and religious groups in India.

Film and cultural theory has usually dealt with the idea of the masquerade in terms of the eliding of gender difference. This gendered understanding of masquerade, while useful, does not address how notions of class, caste, creed, linguistic, and regional difference—in short, the whole range of specificities that inform the body politic of Third World societies—are dissolved in the service of the ideological construction of the nation. The masquerade as a particular form of textual practice in the Bombay cinema elaborates a discourse of social norm-ality (the polyvalent Indian) through the persona of the male star. The star, by virtue of his *national* popularity, is already at once a signifier of immanent and transcendent nationhood. He is, so to speak, a collective creation and object of "transsexual" desire. By presenting the hero's body as eternally changeable and change itself as simply a matter of costume, bodily mannerisms, and performative codes, the binaries of regional/national, self/other, core/periphery are displaced onto each other. In his rendition of these displacements, the hero makes use of particular generic or narrative features that serve as the cultural and historical markers of the Bombay cinema, such as the song-and-dance rituals, the comedian/sidekick routines, the double role, the brotherhood syndrome. Parody is a privileged mode since it effects the destabilization of sociocultural categories *through* entertainment, spectacle, and humor, those occasions that the actor turns to advantage by crossing over from the specific role to the star text.

The Bombay cinema, then, presents the masquerading male body as a site for the elaboration of an Indian identity that can itself ever materialize *as* masquerade, as a mobile field of signifiers open to conscious rearrangements. Forms of masquerade ironically provide the connective tissue, as it were, across the social body so that difference, like beauty, is presented as only skin deep.

The whole picture [Holi (Festival, *1984*), *directed by Ketan Mehta*] *was, I thought, a farrago of borrowed gestures and secondhand beliefs. It had all the blank anger of a punk movie with none of the bravado. It had all the brutality of a kung fu movie with none of the extraordinary stunts. It had much of the behaviorism of* Lord of the Flies *but none of the point. I did not mind that the movie was boring, repetitive and crude. But I did feel cheated by its unspoken assumption that it was addressing a serious problem with serious candor, bravely fighting despair with despair. More than anything, I recoiled from its air of self-importance; it seemed in more ways than one a sub-Continental kind of movie.*

—*Pico Iyer*, Video Night in Kathmandu

The Authenticity Debate

Take Two

One way in which critics may lament and filmmakers seek to contest the hegemony of a commercially based, profit-driven popular cinema is to search for alternatives in the name of a higher calling to the art of the motion picture. In India such attempts, variously called "the parallel cinema," "the art cinema," "the Indian new wave," or simply "regional cinemas," surfaced in the late sixties and had petered out by the mid-eighties. During that period, a government-sponsored cinema had tried to establish a "new tradition" of filmmaking in India, one in which "authenticity" and "realism" were key terms. In 1981, the Indian government showcased a representative selection of such works in a major film festival held in the United States. Among the Hindi language films were titles that have become "passwords" to students of India's new cinema, the keys to its kingdom: *Sara Akash* (*The Whole Sky*, 1968), directed by Basu Chatterjee; *Uski Roti* (*A Day's Bread*, 1970), directed by Mani Kaul; *Bhuvan Shome* (1969), directed by Bengal-based film director Mrinal Sen; *27 Down* (1973), directed by Awtar Kaul; *Maya Darpan* (*The Mirror of Illusion*, 1972), directed by Kumar Shahani; *Garm Hawa* (*Hot Winds*, 1975), directed by M. S. Sathyu; *Chakra* (*The Vicious Circle*, 1980), directed by Rabinda Dharmaraj; *Manthan* (*The Churning*, 1976), directed by Shyam Benegal; *Albert Pinto Ko Gussa Kyon Ata Hai* (*What Makes Albert Pinto Angry*, 1980), directed by Saeed Mirza; and *Aakrosh* (*Cry of the Wounded*, 1980), directed by Govind Nihalani. In addition, films made in the regional languages featured works by G. Aravindan and Adoor Gopalakrishnan (Malayalam), Ritwik Ghatak (Bengali), Girish Karnad, Girish Kasaravalli, and Pattabhi Rama Reddy (Kannada), Ketan Mehta (Gujarati), Ramdas Phutane (Marathi), and Surinder Suri (English). With the exception of Awtar Kaul and Rabindra Dharmaraj, both of whom died shortly after their films were made, all (or nearly all) of these directors have become associated with India's "new" cinema and continue to make films, with varying degrees of success. Lately, however, many have turned to television to survive as artists and to find the audiences they lacked as filmmakers.

It has been customary for so long in Indian film critical circles to adopt hushed tones of respect and awe when confronted with the new cinema that any effort to engage this cinema outside the well-worn parameters of "social concern" and "artistic genius" is likely to arouse resentment and suspicion. It would be only too easy to dismiss such an effort (particularly if it is undertaken in a comparative framework with the popular cinema) as trendy, short-sighted, or partisan. Not that such criticism has not been made occasionally. In recent years, some voices have expressed a disenchantment with the new cinema, although in predictable ways. For instance, Indian film critic Iqbal Masud chastized the Indian new wave in these words, "The new cinema has fallen into its own kind of orthodoxy. They all make films like Godard or Bresson, but they do not convey the reality, the humanity, the warmth of India. They do not bring out the feel of what is happening in India. All these directors are artists. But they are removed from the people. At least in the commercial cinema, there is a connection between the director and the audience; in the New Wave, there is no connection, no sense of the day-to-day experience of the average filmgoer. These films are forms of abstraction."[1] And cultural critic Ashis Nandy has linked the art filmmakers to the *haute bourgeoisie* of India and suggested a "tripartite division of spoils among the high, middle and low-brow cinema" that is rather functionalist as a model and simply extends the binarism in the more familiar approaches to the new cinema.[2] What we need is not a proliferation but rather a problematization of the categories themselves; an analytics of the new cinema that does not polarize but sees it as part of a much larger crisis of articulating the fractures of modernity.

One of the problems that we face at the start is that of terminology and categorization. A single umbrella term like the "new" or "parallel" cinema is simply not sufficient or accurate to designate the diversity of approaches and techniques, aims and intentions that informs the works that are included under its rubric. If, as is generally stated, Satyajit Ray pioneered the new cinema, then its starting point has to be pushed back into the mid-fifties. And if Mrinal Sen and Ritwik Ghatak, along with Ray, are included in the new cinema, we not only have a problem with chronology but with the sheer impossibility of constructing a framework within which the significant differences that mark the work of these filmmakers—differences in style, tone, and texture, in sensibility and inspiration, in politics and ideology—may be accommodated. It is small wonder that serious students of India's new cinema such as Ashish Rajadhyaksha and Geeta Kapur have chosen one small but coherent and self-contained "tradition" of artistic practice within the new cinema, namely the Ritwik Ghatak–Kumar Shahani "line" or "linkage" for discussion and analysis. Filmmakers as diverse as Basu Chatterjee with a penchant for conventional narrative on the one hand and Mani Kaul, who wishes to dispense with narrative altogether, can by no stretch of the imagination be lumped together. The usage of a term like new cinema becomes redundant and problematic as a result.

Moreover, while the terms "new" and "alternative" imply the inscription of difference and separateness vis-à-vis that which is perceived as dominant, the term "parallel" suggests that which runs alongside the mainstream or established genre. The radical potentiality of the former terms is undercut by the latter, which implies the liberal notion of choice and a scenario of coexistence. India, never quite comfortable with the notion of "alternative," has found "parallel" more congenial as a concept. Thus the usage "new cinema" that has been widely adopted by critics is confusing when viewed analytically. The term "elite," which is one way in which Bombay commercial filmmakers designate their "others," is usually missing from critical discussion that focuses on the parallel cinema, although the question of symbolic capital, as French anthropologist Pierre Bourdieu has shown, muddies the neat dichotomies between art and commerce that structure the dominant cinema/new cinema debate in India.[3]

Another common feature underlying the parallel cinema impetus is often stated to reside in Italian neorealism. Many filmmakers, starting with Ray, referred to neorealist cinema as the model and inspiration for their own works. But neorealism was a response to very specific sociopolitical conditions. In post–World War Two Italy, the collective experience of the Resistance and of national reconstruction gave cohesion, a sense of common mission and purpose, and a social vision to the neorealist movement. In India, no comparable collectively shared trauma or event took place in the 1960s that could spark a similar response. The Naxalite,[4] or Maoist movement, in the Bengal countryside and the drought of the mid-sixties, events cited by some new cinema practitioners, did not have the kind of widespread impact that could unleash creative energies on a significant scale. Ghatak's work alone (and he is only ex post facto a new cinema filmmaker) bears the marks of a deeply searing national trauma that took place during independence; that is, the partition of his home state, Bengal, in 1947. We are then left with vague yearnings for change felt by individual filmmakers with individual sources of inspiration and individual conceptions of artistic practice. Moreover, it is perhaps this lack of a vital communication with or articulation of a larger national experience that accounts for the new cinema's inability to make a dent on the international scene. Unlike neorealism, the French new wave, or Latin American Third Cinema aesthetics, India's new cinema was neither revolutionary enough nor culturally distinct enough to influence aspiring filmmakers elsewhere. This is not in itself either good or bad, merely a reflection on the receptivity and long-term significance of new cinema's practices *as a whole*, despite the brilliance and originality of some specific films. The popular cinema, on the other hand, can boast of audiences far beyond the shores of India and the pockets of diasporic Indians scattered all over the globe. Cam-

Social Realism in India's "new cinema": Shabana Azmi and Sadhu Meher in Ankur (The Seedling). *The Museum of Modern Art/Film Stills Archive.*

bodians and Africans, Iranians and Russians have alike found India's Bombay cinema appealing.[5] Again, this fact does not translate into a value judgment, but it is a paradox that has received too little attention from serious analysts of Indian cinema and has implications for questions of cinematic form and content and the relationship between films and society.

This brings us to the question of the new cinema's political project, its self-image as an agent of social change, its vision of the role of the filmmaker as architect of a progressive national consciousness. The new cinema crystallized under the banner of difference from the commercial cinema; that is, the one impulse that united a fairly disparate group of filmmakers or aspiring filmmakers was the need to work outside the structures of the Bombay film industry, in particular the star system and the dominant genres of filmmaking. Apart from the issue of financing such projects, to which we will soon turn, the common resolve on the part of filmmakers was to do away with what were called the "commercial ingredients," mainly the ubiquitous songs and dances of the "formula film." Even if one grants that "songs and dances" must be taken metaphorically (a signifier for "artificiality") rather than literally, the question may still be posed as to whether a concerted film movement can take shape on such flimsy grounds. Can the ideology of difference—in theme and style—without a broader notion of the *politics of difference* create a truly *new* cinema? In other words, how are filmmakers and audiences located vis-à-vis one another? Who defines "difference" and to what end? How may we conceptualize the new cinema's self-projection as an arena of artistic practice and intellectual debate over issues of art and industry, notions of the public, national identity versus regional identities, and the definition of a responsible cinema?

I believe that the way out of this critical quagmire lies in our working back to notions of hybridity and the masquerade and their status as negotiable entities in the ideological and artistic repertoire of the new cinema practitioners. The art cinema is not so successful with hybrid experience because it is tied to sociohistorical specificity. Regional in its moorings, its linguistic and semantic grounding, its production context and audience appeal, it subscribes philosophically and aesthetically to the concept of the authentic. Its ideological task is to demasquerade the dominant cultural form of cinema in the name of "other" borrowings, itself a third hybrid space in which the "purity" of the artistic impulse is mobilized against the messiness of politics. In its ideal-typical mode the new cinema leans toward the intellectual-rational rather than the emotional-mythical. As such, its links are more with the Brahmanic tradition in Indian culture and less so with the popular or little traditions. Although it is ostensibly for the rural, the "true" India, since many of the art filmmakers have Marxist leanings, their well-intentioned critiques of rural power structures are underpinned by rationalist, unilinear principles of change and progress. India's art cinema is wedded to a mimetic view of life that resonates inadequately with the general population.

But it is this general population which the new cinema would like to see as the beneficiary of its modernist project. For the claims to "newness" of the new cinema can only be understood if they are seen in conjunction with the vision of a new society. How else can one explain the enormous psychic and intellectual-rational (in addition to the economic) investment made in the new cinema, much in excess of its actual impact on people in India? Can its third hybrid space, which it claims is neither of the popular commercial cinema nor of the self-absorbed hermeticism of some garden varieties of personal cinema, be precisely that form of cinema that coheres as national allegory? What happens when the third hybrid space becomes the space-time of the nation (rather than of the regions)? How is the issue of social transformation or stasis addressed? What kinds of symbolic elements, textual openings, stylistic motifs, and evocations deconstruct a befogged and tarnished national imaginary? I consider below a few films falling under the rubric of the new cinema but with self-inscribed crossover potential. Made in Hindi, they addressed an all-India audience and used accessible narrative styles (plot-oriented, fast-paced narration as opposed to the "slow" pacing of the regional film) to create an ethos of (national) generality rather than (regional) specificity. These "allegories of underdevelopment" and disenchantment highlight structures rather than characters as emblematic of their ideological shift: away from realism and psychological portrayal to the archetypal mode. One can point, further, to their tableaux-like compositions rendered through architectural and building motifs and metaphors: the historical monuments in *Garm Hawa*, the courthouse in *Aakrosh*, the guesthouse in *Manthan*, the mansion in *Maya Darpan*, the Western-style ranch house in *Godhuli*, to name a few. Buildings are historical and cultural artifacts par excellence, serving here as an incitement to memory and as power structures. As oppressive spatial signifiers for the most part, they are meant to foreground the tensions and contradictions of the Indian experience.

Contours of the Debate

The terms of discussion of India's new cinema have been inflected from the start by what Andreas Huyssen, in another context, has called "the great divide" between the authentic and the imitative, the pure and the impure, the original and the impersonating.[6] A few quotes will make this clear. Here is a statement made in 1981 by Raghunath Raina of the Directorate of Film Festivals:

What really distinguishes the New Indian Cinema is a definitive set of liberal-humanitarian values, embracing progressive solutions to urgent problems, a sensitivity to the plight of the poor and oppressed, a faith in the ultimate movement of man toward change. Drawing its inspiration largely from the neo-realists, it is a cinema of social significance and artistic sincerity, presenting a modern, humanist perspective, more durable than the fantasy world of the popular film.[7]

Film critic Chidananda Dasgupta, insisting on the "brainwashed" masses, asserted, "The difference between 'art cinema' and 'commercial cinema' in India is simply the difference between good cinema and bad—between serious films and degenerate 'entertainment.' The New Cinema in India is the creation of an intellectual elite that is keenly aware of the human condition in India."[8] In fact, images of decay, degeneracy, and cultural and spiritual poverty abound in connection with the commercial cinema and those who frequent it. Kobita Sarkar, in writing about film songs (an index of "unreality" for critics), speaks of "those rotted in the commercial cinema"[9] changing their approach and demanding fewer songs in films. Fewer songs, in her view, translate directly into better cinema. And Andrew Robinson approvingly quoted Chidananda Dasgupta's view of the urban masses flocking to the commercial films as "culturally impoverished," saying that "it is becoming the cinema of the lumpen proletariat, the unemployed half-educated or uneducated vagrant youth, the nouveau riche with more money than education, the hoarder and the black marketeer, the children and adolescents born and brought up on the pavements of large cities and living in the shadow of high-rise buildings."[10]

On the other side, the climate of hope and promise generated by the new cinema is voiced by Barbara Crossette, Delhi correspondent for the *New York Times*, who wrote in 1981, "There is hope, inside and outside India, that the parallel cinema will not only put India on the international film map, bringing to foreign audiences at the same time a better understanding of India and its new, post-Independence generation, but also that it will at least dent the monopoly Bombay holds on the minds of so many million Indian filmgoers. Everyone involved seems to have a gut feeling of great hope, guardedly expressed."[11] Even as pragmatic a statement as this puts on the agenda a bewildering complex of objectives and expectations. Foreign exchange earnings? Cultural prestige? A more art cinema–conscious audience? A gradual weakening of the popularity of the commercial film?

It is perhaps appropriate to start our review with the production context of the new cinema. India's mixed economy policies had outlined a large state sector and a major role in the promotion of "traditional" culture for the government. We have already mentioned the cultural institutions set up in this regard. With regard to film, the Film Finance Corporation (FFC) was established in 1960 with funds from the central government. Modeled on Britain's National Film Finance Corporation, it offered low-interest loans for "quality" films. Mrinal Sen's *Bhuvan Shome* was made with FFC funding and enjoyed reasonable success at the box office. While initially the government required guarantees and hence wished to fund established filmmakers whose works had proven commercial viability, it soon extended support to entirely new film-makers for low-budget productions. Basu Chatterjee's *Sara Akash* and Mani Kaul's *Uski Roti* formed the original triptych of the new cinema. The films had a rural or small-town setting and milieu and, in varying ways, adopted techniques of storytelling which broke with traditional expectations of the fast-paced Bombay film. Perhaps it is the slowness of the rhythm, in these and many other new wave films, that prompted an American film festival official to comment, "You have to relax and get used to a different pace. The films will seem far too long to many people—and the action very slow. But that's the pace of Indian life."[12] While such statements must themselves be read in their "proper" context, the response to the aims and achievements of the Indian new wave did find a critical voice early on. In an article entitled "An Indian New Wave?" and written in 1971, when the new cinema was gathering momentum, Satyajit Ray interrogates the "ideas motivating the new movement," namely, the ideas of experimentation with film language, non-narrative exposition, and improvisation. Providing a historical context for these developments in Western cinema, he cites examples of experimentation from the films of Renoir, Welles, and Godard and the early experimenters, Chaplin, Keaton, and Erich von Stroheim. Turning to Indian cultural conditions and the potential audience for "off-beat" films, Ray writes:

> I understand the new film makers are pinning their faith on the perceptive minority, and the hunt is to track them down and turn them into patrons of the proposed art theatres. Do these film makers seriously believe that this minority is tucked away in odd corners of the country and have only to be ferreted out of their holes to make a bee-line for these art theatres? My own belief is they are all around us, within easy reach and in enough numbers to make a two-lakh proposition pay, waiting for the right kind of off-beat movie to turn up.[13]

Ray cautions aspiring off-beat filmmakers against vague and grandiose statements ("They talk of experiment without clearly specifying what lines the experiment is to take and how far it is to go"), saying that the Indian filmmaker must be prepared to deal with the collective mind, with collective response. "I am not sure I am happy about the minority audience syndrome either," he writes. "They seem suspiciously like a defensive manoeuvre on the part of the new film makers. Why not aim wider? I do not know of a single film maker who has been dismayed by a wide acceptance of his work."[14]

Finally, in deconstructing the so-called newness of one of the first new cinema offerings, *Bhuvan Shome* (1969), directed by Mrinal Sen, Ray finds that it had used some of the most popular conventions of cinema: "a delectable heroine, an ear-filling background score, and a simple, wholesome wish-fulfilling screen story (summary in seven words: Big Bad Bureaucrat Reformed by Rustic Belle)." This was the kind of "newness" likely to appeal to a minority audience, said Ray, "the kind that looks a bit like its French counterpart, but is essentially old-fashioned and Indian beneath its trendy habit."[15]

A major problem in the conceptualization of government support for the Indian new cinema was distribution. While funds were made available to aspiring filmmakers, the government had no way of recouping its investment. By 1982, 84 of the 130 films made with funding from the central government had not been distributed and were still "on the shelf."[16] Despite the substantially expanded role of the National Film Development Corporation (NFDC), which was the result of an amalgamation between the FFC and the Film Export Corporation in 1980, the prospects for receptivity of the new cinema did not effectively change during the 1980s and may even have deteriorated. The NFDC has co-financed more than 200 feature films and has financed 127 theaters in 15 states of India, adding a total of 65,801 seats.[17] Yet there is little evidence that the battle for the hearts and minds of the Indian people through a "better" cinema has been won.

Calcutta-based media educator Gaston Roberge pointed to some of the questionable assumptions underlying the government-sponsored new cinema. In a timely critique of *Report of the Working Group on National Film Policy* that appeared in September 1980, Roberge noted that the report, while reaffirming the importance of film culture in India, lacks conceptual clarity in the very categories it uses to talk about cinema. Distinctions between art and commerce, education and entertainment, creative artist and skilled purveyor of fantasies help to polarize mainstream and parallel cinema. As Roberge comments, "While affirming that cinema disseminates *popular* culture, the Group wants a director's cinema, that is, an individual's, elitist medium."[18] He further notes how repeated injunctions to the popular cinema to act "as a catalyst for social change" not only ignore the real power of the cinema (which is to conjure up illusion) but also its production context. Moreover, because the government, like the Bombay film industry, aims at maximum profit in the form of numerous taxes and levies, it cannot be taken seriously when it calls for major change within the film industry. Finally, the commonplace opposition to "(so-called) bad, commercial, non-educational, unartistic, irresponsible cinema" on the one hand and (in some quarters) equal opposition to "(so-called) good, non-commercial, educational, artistic, responsible cinema" on the other opposes two species of the same genre. "The distinction is maintained even though there is hardly any consensus as to what particular films belong to either side." Roberge states that the distinction is not really between art and commerce but between art and entertainment, where art procures insight and entertainment procures delight. "Scholars who expect cinema to 'become an instrument also of entertainment if its inner content is a true reflection of our everyday experiences' (Report, page 114), nurture a rather drab notion of entertainment."

In his book *Another Cinema for Another Society*, Roberge punctures some of the middle-class pretensions of the art film and its patrons. Supported by the governmental establishment *against* the mainstream popular cinema, the art film would "educate" and "enlighten" the masses. But, notes Roberge:

> A cinema coexisting parallel with a "commercial" cinema that it is supposed to influence and supplant would solely gratify its promoters' personal aspirations. Parallel to a mass cinema would emerge an elite cinema. For a really parallel cinema cannot subsist for a long time unless it caters to a parallel audience. Such an audience—a minority, educated group—may legitimately wish to have a cinema designed to meet their own escapist needs. But would it not be scandalous if funds and talents were mobilized for the promotion of a parallel cinema catering solely to a privileged group? [19]

Ironically, it is to questions of privilege (social/caste/class, bureaucratic/governmental, financial) that the new cinema has most often turned its attention, thereby staking a claim to the distinction of being "anti-establishment." Yet the irony of the situation is not lost on all filmmakers. As Sagar Sarhadi, director of the pretentious *Bazaar* (*Market*, 1982), exclaimed, "The whole system is wrong. . . . You make films against the establishment and then expect the establishment to buy those films. Nonsense."[20] The government confusion is also evident in its censorship policies, often applied haphazardly. *Samskara* (*Funeral Rites*, 1970) and *Garm Hawa* (*Hot Winds*, 1975) were initially banned and then went on to receive national awards.

One of the ironies of India's new cinema is that while the filmmakers belong, for the most part, to a middle-class English-educated elite, the audience they wish to reach is rural and/or urban working class. In the early years of the new cinema project, this desire was reflected in the themes and settings of films, which were invariably rural and focused on age-old customs and social taboos and practices. Soon the practice of trooping out to the villages with camera and crew itself hardened into a predictable genre. Mrinal Sen has satirized this trend in his Bengali film *Aakaler Sandhaney* (*In Search of Famine*, 1980). But Sen himself may have been guilty of wishing to play god to the rural people in laying out for them the entertainment they prefer. In an interview he remarked:

> In a particular area of Bengal dominated by poor, landless farmers, they voted for a communist candidate to Parliament. The margin was overwhelming. But in the same area, where most films never run for more than a week at a time, they thronged to see a film about a miracle man who triumphs over a scientist. The farmers in the film wanted rain but there was no technology to bring rain. So they went to a miracle man who not only helped bring rain but also everything else necessary for a good crop. The film ran for eight weeks in this area. This is a situation difficult to fight—an audience which votes for a man who will be fighting for change, for land reform, but at the same time will flock to a film which accents a mistrust in technology and faith in miracles. This is the kind of dichotomy we suffer from and have to fight.[21]

Given the complexities of the situation, then, it becomes evident that, as Andrew Ross has demonstrated, the history of entertainment and popular forms and of elite forms must be written *together*, as a series of negotiations and accommodations.[22] Thus it is possible, and necessary, to write a new history of the parallel cinema which sees textual negotiation and accommodation not as lapses from the standards of "high art" but as an engagement with the store of images and icons, desires and fantasies in the realm of public culture which is circulated largely (though not exclusively) by the Bombay cinema. As Michael Denning put it, "There is no mass culture *out there;* it is the very element we breathe."[23]

But how does one go about writing such a history? How can one breathe life into the old unresolved philosophical tension between agency and structure, human subjectivity and its social, political, economic determinations? And if we are in the presence of a new global paradigm of mass culture, when "the forms of thought and what it feeds on, together with modern techniques of information, language and dress have dialectically reorganized the people's intelligences and . . . the constant principles which acted as safeguards during the colonial period are now undergoing extremely radical changes,"[24] what sense does it make to retain notions of an authentic or autonomous realm of culture, art, and tradition? Perhaps our task lies rather in determining the ways in which different conceptions of the contemporary are articulated in cinema, how the "hybrid" versions of the new cinema become the metaphoric sites for the construction of a postcolonial Indian sensibility. And what better instance of hybridity than the nation itself?

One of the conflicts in the articulation of a Third cinema—alternative and radical film practices originating in the Third World but now occupying a temporal space of postcoloniality as well—is between what British theorist Clyde Taylor and other marginally located cultural activists would like to see as the "negation" of a dominant aesthetic (in his case Western bourgeois aesthetics) and what Homi Bhabha calls "negotiation" from the "shifting margins of cultural displacement" inherent in the historical hybridity of the postcolonial world.[25] Once the notion of hybridity is taken for granted, we can no longer talk of an "authentic" national culture. Besides, cultures are never unitary in themselves nor simply dualistic in relation to the Other. Thus the polarities of radical purity in Third World aesthetics versus cosmopolitanism or, to extend Bhabha's argument, the genuineness of artistic practice and tradition versus a debased "cosmopolitanism" are not adequate to the terms of discussion. Citing Fanon's model of the phases that a national culture goes through, Bhabha writes:

Fanon's vision of revolutionary cultural and political change as a "fluctuating movement" of occult instability could not be articulated as cultural *practice* without an acknowledgement of this indeterminate space of the subject(s) of enunciation. It is that Third Space, though unrepresentable in itself, which constitutes the discursive conditions of enunciation that ensure that the meaning and symbols of culture have no primordial unity or fixity; that even the same signs can be appropriated, translated, rehistoricised, and read anew.[26]

The Taylor-Bhabha hiatus on the issue of Third World aesthetics has relevance for our discussion of India's new/art/parallel cinema. For the questions facing filmmakers, whether aligned to the popular Bombay cinema or the art cinema, are related, after all, to the politics of representation in which film technology itself is implicated as alien, the originary instrument of cultural difference. How, then, can the art cinema claim for itself the purity of intention and the authenticity of sensibility when the very means employed to suggest a different vision involves "compromise"? Can we take Western technology and reject its ideology (consumerism, commercialism, the free marketplace of ideas, the embattled artist, the vulgar populace)?

Of course it might be pointed out by representatives of the new cinema, artists and critics alike, that their quarrel is not with Western technology per se or even with the West but rather with a "debased" mass culture spawned by an indigenous bourgeois class and its capitalist machinery. But such a response would raise more questions than it answers, for an art protected and sponsored by a capitalist state (as the Indian parallel cinema has been) cannot claim to be "above" the forces of the market. The argument then turns to one of the "integrity" and "personal vision" of the artist as against the "imitative-exploitative" propensities of "commercial" filmmakers. Removed to this rarefied plane, it becomes impossible analytically to distinguish between India's new cinema and that against which it defines itself.

Redefining the Nation: *Garm Hawa*

Of all the new cinema films of the first phase (roughly the period from the late sixties to the end of the seventies), M. S. Sathyu's *Garm Hawa* (*Hot Winds*, 1973) deals most specifically with the politics of the nation. Recalling the harrowing days after the partition of the Indian subcontinent, the film has the distinction of being the first effort to examine inflamed Hindu-Muslim passions and their human costs on the minority community. Based on an unpublished short story by Muslim writer Ismat Chugtai, *Garm Hawa* was developed into a screenplay by two esteemed figures of the Bombay film industry—poet and lyricist Kaifi Azmi and

Sathyu's wife, Shama Zaidi, a scriptwriter. But Sathyu also drew upon the best traditions of the Bombay cinema, not only in selecting a seasoned (non-Muslim) actor like Balraj Sahni to portray the central character but also in using the device of the love story to open up questions of nationalist politics.

The film interweaves the personal and the political, human interest and social critique. Its evenhandedness in presenting both the Hindu and the Muslim communities as self-serving and bigoted in their relations with each other and exploitative of members of their own communities links de-communalization with decolonization as the nationalist project. The story concerns a Muslim family's struggle to survive in post-partition India in an atmosphere of increasing tension and hostility. The "hot winds" of the title, of course, stand for inflamed passions: political, communal, sexual—passions that erupted not only immediately before and after partition but in periodic spurts ever since. The film provides a way to work through those passions by instituting a process of psychic renewal through spectatorial identification with "minority" (Muslim) characters and their family saga. The action is played out against a backdrop of a host of geographical, architectural, and cultural motifs suggestive of the nation as actant. Sathyu himself referred to the larger ramifications of the film's vision, its status as political allegory, when he said, "What I really wanted to expose in *Garm Hawa* was the games these politicians play. Actually there are no human considerations at all. I am not talking only about India, but even in Vietnam, Biafra, Germany . . . it is all the same. How many of us in India really wanted the Partition? Look at all the suffering it caused."[27]

The story focuses on Salim Mirza (Balraj Sahni), owner of a shoe factory in Agra, and on the impact of partition on the lives of him and his family members. These include his aged mother, his wife, his two sons, Baqar Mirza (Abu Siwani) and Sikander (Farouque Shaikh), and his daughter, Amina (Gita). The film begins with one of the most enduring images of the Hindi cinema: a railway platform and a train, that signifier of modern life that is here emblematic of distance, separation, irrevocable otherness. Salim Mirza is bidding farewell to his sister as one more trainload of people heads toward Pakistan, their new homeland. It is a shot that is repeated several times in the film, each time more somber as Mirza's family keeps shrinking and his sense of isolation and desperation deepens. From the railway station, Mirza is shown taking the same *tonga* (a horse-drawn carriage) every time, with the carriage-puller serving as a "voice" commenting on the action. In the opening sequence, Mirza is sad but not unduly worried about his own status in his native Agra, a place that he feels rooted to, and he therefore sees no reason to leave. Mirza is the authentic Indian, a man who is not swayed by spurious emotions and prejudices, in sharp contrast to his brother, Halim Mirza, and other relatives who say one thing and do another. They are visually linked to dogs gnawing at bones, politicians who are both treacherous and cowardly. Halim's son Kazim is engaged to Mirza's daughter, Amina, but is forced by his parents to leave for Pakistan. Amina is now left to suffer the attentions of her other cousin, Shamshad (Jalal Agha), for whom she has little feelings.

Misfortunes start piling up on the stoical Mirza: orders to deliver shoes are canceled; his employees refuse to work for him or banks to loan him money for fear that he will escape to Pakistan; his ancestral home, in the name of the now-absent elder brother, is declared evacuee property and allotted to a Sindhi businessman; Mirza is forced to move to cramped rented quarters; Mirza's eldest son also leaves for Pakistan when the shoe business is on the verge of collapse. But worst of all is the pain that Amina suffers as a result of the political changes. Her lover, Kazim, secretly returns to India to marry her, but before the ceremony can take place, the police arrest him for having entered India illegally. Mirza watches helplessly as his beloved daughter sinks into despondency. Shamshad takes advantage of her situation and woos her; a lonely and vulnerable Amina succumbs to his blandishments. But Shamshad too escapes across the border with his opportunistic parents. Still, Amina hopes for his return, only to have her dreams shattered once more, and this situation culminates in her suicide. Mirza's family has now shrunk to three, a progressive decrease that is signified by the number of plates set during mealtimes, once shared by the whole family. Unable to avoid the move he had resisted so far, Mirza too sadly prepares to leave. On the way to the station, their *tonga* is stopped by a procession of people out to protest injustice. Sikander, drawn to the cause, jumps off the carriage and joins the rally, as, after a few moments, does Mirza. They decide to stay on and struggle for communal harmony and social change.

Within a realist camera style and chronological narrative, *Garm Hawa*'s signification of space is evocative of the film's theme. Mirza is framed in tight shots to signify his shrinking options, while the homes the family occupies are emblematic of their inner states. Bars and grills suggest confinement. In addition, the larger context is portrayed through several Bombay filmmaking conventions—the map of India undergoing mutation and change, the voice-over of the Muslim poet, Kaifi Azmi, commenting on the action, shots of politicians and political leaders (Gandhi, the Mountbattens, Jinnah, Nehru) ushering in a blood-stained birth of a nation, shots of madding crowds in a society gone awry during the violent months of 1947. But the shots also invite distance and calm reflection, for they are still images of newspaper footage of that earlier period and suggest the hope that the nation has forever left those days behind, that the lessons of history have been learned. The open-ended concluding shots and a return to the notion of the stream of humanity (a crowd surging forward waving red flags), this time protesting peacefully in a democratic political tradition, again express a guarded hope of shared experience and coexistence among India's diverse groups.

The narrative itself is centered around a character whose "superhuman" stature marks him as an allegorical figure possessing to a marked degree the culturally valued qualities of moral strength, honesty, nonsectarianism, and traditionalism in the best sense (his attachment to the country of his birth and his sense of rootedness to place are versions of "patriotism," a notion that the film silently interrogates throughout). Salim Mirza is a combination of biblical fortitude (his list of trials and tribulations would humble Job), Gandhian breadth of sympathy, and moral integrity, and he is a true rather than a "false" member of the Indian Islamic community (unlike the rest of his relatives, who migrate to Pakistan at the earliest opportunity). The fact that he is played by a Hindu and not a Muslim actor (certainly not atypical of the Bombay film tradition but significant in the context of what *Garm Hawa* set out to do), an actor, moreover, who could mobilize feelings of strong identification, meant that both Hindus and Muslims could feel secure with the portrayal. The film's effort to build a firmer foundation for the precarious sense of national identity of the Muslim community in India is also especially evident in the evocative use made of architectural monuments from the Mughal era. Here again, both the interests of realism and of allegory are served, for the shots of the Taj Mahal, Fatehpur Sikri, and other buildings are not gratuitous: the setting being Agra, its sights and sounds make for an "authentic" atmosphere, even as a link is being made between individual lives and their historical dimension. But there is an ambivalence here, for a romantic link with the past may not be the best way to confront the problems of national identity in the present.

Indeed, the love story at the heart of the narrative and its tragic out-

Spatial identification: Salim Mirza (Balraj Sahni) framed against the Taj Mahal in Garm Hawa (Hot Winds).

come is a rather conventional device used to symbolize the ruthlessness of external forces and their impact on private lives. Amina's "betrayal" by her two lovers and her subsequent suicide are exploited to the full for their sentimentality, thereby reducing the force of historical and political analysis. Amina's preoccupation with herself makes her a curiously detached creature in a household feeling and responding fully to the currents of history, and her passivity is underscored by a wooden demeanor and expression. Her end seems inevitable, given the way her role is conceptualized, a conclusion strangely at odds in a film that in many ways denies the inevitability of history.

The Historicized Epic: *Kalyug, Tarang*

If *Garm Hawa* suggests that the only way to keep a national consciousness alive is through a courageous interrogation of its suppressed past, *Kalyug* (*Dark Age*, 1981), directed by Shyam Benegal, and *Tarang* (*Wave*, 1983), directed by Kumar Shahani, work with more openly allegorical structures to impose sense on the seeming chaos of contemporary urban experience in India. As efforts to reclaim for the cinema

India's ancient epic and dramatic traditions, to wrest them away from the domain of the "mythological film," these films are self-consciously "academic" and, in the case of *Tarang*, experimental. Both films use structural and thematic elements from the great Indian epic, the *Mahābhārata*, for a modern retelling of the ancient narrative of familial enmity, opposition, and self-destruction. The epic provides the framework for a dramatic representation of power and greed in the business world of contemporary India.

The word *kalyug* or *kaliyug* signifies the dark ages mentioned in the *Māhabhārata* that have followed the earlier epochs (*Satya*, *Treta*, and *Dwa:par*) of three thousand–year cycles, each stage involving the progressive moral decline of the human race. After the battle of Kurukshetra, in which the two clans of the Kauravas and the Pandavas destroy each other, the *kalyug* commences, bringing total destruction till the cycle of epochs can begin all over again. In Benegal's film, the epic framework provides the basis for a star-studded, fast-paced narrative of two giant industrial families whose relationships are graphically presented in Figure 2. Within this framework, the rivalry between Khubchand and Sons and Puranchand, Dharam Raj and Brothers, two engineering companies of Bombay, follows an inexorable path toward mutual destruction. Benegal concentrates exclusively on the upper class here, with their palatial homes and liveried employees, their foreign cars, their tennis games and horse breeding. The main enmity develops between Karan (Shashi Kapoor), the top manager for Dhan Raj (Victor Banerjee), and Bharat, the youngest of Savitri's three sons. As they mar each other's business deals and stage elaborate scenarios of revenge and sabotage, an escalating trend of violence is unleashed. Bharat, whose name recalls "Bharatvarsh," or India, may be said to symbolize the mentality of India's industrial elite in whose hands is concentrated the major percentage of the country's wealth. But Bharat is also the hero, the one who lives till the end and may be said to have won the family battle. Indeed, the last scene in which Bharat's older sister-in-law, Supriya (Rekha), cradles his head in her lap and is both surrogate mother and lover is a rather ambiguous and superfluous intrusion into the allegorical structure of the narrative.

Why are the fortunes of India's business elite given epic dimensions in this film? How is the filmmaker's social critique enhanced by this secular parable of greed, incest, and fratricidal hate? By using the *Mahābhārata* story, Benegal seeks to evoke a widely shared cultural and

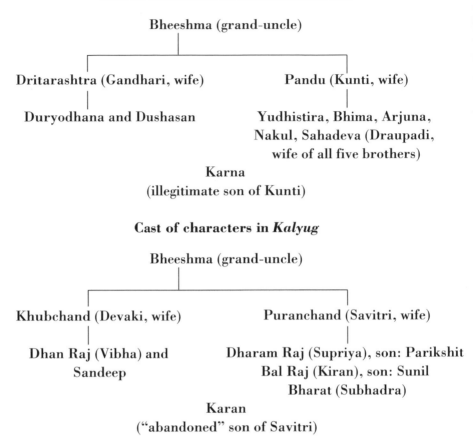

Cast of characters in the *Mahābhārata*

Bheeshma (grand-uncle)

Dritarashtra (Gandhari, wife)   Pandu (Kunti, wife)

Duryodhana and Dushasan   Yudhistira, Bhima, Arjuna,
Nakul, Sahadeva (Draupadi,
wife of all five brothers)

Karna
(illegitimate son of Kunti)

Cast of characters in *Kalyug*

Bheeshma (grand-uncle)

Khubchand (Devaki, wife)   Puranchand (Savitri, wife)

Dhan Raj (Vibha) and   Dharam Raj (Supriya), son: Parikshit
Sandeep   Bal Raj (Kiran), son: Sunil
Bharat (Subhadra)

Karan
("abandoned" son of Savitri)

Figure 2

moral frame of reference whereby the maneuverings of industrial power
can be collectively grasped. The larger story is of course that of Indian
politics itself, its fractiousness and corruption. Yet Benegal's symbolic
gesture also confers dignity and legitimacy to a level of experience that
is remote from the life of the average Indian, even as he seeks to open it
up to scrutiny. *Kalyug* presents both Indian business and labor as corrupt, but the very speed at which events unfold discourages reflection.
The greatness of the *Mahābhārata* as epic lies precisely in its inter-
weaving of philosophical and "historical" discourse, its ability to suggest
the infinite ambiguity of human life and motivations. *Kalyug*'s archetypes do not sufficiently resonate with the contradictions of the contemporary experience. The mythic framework suggests an inevitability to the
course of action pursued by the two clans, so that the lessons of destruc-

tive violence are lost in the process of identification of the overall pattern. Moreover, it might be too easy to see the film's parable of greed and destruction as applicable only to the already affluent, of their getting their just desserts. The class relationships are not developed in the film, although the consciousness of family background and pedigree that affects the rich is brought out by Bharat's reference to Karan as a bastard and a foundling. The ironies of birth and upbringing are reflected through the theme of incest and inbreeding that underlies the film. Money seduces money in high places, and it also kills. The epic framework serves as a warning for the kind of future that India might be headed toward.

Tarang's exploration of the many aspects of Indian social and class relations, its more subjective approach, its blending of the lyrical and the historical make it at once a more complex but ultimately unsatisfactory work. There are several levels of discourse here involving "technology, class-antagonisms, relations between male and female, and finally the universe itself beyond the realm of the 'known' which, in the bourgeois world, equates with what can be 'possessed.'"[28] This is all to the good, but the film's intellectuality seems to submerge the epic form. *Tarang* gives the impression of simultaneously freezing and freeing the play of meanings. Shahani comments that in his experiment with the form of the epic, a kind of oscillating movement was involved, revealing the transitions from the social to the psychological, to the spiritual and back. He explains his use of the epic structure in this way:

> As I viewed it, the epic always has to find its expression through the dominant mode of exchange. I had to place it in the present, in a historical situation where it had to articulate itself with the positive aspects of commodification. I had to realise the languages that revealed the material states of oppression, as formulated in the ideologies that emerged, and a universe of experience, contained by mythology, that was equally shaped by those material states. With a lyrical construction I would have had to work only with sensuous experience, and to give it a metrical structure; or with the dramatic I would have had to turn the social environment into a metaphor, of death possibly.[29]

The characters in *Tarang* are representatives of this "dominant mode of exchange": the petulant industrial father figure, self-made and self-centered; the nephew who represents multinational capital; the son-in-law who is an emblem of a nationalist bourgeoisie. The film uses the epic tradition to deal with the tensions of a modern industrial family. Then there is the "proletariat," the workers in the factories denied decent wages, hounded by the police, incited to self-inflicted and intercommunal violence. And finally there are the middlemen, the corrupt union leaders who betray the workers and live in the pay of the businessmen. The epic struggle in the *Mahābhārata* is here the class struggle conceived in classic Marxist terms. But Shahani's interest in the Indian tradition finds expression in the construction of female archetypes. Primary among them is Janaki (Smita Patil), who is the wife of a deceased worker of the industrialist killed on the job. She is a composite icon of the Mother Goddess and embodies both nurturing and destructive tendencies. She is also a foil to the upper-class, remote, and sexually repressed Hansa, only daughter of the industrialist and the wife of Rahul the protagonist, played by Amol Palekar.

Tarang is only partially successful in its ambitious project of constructing a modern language of epic, both cinematic and lexicographic. Conceived within an overall illusionist and narrative style, the self-reflexive moments seem to stick out as gratuitous. For instance, in two sequences the lead characters, Smita Patil and Amol Palekar, are referred to by "the public" (ostensibly the actual people watching the film's shooting) by their own names and are the butt of the usual remarks made by fans. It is difficult to see what purpose this level of "reflexivity" serves within the general scheme of the film. The interactions between the two women, Hansa and Janaki, are also marred by a confusion of codes. Their girl-to-girl talk is meant to suggest realism, and yet it undercuts the "feminist" stance of the film, reinforcing traditional expectations of how women converse. Also, there is an inherent contradiction in Janaki's portrayal, for she is supposed to be a crucial member of the workers' struggle and yet is purely a sexual symbol in the context of Rahul's milieu, a contradiction that she seems in no sense to be aware of and in fact willingly subjects herself to.

Stylized performances, static images, and the straining for epic effects clash with the illusionist conventions of the dominant cinema in the enunciation of *Tarang*. There are also the utopian dimensions of the film—Janaki's Muslim admirer, Abdul, who wishes to marry her, and Janaki's own "reunion" with Rahul on a spiritual plane, with which the film ends. The sea as regenerative metaphor comes to life as Janaki, and earlier Hansa, find refuge in water from the evils of the system and the manipulations of patriarchy.

Allegories of Nation Building: *Godhuli, Manthan*

Godhuli (*The Hour of the Gods*, 1977) and *Manthan* (*The Churning*, 1976) are, literally, allegories of nation *building*. That is, they are centrally informed by building and construction motifs and themes, as these are introduced into the Indian village in the name of modernization. Although presenting almost exclusively the micropolitics of village life, it is the ideological control of the village by the city that is being explored here. This is evident from the fact that the protagonists in both films are "outsiders" in some sense and represent Westernized scientific rationality and technique, which they seek to dispense in the rural areas. It is the familiar problematic of tradition versus modernity, rendered forceful and urgent here by the nature of the energies (destructive and constructive) unleashed as the balance of forces in the village is upset. The films' message: on this side darkness, on the other chaos.

Godhuli, directed by Girish Karnad and B. V. Karanth and made in both Hindi and Kannada versions, is the weaker of the two films. Part of the reason is that both "tradition" and "modernity" are schematized. The polarizations of the dumb mother, representing a primitive level of feeling and thinking, according to one critic, and the American girl who vainly tries to understand village mores and customs, with the protagonist caught in between, reduce complex forces into essentialized positions. The film's opening scene sets the tone of contemplative distance through which village life is to be apprehended: it involves a staged masquerade, suggesting in some sense the impenetrability of village codes by outsiders. A group of village children with masks that represent the sacred cow are singing and performing before a big gathering of adults, offering thanks to the gods and affirming togetherness. The camera pans to show the rapt faces of those in the audience and is meant to signify the peace and calm of village life, the lull before the storm. For soon outside forces are shown descending on the people here, threatening their traditional beliefs, values, and life-style.

The first disruption comes when the Public Works Department wishes to build a road through open fields which are sacred to Amma, the dumb woman who represents all that is unyielding and instinctive in rural existence. She owns several cows, which are the central symbols of material and spiritual wealth to the villagers. Amma's son, Nandan (Kulbhushan Kharbanda), next returns after having spent several years abroad, bringing in winds of change—and of war. He wishes to introduce modern farming techniques and to use the lands of his ancestors to produce more grains for the villagers. However, to draw water to irrigate the fields, he has to use a well that is sacred because it is near the local temple. The Brahmin priest, Venkatesh (Naseeruddin Shah), is a fiery and stern believer in what the scriptures have laid down and, although he and Nandan had played together as kids, he now opposes Nandan's projects. Matters get much worse when Nandan reveals he has an American wife, and she arrives soon after. As a beef-eating foreigner, Lydia (Paula Lindsay) is suspect from the start, an object of curiosity and hate. Nandan builds a Western-style ranch house for the two of them to live in, cutting himself off further from his mother and her ways. Although Lydia makes some attempts to understand the village folk and their customs, she is angered at their rejection of her. Defiantly, she orders one of Amma's cows to be slaughtered and its meat cooked for her. This action, taken in Nandan's absence on one of his frequent trips to the city, irrevocably pits the villagers and Amma against her son and his wife. Although he pays the fine and performs the rituals decided by the village elders, his mother does not forgive him. When she dies, partly through shock and grief, Nandan is not allowed to cremate her. He decides to sell his house and cows and leave the village with his wife and newborn son. Venkatesh and others urge him not to leave his ancestral place and to buy back the cows he has sold. In a last-attempt act, Nandan rushes to the cow dealer and is asked to identify his own cows. He is unable to do so, and as hordes of the animals surge past him toward the sunset, he stands there helplessly, a lone figure caught in the midst of modernity and tradition.

The word *godhuli* means dusk or sunset, that time of day which is neither light nor dark. Perhaps the state that the film suggests is that of those torn between the old and the new, the problem of identity of the educated Indian. Yet the village is too easily symbolic of tradition, of resistance to change, and of suspicion of the outsider. Such neat dichotomies do not begin to address the complex dynamics of village life, nor can such a framework provide an adequate basis for understanding modern India itself.

Shyam Benegal's *Manthan* does provide a more powerful sense of the divergent interests and clashes that motivate village life and the contradictions of even the most well meaning interventions from the larger entity that is the nation-state. It is arguably the best of Benegal's works (with the possible exception of *Bhumika* and *Mandi*), both for its concentrated social critique and its cinematic feel for the tempo of change in postcolonial India. *Manthan* is well known for its unusual mode of sponsorship. It was produced by 500,000 farmers of the state of Gujarat who had organized a milk cooperative and who each contributed two rupees for the film. Like *Godhuli*, *Manthan* too portrays the impact of Westernized technique on the village structure and its local "politics." Here again it is the metaphor of building or creating a new setup which opens onto the larger issues of power relationships and elite identity in contemporary India. The protagonist in this case does not belong to the village but is a complete outsider, a government official sent with his team to start a dairy cooperative in a small village. Dr. Rao (Girish Karnad) is a veterinarian, a professional anxious to do a job well but slightly condescending toward the villagers. His assistants, Deshmukh (Mohan Agashe) and Chandravarkar (Anant Nag), are also outsiders, the former urging separation from local rivalries and the latter with a roving eye, satirically portrayed as either given to sleep or sex.

In establishing the dairy cooperative, Dr. Rao and his colleagues meet with resistance from three directions, representing the three nodal points of power and powerlessness in the village. There is first Mishraji (Amrish Puri), owner of a private dairy, who has been underpaying the villagers for years and who stands most to lose if a cooperative is formed. Then there is the *sarpanch*, or village headman (Kulbhushan Kharbanda), who has a political stake in retaining control of the opinions of the villagers. And finally there is Bhola (Naseeruddin Shah), a fiery untouchable who has the capacity to make a difference in the balance of power because he represents the group that is most exploited and constitutes the bulk of humanity in the society. Rao and his associates attain a measure of success in their endeavors before the tide turns against them and vested interests assert themselves. Rao is charged with having seduced a village woman, Bindu (Smita Patil), and finally recalled to headquarters. But Bhola has taken up the cause with the untouchables, convincing them that the cooperative is theirs, not the outsiders', and the ending of the film suggests that change must come from within the ranks of the most oppressed social groups.

After its completion, *Manthan* was shown on super 8 in villages and was even part of a UN-sponsored seminar held in Seattle.[30] A frankly consciousness-raising film, *Manthan* combines a feel for the texture of village interactions with a cinematic rhythm of palpable energy. Its metaphor of the churning of village society and Indian consciousness in general serves well to capture a high moment in the new cinema's commitment to bring fresh insights into the politics of change.

Allegories of Aggression: *Aakrosh, Ardh Satya*

Aakrosh (*Cry of the Wounded*, 1980) is considered a "film of the second break"—it introduced fast-paced narrative and hence broke with the expectations of slowness that had become associated with the new cinema, particularly its regional variants. Structured like a political thriller in the style of Costa Gavras's *Z*, *Aakrosh* creates a tense atmosphere of lurking danger, unidentified assailants, and erupting violence in a world polarized into the powerful and the powerless (who are also voiceless). Directed by Govind Nihalani, its screenplay was written by the noted Marathi playwright Vijay Tendulkar. *Aakrosh*, which literally means "anger," is meant to evoke the anger of the average citizen-spectator through a vicarious positioning and identification with the exploited in the film. Its tight shots of the eyes of actor Om Puri (in the role of the captive tribal) that seem to burn holes in the screen suggest at once the need for penetrating vision as well as the failure of vision alone (cinema alone?) to alter social reality. The high-key lighting draws attention to the allegorical nature of the tale, to a national mood and ethos.

A bitter film, *Aakrosh* takes the complicitous corruption of those in high places so much for granted that it makes no pretense at well-developed characterization. Rather, the rottenness of the system is symbolized by the caricatures of its representatives: the politician, the district superintendent of police, the government doctor, the forest contractor, the public prosecutor, himself a tribal but with a deadened conscience. Grown fat on the system, they are men in middle age, too set in their ways to want any challenge to their power and authority. As in the films of Shyam Benegal, the exercise of social power is linked with sexuality and machismo. These men, particularly the forest contractor and his buddy, leer and smack their lips at the sight of women (there is a representative scene of a local woman dancing in a folk performance) and share smutty jokes. Against them the film pits youth—a struggling young defense lawyer, a leftist organizer working among the tribals, a jailed tribal and his beautiful dead wife. The hermeneutic code—who killed Bhiku's wife—does not need to be resolved because the film provides enough signals to implicate the authority figures. Rather, the question becomes whether Bhiku can be saved, and the answer we get is predetermined through a violent climax. By providing the accused with a symbolic noose to hang himself, to become the agent of his own condemnation, the film dilutes its social critique and substitutes a message of reform for that of radical change.

The narrative focus is on an Adivasi (tribal) named Lahanya Bhiku (Om Puri) who has been accused of killing his wife, Nagi (Smita Patil). His court-appointed lawyer is Bhaskar Kulkarni (Naseeruddin Shah), to whom Bhiku will say nothing and who tries earnestly to gather some evidence regarding the case. Bhiku's aged father and younger sister also refuse to talk. So does the editor of the local newspaper. But other sinister voices are heard. The public prosecutor, Dusane (Amrish Puri), gets abusive phone calls. The inane conversations of bridge-playing power brokers tell us what Bhiku's chances of a fair trial really are. Bhaskar himself is victimized by unknown attackers as he tries to unmask the actual people who he learns are responsible for Nagi's rape and death. Then Bhiku's father dies, and as his only son, Bhiku is allowed to perform the last rites. The fire that had burned at the beginning of the film when Bhiku's wife was being cremated now burns again, an obvious emblem of destruction and purification in the filmic text. Surrounded by the police, some tribals, including his weeping sister, and with his lawyer also present, Bhiku performs the ritual. Then, either in the heat of the moment or through long contemplation, we are not sure which, he takes this opportunity to strike a blow at the system that suppresses his group. Ironically the blow is self-directed—Bhiku axes down his own sister in an effort to "save" her from a fate similar to his wife's. Then his anguished cries rend the sky as he is overpowered by policemen. Bhaskar determines to carry on the fight on Bhiku's behalf through the judicial system. The upheavals of the individual conscience are made to signify systemic upheaval.

The events in the film are filtered through the perceptions, consciousness, and, occasionally, the body of the lawyer-protagonist, Bhaskar. The film is really about the consciousness-raising of the professional and middle classes, long the beneficiaries and representatives of Indian polity. Bhaskar's earnestness, good faith, and youthful energy at the be-

The wall of silence: Naseeruddin Shah as the well-meaning, ineffectual lawyer and Bhiku (Om Puri) as the wronged tribal, in Aakrosh (Cry of the Wounded).

ginning of the film are those of a naïve and well-intentioned person motivated by individualistic professional ambitions. A newcomer to the
area and a loner, he is anxious to build his own legal practice by winning
Bhiku's case. As the difficulties of getting evidence confront him, however, he is drawn into the "politics" of the region and senses invisible
forces at work. Physically attacked, pursued, and harassed, he is at last
able to identify with the tribals and distance himself from his mentor,
Dusane, the public prosecutor. The last scene of the film shows him
taking a stand by challenging Dusane's authority to determine the parameters of Bhaskar's actions and investigations. As he leaves Dusane's
office, the freeze frame indicates both the enormity of the struggle ahead
and the hope that the effort is alive.

Aakrosh presents self-enclosed worlds that have no means of communicating with one another. Three such worlds are depicted: that of the
tribals, representing the exploited underclass; that of the higher-ups,
representing political, bureaucratic, and business interests; and that of
the professional and educated class, exemplified by a lawyer, an editor,
and a Naxalite social worker. While the last group seeks to mediate
between the other two worlds, their inability to succeed (the editor gets

Aakrosh: *Bhiku's anguished cry against an oppressive system. The Museum of Modern Art/Film Stills Archive.*

beaten up and refuses to talk to Bhaskar, the social worker is kidnapped and presumed killed, Bhaskar is unable to win Bhiku's confidence) denotes a vision of social paralysis in contemporary India. But the most disturbing note in the film is that, ultimately, the exploiters and the exploited become mirror-images of one another. They are linked through violence and through a kind of self-protective inner solidarity. Since neither world is fleshed out, we have no means of understanding their inner dynamics. Power is a monolith concentrated in a government-business-landlord complex. And the oppressed are the objects of a paternalism on the part of well-meaning outsiders. Neither scenario is equipped to channelize the anger that the film's title and theme evoke.

Finally, mention must be made of the filmic references in *Aakrosh*, particularly the use of a stanza from a very popular song "sung" by the poet-hero in Guru Dutt's classic *Pyaasa*. "Burn up! Burn up! Burn up, erase this world," is the frustrated and anguished cry of the character who feels misunderstood and exploited by society. The viewer's recognition of the soundtrack is followed by the shot that reveals the mundane setting of the song excerpt: a cheap restaurant in which Bhaskar is having a meal and the song is coming from an overhead radio. Despite its "realistic" context and the obvious thematic parallel being drawn between the two films, this tribute to the commercial cinema suggests a vision of collectivity and a shared cinematic memory denied within the terms of the film's narrative. A "flashback" to the fifties, the Bombay cinema's golden age, the song serves as a nostalgic evocation of "popular" cinema as well as a more "hopeful" period of Indian nationhood. (The irony, of course, is that the text of the song belies the hope the fifties generation is supposed to have felt.) The moment of collective awareness is brief and itself becomes a memory studded in the harsh texture of the film's allegorical surface.

Ardh Satya (*Half-Truth*, 1983), also directed by Govind Nihalani from a script by Vijay Tendulkar, evokes the notion of liminality and ambiguity in its very title. The film works its message on several levels: poetic and philosophical, sexual-pathological, social and political. It is the way all the levels are articulated together that makes the film an artistic and popular triumph. In an early scene, the protagonist-hero reads a poem by Dilip Chitre, a Marathi poet, which encapsulates the film's mood and tone. Referring to life as a maze and to death as oblivion, it is a philosophical rumination on border states of consciousness, the half-truth, the feeling in between impotence and masculinity as metaphors for action.

Generically, *Ardh Satya* spreads itself in different directions. Part action film, part social tract, part psychological drama, the film is able to match the demands of a fast-paced narrative with the probing of social and psychological issues through mechanisms of viewer identification and vicarious fantasy. The action revolves around a police officer, Anant Walenkar (Om Puri), who is stationed in crime-infested Bombay, signifier of contemporary urban India. The opening scene of the film evokes this milieu by showing Walenkar in a disco party where loud music and flashing lights mark the rhythm of swaying bodies. Such settings in the new cinema suggest Western-style affluence, the aspirations of the middle class, the backdrop of urban life, and the lure of the popular cinema. Here it serves the function of the meeting between Walenkar and Jyotsna Gokhale (Smita Patil), the female lead in the film.

Thematically, *Ardh Satya* takes on the Indian police department in order to expose the corruption within. This world is signified through the vicissitudes of Anant's professional career and its link with his personal degradation. The early sequences show him as an enthusiastic police officer, locking up petty criminals and street hooligans. One such occa-

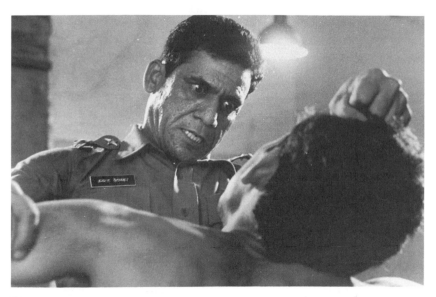

The psychopathology of violence: police brutality in Ardh Satya (Half-Truth).

sion brings him in contact with Rama Shetty, an underworld boss who also happens to have access to the highest echelons of the police service and government. Shetty tries to buy off Walenkar at their first meeting, but Walenkar spurns his offer and the two become sworn enemies. Thereafter, events show Walenkar paying the price for confronting Shetty, who is well-connected politically. As the protagonist evokes the wrath of his superiors, he is demoralized and starts drinking heavily. ("I felt I had been stripped naked and someone was spitting on me," Walenkar recalls later in an image reminiscent of Ousmane Sembene's *Xala.*) In an violent outburst, he kills a man in police custody and loses his job and, soon, his girlfriend. As events reveal the unlimited power of the villain, Shetty, Walenkar sees only one way out. He kills Shetty and delivers himself up to the police.

The half-shades evoked by the title of this film find visual dramatization through the systematic alternation of night sequences with day sequences, the former filmed in a bluish and high-key lighting, the latter in more even lighting. More significantly, violence as a lurking underside to the individual and social psyche is aligned to the diurnal cycle, the most violent episodes taking place at night and the "lighter" sequences taking place during the day (although there are exceptions). Violence, it is suggested, is as inevitable as night following day, the day-night continuum representing the social system and not the natural world. The film brings together different kinds of violence within its national-allegorical universe: male violence toward women (Walenkar's father routinely strikes his wife), police brutality, mob and gang brutality. Critics have read the violent/masculine discourse of the film only in personal-psychological terms, but that provides a very schematic interpretation and misses its moral, philosophical, and political implications and imbrications. For it is with the corrosive effects of brutalization on the soul that the film is concerned.

Violence as theme and metaphor sustains both the social critique and the dramatic tension of the narrative. The verbal-thematic play on the contradictory forces of masculinity and impotence is important here. It is ironic that the very masculinity that is Anant Walenkar's source of strength (he is commended as a conscientious police officer, which in India's widely acknowledged corrupt police system must be taken as a positive sign) also contains the seeds of his uncontrollable fits of anger and brutality. But these "fits" are most often brought on by what he perceives as disrespect and offensive behavior of males toward women. By contrast, the masculinity and male chauvinism associated with his father, a former police inspector himself, is portrayed decidedly as a negative force. Anant's sense of masculinity is his Achilles' heel: simultaneously his strength and weakness. Jyotsna, a college teacher and embodiment of rational thinking, cannot understand it. She abhors Anant's violent outbursts and in rejecting them rejects him.

Impotence, on the other hand, is associated with moral cowardice (he was never able, in flashback sequences, to intercede with his father on his mother's behalf), frustration on the job, and despair after losing it. His final act to reclaim his masculinity at once redeems and destroys him. By killing Shetty he has rid the Bombay underworld of a powerful crook but only through the ultimate act of violence and pent-up hatred. His grand gesture of social service must nevertheless remain pitiful as a single hollow blow against a mountain of political and systemic corruption.

The new cinema impetus in India has been governed by the desire on the part of some filmmakers to present viewers with an alternative to the dominant popular "song-and-dance" film. Film, they believed, should be a truer reflection of social reality, an instrument of social critique, and a site of formal experimentation. In practice, these aims tended to remain separate, at least in the early instances of the new cinema.

(Roughly, *Sara Akash* represented the first type, *Bhuvan Shome* the second, and *Uski Roti* the third.) More generally, the new cinema has shared an interest in linear narrative, "realistic" mise-en-scène, psychological portrayal of character, the "motivated" use of songs and dances (as and when required by the context of the film), explicit scenes of sexuality, and a disenchantment with the workings of the Indian political system. It is the latter dimension that has been of interest in the films discussed above. The choice of language (Hindi) in these films determines to a large extent their terms of address and their stylistic components. Addressing a national, as opposed to a regional, audience, they strain toward a language of common identity and employ many crossover elements: background songs (*Tarang*), pop music and a Westernized milieu (*Kalyug, Ardh Satya*), the love story with a tragic ending (*Garm Hawa*), iconographic presentation of moral forces (*Aakrosh, Manthan*), the rural-urban divide (*Godhuli*). Perhaps it is a reflection of the current state of intellectual crisis in India that the vision embodied in each of these films is exceedingly bleak. With the exception of *Garm Hawa*, each film ends with death and destruction.

But the question ultimately to be faced by the new cinema is: Can a progressive and secular national culture be based on negativity? Can the ideology of regionalism and authenticity spark a substantive change in consciousness? The history of other art movements which have been rooted in nationalist concerns (for example, in Latin America) shows that writers and artists can spark a response when their works explore a utopian dimension of the communitarian experience, when they build as well as break. Structures of myth and memory are important for the mobilization of consciousness toward change. Even as enjoyable a film as *Jaane Bhi Do Yaro* (*Let It Go, Guys!*, 1984), which uses parody and a combination of the buddy film and the detective thriller to mercilessly satirize political corruption in contemporary India, ultimately only gives in to the feeling of frustration and helplessness on the part of the average citizen. As its two lower-middle-class protagonists become scapegoats of the machinations of the unscrupulous power brokers of society, including politicians, big business, and the press, the bleakest of scenarios emerges. The solution is not, of course, to introduce facile happy endings, as the commercial cinema is accused of doing, but to consider the possibilities of a language of the popular that people can identify with.

Given the complicated situation in which filmmakers have found themselves, not only in terms of production and distribution opportunities but in terms of the more "invisible" factors of taste and upbringing, including class differences between the filmmakers and the bulk of India's movie-going population, even trenchant social critique may fail to make inroads on the legitimacy of the powers that be and may even strengthen them by making them patronize works critical of the establishment. Ultimately, India over the last three decades or so has lacked a unifying revolutionary movement or experience that might abolish the distance between the creators of culture and the consumers of culture. The cultural elite's traditional hostility to mass culture has been shared by the new cinema. Although the new filmmakers and their critical exponents often invoke the names of Walter Benjamin and Bertolt Brecht as sources of inspiration in radical art, they do not share these Europeans' larger social vision or their technological optimism. Rather, in identifying commercial culture with the American influence, they have sought refuge in different forms of European modernism with its aversion to mass culture. Maybe what we have witnessed so far is the first phase of the new cinema, its destructive phase; the regenerative phase, that which can fashion out of destruction and the signs of social and moral decay a new language of collective desire, is yet to come.

Who will listen to the tale of my woeful heart?
Far and wide I have wandered on the face of this earth
And I have much to impart.
—*Umrao Jan Ada*, The Courtesan of Lucknow

Woman and the Burden of Postcoloniality

The Courtesan Film Genre

The courtesan, as historical character and cinematic spectacle, is one of the most enigmatic figures to haunt the margins of Indian cultural consciousness. Variously described as dancing girl, nautch-girl, prostitute, or harlot, she appears again and again in Indian cultural texts, at once celebrated and shunned, used and abused, praised and condemned. Socially decentered, she is yet the object of respect and

269

admiration because of her artistic training and musical accomplishments. The embodiment of a charged sexuality, she is as often associated in popular culture with the madonna. A bazaar entertainer, she is paradoxically the repository of the traditions of a vanished age and a lost way of life. Economically independent, she is portrayed as yearning for the affections and protection of a man. Because the figure of the courtesan lends itself to a whole range of interpretations, it is richly invested with allegorical possibilities. Skirting the boundaries of the legitimate and the illegitimate, an intricate blend of Hindu and Muslim social graces, this ambiguous icon of Indian womanhood and female power-cum-vulnerability serves as the analog of a national palimpsest inscribed with contradictory social meanings. In the postindependence era, the representation of the courtesan and/or prostitute[1] projects a view of woman at once humiliating and tantalizing, essentialized and active. Her identity a play upon impersonation, the figure of the prostitute allows the culture to probe some of its own assumptions regarding sexuality, social mores, and human growth.

The courtesan/prostitute film has enjoyed wide and consistent popularity in India and has been a favored subject of even the respected Bombay filmmakers. From *Mamta* (*Mother Love*, 1966) to *Mandi* (*Marketplace*, 1983), *Pakeezah* (*The Pure One*, 1971) to *Bhumika* (*The Role*, 1977), *Amar Prem* (*Eternal Love*, 1971) to *Utsav* (*Festival*, 1985), from *Chetna* (1970), *Dastak* (1970), and *Khilona* (*Toy*, 1970) to *Ram Teri Ganga Maili* (*Ram, Your Ganges Is Polluted*, 1987) and *Salaam Bombay!* (1987), filmmakers have repeatedly turned to the oldest profession in the world to make their statements about the present. Nor is the prostitute of less significance in those films in which she does not occupy the primary narrative and visual space. As the "other" woman, her role often supersedes that of the heroine: Chandramukhi in *Devdas* (1955), Gulab in *Pyaasa* (*The Thirsty One*, 1957), Kishori in *Kala Pani* (*Prison*, 1958), and Tulsi in *Main Tulsi Tere Angan Ki* (*I Am the Basil Plant in Your Courtyard*, 1978) come most easily to mind. These outcast women are nurturing and sacrificing, beautiful and gentle, prostitutes with golden hearts who help and nourish the hero. Whether as a poignant reflection of dependence on the values of a manmade world or as a searing metaphor of postcolonial political corruption and moral decay (for example, in Satyajit Ray's *Jana Aranya* [*The Middleman*, 1975]), prostitution denotes a masquerading social and moral universe. Men must enter the

The prostitute with a heart of gold: Chandramukhi (Vyjayantimala) and Devdas (Dilip Kumar) in Devdas. *Courtesy Bimal Roy Productions. The Museum of Modern Art/Film Stills Archive.*

prostitute's quarters shamefacedly or in some form of disguise. She herself is no more real than her reflection in a mirror.

Indeed, mirror imagery is abundant in courtesan films, giving added dimension to the metaphor of woman as essentially "split" (virgin/whore, for example) and as the looking-glass held up to man. For if, as Virginia Woolf said, "women have served all these centuries as looking-glasses possessing the magic and delicious power of reflecting the figure of man at twice his natural size,"[2] what is the significance of woman being placed in front of a mirror, in short, the mirroring of the mirror? Does woman, in a reversal of Woolf's statement, appear at half *her* natural size? Or does this doubling of the image suggest a simultaneous distantiation of woman from herself, a sign of her emptiness and social negation *and* a displaced narcissism on the part of the (Indian) male? And then, is man to be the agent of her problematic (because necessarily partial) reentry into the "fullness" of a social subjecthood? Her identity

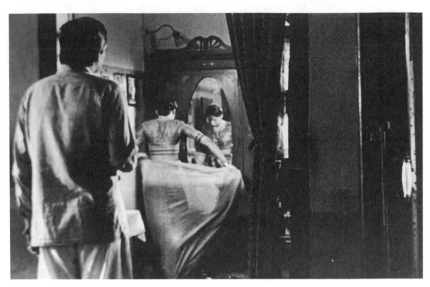

Mirror imagery as motif in the courtesan film: Smita Patil and Amol Palekar in Bhumika (The Role).

as various and dispersed as her lovers, the prostitute of the Bombay film is on a perpetual quest, seeking the answer to the enigma of herself.

The enigma has relevance for feminist film theory as well. For the woman viewers in the audience, does the primacy of the female image (courtesan films are woman-centered), whether or not deflected through a mirror, allow forms of identification that legitimize a female subjectivity? Does the representation of the courtesan as subject and as a producer of culture (positionalities traditionally denied to women in systems of symbolic exchange) alter the terms of address of this cinema? The courtesan film provides a space to raise these concerns as well. In the matriarchal universe signified by the courtesan culture, at once economically dependent on and yet distinct from the world of men, can female values be nurtured and a female utopia visualized? And what is the significance of this utopia being conceived by men (since all courtesan films are by male directors)? What, in short, is the courtesan film's social and cinematic currency in postcolonial India? Herself a colonized image, can the courtesan narrative suggest decolonization? As both a threatened and threatening icon of cultural (in)difference, the figure of the courtesan allows us to explore the psychosexual dimension of the Indian national imaginary.

Identifying Generic Elements of the Courtesan Film

Variations on the motif of imminent prostitution are to be found in almost every commercial film: stagings of the attempted rape scene, the cabaret dancer scene, the misfortunes and social ostracism of the unwed mother, the Westernized heroine or vamp lurching, wineglass in hand, toward sinister-looking men at a bar or club, the orphan girl trapped in a den of vice, the village woman assaulted by phallic glances (if not actually molested) in the big bad city. Apart from the dramatic potentialities and voyeuristic elements of these scenarios of libidinal excess, these scenes reinforce the sense of female vulnerability in the face of male power and aggression. These stereotypical portrayals have led to a blanket critical denunciation of the "negative" images of woman in the Bombay film, images that cast woman, to use Aruna Vasudev's phrase, as either "vamp or victim."[3]

On the face of it, the prostitute/courtesan film would seem to be the classic instance of female objectification in the cinema. Here is the representation of woman as spectacle par excellence: she is a body to be looked at, the place of sexuality, an object of desire—everything, in short, that the apparatus of cinema purveys and that the misogynistic tendencies prevalent in Indian culture exploit. Indian feminists have followed their Western sisters in denouncing a Hollywood-informed Indian cinema whose symbolic language is given to sexist stereotyping of women. We are indebted to (the first phase of) feminist film theory for our awareness of woman in cinema as "object of the male gaze," the commodified image as fetish, and the independent woman who is not so independent after all. But cinemas are culture-specific and nation-specific, so that distinctive Indian modes of critique have to evolve that directly address different systems of meaning and signification. A feminist reading of patriarchy that would view all versions of woman as signifier as one and the same is in danger of producing its own brand of essentialism and universalism. The focus, by contrast, has to be on the cultural notions of femininity that inform different symbolic systems. The Bombay film's vast repertoire of female representation has not been explored in any systematic way so far, although its dominant forms (encapsulated by the vamp or victim formulation) have been recalled often enough by feminists and critics in India. However, the "reflection theory" (how images of women fail to reflect their actual lives or identities) does not begin to address the power of these images and their pleasurable address to spectators, both male and female. A more generic approach, inflected by history and culture, to films depicting women may provide a better grasp of the elements that construct their distinctive appeal.

Courtesan films, although a staple of the Bombay cinema, have changed over the years. In the thirties, forties, and fifties, filmmakers like B. R. Chopra and V. Shantaram, who used the film medium for overt social messages, portrayed the trajectory of the prostitute from that of fallen woman to one restored to social respectability through marriage. The "rescue" scenario, wherein the unfortunate woman trapped in a life of moral degradation is rescued by a good man, dominated these films. *Aadmi (Man,* 1939), *Sadhana (Prayer,* 1958), and *Kanch ki Guriya (Glass Doll,* 1961) are some well-known instances. A combination of economic necessity and the desire to escape from unscrupulous men also served as diegetic motivations that portrayed woman's "fall." *Adalat (Court,* 1957) contains some of the seeds that were to find more complete and separate development in later versions of the courtesan film genre. A melodrama, *Adalat* is about a young girl (Nargis) from a poor family who secretly marries her rich college sweetheart (Pradeep Kumar) in a temple and soon after has a son. Her husband goes abroad for further studies, and in his absence the girl is thrown out into the streets by her in-laws, who refuse to accept her as their son's wife. She experiences extreme misery and hardship and is reduced to begging, unable even to feed her baby. In this condition she is spotted by a pimp (Pran) and lured to a brothel, where she is forced to sing and dance to earn her living. Unable to escape, she gives up her son to the care of a woman doctor friend so that her disreputable existence will not cast a shadow on his life. Gradually, she becomes a famous singer/courtesan and years later is able to meet her long-lost husband. She convinces him that even though her life-style was disreputable, her body had been untouched by strange men (in keeping with the fifties' image of the "pure" heroine). But the pimp-villain does not leave her alone and continues to blackmail her. Driven to desperation, she kills him, is jailed, and faces prosecution by her own estranged son, now a lawyer. She dies in the courtroom after her identity is revealed to her son and the madonna image is reinstated. (A variation of this plot appeared in the popular film *Mamta,* discussed later, in which the famous Bengali actress Suchitra Sen played a double role as the prostitute/destitute mother and her respected/educated lawyer daughter.) A discourse on the nature and definition of public and private (home and brothel, morality and legality, body and "art"), *Adalat* articulates the themes circulating around the representation of woman as at once central and marginal, idealized and tragic.

Adalat, as a precursor text, has several features of note. First, the courtesan film emerges as a vehicle for the acting talents of women. Nargis, Meena Kumari, Vyjayantimala, Suchitra Sen, and Sharmila Tagore, all top-rated actresses, took these roles at the height of their careers. Later, when women's roles were somewhat eclipsed by the male-oriented violent action films of the postsixties era, actresses found their histrionic abilities fully engaged by the courtesan film. Rekha, Smita Patil, and Shabana Azmi, the foremost names of recent times among film actresses, have given fine performances in courtesan films. Like the Hollywood film noir, this genre signaled a woman-centered film. Second, the "normal" world and its values are overturned in the courtesan film, primarily definitions of "home." Threatening parental figures are often responsible for turning daughters out into the streets. And finally, different social worlds collide and meet across the body of the courtesan, primarily to disrupt or challenge notions of justice as impartial and objective. If the home is alien, the courtroom often becomes a "home" in terms of the familial relationships that are revealed in the course of testimony to exist between key characters and the reconciliations that take place.

The full-fledged courtesan film of recent decades may be said to be of three types. Of the first type are those that present famous courtesans from Indian history or ancient texts. Amrapali, the celebrated courtesan of the time of King Bimbisara of Magadha (second century B.C.), Chitralekha, known to have existed in the time of Chandragupta Maurya (second century B.C.), and Vasantsena, from a fourth-century play, belong to this category. A modern variation of some of the features of this mode can be found in *Bhumika,* based on the life of a Marathi stage actress who was known for her "colorful" life-style. The second category encompasses those films in which prostitution is a condition into which young girls are initiated as a result of unfortunate or impecunious circumstances. *Umrao Jan, Pakeezah,* and to a lesser extent *Dastak* as well as the earlier *Sadhana, Adalat,* and *Kala Pani* belong to this type. The third category explores the prostitute as the embodiment of maternal love and self-sacrifice, as in *Mamta* and *Amar Prem.* A recent film like *Mandi* defies the above categories, portraying life in a brothel in a parodic vein of macabre humor and irony.

A key element in this genre is the idea of woman's social and psychic transformation. Unlike the physical transformations possible for male figures, here it is a change that is primarily one of semantics and involves a process of renaming. And while the adoption of different disguises by male characters does not preclude a return to a prior state, in the case of the women of this genre, the change or cross-over is irrevocable. As women who are renamed (resemanticized) and thereby take on the identity of a radically social other, the move can only be in one direction. "Jan" and "Bai" (as in Umrao Jan or Akhtari Bai) are name-suffixes that discursively mark differences of social status and respectability among women. Within the available literature on the woman's film in the Western tradition, not much has been written on the figure of the prostitute,[4] although attention has been devoted to representations of the prostitute in nineteenth-century Western literature and painting.[5] The treatment of the ambiguously sexualized female figure as an example of androgyny, particularly the androgyny of the Marlene Dietrich persona in *Blonde Venus* who is dressed in a man's clothes, is not very helpful for our purposes.[6] For the figure of the Indian film courtesan raises the interesting problem of woman's impersonation of/as woman.

One might consider here the ramifications of the courtesan taking on a different name and identity. While losing social prestige, she gains the earning capacity of a man. The courtesan "impersonates" (in the sense of standing in for) a man in her economic independence, her ability to turn the tables on men by having them beg (or threaten) her for money. (Popular cultural stereotypes still depict the working woman as desexed/defeminized.) Money as a sexualized metaphor as well as an item of exchange becomes the basis for women's simultaneous dependence and independence. In Kumar Shahani's *Tarang* (*Wave*, 1984), the capitalist boss makes love to a deceased worker's wife and then offers her money, thereby treating her like a common prostitute. Stung, she cries out against this humiliation. On subsequent occasions, however, she insists on being paid and uses the money to further the workers' struggle for better wages and living conditions. Like the phallus, it (money) passes from man to woman, weakening (according to Hindu tradition) the former (through repeated loss of semen, the life-force) and empowering the latter. The prostitute's autonomy is linked to money, which nevertheless may also serve to identify her as a loose woman. In this way Indian mass culture links the taint of money with the taint of woman.

The Courtesan in Indian Culture

Our understanding of these films as well as the significance of courtesans in general can be enhanced if we examine their role and function
in Indian society through the ages. Two studies are particularly helpful
in this regard, Moti Chandra's *The World of Courtesans* and Frédérique
Apffel Marglin's *Wives of the God-King*.[7] While Marglin's is a contemporary study of the last traces of religious prostitution as practiced by
the *devadāsīs* (literally, female servants of the deity) of Puri, Chandra
reconstructs the secular "classical phase" of this phenomenon as revealed in a variety of Sanskrit texts. As Havelock Ellis has shown in the
case of ancient Greece,[8] Chandra finds prostitution well established and
respected in ancient India. He traces the existence of courtesans all the
way to the Rig Vedic age, thousands of years ago, cataloging the available references to them in the major treatises and literary works of both
ancient and medieval times. A complex picture emerges of an institution
that was prevalent in all parts of India and toward which moral oppro-
brium existed side by side with widespread social acceptance.

The concepts of pleasure, luxury, physical adornment, and sexual
enticement seem to predominate in the references to courtesans. They
were employed by kings, rich merchants, and bankers, and the harem
was a well-built structure in the palace provided with many luxuries.
But although appreciated (often secretly), courtesans were called har-
lots, wenches, streetwalkers, and even murderesses. Chandra writes:
"Whether she evoked pity or whether she was condemned, the courtesan
flourished and no stigma seems to have been attached to the profession."[9] Marglin corroborates this stance when she writes· "Clearly, *ap-
saras, ganikās, veśyās* and *devadāsīs*, even though contrasted to chaste
wives and even sometimes reviled in the texts as low and not deserving
of respect because of their lack of chastity, have a place and a time in
which their function is required, highly appreciated and, in its context,
highly respected."[10]

The most crucial aspects relate to the economic organization of the
prostitute's body and the social worth of her cultural attainments. The
Arthaśāstra states that different grades of courtesans and prostitutes paid
money to the state by way of taxes. Their profession being an important
source of revenue to the state, their rights and privileges were naturally
recognized. Social stratification is also indicated by the profusion of

names by which they were called: *gaṇikā, pratigaṇikā, rūpājīvā, veśyā, dāsī, devadāsī, puṁśchalī, śilpakārikā, kauśikastrī,* and *rūpadāsi.*[11] Texts from the early centuries of the Christian era, notably Vatsyayana's *Kamasutra* and Bharata's *Nātyaśastra,* bring together the arts of erotic play and acting and entertainment through the person of the accomplished courtesan.

According to Chandra, courtesans gained dignity up to the Gupta period (as witnessed in the poetry of Kalidāsa, with its vivid descriptions of their beauty, grace, and charm). In the medieval period, however, emphasis is placed on "the sex aspects of the profession and on its perfidies."[12] Some commentators have seen further decline with the advent of the Muslims. However, other accounts are more persuasive, and it is perhaps not incorrect to say that it is their cultural contributions during Mughal times that most informs contemporary notions of the courtesan. During the later Mughal period in the eighteenth and nineteenth centuries, courtesan culture was patronized by the nawabs and flourished in North India, particularly Lucknow. Essayist, historian, and novelist Abdul Halim Sharar (1860–1926) commented on the social standing of famous courtesans. In contrast to Europe, he wrote, these women "participated more or less as equals in the gatherings of refined and polished people. . . . The houses of Chaudhrayan Haidar Jan and some other courtesans of high status were the 'clubs' of genteel people."[13]

Marglin's sensitive awareness of the ambivalence surrounding the *devadāsī* and dancing-girl tradition ascribes a change in native consciousness to the influence of Western ideas that followed in the wake of colonialism. Quoting an early European viewpoint (that of the Abbé Dubois in the late eighteenth century), she notes the terms of moral condemnation used, along with a reluctant admiration. "This mixture of the sinful and the sensuously beautiful is Europe's classical recipe for the exotic," she writes.[14] It was not Europe's fascination with the subject but rather its moral censure that entirely influenced Indian reformers, who felt "they could reclaim the beauty only at the cost of separating it from what they themselves came to see as sinful and deserving of moral condemnation."[15] A virulent antinautch campaign was mounted, and temple dancers, now reidentified as prostitutes, were legislatively controlled. (Singing and dancing, the millennia-old practices of courtesans, evoke mixed reactions among many Western-educated Indians.)

British legislation wrought significant changes in the social standing of courtesans, as in so much else. In her study of the nawabi culture of

Lucknow, Veena Oldenburg writes that the health concerns of British soldiers visiting prostitutes led to laws regulating the latter's conduct and life-style. As a result of British interference, this profession was gradually debased into common prostitution. Oldenburg notes: "The world of the courtesans of Lucknow was as complex and hierarchical as the society of which it was part. Under the generous patronage of the nawabs of Oudh and the town notables during the eighty-odd years that Lucknow served as the nawabi capital, the apartments in the Chowk bazaar, where these women lived and entertained in decadent opulence, were centers for musical and cultural soirees."[16]

The highly organized world that Oldenburg describes finds many echoes in films. A courtesan was usually part of a household establishment under the chief courtesan, or *chaudhrayan*. The latter owned and maintained apartments, having acquired wealth and fame through her beauty and musical accomplishments. It was typical for a wealthy patron, often the king himself, to set her up in pleasant quarters and maintain her household in the style in which he wished to be entertained. She in turn recruited budding young singers, dancers, and musicians to compete with other reputable establishments. We are told that Ameer Jan (later Ameer Mahal), a dancing girl, made her debut in Wajid Ali Shah's *parikhana*, or "fairy house," was later married to the king, and was then divorced. She resumed her career as a courtesan along with the king's other divorced wives.

Oldenburg provides several historical details of interest. Every reputable house maintained a team of skilled male musicians who were often connected to famous lineages, or *gharana*s, of musicians, thereby enhancing the prestige of the establishment. Doormen, touts, and other male auxiliaries, often sons or nephews of the chief courtesan, screened clients at the door and acted as sentries of the house. The other members of the house were females, often related to or close associates (daughters, nieces, cousins) of the *chaudhrayan* who formed a core group of *tawaʔif*s (courtesans). They were intensively trained from an early age (seven or eight years old) to dance, sing, converse, amuse, and excel in the "exaggerated politeness for which Lucknow had acquired a special reputation during the *nawabi*." To acquire social fastidiousness, the young sons of the gentry were sent to the salons of the best-known *tawaʔif*s for lessons in etiquette and the proper appreciation of Urdu poetry.

If the nawabs had perceived these women as a cultural asset, the British Raj saw them as a necessary evil, if not a threat, and sought to make of them an inexpensive answer to the sexual needs of single European soldiers by insisting on clinical standards of personal hygiene. The government taxed their income and regulated their contact with Europeans, which had interesting effects on patrons and clients alike. With Wajid Ali Shah in exile after 1856, the profession lost its chief patron and several lesser ones but gained numerous practitioners from among the abandoned wives of the ex-king and the nobles who went into exile. These women resumed their careers (for several of the royal harem had been singing and dancing women) to support themselves, the profession having become more competitive with hard times.

Their new patrons were a breed created by the new rulers, whether they were landowners on frequent trips to the capital or European soldiers roving the city after dark. The soldiers understood little or none of the urbane Urdu speech used in the salons. Having neither taste, time, nor money to partake of the pleasures of the nautch, they made short businesslike trips to the *chaklakhana* (brothel). In time prostitutes displaced the old-world courtesan to meet the demands of the new ruling elite. The heyday of the retired *tawaʾif*s of Lucknow was the period between 1920 to 1940. Oldenburg informs us that the final blow to the profession came from the Indian government, which abolished *zamindari* rights in 1957 and declared existing salons illegal. "To this must be added the change in taste wrought by the British: a garden party, a cricket match, a play, or the races now competing with the *mujara* or 'nautch' to amuse those with means."[17]

Courtesans of the Screen

Courtesans, therefore, occupy a separate though special place in Indian culture and consciousness. The Hindi cinema explores this "otherness" through modes of impersonation that hauntingly play upon questions of identity and difference. Since courtesans are regarded both as cultural capital and as social disease, their self-perception is portrayed as a fragmented one. As mentioned earlier, mirrors and caged birds serve as dominant imagery to denote the relationships of courtesans to themselves and the outside world. The journey motif, including the journey of life itself encapsulated in "biographical" films, also underscores the lack of stability and the certainty of change as endemic to the courtesan culture. At once dependent on and insulated from the world of men, the brothel nurtures talent as well as illusion, provides emotional support together with the longing for escape. This tension is maintained through the generic stability of these films. Most of them have excellent song and dance sequences (*mujras*) performed in the presence of male clients and patrons through which the public nature of a prostitute's life unfolds. The narrative is one of romantic love and longing, passion and forbidden dreams. Although men exploit her body and her talents, it is to men (or, rather, to a special man) that the screen courtesan/prostitute turns to fulfill her dreams.

These woman-centered films, then, raise a number of questions regarding male projections of female power and vulnerability in postcolonial India. How has the Bombay film projected the image of the courtesan? How are the notions of art and entertainment associated with the nautch-girl articulated with the cinema's own discursive regime? Can the brothel signify an alternative female space? Is the brothel setup a prototype of a matriarchal culture in which the normal male-female hierarchies of the social world are subverted? How does the courtesan film negotiate the boundary that separates woman (fictional construct) and women (historical beings), as Teresa de Lauretis has distinguished the terms? What follows are some analyses that illuminate these concerns. My readings are inflected by the premise that the figuration of the whore's body is one more form of impersonation through which the narrative of the nation constructs itself.

The Courtesan as Historical Artifact

In 1984, Girish Karnad made *Utsav*, a big-budget film adapted from a classic Sanskrit play of the fourth century A.D. entitled *Mrichchhakatikam* (*The Little Clay Cart*) by Sudraka. A story of "pimps, prostitutes and common life," the film was made simultaneously in Hindi and in English for the international as well as the Indian market and cost Rs. 1 crore (one hundred million). The double task involved in this enterprise was matched by other well-publicized crossover elements. Girish Karnad, himself a playwright turned filmmaker who had the reputation of belonging to the "new cinema" but acting in commercial films, was now moving from a low-budget film to a big-budget one. Moreover, Rekha, the foremost star of the commercial cinema, had the leading role in *Utsav*. Whether the making of this film signaled Karnad's disenchant-

Nostalgia for an erotic past? Vasantsena (Rekha) as the legendary courtesan of ancient India in Utsav *(Festival).*

ment with the parallel cinema, or an effort to "redeem" the popular cinema, or to put a fresh aspect on it is difficult to say. Perhaps all three motivations were at work.

As a period film centered around the life of a courtesan, *Utsav* both draws upon and seeks to detach itself from the tone and thematic concerns of the by now well-established courtesan genre. Adopting a stage convention, *Utsav* opens with a prologue: a man and a woman in contemporary dress directly address the spectators, inviting them to symbolically enter the ancient world. These figures, we find, soon "reenter" the diegesis and double as characters. Other distantiating devices are humor and exaggerated characterization. Karnad noted that "the film has no message, political, social, or of any other kind. The basis is the Sanskrit theory that a work of art should create a *rasa*, a mood, an evocation of emotion—not preach. What I hoped to do was to revive the two qualities which ancient Indian literature had, but which we seem to have lost in the course of the last thousand years—sensuousness and humour. Not sex, but sensuousness, the poetic, tactile quality of it." [18] These two designated modes, however, remain separate in the film, sensuousness being the property of the sequences associated with the courtesan and humor that of the larger social world represented in the film. There is a romanticism, an etherealization of the courtesan, as well as a fetishization of her body that contrast sharply with the earthiness of many of the other characters. Thus the effect of authentic historical details that the film achieves ("since we wanted to retain the 4th century background, a lot of spadework and considerable research were required"—Karnad) does not extend to the depiction of its central character, Vasantsena, the legendary courtesan of Ujjain.

Like other courtesan-heroines, Vasantsena is beautiful, generous, passionate, and emotionally vulnerable. Although she reputedly commands wide influence and respect, she is presented as weak and in need of male protection. The first sequence shows her being pursued by two ruffians, Samasthanaka, the king's comical and bull-headed brother-in-law, and his companion. By a series of mistaken identities, Vasantsena is able to get into Charudutt, a Brahmin's house, where he is all alone, his wife and son having gone away for a few days. Here we get our first look at the beautiful courtesan, as seen through the eyes of an admiring Charudutt. Heavily adorned with gold ornaments, Vasantsena is temptation incarnate, and Charudutt does not need much persuasion to succumb to the proffered pleasures of the flesh. Afterwards, Vasantsena leaves her ornaments behind to avoid being attacked by thieves on the way home. The ornaments now seem to take on a life of their own as they change hands in rapid succession and contribute to the complications of the plot. As an extension of their owner, the gold ornaments serve "magically" to solve many problems and to link the several characters in the film. Charudutt gives the bundle for safekeeping to his friend Maitraya, who sleeps with it under his head. From there it passes into the hands of the thief, Sajjal, who has come to rob Charudutt's home in order to have money to purchase the freedom of his beloved, Madanika, who is Vasantsena's personal maid. When Madanika finds out about Sajjal's theft, she thinks the jewelry was stolen from Vasantsena herself and approaches her mistress in fear. But Vasantsena knows the truth and, accepting her ornaments back, grants Madanika her freedom.

The ornaments also serve the function of bringing Vasantsena and Charudutt's wife together. As a dutiful Hindu wife, Kamala tries to compensate for Charudutt's carelessness in losing Vasantsena's ornaments by sending her own last piece of jewelry to the courtesan. She then leaves home in seeming anger at her husband's infidelity, only to return the next day to meet Vasantsena, who she knows will enter the house as she exits. Relaxing in Charudutt's bed after a night of passionate love-

making, Vasantsena jumps up when Kamala announces herself. Charudutt's wife is not offended but, rather, proud that the famous and beautiful courtesan is in love with her husband. Thereafter the two women
develop a warm friendship, in the course of which Vasantsena puts her
ornaments on Kamala; she even gives some to Charudutt's little son to
play with and to turn his little clay cart into a golden one. The female
bonding shown between the good, understanding wife and the courtesan
plays out the ultimate male fantasy: the freedom of a man to move without guilt between a nurturing wife and a glamorous mistress.

The jewelry finally brings Samasthanaka and Charudutt together as
rivals for Vasantsena's affections. In the culminating episode of the film,
when Samasthanaka seeks revenge on both Charudutt and Vasantsena
for outwitting him, he accuses Charudutt of killing the courtesan (whom
he has himself rendered unconscious in a fit of jealousy) in order to steal
her jewelry. With his head on the executioner's block, Charudutt pro-
tests his innocence but is reconciled to his fate. As his death is comi-
cally averted through repeated interventions and finally by the birth of a
new political order in the land which decrees a pardon for all prisoners,
the tables are turned on Samasthanaka, the ousted king's relative.
Bruised and beaten by the newly freed people, he slinks away while
Charudutt is happily reunited with his wife. By a further reversal, Vasantsena is aligned with the defeated, for Charudutt forgets her in the joy
of being alive again and in his wife's embrace. Realizing the hopeless-
ness of her situation as the other woman, she runs from the scene, and
the last shot shows her accepting the attention of a now humbled
Samasthanaka.

An important feature in this film is the iconography and symbolic
function of money (and by extension the courtesan). By showing money
(signified by the ornaments) as a facilitative agent, harmless in itself,
Girish Karnad no doubt wants to evoke an Indian golden age when life
was not only more joyous but also free from want. Women, and courtesans in particular, were wealthy and respected. It is revealing in this
connection that the director refers to the spirit of Sudraka's play as that
of "a marketplace, presenting life in all its fun, vitality, exuberance."[19]
But a marketplace is primarily an arena where commodities are bought
and sold. In one sense, Vasantsena is literally the "pot of gold" that
passes from Charudutt to Samasthanaka. The carnivalesque elements of
the film are recuperated by this larger ideological framework.

One of the most interesting characters in *Utsav* is that of a masseur who is being pursued by his creditors. He escapes them by climbing into the courtesans' dwelling, where he overhears a conversation about Vasantsena's infatuation with Charudutt. When discovered in this female world, he pretends to be Charudutt's emissary, and Vasantsena immediately pays off the men to whom the masseur owed money. Astonished that one man's name can change his destiny, he decides to give up the world of illusions and become a hermit. Later, it is the masseur who is meditating in the garden where Vasantsena is to meet Charudutt and is intercepted by Samasthanaka. He revives the unconscious courtesan with his skilled hands and departs, searching (in vain, it would appear) for a quiet spot to resume his meditations.

Utsav, then, is an orchestration of gazes and perspectives through which the discourses of history, sexuality, and cinematic representation are played out. Overtly, the film seeks to both glamorize and enliven the (imputedly drab and prudish) present by framing ancient courtesan culture as spectacle, farce, caricature, and romance. These male "writerly" tendencies of the text are fecundated and carnivalized through the agency of the female sexual figure of the courtesan. "History" as the male gaze (the brothel scenes are presented through the eyes of a fat Vatsyayana) and source of authority is satirized on the one hand and authenticated on the other through the more "eternalized" visual and social coding of the woman/courtesan. By suggesting the communal image of "feast" or "festivity" as controlling metaphor, *Utsav* prescribes a mode of historical and gendered understanding. It is thereby able to elide the question of female desire and its own problematic investment in the representation of female sexuality.

The displacement of sexuality by spiritual considerations is the central theme of *Chitralekha* (1964), a film ostensibly about a legendary courtesan from the Gupta period. It portrays the "public" woman as epitomizing the clash between the attractions of the body and sensual indulgence on the one hand and the spiritual search on the other. Woman is at once the cause and the ground for the playing out of man's struggle with the demons of his inner self. Notions of purity and impurity, illusion and reality, entertainment and enlightenment convey a discourse on the cinema as well as on womanhood in this film.

The ideas of duality and masquerade are inscribed at the very beginning when Chitralekha (Meena Kumari), the famed courtesan, is introduced. In a dance sequence before the king's son, Bijgupta (Pradeep Kumar), two women whose faces are hidden behind masks dance for the royal visitor, who is asked to guess which one is Chitralekha. Bijgupta guesses rightly and thereafter begins his daily visits to the courtesan's house. The affluence and luxurious life-style associated with such women are presented through some of the typical images of the courtesan film: marble floors, pools, and baths, fleet-footed maidservants, and shimmering curtains. The very popular songs and music by Roshan draw upon classical ragas to create the aura of cultural attainment. Apart from costumes, however, little attempt is made to evoke another era; the focus is on the drama of personalities, particularly that of Chitralekha and the holy man/guru, Kumar Giri (Ashok Kumar). The film spans many years in Chitralekha's life as she attains maturity and self-realization through her transformation from proud and sensuous courtesan to humble ascetic.

The film roughly divides into two parts, as is usual in the commercial Bombay cinema, where the period before the intermission sets the stage (here the life of sensuality and romance) and the period after it alters or reverses the prior condition (the spiritual struggle). In *Chitralekha*, the action moves between the courtesan's house and the royal palace, with characters passing between the two. Bijgupta's visits to Chitralekha make him forget his royal duties (his promise to marry the young and innocent Yashodara), and who could be a more suitable figure to show the path of duty than a stern and powerful guru? Kumar Giri pays Chitralekha a visit and warns her of her impending doom: to be shunned by men once her youth and beauty decline. Chitralekha sends him away but cannot forget his words. After much agonizing, she decides to sacrifice her love for Bijgupta by removing herself from his path and renouncing her worldly possessions. Shorn of her jewelry now and draped in a white saree, she sets off for the guru's ashram to become his disciple and embark on a spiritual quest. At first reluctant to accept a prostitute into his holy place, the guru finally relents, hoping to prove once again his own invincibility to the lure of woman. However, he finds his resolve progressively weakening and his desire to possess Chitralekha physically becoming more acute. He even lies to her that Bijgupta is marrying Yashodara so that she has nowhere to go. Shocked by his degradation, Chitralekha runs away, and only then does the *sanyasi* repent of his fall and decide to kill himself. Chitralekha is reunited with the now penniless prince, who has himself renounced his kingdom in order to make his own peace with the gods.

Unlike many other Bombay films, *Chitralekha* contains long conversations between the principal characters on the nature of the courtesan's life and its relationship to love and attachment, beauty and pleasure. The range of fulfillments promised by the pleasure house seems to parallel that of the cinema, and one is tempted to make the connection between two illusory systems as projected by the film's discourse. The courtesan functions as the embodiment for the cinema's lure, suggesting illicit pleasure, and must be superseded by "true art" (spirituality). But more important, it is through moral victory that a whore can transcend her circumstances and avoid the pain of the body's inevitable decay.

Umrao Jan and the Subaltern Consciousness

Umrao Jan (1981) is the quintessential courtesan film of the Bombay cinema. Here the narrativization of female subjectivity through the "double inscription" of a poetic sensibility, the meshing of eroticism, song, and dance with the spectacle of woman as feminine beauty and grace, the recreation of a past era (the turn of the century) through a historico-biographical structure, the naturalistic presentation of a cultural institution (the famed nawabi culture of Lucknow)—all these find evocative utterance. Directed by Muzaffar Ali, the film is based on a very popular novel with the same title by Mirza Mohammed Ruswa (1857–1931) which is itself supposedly an account of the real-life reminiscences of a prostitute living in Lucknow's Chowk area (red light district) known to the author. The novel transforms the character from a "dark, tall, flirtatious pockmarked" woman to one passably attractive, "a woman of culture, with great charm of manner and with a reputation as a singer."[20] The film *Umrao Jan* effects a further transformation by having the beautiful Rekha play the role of the Lucknow courtesan. The film constructs a visual and musical treat through its social tapestry, lavish sets, personalized star appeal, romantic drama, and pathos. It recreates the milieu of the mid- to late-nineteenth-century Lucknowi culture, particularly that of the brothel and its support-system of effete noblemen and nawabs. Drawing upon the prurient fascinations of "Lucknow's aristocrats and their pleasure houses, the courtesans and their elegant boudoirs, the colorful vagabonds and their frolics, an epicurean life with extraordinary refinements, and the ups and downs in the life of a girl forced into the oldest profession,"[21] the novel and the film have enjoyed great popularity.

Although the story has primarily Muslim characters, the film draws upon Hindu elements as well in its music and lyrics. This point is worth emphasizing, since courtesan culture is celebrated precisely because of this cultural fusion, a fusion highly desired ideologically in the discourse of Indian nationhood if not quite in actual social life, where Hindu and Muslim social practices remain fairly distinct. One might add that, as Anne McClintock has suggested in another context, the body of the prostitute effects a mixture of diverse racial and subcultural "liquid assets,"[22] and hence the courtesan is a national projection of a literal embodiment of Hindu-Muslim unity. It is small wonder that courtesan life is closely associated in the popular imagination with North Indian classical music, perhaps the paradigmatic and most celebrated instance of the blend of Hindu and Muslim artistic traditions. And if culture must subsist in time and place, it is Lucknow of the nawabi era that represents the best of the Hindu-Muslim amalgam. Although courtesans were located in all parts of India, it is Lucknow that popular culture has identified as their representative site. For the minority Muslim population and for Indians generally, Lucknow connotes the "civilized" outpost or remnants of bygone Muslim imperial splendor, the elegance of the Urdu language, and lived social graces. Such a complex of sentiments, in light of occasional but ongoing tensions between communal groups, makes the task of the Bombay film a delicate one and notions of authenticity (to a prior text, to history, to contemporary life) highly complicated at best. *Umrao Jan* does not mix its cast of characters and in general devotes itself to portraying a Muslim familial and cultural milieu. Therein lies its claim to "authenticity." However, as this study suggests, the courtesan is a masquerading and liminal figure, an impersonation writ large—culturally, individually, sexually. Echoing this masquerade, the film positions itself as part "historical" drama, part tragic romance. *Umrao Jan* also suggests a bazaar woman's consciousness as subaltern space, wherein the private is invaded and determined by the public, imprinted upon by men's desires and actions. Umrao's travels are along both inner and outer landscapes, and her circular trajectory tells the tale of a woman imprisoned by the chimera of her dreams and the reality of her social standing.

The narrative of *Umrao Jan* starts in Faizabad in 1840 in an average middle-class Muslim family. The father has made an enemy of the unscrupulous and criminal Dilawal by testifying against him in court, as a result of which Dilawal spends twelve years in jail. In revenge he kidnaps the man's young daughter Ameeran and sells her to Khanum Jan, a madam who runs a brothel in Lucknow. Ameeran's name is changed to

Rekha performing the mujra *in* Umrao Jan.

Umrao and she grows up in Khanum's establishment. Here girls are taught singing, dancing, reading, and writing. Although initially unhappy, Umrao soon forgets her former existence and learns the techniques of being an accomplished courtesan. She is courted by Gauhar Mirza, a harlot's son and resident pimp, but Umrao loses her heart to Sultan Sahib, who is rich, handsome, cultured, and well-mannered. After a short-lived romance, however, he leaves her to get married and Umrao is left disconsolate. Her next client, Faiz Ali, is a robber with whom she elopes, but he is killed on the way, and Umrao slowly makes her way to Kanpur. She earns fame as a poetess and is celebrated as a courtesan. She finally arrives in Faizabad, her point of origin, and enters her long-lost home. There is a surprise and tearful reconciliation with her mother, but her young brother, now grown up, will have nothing to do with the likes of her. Saddened and truly alone, Umrao's circle of victimization is complete. The final shot of the film presents a double image of the heroine as she is left facing her reflection in a mirror.

Like other courtesan films, we have here a microcosm of a social and historical world and of woman's place within it. The hustle and bustle of a household, the petty or smart economic transactions, the comings and goings of men in search of pleasure, the clink of glasses, the jangle of anklets, the storms of love and passion all contribute to the felt impres-

Identity as alienation: the metaphor of doubling in Umrao Jan.

sion of a rich and vibrant culture under scrutiny with the help of rose-tinted glasses. Because we are rarely outside the ambience of the whore-house, the effect is simultaneously one of claustrophobia and intense involvement. The courtesan herself shares this feeling of belonging and not-belonging, for while her body is trapped within the walls of the plea-sure palace, her thoughts range far and wide as she dreams of love and romance and personal fulfillment. Thus social detail and the critique of woman's exploitations become incidental to individualized and psychic representations of the world.

In all three of the films discussed above, the prostitute's conscious-ness may be said to be constructed out of a pattern of nature overlaid by culture. The emotional turmoil of the heroine results whenever she is swayed or affected by deep personal emotion and self-realization that clash with her socialized role as public "entertainer." Even in *Utsav*, where the courtesan enjoys social prestige and is happy in her surround-ings, her "natural" yearnings to belong to one man ultimately make her a desolate and pitiable being, forced, in a sense, to accept the attentions of a man she has abhorred. In all these films, the mise-en-scène of opu-lent and/or garish trappings of the whorehouse is at once a silent re-proach to the courtesan's "sinful" way of life and a mark of difference between this life and the subjectivity that develops independently of it.

Ultimately it is through her higher yearnings, rather than through her cultural attainments, that the screen courtesan redeems herself. Nature wins out over culture, at least insofar as the personal growth of the woman is concerned. Thus while these quintessential courtesan films ostensibly celebrate her artistic talents and enrichment of social life, it is as (im)pure woman that she is judged and elevated only when the threat of her sexuality is suppressed.

If Umrao Jan is a victim of a vengeful male world, the heroine of *Pakeezah* (*The Pure One*, 1971) is the classic subaltern figure, silently acquiescing to the buffetings of "fate" and caught in a web of social and familial intrigue. More than any other courtesan film, *Pakeezah* recreates the decadent milieu of this subculture as well as the artistic and linguistic refinement which characterized it. For these and other reasons, *Pakeezah* enjoys the status of a cult classic. Starring the highly acclaimed actress Meena Kumari, the film was a huge box-office hit when it was released and continues to draw crowds when it is shown. Its outstanding musical score has become indelibly stamped on the popular mind as the actress's swan-song. The history of the film's genesis has itself become part of the mystique of the film. Produced, directed, and written by Kamal Amrohi, who in fifty years had directed only four films and whose third wife was Meena Kumari, *Pakeezah* is poetry and fantasy and nostalgia all orchestrated together on a grand scale. Film researchers Shampa Banerjee and Anil Srivastava write, "After he [Amrohi] had completed shooting five reels of the film, *Pakeezah* was stalled for seven and a half years, mainly due to Amrohi's differences with Meena Kumari which eventually led to their separation. When it was finally taken up again, Meena Kumari was already an alcoholic and the film was one of her last. She died soon after its release; yet it is impossible to find any lack of consistency in her portrayal, or any sign of the passage of the years."[23]

Like *Umrao Jan*, *Pakeezah* is also a film in which high drama and spectacle combine with a fine evocation of the niceties of Muslim culture and the beauty of the Urdu language. But if *Umrao Jan* uses specific historical references and types, *Pakeezah* creates the mood and sensibility of the grand romance. For events and characters are all larger than life. While this is hardly a novelty in the context of the Hindi cinema, *Pakeezah* has a curious other-worldly air that is in tension with the social and historical concreteness of the institution being portrayed. The central character is named Pakeezah (meaning "the pure one") by her lover when he seeks to give her a new identity from her past one of a dancing girl. She is actually Sahebjan (Meena Kumari), the daughter of a courtesan, abandoned in a graveyard when her mother dies after giving birth. She is brought up by her aunt, Nawabjan (Veena), who wants to take revenge on her dead sister's husband for her tragic end. So the father, Sahabuddin (Ashok Kumar), the scion of an aristocratic household of North India, is told that his daughter is alive, but when he goes to the salon to fetch her, the place is locked. Nawabjan and her entourage are escaping to another town; in the railway carriage where Sahebjan is asleep, a strange man slips a note between her toes which says, "Your feet are beautiful. Do not let them touch the ground or they will be soiled." On reading the note, Sahebjan loses her heart to the stranger and dreams about him night and day. Although a famous courtesan herself, she often appears preoccupied, rushes to the balcony every time a train passes at night, and reads the note countless times.

One of her rich and aristocratic admirers takes her sailing on his boat, which is attacked by a herd of elephants. As the party get scattered, Sahebjan finds herself in a strange spot on the shore and enters a tent pitched there. Inside she finds a diary that reveals the owner to be none other than the man on the train. The two finally meet, but Sahebjan's aunt forces her back to her life as a courtesan. She runs away but is found by Salim, her lover, who wants to marry her. Unable to tell him of her past, she runs away again, returning to an empty Rose Palace. Salim sarcastically invites her to perform at his wedding, and Sahebjan gives the performance of her life on the broken glass pieces of a chandelier. Her aunt sees Sahabuddin among the hosts and reveals to him the identity of his daughter. When he tries to rush to her, his own father, the old aristocrat who had objected to his marrying the courtesan Nargis, shoots him dead. Before dying, however, Sahabuddin tells his nephew Salim that Sahebjan is indeed his daughter, and Nawabjan insists that Salim marry her to wipe out the injustice committed against Sahebjan's mother. In a grotesque finale, the *nikah,* or wedding ceremony, is performed in front of the body of the dead Sahabuddin. Sahebjan is finally freed from her life of shame.

This overdetermined plot perhaps symbolizes the complexity and ambiguity that surrounds the courtesan culture and what might be termed the "courtesan consciousness." Many of the visual and thematic elements of the genre are present here: the struggle over definitions of pure and impure, the tension between the glamor of the settings and the suggested emotional emptiness of the courtesan, the empathic male, the taunts of society, the ultimate triumph of the heroine's "better" instincts. But the courtesan's body is also the site where cultures and values and generations clash, where the trade of the flesh is sublimated into a metaphor of the purity of the soul, where the pain of foiled expectations is transmuted into the insubstantiality of dream.

More than any other film in this genre, *Pakeezah* captures the ambience of surface glitter masking the exploitative nature of institutionalized prostitution. Here we have the most substantive expression of the prostitute's subjective longing to escape the prison house of sexualized ritual and commodification—the series of acts (adornment, a song-and-dance routine, retiring for the night with a wealthy patron) through which the courtesan must conduct herself through unfailing regularity until she is rescued by a good man. Oddly enough, the moment of self-awakening also comes about through a form of fetishization: Salim falls in love with Pakeezah's dainty feet, which are offered to the cinematic gaze as she sleeps in the railway carriage. The feet become a motif throughout the film and are invested with layers of meaning. They are, simultaneously, an emblem of prostitution, of escape from prostitution through self-sufficiency (her ability to stand on her own feet), of displaced emotion (as when Pakeezah, in the climactic scene of the film, dances on broken glass to show her defiance of aristocratic norms and values). One of the symbols, then, of decommodification is the dancing girl's ability to, literally, take the weight off her feet. Pakeezah's relationship to her body may be said to reproduce society's relationship to courtesans: a relationship of fixity and flux, attachment and alienation, stigma and transcendence.

Sexual Sublimation and the Ideal of Motherhood

Of all the courtesan films, those that portray her as the sacrificing mother are the closest to Bombay film melodrama and the least ambiguous in terms of representational strategies. Given the importance of the mother in Indian social and psychic life and the generic stability of the maternal melodrama, questions of female sexuality and independence can be dealt with relatively easily by being subordinated or silenced before the obligations and intense emotional affect of motherhood. The prostitute sings and dances before a paying public because she needs the money to support her offspring and to give the latter a better chance in the world than she has had. Beneath the veneer of the gaudy or disreputable life lies the pure instinct of the mother. In both *Mamta* (*Mother Love*) and *Amar Prem* (*Eternal Love*), the courtesans are selfless women who are trapped in the profession and redeem themselves through death or much suffering.

Mamta, based on a popular Bengali novel, *Uttar Phalguni*, written by Nihar Ranjan Roy, portrays the heroine, Deviyani (Suchitra Sen), as driven to the brothel through a combination of patriarchal oppression and (lower) class positioning. Her beauty and virginity are the assets her father turns into cash in the marriage market (appeasing an unscrupulous creditor), to be followed by her husband, who tries to use her as a source of income through prostitution. Escaping this fate, a pregnant Deviyani is picked up by a madam. The story is told in flashback, when Deviyani has already taken on a courtesan's name and identity. As Panna Bai, she gives pleasure to men in order to raise her daughter. Threatened with blackmail by her former husband, she entrusts the guardianship of her child to Manish, her first and true love from whom she was separated early on in the narrative. The bulk of the film deals with a mother's sacrifice and love for her daughter as the latter grows up away from her mother's "contaminating" presence. The final episode brings the two women together in a courtroom as criminal and defense lawyer, respectively. Panna Bai has shot to death her blackmailing husband in her final attempt to protect her daughter, Suparna, from her biological father. She dies in court, her love vindicated, her daughter having achieved both social respectability and a moral victory in acknowledging her "lowly" parentage.

The courtesan film as maternal melodrama, of which *Mamta* is a prime instance, projects the problem of woman and of prostitution onto the terrain of empathic identification associated with motherhood. In doing so, however, it incorporates kinship itself into the idea of the masquerade, for kinship, like the prostitute's social identity, is double-edged. In *Mamta*, the institutions of the family and of arranged marriage are depicted as exploitative and abusive, not nurturing and protective. The courtesan, then, is both its product and its nemesis. As a single woman semantically linked to the bazaar or marketplace, she is a challenge to the social order yet a vital part of it. For if prostitution is a metaphor for the social circulation of sexual currency (with the consequent debasement of ethical values), what maternal sacrifice is meant to achieve is personal redemption as well as the redistribution of social wealth and prestige (through the incorporation of the heroine's daughter into the upper middle class). In keeping with the postcolonial ideology of individual responsibility, such a redistribution must alter traditional maps of family and kinship. The film's trajectory follows the process of first destroying and then reconstructing the family. The trajectory here is the replacement of the real family with a substitute one, what Thomas Elsaesser has called displacement-by-substitution.[24] Melodrama also displaces the courtesan genre in that it is fear and violence rather than passion which punctuates the action. Blackmail, mental abuse, murder, imprisonment—these foreclose the courtesan's chances of social rehabilitation except through death.

A similar ambience of violence and psychological abuse, albeit with a happy ending, pervades *Amar Prem*, also a remake of a popular Bengali version. Here the odyssey of suffering of the courtesan figure is all but total. Beaten and turned out by a ruthless husband, disowned by a punitive mother, the protagonist, Pushpa (Sharmila Tagore), is further sold into prostitution by a trusted friend. Innocence, simplicity, and/or virginity as inherent snares for young women are a pervasive theme and source of dramatic action in the Bombay film, projecting the anxiety felt by the breakdown of old family structures and the pressures of urban living. Pushpa acquires a rich client, himself lonely and embittered, and together the two form a new "family." Into this setup arrives a little boy from Pushpa's village whom she befriends because he is ill-treated by his stepmother. The film devotes its psychic energies to the transformation of the courtesan to mother figure. Although the boy disappears from her life, Pushpa redeems herself by abandoning her profession and taking up menial jobs to support herself. Female masochism becomes the means for a symbolic cleansing of the body and material want the means of spiritual salvation. Time itself, its suggested passage a feature of the biographical mode of this genre, serves to reinforce the metamorphosis. Cathartic release is provided at the end of the film as the main characters are reunited and Pushpa is accorded the right to a place in her "son's" home.

Stock images of feminine/maternal purity circulated in countless films are used to define the modest, self-effacing courtesan. Anand insists that she is pure like the holy Ganges, and later she is compared to sweet-smelling flowers that bloom in the night. At the same time, more specialized information is also communicated to the audience, for instance, that the clay figurine of the goddess Durga worshiped during the Dushera festival in Bengal incorporates a clump of mud taken from the courtyard

of a whorehouse. A standard melodrama with conventional characterizations and episodes, *Amar Prem* nonetheless points to some real social
contradictions pertaining to the deviant woman.

Body/Transgression/Nation

Bhumika (1977) and *Mandi* (1983) are two films by Shyam Benegal
that both draw upon and problematize the conventions of the courtesan
film. They are not only woman-centered but are self-consciously allegorical, suggesting the larger historical forces and movements shaping
contemporary India. *Bhumika*, although not a courtesan film in the strict
sense in that the lead character is not associated with a brothel at any
time and her sexuality is not potentially for sale, nevertheless deserves
to be considered here for a number of reasons. The film raises many of
the same issues—about art, entertainment, and female sexuality as
economy—as those films in which the central character is a prostitute.
(In an interesting link made between acting and prostitution, it might be
pointed out that even prostitutes were unwilling to appear in movies of
the 1930s, the time-frame of this film.[25]) Based on the life of Hansa
Wadkar, a famous Marathi stage and film actress of the 1930s, *Bhumika*
explores the tortuous labyrinths of female subjectivity. The film has
many explicit ties to the generic features we have isolated as specific to
the courtesan film: a biographical approach to the subject, an extremely
complicated plot structure, a matriarchal setup which is both supportive
and oppressive, songs and dances rendered through a female performer-
heroine, and the work-money-sexuality nexus.

Moreover, the very title of the film raises intriguing questions about
impersonation and identity. Whose "role" is being referred to here? Are
we to understand the word in terms of the diverse roles an actress plays
in the course of her career? Or is reference being made to a female role,
the parameters of which are socially designated and which the heroine
rebels against by her "promiscuity" and yet adheres to naïvely? Or perhaps we are to go further and consider the role of the cinema as a national archive of bygone eras? A self-reflexive film, *Bhumika* pays obvious homage to the Bombay cinema, recreating the studio atmosphere
of the thirties and forties. Its intricate intertextual network provides the
proper ground to explore a woman's artistic and sexual longings.

Where *Bhumika* goes beyond the normal range of the woman-centered
film is in its attempt to link a postcolonial Indian political reality (evoked

through the background use of radio news bulletins) with the drama of struggle and conflict involving the central character. In this endeavor, the film is only partially successful because it sets up a hierarchy of representational values which is spurious. That is, a rhythm is established between the "real" and the "make-believe," the former inhering in the larger text of history and the latter in the films-within-the-films that signify Usha's acting career. Structurally and stylistically, *Bhumika* sets up an internal opposition or dynamic, dividing itself rather too neatly (and problematically) into "serious" and "entertaining" segments. "Realism" (Usha's life) and "fantasy" (her public personas as rendered through different movie roles) are presented as self-evident categories, and this model is projected onto the national level. Radio becomes a "realistic" medium and cinema an "entertainment" medium, a form of signification which is too simplistic.

The story concerns Usha (Smita Patil), whose screen name, Urvashi, connotes beauty as well as the mythological role of "temptress" (Urvashi being the siren sent by Indra and the gods to distract the sage Vishwamitra from his meditations in the *Mahābhārata*). This suggestion of wantonness hangs over the film like a stench that threatens to smother the main characters: Usha's mother and her lover, Keshav Dalvi (Amol Palekar), who becomes Usha's husband. The household includes Usha's father, a sick alcoholic, and her grandmother, who was a singer-courtesan in her time and thus denied the social respectability conferred by marriage. Usha's mother is an embittered and angry woman, conscious that her illegitimacy means a lack of social standing. She often scolds Usha for singing, a pastime that Usha's grandmother encourages. Shanti, the mother, would rather have Usha find a husband and lead a "normal" life.

Usha often escapes to the woods to be alone. Sometimes she is pursued there by Dalvi, who once extracts a promise of marriage from the young girl. When Usha's father dies, Dalvi becomes their sole support, and he takes Usha to Bombay for entry into films. Her good singing voice lands her a role and her career takes off. As she grows up, her fights with her mother become increasingly intense, and she takes refuge in Dalvi's arms. She gets pregnant, marries Dalvi, and has a daughter, Sushma. Reluctant to see her end her lucrative career, Dalvi appoints himself her manager and signs many contracts on her behalf. While pushing her to work, he is also intensely jealous and even violent with her. The marriage sours and Usha drifts from one lover to another, but she is unable to find the emotional security she needs. Finally, tired of

Undressing evokes visceral subjectivity in the succession of roles that Usha (Smita Patil) inhabits in Bhumika.

the world of men and their attempts to curb her independence, she decides to live alone, refusing even a space in her now grownup daughter's home. Loneliness, she realizes and accepts, is the price she must pay if she is to retain her autonomy.

The highly complicated weave of this psychological narrative (there are five long flashbacks roughly corresponding to Usha's childhood, young adulthood, and mature years and her extramarital affairs) and the frequent temporal shifts leave the viewer engrossed but disoriented. This sense of confusion is compounded by the impersonating nature of Usha's job as actress. The very opening scene is calculated to introduce ambiguity. It "impersonates" the typical Bombay film: a heavily made-up heroine is seen performing a coquettish song-and-dance number in an obviously contrived setting for the benefit of a waiting hero. The liveliness of the music and orchestral accompaniment further reinforces viewer expectations of being in the presence of the "normal" commercial film. Only when the heroine suddenly stops, the director calls out, "Cut!" and the music trails off do we realize that a film shooting was in progress. Usha's co-star and emotional support, Rajan (Anant Nag), is also introduced here. Presented as a foil to the more grasping and exploitative husband, Rajan functions as the idealized lover in courtesan

Experimenting with sexual freedom: Smita Patil and Naseeruddin Shah in Bhumika. *Courtesy the Asia Society.*

films whom the woman can never fully attain. In *Bhumika*, Rajan accompanies Usha in her many roles: these roles simultaneously "educate" the film viewer in Indian cinematic history. The dominant genres of Indian filmmaking (the mythological, the stunt film, the historical, the romantic drama) are recreated through the career of Usha/Urvashi as the utopian possibilities of these impersonating forms are recalled. These provide the moments of "comic relief" as they punctuate the tense drama of Usha's life. As Rajan fades in and out of Usha's existence to be replaced by other patriarchal figures whom Usha takes as lovers (a poetic, smooth-talking film director, Sunil Verma, and a feudal authoritarian, Kale), so also the impossibility of a complete relationship becomes clear to her. Ultimately, even Rajan can only signify dependence, and Usha cuts loose.

Although biographical in intent, *Bhumika*'s structural complexity seems to suggest that the journey of self-exploration undertaken by Usha (and the film's own exploration of a woman's consciousness) is circular, full of snares, forever incomplete. Usha's consciousness is a hall of mirrors where past and present are merely reflections that mock each other. And indeed, the dominant visual motif in the film is that of the mirror, of its proliferating and static images. Usha seems to contest the mirror's inert reflections by changing her sarees (another recurring image). As she "peels off" one identity to take on another, she is both asserting her will to change and capitulating to the mirror's ability to make of it yet another image. For an entertainer (courtesans were traditionally actresses too), the public and the private selves cannot be differentiated.

The motif of travel underscores psychological exploration as well as the biographical mode. Usha is shown constantly moving, and there are excellent traveling shots which present landscape as visual metaphors for the protagonist's inner state. Three such shots appear at key moments: in the childhood segment, Usha running with Dalvi in pursuit, a scene with heavy symbolic overtones; Usha in a taxi speeding along the streets of Bombay after she has left her husband, the city and herself aligned in their alienation; and again, in the final flashback, as she embarks on a new relationship with hope, the openness of the country-side provides visual and narrative relief from the claustrophobic site/ sight of hotel rooms and confining living spaces, yet it is an ironic prelude to the more hellish claustrophobia she is to experience as the feudal landowner's mistress. Movement in the film suggests a world in flux, an autonomy just beyond the protagonist's grasp.

Bhumika's preemption of the specificities of the courtesan film genre is located most directly, however, in the sexuality-as-labor analogy. Actresses and courtesans both live by their bodies; they are driven by a sexual economy. In *Bhumika*, Usha's earnings, like those of other young singer-courtesans, support her mother and her husband. The conflicts between them originate because he "pimps" for her while she would like to rest for a while and raise a family. It is financial need rather than artistic drive that lands Usha in the film world. Like other courtesan films, *Bhumika* portrays women as romantic seekers of love and security, not enthusiastic purveyors of a cultural tradition. The "immoral" traffic of the body, even if entered into consciously and not overtly for money, as in the case of Usha, must be transcended in order to attain self-fulfillment. Female sexuality, on balance, is an aberration that is both exploiter and exploited, a monster that needs to be harnessed for legitimate ends.

If *Bhumika* presents female sexuality at the intersection of cultural capital and as a form of emotional currency, the notion of prostitution as

The whorehouse as menagerie: Mandi (Marketplace).

a commodity form virtually animates *Mandi* (*Marketplace*, 1984). Directed by Shyam Benegal, who also was the director of *Bhumika*, the film is unique in that it uses burlesque as the mode to examine the dynamics of a whorehouse. Benegal said of the film, "I was very keen on creating a whole microsystem of Indian life—the survival instinct, as evident in Shabana's character, middle class hypocrisy, the manipulation that goes on constantly, the young pecking the old." [26] *Mandi* substantially extends the parameters of the courtesan film genre. Here the life of prostitutes and courtesans-in-training is not glamorized, set in the past, or linked to an idealized male. However, the pleasures provided by the motivated use of songs and dances are not eschewed nor are the "utopian" dimensions of a matriarchal domain entirely negated. Rukmini Bai (Shabana Azmi), the madam who runs the whorehouse, is tenderly solicitous of all her girls and adores her favorite ward, Zeenat (Smita Patil), who is reserved for special clients. The other prostitutes sing and joke together, help each other, and generally stick together.

The film avoids the stance of moralism, which dictates that the duality implicit in the courtesan's profession is a version of nature masquerading as culture. *Mandi* foregrounds the "nature" part of this equation and presents the whorehouse as a menagerie of temperamental creatures. An early sequence with a monkey makes this explicit. Performing monkeys and their trainers are a familiar sight in neighborhoods in Indian towns and cities, where monkeys perform tricks and receive some money from passersby. In the film, a monkey darts away from its owner and rushes up to Zeenat's room in the top floor of the house. Pandemonium breaks loose as Rukmini Bai runs up and down shouting to the manservant, Tunglus, to capture the animal. Apparently even the monkey knows where the goods are, but Zeenat is not afraid of it and has a good deal of fun watching the monkey imitate her imitations of *its* acts. Although trite, the analogy is calculated to anticipate and dispel judgmental, ponderous attitudes toward whores. The burlesque form is also meant to create a double-edged awareness of the social meanings surrounding prostitution. By presenting the whores, particularly Rukmini Devi, as caricatures rather than as psychologically developed characters, the film undercuts the pretensions of the middle class, who are presented as the self-appointed guardians of society's moral health and well-being. Thus "feminists" and city officials are equally objects of ridicule. Among them is Shanti Devi, who has established a women's center (Nari Niketan) and would like to rid the city of Rukmini Bai's establishment. Shanti Devi is a "colorless" character: she is always shown dressed in a white saree, whereas Rukmini Bai dresses in bright shades and has a pleasing appearance. The encounters between the two show Rukmini Bai turning on her charms, although she fails to avert the tide of social forces against her.

But not all is comedy inside the whorehouse. A pimp brings in a deaf and dumb girl, gets his commission, and leaves. The girl, Phoolmani (Srila Majumdar), is like a caged bird and is literally imprisoned inside a room so that she can't escape. When she is forced to gratify a client she goes into a coma and later tries to kill herself. The incident lands all the inmates of the whorehouse in jail for a few days. Other incidents are harbingers of other complications. *Mandi* is not only about pimps and prostitutes but incestuous liaisons and shady deals. Indeed, a distinct link is made between whoring and the Indian business community. One influential businessman, Mr. Agarwal (Sayeed Jafri), is trying to forge a family-cum-business relationship with another notable, Mr. Gupta (Kulbhushan Kharbanda), the owner of the building Rukmini Bai and her girls inhabit. A marriage is being arranged between their son and daughter, both of obviously tender age. As is customary with the wealthy, a *mujra* (the performance by a courtesan before an audience) is arranged and the town's notables are invited. Zeenat performs in the *mujra* and succeeds in exciting the erotic fantasy of the prospective groom and the host's son, Sushil. He falls in love with Zeenat, visits the brothel, and wants to elope with her. But she is revealed to be the illegitimate off-spring of Sushil's father, Mr. Agarwal, and therefore Sushil's half-sister. The hypocrisy of the so-called respectable members of society, indeed of the institution of marriage itself, is also suggested since Sushil's mar-riage is being arranged with a rich man's daughter so that the dowry can pay the mortgage on his father's house.

The brothel, then, serves as the hiding place for so-called respectable society's moral lapses and sexual excesses. It is also caught between the political machinations of different social groups—the business class on the one hand and middle-class moralistic "social workers" on the other. The marginal status of the prostitutes is literally and figuratively evoked as the township orders the brothel closed and the inmates are "relo-cated" by Mr. Gupta in a distant and rocky undeveloped area at the very edge of the city. In an ironical twist in a film loaded with irony, the site happens to be a shrine of a local holy man to whom Rukmini Bai prays at the behest of a madman who lives in those parts. As though by magic, her business starts flourishing again and what was a desolate place be-comes a bustling center of business and carnival. Only Zeenat, forcibly separated from her would-be lover, Sushil, pines for him and refuses to come out of her isolation. In a parody of the commercial Hindi film, we have a lengthy sequence of an attempted elopement by Sushil and Zeenat, with Mr. Agarwal and Rukmini Bai in hot pursuit. Zeenat takes the opportunity to escape from a doomed relationship with her half-brother and a caged life as a courtesan and is never found, while a whimpering Sushil is taken home by his father. As Rukmini Bai mourns the "loss" of her favorite ward, the other prostitutes threaten to leave as well and stage a minor rebellion against the madam. Reduced to a pa-thetic helplessness, Rukmini Bai, with the faithful and desexed atten-dant, Tunglus (Naseeruddin Shah), takes off for Tirupati (a place of pil-grimage), only to be recalled by the echoing voice of the madman in the wilderness. "Pray," he urges her, "pray again to Baba Kharadsha!" A second "miracle" occurs as Phoolmani appears on the horizon, running toward them. Delighted and thankful, Rukmini Bai retraces her steps to the brothel.

As a metaphor for life in postcolonial India, *Mandi's* social Darwinism has a harsh and cutting edge. Stark juxtapositions, overdrawn charac-ters, outrageous situations, sinister dealings: these are the visual images and discursive patterns with which the audience is invited to apprehend the national ethos, augmented by restless camera movements and an overbusy soundtrack. The brothel as symbol of corruption is superseded by a more general lack of scruples masquerading as charitable aims and agendas. In such a situation, the prostitute is plying her trade like everybody else, only with more honesty. The break with a nostalgia-ridden past is complete.

What is the significance of the tendency within Indian cinema to evoke the female vision through the image of the prostitute? Part of the motivation of filmmakers is no doubt to recapture the "magic" of a deceased institution and a lost art (the poetry and classical song-and-dance traditions preserved by the courtesans over the centuries). Courtesans thus provide a sense of continuity, a connection with the past that is glamorous and erotic, even if laced with pathos. Courtesans also embody a fusion of the best in the Hindu and Muslim cultural traditions, a feature that is foregrounded in different ways in the Bombay film. But these features, which may be termed "cultural," clash with the social meanings adhering to the presence of the whore. Stigmatized by a society whose conventions she flouts, the prostitute must be denied space in the company of "decent" men and women. Hence she remains a lonely and tragic figure in most films. Clearly the courtesan is also meant to be a symptom and symbol of a larger social malaise in contemporary India, for the social forces unleashed on the road to modernization can only be understood through mediating figures like that of the prostitute. As an image of female oppression, of class oppression, and of psychic and moral ambivalence, the haunting figure of the prostitute can be a searing indictment of social hypocrisy and exploitation. To these too the viewer must be reconciled. And so the prostitute herself is the agent of redemption, her own and that of others. Like the cinema itself, the screen prostitute impersonates the real.

The courtesan film also reconnects us to the concerns of this study as a whole. I have contended that impersonation both literal and figurative, lies at the core of the Bombay cinema's structural dynamics and thematic preoccupations. Imperso-nation, I have tried to show, throws into question the notion of a stable (individual) identity in order to configure the possibilities of a pluralized (national) identity as the expression (conscious or unconscious) of the ideology of a "benevolent" nationalism; that is, a nationalism that seeks to incorporate the margins into the mainstream. Unlike other studies, where impersonation is considered solely or largely in terms of gender, what I wish to draw attention to in the

Bombay film is the range of use and depth of evocative power that the concept attains. Straddling comic, satiric, and tragic forms, employing visual and verbal mechanisms, anchored in both metaphor and metonymy, imperso-nation becomes our way of grasping our lived relations with our fellow beings. Therein perhaps lies the power and popularity of this cinema.

Thus, contrary to what various commentators assert, my investigation has found that the commercial popular film is the site where meanings and values that have long held sway in Indian culture are reworked, updated, renegotiated. The worlds of high culture and popular or "mass" culture are not polarized opposites but feed off each other. As such they perform complementary functions in the society, the one to affix points of reference and to suggest continuity, the other to scatter those points, to collect, *bricoleur*-fashion, the rags and pickings of the culture, to itemize the baubles of the moment, to keep, as it were, an ear to the ground. Knowing its own precariousness, subject as it is to changes in the economy, technology, and audience preference, it shamelessly raids high culture, nursing its "other" at its very heart. It is thus that yesterday's pop culture becomes today's high culture.

These shiftings back and forth designate Bombay cinema's basic instability, an instability it manifests less in its rhetoric than in its generic compositions and tendencies. The courtesan genre, as we saw, is the limit-case of this cinema's ideological inconsistencies, the point at which it is willing, as it were, to wear its contradictions on its sleeve. For a cinema that seeks to address the whole of Indian nationhood (if only as a market), to take in the whole of Indian culture, both magnified and reduced to manageable entities and constructs, can hardly avoid the consequences of its own hubris. And so the critical space that the Bombay film opens up for itself through the aestheticization of the courtesan figure and the turning of this figure into a valorized cultural emblem must be at the cost of a repression. The possibilities of playful impersonation and of the masquerade that are available to men are not extended to woman as sexual being. Defined as a courtesan, she remains trapped within that definition and the social ostracism that goes with it. At best, she is a romanticized Other whose cultural contributions the dominant society has already acknowledged but whose sexuality remains outside its normative horizons.

*If banality keeps on coming back around in our polemics, it
is less because of the residual elitism of individual intellectuals,
and populist reactions to it, and more because "banality" as
mythic signifier is always a mask for the question of value, and
of value-judgment, or "discrimination."*
—Meaghan Morris, "Banality in Cultural Studies"

Conclusion

This book has dealt with a master narrative and a mistress
narrative: Indian national identity and Indian entertainment cinema.
The latter has classically enjoyed, in relation to the former, all the ambivalence, anxiety, and otherness that the sexualized semantics of the
word "mistress" is likely to conjure up in the dominant social imaginary—a relationship always fractious, occasionally tender, somewhat
contingent that underlies the politics of pleasure. The discourse of identity is a power play in which victory does not necessarily accrue to the
dominant and in which the categories are always already contaminated.
The nation, female in its fecundity, its ideological openness to nurture

(collective participation) and nature (naturalized citizenship), is never-theless most often apprehended in the guise of a rhetoric of virility, a symbolic landscape of borders and margins, laws and policing. Com-mercialized mass culture leaks and insinuates itself into every available space in a triumph and self-test of survival, transgressive and familiar, flamboyant and self-deprecating at the same time. It is thus that the nation both recognizes and misrecognizes itself in its cinema, so mun-dane and routinized in its production, so volatile and unpredictable in its products.

The interpretation of Indian popular cinema in the preceding pages has sought to chart this dual process, to inflect the question of economic production, always germane to any accounts of the commercial cinema, with questions of feeling, memory, and desire aroused by the machinery of circulating images, songs, and discourses. Rather than provide a strictly chronological account, I have appropriated specific instances of cinematic production and examined them as "moments" of cultural self-reckoning and national self-examination. My justification for doing so lies in the fact that "objective" accounts of popular cinema invariably involve the stance of what Meaghan Morris and others would call the masculine-critical gaze on "mass culture as woman."[1] A recent desig-nation of mainstream film industries (those of India, Egypt, Turkey, Mex-ico, Argentina, the Philippines) as churning out "fulp (film + pulp),"[2] while calling attention to the structures of commodity production (an inalienable fact of life in cinema as in much else) does not then go on to suggest any residual interest in how one can deal with "one's pleasure, fascination, thrill and sense of 'life,' even birth, in popular culture."[3] Silence, then, prepares the ground for a search for the theoretical object elsewhere, in the marginalized and "alternative" film practices that lend themselves to more "universalist" constructions such as "third cinema." Such evacuation of theoretical space in the name of a more engaged film politics seems to me to be regrettable and short-sighted, since "the global" is increasingly shaped and apprehended in the realm of mass culture. And what has spawned more "universalism" in film than Holly-wood, more far-flung cultural crossings in the Third World than the Bombay film and the film song? I believe that the critical vocabulary of ideology and imitation alone is not sufficient to deal with these interar-ticulations. A popular national cinema is a social investment, not just in patternings of image and sound but in complex bargains over technology, national autonomy, and identity. A more productive concept to orient the study of the everyday experience of mass culture is what Meaghan Morris has termed "banality" and what, giving a national complexion and resonance to its contradictions, I have in this study described as "impersonation." I shall return below to these concepts and how they might work together.

The broad(er) objective of this work has been to provide a sense of a "Third World" cultural ethos whereby what Raymond Williams would term the "lived experience" of decolonization may be apprehended as a peculiar instance of the local and the global, where the immediate concerns of defining/contesting notions of the popular are inflected by how "others" do things. Questions of art/commerce, high art/low art, spirituality/material needs, taste/appetite, while posed as Manichaean opposites, actually serve to underscore the multiplicity, the multiaccentuality of this lived experience in which the East is never just the East and the West a little more than the West. But this study has had more specific concerns. Foremost among them is the construction of a critical framework for the understanding of Indian popular cinema that is conjunctural—that is, one which can articulate the dynamics of popular form with a historically differentiated notion of receptivity to that form. Admittedly, this is an ambitious undertaking, and one that perhaps can only be accomplished over the course of several studies. In the present instance, my efforts have run along two interconnected lines: first, I have tried to isolate certain modalities of cinematic genre and expression in the Bombay film, and second, I have treated them as openings onto larger cultural and national debates. The first impulse was motivated by the desire to look more closely at actual filmic texts in order to identify, categorize, and systematize their economy of pleasures, both narrative and visual. Realism, myth, and historical drama in the late forties and fifties, the romance and the courtesan film, as well as some popular versions of an "oppositional" cinema in the sixties, seventies, and eighties are identified as major "genres" inhabiting, exploring, and perhaps bending contemporary structures of feeling. I claim the status of "genre" for these groups of films because they seem to be governed by distinctive structural elements and signifying codes.

Generally, the Hindi cinema has been referred to exclusively as the "masala film," the "song-and-dance film," or "melodrama." The expressive modes identified in this study help us to see the Bombay film as "cultural form," as artifacts located within certain traditions of local (and "foreign") filmmaking, traditions that are continued as well as reworked.

These genres serve as cues for identification, both the identifiability of directors, studios, and stars, and the "mobile identification" on the part of the audience sought by the Bombay cinema apparatus. For what runs as a common thread through these genres may be described as the "thematics of transformation," an inscription of a *national* identity as a *bricoleur*-inspired camouflage of the actantial body. I believe it is to this "participatory" strategy that we owe the popularity and coherence of the Bombay cinema.

The second impulse noted above arose in conjunction with the first; namely, it sought to give textual analysis "a local habitation and a name." It raised the following questions: to what extent did the Bombay cinema (including the entity called the "film industry people") generate, contest, and circulate discourses relating to culture in postcolonial India? How did it distinguish itself discursively from other "entities" such as artists and writers, the state, the people? How were more "authentic" narrative and dramatic, musical, and philosophical traditions appropriated, cast aside, contested? Above all, how were the two dominant "national" traditions—Hindu and Muslim—fused, highlighted, or problematized? I have tried to chart the contours of certain debates, illustrating their allegorical significance for the films themselves, my theoretical premise being that cultural texts are not hermetically sealed systems of meanings but processes of negotiation with the bounds of legitimacy set up by a society. Thus Indian entertainment cinema is seen as embroiled in controversy, the subjects of which have ranged from high fashion to historiography, politics to pedagogy. The size of the film industry, its seemingly boundless energy on the one hand (along with a flourishing black market and income-tax evasion), the size of the Indian populace on the other are yoked together in various scenarios of threat and victimization, power and powerlessness, order and chaos. This book has concentrated on the issue of *national* self-representation, certainly the source of the Bombay cinema's own regenerative power. Indian entertainment cinema *is* ironically India's sole model of national unity, and the model it is least prepared to come to terms with.

The trope of impersonation and masquerade is presented in this study as central to the process of movement and translation from social macrocosm to filmic microcosm. I have tried to divest the word "impersonation" of its negative connotations of false identity, deceit, and duplicity; rather I have tried to test it as a concept in film studies which would allow us to raise issues of how the play on presence/absence as integral to notions of a national collectivity is embodied in cinematic discourse and performance. While impersonation and masquerade are familiar devices in traditional drama, their use in narrative cinema has not drawn much attention. I have suggested that the reason might lie in our inability to dissociate the camera from the realist conventions established early on in its history. The fact that in (Western) film criticism the masquerade (in specific instances of the classic Hollywood cinema) has been discussed in individualized, psychoanalytic terms, primarily insofar as cross-dressing subverts gender lines, is significant for our purposes at least in one respect: the masquerade's relation to marginality, social and psychic. The Bombay film's prime social function may be said to be the symbolic "return" of the marginalized and the rejects of society into the body politic. Marginality, then, is the prior condition of the masquerade, the inner logic of impersonation. But the return is also to the resources of the body, the actor's body treated as a plane of signification. Michael Denning usefully draws attention to Raymond Williams's suggestion along these lines:

> In his chapter on "Means of Production" [in his book *Culture*], Williams discusses the development of cultural forms in terms of the "inherent resources" of the species (beginning his account not from "literature" or the "novel" but from the social development of physical movement and voice in dance and song) and the degree of popular access to the form: "while anyone in the world, with normal physical resources, can watch dance or look at sculpture or listen to music, still some forty percent of the world's present inhabitants can make no contact whatever with a piece of writing, and in earlier periods this percentage was much higher."[4]

While neither Denning nor Williams talks about "impersonation" and what they, as Janice Radway suggests in her critique, overlook is the fact of the mediation of all cultural forms, "impersonation" draws attention to itself as construct, to the viability and provisionality of all identities.

The Bombay film's use of the masquerade is motivated, as mentioned earlier, by ideas of the fragmentation and disintegration of the social/ national body and its recuperation and regeneration. It serves as a crossover phenomenon: between the individual and the social, between one's current state and a future state, between the private citizen and the public official, between dis-ease and well-being. As utopian moments interspersed in filmic texts, the masquerade signifies the triumph of social ideals within the context of the modern nation-state. However, the Bombay film treads its ground gingerly, not willing or capable of upsetting the two major divisions in Indian society: those of religion and language. (Intercommunal or interlinguistic love-affairs or attachments have been taboo on the Indian screen.) Class, the other major division in Indian as in all societies, on the other hand, is seen as less crucial a barrier to peaceful co-existence and citizenry and is routinely transcended through "magical" upward mobility.

Finally, we might ask, is the masquerade capable of embodying the aspirations of "the people"? The question of "the popular" is a thorny one for film studies, one that we still have very little purchase on. Our ways of verifying the popular—box-office success *or* work that somehow "arises" from the people, hence the "voice" of the disenfranchised—have to be seen together rather than as mutually exclusive. More and more, it is in the banality of mass culture that we have to theorize our notions of inclusiveness, of nationness. Meaghan Morris has provided a very useful discussion of this concept, weaving together notions of media analysis with the specificity of gendered and national-cultural discourses. "Banality," she writes, "is one of a group of words—including 'trivial' and 'mundane'—whose modern history inscribes the disintegration of old ideals about the common people, the common place, the common culture. In medieval French, the 'banal' fields, mills, and ovens were those used communally. It is only in the late eighteenth century that these words begin to accumulate their modern sense of the trite, the platitudinous, and the unoriginal."[5] The concepts of "impersonation" and "masquerade" for the study of Indian popular cinema would reveal, I have argued, a similar if far more lost and buried history. As a "banal" signifier of national-cultural belief and anxiety, of the lure of cinematic spectacle shining through the "false glitter" of a devalued cinema, imperso-nation as theoretical construct enables us as critics to "move *between* polemological and utopian practices."[6]

Notes

Introduction

1. See Chidananda Dasgupta, "The Painted Face of Politics: The Actor Politicians of South India," in *Cinema and Cultural Identity*, ed. Wimal Dissanayake, p. 143.

2. *India Today* (August 1982): 32.

3. See Alison Arnold, "Hindi Filmi Git: On the History of Commercial Indian Popular Cinema" (Ph.D. dissertation, University of Illinois, 1991).

4. Michael Denning, "The End of Mass Culture," *International Labor and Working-Class History* 37 (Spring 1990): 15.

5. Two films—Ismail Merchant and James Ivory's *Shakespearewallah* and Buddhadev Dasgupta's *Phera* (The return, 1986)—deal with this phenomenon.

6. David Napier, *Masks, Transformation and Paradox*, p. xxv.

7. Impersonation associated with courts and ideas of kingship was mentioned to me by historian Carol Breckenridge, editor of *Public Culture*.

8. Timothy Brennan, "The National Longing for Form," in *Nation and Narration*, ed. Homi Bhabha.

9. Edwin Gerow, "Rasa as a Category of Literary Criticism," in *Sanskrit Drama in Performance*, ed. Rachel Baumer et al., p. 249.

10. Iain Chambers, *Popular Culture: The Metropolitan Experience*, p. 43.

11. Ibid.

12. Salman Rushdie, "In Good Faith," *Newsweek*, February 12, 1990, p. 52.

13. I refer to India as a nation throughout this study in this commonly understood way, as we would refer to the United States or Australia or Senegal as nations. But I also suggest that the idea of "unity" implied by the term is always being contested and reaffirmed by the citizens of a given nation.

14. Gerow, "Rasa."

15. Slavoj Žižek, *Looking Awry: An Introduction to Jacques Lacan through Popular Culture*, p. 163.

16. Ibid.

17. Benedict Anderson, *Imagined Communities*, p. 14.

18. Homi Bhabha, ed., *Nation and Narration*, p. 3.

19. Philip Rosen, "History, Textuality, Nation: Kracauer, Burch and Some Problems in National Cinemas," *Iris* 2 (1984): 69.

20. Bhabha, *Nation*, p. 4.

21. Some characteristics of Ozu's distinctive filmic style include graphic continuity in editing and violation of the 180-degree system favored by the classical Hollywood film. See David Bordwell and Kristin Thompson, *Film Art*, and Noel Burch, *To the Distant Observer: Form and Meaning in Japanese Cinema*.

22. The term "interpellation" is now widely used in film and cultural criticism. Originating in Althusser's work, it refers to the pulling of individuals into social positions through

the discursive address of institutions. See Louis Althusser, "Ideology and Ideological State Apparatuses (Notes towards an Investigation)," in *Lenin and Philosophy*, pp. 170–183.

23. See Paul Willemen, "The Third Cinema Question: Notes and Reflections," in *Questions of Third Cinema*, ed. Pines and Willemen, pp. 1–29.

24. Fredric Jameson, "Third World Literature in the Era of Multinational Capitalism," *Social Text* 15 (Fall 1986): 65.

25. Andrew Ross, *No Respect: Intellectuals and Popular Culture*, p. 3.

26. Ashis Nandy, "An Intelligent Critic's Guide to Indian Cinema— III," *Deep Focus* 2, no. 1 (December 1988): 58.

1. Culture/Nation: Reclaiming the Past

1. Gayatri Spivak, *The Post-Colonial Critic*, p. 39.

2. Ibid.

3. *Film India: Satyajit Ray*, pp. 138–139.

4. See Hugo Munsterberg's review of books on Indian Art in *Literature East and West* 10, no. 1/2 (1966): 174.

5. Jawaharlal Nehru, *The Discovery of India*. Hereafter cited in text as *DI*.

6. Tariq Ali, *An Indian Dynasty*.

7. Judith Brown's *Modern India: The Origins of an Asian Democracy*, has a solid bibliography, but I want to draw special attention to *Subaltern Studies: Writings on South Asian History and Society*, ed. Ranajit Guha, 4

vols., for a revisionist historiographic project.

8. Francine Frankel, *India's Political Economy, 1947–1977*, pp. 11–22.

9. Interview with the author, April 1984.

10. Ibid.

11. Bipan Chandra, ed., *The Indian Left: Critical Appraisals*, p. 390.

12. Akhil Gupta, "The Political Economy of Post-Independence India—A Review Article," *Journal of Asian Studies* 48, no. 4 (November 1989): 787.

13. Cited in ibid., p. 788.

14. Barbara Stoller Miller, "Contending Narratives—The Political Life of the Indian Epics," *Journal of Asian Studies* 50, no. 4 (November 1991): 783–792.

15. Jabbar Patel in the *Statesman*, November 6, 1983.

16. "Interview with Nirmal Verma," *Illustrated Weekly of India*, November 20, 1983.

17. See Judith Mara Gutman, *Through Indian Eyes*, pp. 84–100.

18. Firoze Rangoonwalla, *Indian Cinema: Past and Present*, p. 15.

19. Ibid., p. 28.

20. J. B. H. Wadia, "The Indian Silent Film," in *Seventy Years of Indian Cinema, 1913–1983*, ed. T. M. Ramachandran, p. 24.

21. *Studies in Film History: D. G. Phalke*. All the quotes regarding Phalke and his work are taken from this publication.

22. Rangoonwalla, *Indian Cinema*.

23. Ibid.

24. Wadia, "Indian Silent Film."

25. *Illustrated Weekly of India*, November 20, 1983.

26. Ramachandran, *Seventy Years,* p. 50.

27. Rangoonwalla, *Indian Cinema,* p. 25.

28. K. A. Abbas, *Indian Talkie, 1931–56.*

29. Ibid.

30. Ibid.

31. Erik Barnouw and Krishnaswamy, *Indian Film,* p. 121.

32. "The Changing Scene," *India Today,* July 16–31, 1981.

33. Ibid.

2. The Film Industry and the State

1. Satyajit Ray, "Under Western Eyes," *Sight and Sound* (Autumn 1982): 269.

2. David Bordwell, Janet Staiger, and Kristin Thompson, *The Classical Hollywood Cinema,* p. xiv.

3. Thomas Schatz, "Authorship, Authority and Studio Filmmaking: Notes Toward a Classical Management Paradigm," paper presented at the Society for Cinema Studies conference at Los Angeles, May 1991.

4. See John Downing, ed., *Film and Politics in the Third World,* and Jim Pines and Paul Willemen, *Questions of Third Cinema.*

5. Ibid.

6. Ashish Rajadhyaksha, "Neo-Traditionalism: Film as Popular Art in India," *Framework* 32/33 (1986): 41.

7. *Indian Talkie, 1931–56,* p. 81.

8. Girish Karnad, "When Stunt Was King," in Ramachandran, *Seventy Years,* p. 264.

9. Ibid., p. 263.

10. "Interview with Rajinder Singh Bedi," *Mahfil* 8, no. 2/3 (1972): 139–155.

11. Ibid., p. 154.

12. *Indian Talkie, 1931–56,* p. 34.

13. Nirad C. Chaudhari, "Is India a Cultural Vacuum?" *Illustrated Weekly of India,* August 15, 1954.

14. Donald E. Smith, *India as a Secular State,* pp. 372–374.

15. R. K. Narayan, "The Writer in India," *Illustrated Weekly of India,* October 2, 1960.

16. Gangadhar Gadgil, in ibid.

17. *Indian Talkie, 1931–56,* p. 35.

18. Ibid., pp. 37–41.

19. B. V. Dharap, film historian in interview with the author, November 1982.

20. *Report of the Film Enquiry Committee,* Government of India (1951), p. 3.

21. Ibid., p. 16.

22. *Filmfare,* April 18, 1952.

23. *Filmfare,* April 26, 1957.

24. *Filmfare,* January 4, 1957.

25. *Filmfare,* July 10, 1953.

26. John Ellis, *Visible Fictions,* p. 97.

27. *Filmfare,* March 20, 1953.

28. Raymond Williams, *The Sociology of Culture,* pp. 102–103.

29. *Filmfare,* May 15, 1953.

30. *Illustrated Weekly of India,* May 2, 1954.

31. *Filmfare,* February 19, 1954.

32. *Filmfare,* August 7, 1953.

33. *Filmfare,* July 9, 1954.

34. Ibid.

35. *Filmfare,* June 13, 1952.

36. Cited in Aruna Vasudev, *Liberty and License in the Indian Cinema,* p. 73.

37. *Filmfare*, May 1, 1953.

38. Ashis Nandy, *The Intimate Enemy: Loss and Recovery of Self under Colonialism*, p. xviii.

39. See discussion of this episode in Barnouw and Krishnaswamy, *Indian Film*, pp. 207–214.

40. *Filmfare*, July 19, 1957.

41. *Filmfare*, February 27, 1959.

42. Ibid.

43. *Report of the Enquiry on Film Censorship*.

3. National Identity and the Realist Aesthetic

1. The question of realism has been crucial to the discussion of cinema from the very beginning but received its most systematic formulation in the 1940s and 1950s in the work of Andre Bazin, *What Is Cinema*. Siegfried Kracauer's *Theory of Film: The Redemption of Physical Reality*, also adopts a realist stance. During the 1970s, issues of realism were central to the ideological and aesthetic debates that flourished in *Screen*. See, for instance, Paul Willemen, "On Realism in the Cinema," *Screen* 13, no. 1 (Spring 1972): 37–44; Colin MacCabe, "Realism and the Cinema: Notes on Some Brechtian Theses," *Screen* 15, no. 2 (Summer 1974): 7–27; and Colin MacCabe, "Theory and Film: Principles of Realism and Pleasure," *Screen* 17, no. 3 (Autumn 1976): 7–27. Other journals that have taken up the debate on realism are *Cinema Journal*, *Camera Obscura*, and *Quarterly Review of Film Studies*.

2. Ananda Coomaraswamy, *Dance of Siva: Essays on Indian Art and Culture*, p. 104. The concept of *maya*, or illusion, in the Hindu philosophical tradition is a complex and difficult one. Material reality as *maya* should not be taken to mean that this view holds the world to be a figment of one's imagination. For a brief clarification of the concept, see Mircea Eliade, *Myths, Dreams and Mysteries*, pp. 238–245.

3. An extensive literature is available on the "Rasasutra," the basis of Sanskrit classical drama and aesthetics. For an introduction to the concept, see Edward Dimock et al., *The Literatures of India: An Introduction*, pp. 115–136, 216–227.

4. Meenakshi Mukherjee, *Realism and Reality: The Novel and Society in India*, p. 15.

5. Ibid., p. 89.

6. Ibid., p. 80.

7. See, however, a critique of Mukherjee's position in a review of her book by Nancy Fitch, *Journal of South Asian Literature* 22, no. 1 (Winter/Spring 1987): 238–244.

8. Gordon Roadarmel, "The Modern Hindi Short Story and Modern Hindi Criticism," in Dimock, *Literatures*, p. 241.

9. Ibid., pp. 241–243.

10. Ibid., p. 245.

11. For detailed background information on developments within the Bombay film industry during the fifties, I have relied primarily on *Filmfare* and *Filmindia* for reasons of availability and also for the fact that as English-language film magazines they had a pan-Indian readership. I have also consulted the *Journal of the Film Industry* and the film page in the *Illustrated Weekly of India*.

12. See Edward Shils, *The Intel-*

lectual between Tradition and Modernity.

13. Aruna Vasudev and Philippe Lenglet, eds., *Indian Cinema Superbazaar*, p. 222.

14. *Filmfare*, July 24, 1953.

15. *Indian Talkie, 1931–56*, p. 4.

16. *Filmfare*, March 18, 1955.

17. Interview with Nabendu Ghosh by the author, March 13, 1984.

18. Even as astute a filmmaker as Shyam Benegal felt that the editing out of songs from Guru Dutt's *Sahib Bibi aur Ghulam* would enhance it as a "realistic" film. See Vasudev and Lenglet, *Indian Cinema*, pp. 161–162.

19. Kumar Shahani, interview with the author, March 1984.

20. Satyajit Ray, quoted in *Film India: Looking Back, 1896–1960*, p. 134.

21. Stanley Corkin, "Realism and Cultural Form: The Common Structures of American Cinema and Realistic Literature in the Late 19th and Early 20th Centuries" (Ph.D. dissertation, New York University, 1984), p. 93.

22. Interview with the author, February 1984.

23. Rustom Bharucha, *Rehearsals of Revolution*, p. 40.

24. Ibid., p. 42

25. Ibid., p. 48.

26. Kobita Sarkar, *Khwaja Ahmad Abbas as a Film-Maker*.

27. Interview with the author, December 1982.

28. Review of *Do Bigha Zamin* in *Film India: Looking Back*, p. 134.

29. Balraj Sahni, *Balraj Sahni*, p. 205.

30. Ibid., p. 212.

31. Fredric Jameson, "Class and Allegory in Contemporary Mass Culture: *Dog Day Afternoon* as a Political Film," in *Movies and Methods*, part 2, ed. Bill Nichols, p. 722.

32. Janice Radway, "The Error of Her Ways," Book Review Section in *Journal of Communication* 35, no. 4 (Autumn 1985): 181.

33. Jameson, "Class," p. 719.

34. Ibid.

35. Richard Lannoy, *The Speaking Tree: A Study of Indian Culture and Society*, p. xix.

36. Richard Dyer, "Entertainment and Utopia," in *Movies and Methods*, ed. Nichols, p. 222.

37. Ibid., pp. 228–229.

38. Vijay Mishra, "Towards a Theoretical Critique of Bombay Cinema," *Screen* 26, no. 3–4 (May–August 1985): 139.

4. New Uses of the Romantic-Mythic Tradition

1. Mark Schorer, "The Necessity of Myth," *Daedalus* 88 (Spring 1959): 359.

2. William Rowe and Vivian Schelling, *Memory and Modernity*, p. 155.

3. D. D. Kosambi, *Myth and Reality*, p. 1.

4. Ibid., p. 2.

5. Roland Barthes, *Mythologies*, p. 114.

6. Roger Silverstone, "Television: Myth, Science, Commonsense," paper presented at the International Communication Association conference in May 1986, p. 2.

7. Doris Sommer, "Irresistible Ro-

mance: The Foundational Fictions of Latin America," in *Nation and Narration*, ed. Homi Bhabha, p. 75.

8. Chidananda Dasgupta, *Talking about Films*, p. 25.

9. Ibid.

10. Mircea Eliade, *Myths, Dreams and Mysteries: The Encounter between Contemporary Faiths and Archaic Realities*, p. 165.

11. Quoted in ibid.

12. Christopher Baker, "Introduction," in S. Theodore Baskaran, *The Message Bearers: The Nationalist Politics and the Entertainment Media in South India, 1880–1945*.

13. Ibid., p. 1.

14. See Ainslie Embree, *India's Search for National Identity*, p. 27.

15. Shampa Banerjee and Anil Srivastava, *One Hundred Indian Films*, p. 114.

16. Sudhir Kakar, *The Inner World: A Psycho-analytic Study of Childhood and Society in India*, p. 32.

17. Ibid., pp. 32–33.

18. Ibid., p. 33.

19. Ashis Nandy, *At the Edge of Psychology*, p. 1.

20. Kakar, *The Inner World*.

21. Girish Karnad, "Comments from the Gallery," in "Indian Popular Cinema: Myth, Meaning and Metaphor," *India International Centre Quarterly* 8, no. 1 (1981): 104.

22. Farrukh Dhondy, "Keeping Faith: Indian Film and Its World," *Daedalus* (Winter 1985): 126.

23. Punita Bhatt, "The Cinema of Raj Kapoor," in Ramachandran, *Seventy Years*, p. 132.

24. *Filmfare*, January 4, 1957.

25. *Filmfare*, August 8, 1952.

26. *Filmfare*, April 26, 1957.

27. Kakar, *The Inner World*, pp. 125–126.

28. Ibid., p. 137.

29. Edward Hotspur Johnson, "Indian Cinema," BFI Dossier #5 (London). Unpublished.

30. *Filmfare*, August 16, 1957.

31. See Jawaharlal Nehru, "The Quest," in *Modern India: An Interpretive Anthology*, ed. Thomas Metcalf, p. 9.

32. Erich Neumann, *The Great Mother: An Analysis of the Archetype*.

33. E. O. Cousins, *The Awakening of Asian Womanhood*, p. 95.

34. Also see Rosie Thomas, "Sanctity and Scandal: The Mythologization of Mother India," *Quarterly Review of Film and Video* 11, no. 3 (1989): 11–30.

35. Neumann, *The Great Mother*, p. 128.

36. Nandy, *At the Edge*, p. 36.

37. Wendy Doniger O'Flaherty, *Women, Androgynes and Other Mythical Beasts*, p. 4.

5. The Recuperation of History and Memory

1. See Stephen Heath, "Contexts," *Edinburgh Magazine* 2 (1977): 38.

2. Philip Rosen, "Securing the Historical: Historiography and the Classical Cinema," in *Cinema Histories, Cinema Practices*, ed. Patricia Mellencamp and Philip Rosen, pp. 17–18.

3. Thomas Elsaesser, "Film History and Visual Pleasure: Weimar Cinema," in ibid., p. 77.

4. V. S. Naipaul embodied this view in most of his books on India.

5. Romila Thapar, *Ancient Indian Social History: Some Interpretations*, p. 2.

6. Meenakshi Mukherjee, *Realism and Reality: The Novel and Society in India*, pp. 38–67.

7. Quoted in ibid., p. 57.

8. Thapar, *Ancient Indian Social History*, p. 285.

9. Kakar, *The Inner World*, p. 46.

10. Mircea Eliade, *Myth and Reality*, pp. 114–125.

11. Ibid., p. 116.

12. Thapar, *Ancient Indian Social History*, p. 273.

13. S. Radhakrishnan and Charles Moore, eds., *A Sourcebook in Indian Philosophy*, p. xvii.

14. Thapar, *Ancient Indian Social History*, p. 273.

15. Ibid., p. 326.

16. Ibid., p. 275.

17. Mukherjee, *Realism and Reality*, p. 41.

18. Rabindranath Tagore, "A Vision of India's History," in *A Tagore Reader*, ed. Amiya Chakravarty, pp. 189–190.

19. Ibid., p. 194.

20. Kalyan Chatterjee, "Renaissance and Modernity: Tagore in Perspective," in *Review of National Literatures: India* 10 (1979): 36.

21. Vijay Mishra, "Decentering History: Some Versions of Bombay Cinema," *East-West Film Journal* 6, no. 1 (January 1992): 111–155.

22. Hayden White, *Metahistory: The Historical Imagination in Nineteenth Century Europe*.

23. Following the French linguist Emile Benveniste, film theorists in the 1970s employed the distinction between "history" and "discourse" in order to signal two styles of narration. The classic narrative film conceals the marks of enunciation and is thus considered historical: events unfold, as it were, by themselves, with no narrators or viewers acknowledged. Those films which draw attention to themselves as constructs are discursive, foregrounding the act of enunciation or address. See Christian Metz, "History/Discourse: Note on Two Voyeurisms," and Geoffrey Nowell-Smith, "A Note on History/Discourse," in *Edinburgh '76 Magazine* 1 (1976): 21–32. Also see Robert Stam, Robert Burgoyne, and Sandy Flitterman-Lewis, *New Vocabularies in Film Semiotics*, pp. 105–107. In the present instance, I believe that the historical film genre as an instance within Indian popular cinema considerably complicates issues relating to the representation of social reality on the screen.

24. Heath, "Contexts."

25. Fredric Jameson, *The Political Unconscious*, p. 75.

26. *Anarkali* (1953) was directed by Nandlal Jaswantlal.

27. R. C. Majumdar, *Historiography in Modern India*, p. 48.

28. Ibid., p. 51.

29. Romila Thapar, *Communalism and the Writing of Indian History*.

30. Alison Arnold, "The Overt and Covert Expression of Hindu-Muslim Unity in Popular Hindi Film Song," unpublished paper, 1986.

31. S. Bhattacharya, *A Dictionary of Indian History*.

32. Edward Balfour, *The Cyclopaedia of India*, vol. 2, p. 655.

33. Rangoonwalla, *Indian Cinema*.

34. Michel Foucault, *Power/*

Knowledge: Selected Interviews and Other Writings: 1972–1977, trans. Colin Gordon et al., pp. 73–74.

35. Heath, "Contexts," pp. 41–42.

36. Leger Grindon, "Romantic Archetypes and Political Meaning in the Historical Fiction Film," *Persistence of Vision* 3/4 (Summer 1986): 16–17.

37. Bimal Mitra, *Saheb Bibi Golam*, preface. The translations from the book are mine.

38. Ibid., p. 14.

39. Arun Khopkar, *Guru Dutt*, pp. 102–117.

40. Thomas Elsaesser, "Film History and Visual Pleasure," p. 51.

41. Andrew Robinson, "Introduction," in Satyajit Ray, *The Chess Players and Other Screenplays*, p. 3.

42. Prem Chand, *A Game of Chess*, in ibid., p. 62.

43. Satyajit Ray, "Reply to Rajbans Khanna," *Illustrated Weekly of India*, December 31, 1978, p. 50.

44. *Film India: Satyajit Ray*, p. 115.

45. Rajbans Khanna, "Ray's Wajid Ali Shah," *Illustrated Weekly of India*, October 22, 1978, pp. 49–53.

46. Ray, "Reply."

47. See Robinson, "Introduction," p. 7.

48. Ibid.

49. Teresa de Lauretis, *Alice Doesn't: Feminism, Semiotics, Cinema*, p. 3.

50. Ray, "Reply."

51. Ibid.

52. Ibid.

53. M. Bhaktavatsala, "Attenborough's Experiment with Truth," *Illustrated Weekly of India*, November 21, 1982, pp. 42–43.

54. David Denby, *Sight and Sound*.

55. Timothy Brennan, "The National Longing for Form," in Bhabha, ed., *Nation and Narration*, p. 44.

6. The National-Heroic Image

1. Jean Franco, "Beyond Ethnocentrism: Gender, Power and the Third World Intelligentsia," in *Marxism and the Interpretation of Culture*, ed. Cary Nelson and Lawrence Grossberg, pp. 503–515.

2. Ashis Nandy, "The Popular Hindi Film: Ideology and First Principles," *India International Centre Quarterly* 8, no. 1 (1981): 93.

3. Vijay Mishra, Peter Jeffery, and Brian Shoesmith, "The Actor as Parallel Text in Bombay Cinema," *Quarterly Review of Film and Video* 11, no. 3 (1989): 52.

4. See, for instance, the essays in the volume *Formations of Fantasy*, ed. Victor Burgin, James Donald, and Cora Kaplan, in particular, Joan Riviere's "Womanliness as a Masquerade" and Stephen Heath's commentary on it. In Heath's words, "In the masquerade the woman mimics an authentic—genuine—womanliness but then authentic womanliness is such a mimicry, *is* the masquerade ('they are the same thing'); to be a woman is to dissimulate a fundamental masculinity, femininity is that dissimulation" (p. 49).

5. Marjorie Garber, *Vested Interests: Cross-Dressing and Cultural Anxiety*.

6. See Mary Ann Doane, "Film and the Masquerade: Theorising the

Female Spectator," *Screen* 23 (September–October 1982): 74–87.

7. James Naremore, *Acting in the Cinema*, p. 2.

8. Charles Affron, "Generous Stars," in *Star Texts*, ed. Jeremy Butler, p. 92.

9. Joseph Campbell, *The Hero with a Thousand Faces*.

10. Napier, *Masks*.

11. Robert Ezra Park, quoted by Naremore, *Acting in the Cinema*, p. 22.

12. Roland Barthes, "The Face of Garbo," in *Mythologies*, p. 56.

13. I have used Farrukh Dhondy's translation of this stanza that appeared in his article, "Keeping Faith: Indian Film and Its World," *Daedalus* (Winter 1985): 130. Dhondy wrongly attributes the song to the film *Awaara*.

14. See Ashis Nandy, *The Intimate Enemy: Loss and Recovery of Self under Colonialism*, pp. 1–63.

15. Sudhir Kakar, *Intimate Relations: Exploring Indian Sexuality*, p. 37.

16. *Filmfare* 38, no. 4 (April 1989): 77.

17. Kashmir as limit text of the Indian national imaginary is replayed in David Lean's *A Passage to India* when Lean departs from Forster's text at the end of the novel and effects a reconciliation between Aziz and Fielding in Kashmir, where Aziz has retired after the trial.

18. Sharmila Tagore's "bikini outfit" worn in the film provided grist for the fanzines. Here we have a transgression of female identity through a reversal of the state of modesty, which functions as a signifier of femininity in the Bombay film.

19. Naremore, *Acting*, p. 158.

20. There has been much theoretical work in the area of the gaze since Laura Mulvey's pioneering essay "Visual Pleasure and Narrative Cinema," *Screen* 16, no. 3 (Autumn 1977): 6–18. The articles are too numerous to mention, but in general applications of Mulvey's ideas to the classical Hollywood film were followed by a questioning of the theory itself because of its view of the female spectator as absent. More recent work has sought to correct that imbalance by positing the historical female spectator as well as the male star as subject and object of the gaze. For a review of these issues, see Miriam Hansen, "Pleasure, Ambivalence, Identification: Valentino and Female Spectatorship," *Cinema Journal* 25, no. 4 (Summer 1986): 6–32. However, the focus on the gendered gaze has obscured other visual paradigms to which oedipal conflict and resolution is less applicable and where different cultural and narrative patterns would call for the structuring of other modes of identification and pleasure.

21. Mishra, Jeffery, and Shoesmith, "The Actor," p. 52.

22. Claude Lévi-Strauss, quoted in Elizabeth Cowie, "Woman as Sign," *m/f* 1 (1978): 49–63.

23. Ibid., p. 54.

24. Ibid.

25. Napier, *Masks*, p. 3.

26. Wimal Dissanayake and Malti Sahai, *Raj Kapoor's Films: Harmony of Discourses*, p. 73.

27. Ibid., pp. 73–74.

28. Gayle Rubin, "The Traffic in Women: Notes on the 'Political Economy' of Sex," in *Toward an An-*

thropology of Women, ed. Rayna Reiter, p. 195.

29. *Filmfare* 38, no. 6 (June 1989).

7. The Authenticity Debate

1. Quoted in Pico Iyer, *Video Night in Kathmandu*, p. 283.

2. Ashis Nandy, "An Intelligent Critic's Guide," 53.

3. Pierre Bourdieu, *Distinction: A Social Critique of the Judgment of Taste*.

4. The Naxalite movement was a Maoist-inspired movement that originated in Naxalbari in rural Bengal in the early seventies and was conducted with the use of terror tactics and a campaign of violence.

5. Many anecdotal accounts, recounted to me, support this assertion.

6. Andreas Huyssen, *After the Great Divide*.

7. Raghunath Raina, "Foreword," in *The New Generation, 1960–1980, Film India*, p. 5.

8. Chidananda Dasgupta, "The 'New' Cinema: A Wave or a Future?" in *Indian Cinema Superbazaar*, ed. Aruna Vasudev and Philippe Lenglet, p. 41.

9. Kobita Sarkar, "Indian Cinema: New Directions," in *Indian Horizons*, p. 30.

10. Andrew Robinson, "The New Indian Cinema," *Films and Filming* 338 (November 1982): 16–18.

11. *New York Times*, June 21, 1981.

12. Ibid.

13. Satyajit Ray, *Our Films Their Films*, p. 93.

14. Ibid., p. 98.

15. Ibid., p. 99.

16. Mira Reym Binford, "The Two Cinemas of India," in *Film and Politics in the Third World*, ed. John Downing, p. 150.

17. Manji Pendakur, "India," in *The Asian Film Industry*, ed. John Lent, pp. 229–252.

18. Gaston Roberge, "A New Film Policy for India," *Media Development* 3 (1981): 8–11.

19. Gaston Roberge, *Another Cinema for Another Society*, pp. 89–90.

20. *Illustrated Weekly of India*, December 19, 1982.

21. "Interview with Mrinal Sen," *Cineaste* 11, no. 4 (Winter 1982): 19.

22. Andrew Ross, *No Respect: Intellectuals and Popular Culture*.

23. Michael Denning, "The End of Mass Culture," in *Modernity and Mass Culture*, ed. James Naremore and Patrick Brantlinger, p. 267.

24. Frantz Fanon, quoted in Bhabha, "Commitment."

25. Clyde Taylor, "Black Cinema in the Post-aesthetic Era," and Homi Bhabha, "The Commitment to Theory," in *Questions of Third Cinema*, ed. Jim Pines and Paul Willemen, p. 113.

26. Bhabha, "Commitment," p. 130.

27. *Film India: The New Generation*, p. 149.

28. Ashish Rajadhyaksha, "Dossier: Kumar Shahani," *Framework* 30/31 (1986): 69.

29. Ibid., p. 103.

30. "Interview: Shyam Benegal," in Vasudev and Lenglet, *Indian Cinema Superbazaar*, p. 166.

8. Woman and the Burden of Postcoloniality

1. In this discussion, I have used the terms "courtesan" and "prostitute" interchangeably, as most scholars on the subject have tended to do, although historically the courtesan's social status was no doubt higher than that of the common prostitute. Moreover, their representation in the Bombay cinema tends to support a conflation of the terms, since it is precisely the moral and social ambiguity of the courtesan's "state of being" that is explored.

2. Quoted in Teresa de Lauretis, *Alice Doesn't: Feminism, Semiotics, Cinema*, p. 6.

3. Aruna Vasudev, "The Woman: Vamp or Victim?" in Vasudev and Lenglet, *Indian Cinema Superbazaar*, pp. 98–105.

4. To my knowledge, the only book devoted to the "fallen woman" genre in Hollywood is Lea Jacobs's *The Wages of Sin*, a study of censorship rather than of representation per se. This is itself an indication of the lack of cultural resonance of the courtesan figure in American society.

5. Two recent studies of interest are Alain Corbin, *Women for Hire*, and Charles Bernheimer, *Figures of Ill Repute*.

6. Most studies of female impersonation hinge on the issue of gender identity, following Joan Riviere's classic essay "Womanliness as a Masquerade" in Victor Burgin et al., eds., *Formations of Fantasy*. For a recent study of androgyny, see Marjorie Garber, *Vested Interests: Cross-dressing and Cultural Anxiety*.

7. Moti Chandra, *The World of Courtesans*; Frédérique Apffel Marglin, *Wives of the God-King: The Rituals of the Devadasis of Puri*.

8. Havelock Ellis, *The Psychology of Sex*, pp. 218–318.

9. Chandra, *World of Courtesans*, 23.

10. Marglin, *Wives*, p. 10.

11. Chandra, *World of Courtesans*, 44.

12. Ibid., 192.

13. Abdul Halim Sharar, *Lucknow: The Last Phase of an Oriental Culture*, p. 145.

14. Marglin, *Wives*, p. 5.

15. Ibid., p. 6.

16. Veena Oldenburg, *The Making of Colonial Lucknow, 1856–1877*, p. 108.

17. See ibid., p. 110.

18. "Girish Karnad: Doing a Double Take," *Express Magazine*, January 26, 1984.

19. Ibid.

20. Mirza Mohammed Ruswa, "Introduction," *Umrao Jan*.

21. Ibid.

22. Anne McClintock, "The Scandal of the Whorearchy: Prostitution in Colonial Nairobi," *Transition* 52 (1991): 92–99.

23. Shampa Banerjee and Anil Srivastava, *One Hundred Indian Feature Films: An Annotated Bibliography*, p. 78.

24. Thomas Elsaesser, "Tales of Sound and Fury: Observations on the Family Melodrama," in *Movies and Methods*, vol. 2, ed. Bill Nichols, pp. 166–189.

25. See Alison Arnold, "Hindi Filmi Git: On the History of Commercial Indian Popular Cinema" (Ph.D. dissertation, University of Illinois, 1991), p. 21.

26. *India Abroad*, September 7, 1984.

Conclusion

1. See Meaghan Morris, "Banality in Cultural Studies," *Discourse* 10, no. 2 (Spring–Summer 1988): 18.

2. John D. H. Downing, ed., *Film and Politics in the Third World*, p. 312.

3. Morris, "Banality," p. 11.

4. Michael Denning, "The End of Mass Culture," *International Labor and Working-Class History* 37 (Spring 1990): 15.

5. Morris, "Banality," p. 26.

6. Ibid., pp. 24–25.

Selected Bibliography

Abbas, Khwaja Ahmad. *I Am Not an Island: An Experiment in Autobiography.* New Delhi: Vikas, 1977.

Ahmad, Aijaz. *In Theory: Classes, Nations, Literatures.* London: Verso, 1992.

Ali, Tariq. *An Indian Dynasty.* New York: G. P. Putnam's Sons, 1985.

Allen, Robert, and Douglas Gomery. *Film History: Theory and Practice.* New York: Knopf, 1985.

Altekar, A. S. *The Position of Women in Hindu Civilization: From Prehistoric Times to the Present Day.* Delhi: Motilal Banarsidass, 1973.

Althusser, Louis. *Lenin and Philosophy and Other Essays.* Translated by Ben Brewster. New York: Monthly Review Press, 1971.

Anderson, Benedict. *Imagined Communities: Reflections on the Origin and Spread of Nationalism.* London: Verso, 1983.

Anderson, Perry. "Modernity and Revolution." *New Left Review* 144 (March/April 1984).

Armes, Roy. *Third World Film Making and the West.* Berkeley: University of California Press, 1987.

Auerbach, Erich. *Mimesis: The Representation of Reality in Western Literature.* Translated by Willard Trask. Princeton: Princeton University Press, 1953.

Bald, Suresht Renjen. *Novelists and Political Consciousness: Literary Expression of Indian Nationalism 1919–1947.* Atlantic Highlands, N.J.: Humanities Press, 1982.

Banerjee, Shampa, and Anil Srivastava. *One Hundred Indian Feature Films: An Annotated Bibliography.* New York: Garland Publishing, 1988.

Barnouw, Erik, and S. Krishnaswamy. *Indian Film.* 2d ed. New York: Columbia University Press, 1980.

Barthes, Roland. *Image, Music, Text.* Translated by Stephen Heath. New York: Hill and Wang, 1977.

———. *Mythologies.* Translated by Annette Lavers. New York: Hill and Wang, 1972.

Baskaran, S. Theodore. *The Message Bearers: Nationalist Politics and the Entertainment Media in South India, 1880–1945.* Madras: Cre-A, 1981.

Baumer, Rachel, and James Brandon, eds. *Sanskrit Drama in Performance.* Honolulu: University of Hawaii Press, 1981.

Bazin, Andre. *What Is Cinema?* 2 vols. Berkeley: University of California Press, 1967.

Berman, Marshall. *All That Is Solid Melts into Air: The Experience of Modernity.* New York: Simon and Schuster, 1982.

Bernheimer, Charles. *Figures of Ill Repute: Representing Prostitution in Nineteenth Century France.* Cambridge, Mass.: Harvard University Press, 1989.

Bertrand, Ina. "'National Identity'/'National History'/'National Film': The

Australian Experience." *Historical Journal of Film, Radio and Television* 4, no. 2 (1984): 179–188.

Bhabha, Homi. *Nation and Narration.* New York: Routledge, 1990.

———. "The Other Question: Difference, Discrimination and the Discourse of Colonialism." In *Literature, Politics and Theory: Papers from the Essex Conference, 1976–1984.* Edited by Francis Barker et al. London: Methuen, 1986.

Bharucha, Rustom. *Rehearsals of Revolution: The Political Theater of Bengal.* Calcutta: Seagull Books, 1983.

Bhatia, Krishan. *The Ordeal of Nationhood: A Social Study of India since Independence, 1947–1970.* New York: Atheneum, 1971.

Bordwell, David, Janet Staiger, and Kristin Thompson. *The Classical Hollywood Cinema.* New York: Columbia University Press, 1985.

Bordwell, David, and Kristin Thompson, eds. *Film Art,* 3d rev. ed. New York: McGraw Hill, 1990.

Bourdieu, Pierre. *Distinction: A Social Critique of the Judgment of Taste.* Cambridge: Harvard University Press, 1986.

Brooks, Peter. *The Melodramatic Imagination.* New York: Columbia University Press, 1985.

Brown, Judith. *Modern India: The Origins of an Asian Democracy.* New York: Oxford University Press, 1985.

Burch, Noel. *To the Distant Observer: Form and Meaning in Japanese Cinema.* Berkeley: University of California Press, 1979.

Burgin, Victor, James Donald, and Cora Kaplan, eds. *Formations of Fantasy.* London: Methuen, 1986.

Burton, Julianne. "Marginal Cinemas and Mainstream Critical Theory." *Screen* 26, no. 3/4 (May–August 1985).

Butler, Jeremy, ed. *Star Texts.* Detroit: Wayne State University Press. 1991.

Butler, Judith. "Sex and Gender in Simone de Beauvoir's *The Second Sex.*" *Yale French Studies* 72 (1986): 35–49.

Campbell, Joseph. *The Hero with a Thousand Faces.* New York: Bollingen Foundation, 1968.

Chakravarty, Amiya, ed. *A Tagore Reader.* Boston: Beacon Press, 1966.

Chambers, Iain. *Popular Culture: The Metropolitan Experience.* London and New York: Methuen, 1986.

Chanan, Michael. *The Cuban Image.* London: BFI Publishing, 1985.

Chandra, Bipan. *The Indian Left: Critical Appraisals.* Delhi: Vikas Publishing House, 1983.

———. *The Rise and Growth of Economic Nationalism in India: Economic Policies of Indian National Leadership, 1880–1905.* New Delhi: Peoples' Publishing House, 1966.

Chandra, Moti. *The World of Courtesans.* Delhi: Vikas Publishing House, 1973.

Chatterjee, Kalyan. "Renaissance and Modernity: Tagore in Perspective." In *Review of National Literatures: India.* Vol. 10, 1979.

Chatterjee, Partha. *Nationalist Thought and the Colonial World: A Derivative Discourse?* London: Zed, 1986.

Chaudhari, Nirad. "Is India a Cultural Vacuum?" *Illustrated Weekly of India,* August 15, 1954.

Clark, T. W., ed. *The Novel in India: Its Birth and Development.* Berkeley: University of California Press, 1971.

Coomaraswamy, Ananda K. *The Dance of Siva: Essays on Indian Art and Culture.* New York: Dover Publications, 1985.

Corbin, Alain. *Women for Hire.* Cambridge, Mass.: Harvard University Press, 1990.

Dasgupta, Chidananda. "Indian Cinema: Dynamics of Old and New." In *India 2000: The Next Fifteen Years.* Edited by James R. Roach. Maryland: Riverdale Company, 1986.

————. *Talking about Films.* Delhi: Orient Longman, 1981.

D'Cruz, Edward. *India: The Quest for Nationhood.* Bombay: Lalvani Publishing House, 1967.

de Lauretis, Teresa. *Alice Doesn't: Feminism, Semiotics, Cinema.* Bloomington: Indiana University Press, 1984.

Dhondy, Farrukh. "Keeping Faith: Indian Film and Its World." *Daedalus* 114, no. 4 (Fall 1985).

Dimock, Edward C., et al. *The Literatures of India: An Introduction.* Chicago: University of Chicago Press, 1974.

Dissanayake, Wimal, ed. *Cinema and Cultural Identity.* Hawaii: East-West Center, 1988.

Dissanayake, Wimal, and Malti Sahai. *Raj Kapoor's Films: Harmony of Discourses.* Delhi: Vikas, 1988.

Doane, Mary Ann. "Film and the Masquerade: Theorising the Female Spectator." *Screen* 23 (September–October 1982).

Downing, John, ed. *Film and Politics in the Third World.* New York: Autonomedia, 1987.

Eagleton, Terry. *Ideology.* London: Verso, 1991.

Eliade, Mircea. *Myth and Reality.* New York: Harper Torchbooks, 1963.

————. *Myths, Dreams and Mysteries: The Encounter between Contemporary Faiths and Archaic Realities.* New York: Harper and Row, 1967.

Ellis, John. *Visible Fictions.* London: Routledge and Kegan Paul, 1983.

Elsaesser, Thomas. "Film History and Visual Pleasure: Weimar Cinema." In *Cinema Histories, Cinema Practices.* Edited by Patricia Mellencamp and Philip Rosen. AFI Monographs, vol. 4. Maryland: University Publishers of America, 1984.

————. "The New Film History." *Sight and Sound* (Autumn 1986).

Embree, Ainslie T. *India's Search for National Identity.* New York: Alfred A. Knopf, 1972.

Erikson, Erik. *Gandhi's Truth.* New York: W. W. Norton, 1969.

Fane, Hanna. "The Female Element in Indian Culture." *Asian Folklore Studies* 34 (1975).

Fanon, Frantz. *The Wretched of the Earth*. New York: Grove Press, 1968.

Filmfare. Bombay, weekly.

Fimindia. Bombay, monthly. Succeeded by *Mother India*, 1961.

Film India: Looking Back, 1896–1960. New Delhi: Directorate of Film Festivals, 1981.

Film India: The New Generation, 1960–1980. New Delhi: Directorate of Film Festivals, 1981.

Film India: Satyajit Ray. New Delhi: Directorate of Film Festivals, 1981.

Film Miscellany. Poona: Film and Television Institute of India, 1976.

Fischer, Michael, and Mehdi Abedi. *Debating Muslims*. Madison: University of Wisconsin Press, 1990.

Formations of Fantasy. London: Methuen, 1986.

Formations of Nation and People. London: Routledge and Kegan Paul, 1984.

Foucault, Michel. "Film and Popular Memory." *Radical Philosophy* 11 (Summer 1975).

———. *Power/Knowledge: Selected Interviews and Other Writings: 1972–1977*. Translated by Colin Gordon, L. Marshall, J. Mepham, and K. Soper. New York, 1980.

Frankel, Francine. *India's Political Economy, 1947–1977*. Princeton, N.J.: Princeton University Press, 1978.

Garber, Marjorie. *Vested Interests: Cross-dressing and Cultural Anxiety*. New York: Routledge, 1992.

Ghatak, Ritwik. *Cinema and I*. Calcutta: Ritwik Memorial Trust, 1987.

Gilmore, David. *Manhood in the Making: Cultural Concepts of Masculinity*. New Haven: Yale University Press, 1990.

Gombrich, E. H. *Art and Illusion: A Study in the Psychology of Pictorial Representation*. New York: Pantheon, 1960.

Grindon, Leger. "Romantic Archetypes and Political Meaning in the Historical Fiction Film." *Persistence of Vision* 3/4 (Summer 1986).

Guha, Ranajit, ed. *Subaltern Studies: Writings on South Asian History and Society*, 4 vols. Dehli: Oxford University Press, 1982–1986.

Gupta, Akhil. "The Political Economy of Post-Independence India—A Review Article." *Journal of Asian Studies* 48, no. 4 (November 1989): 787–796.

Gutman, Judith Mara. *Through Indian Eyes: Nineteenth and Early Twentieth Century Photography from India*. New York: Oxford University Press, 1982.

"History/Production/Memory." *Edinburgh Magazine* 2 (1977).

Hobsbawn, Eric, and Terence Ranger, eds. *The Invention of Tradition*. Cambridge: Cambridge University Press, 1983.

———. *Nations and Nationalism since 1780*. Cambridge: Cambridge University Press, 1990.

"Indian Popular Cinema: Myth, Meaning and Metaphor." *India International Centre Quarterly* 8, no. 1 (1981).

Indian Talkie, 1931–56 (Silver Jubilee Souvenir). Bombay: Film Federation of India, 1956.

Iyer, Pico. *Video Night in Kathmandu: And Other Reports from the Not-so-Far East*. New York: Vintage, 1988.

Jacobs, Lea. *The Wages of Sin: Censorship and the Fallen Woman Film, 1928–1942*. Madison: University of Wisconsin Press, 1991.

Jameson, Fredric. *The Political Unconscious: Narrative as a Socially Symbolic Act*. Ithaca, N.Y.: Cornell University Press, 1981.

———. "Reification and Utopia in Mass Culture." *Social Text* 1, no. 1 (1979).

———. "Third World Literature in the Era of Multinational Capitalism." *Social Text* 15 (Fall 1986).

JanMohamed, Abdul, and David Lloyd, eds. *The Nature and Context of Minority Discourse*. New York: Oxford University Press, 1990.

Jayakar, Pupul. *The Earth Mother*. New Delhi: Penguin Books, 1989.

Jha, B., ed. *Indian Motion Picture Almanac: 1971*. Calcutta: Shot Publications, 1972.

Johnson, Edward H. "Indian Cinema." BFI Dossier No. 5. London. Unpublished.

Johnson, Richard, et al. *Making Histories: Studies in History Writing and Politics*. Minneapolis: University of Minnesota Press, 1982.

Kakar, Sudhir. *The Inner World: A Psycho-analytic Study of Childhood and Society in India*. 2d ed. Delhi: Oxford University Press, 1981.

———. *Intimate Relations: Exploring Indian Sexuality*. Chicago: University of Chicago Press, 1989.

———. "The Theme of Authority in Social Relations in India." *Journal of Social Psychology* 84 (1971).

Kosambi, D. D. *Myth and Reality: Studies in the Formation of Indian Culture*. Bombay: Popular Prakashan, 1962.

Kracauer, Siegfried. *Theory of Film: The Redemption of Physical Reality*. New York: Oxford University Press, 1960.

Kuhn, Annette. *Women's Pictures: Feminism and Cinema*. London: Routledge and Kegan Paul, 1982.

Lal, P. *The Concept of an Indian Literature*. Calcutta: Writers Workshop, 1968.

Lannoy, Richard. *The Speaking Tree: A Study of Indian Culture and Society*. New York: Oxford University Press, 1974.

Lent, John. *The Asian Film Industry*. Austin: University of Texas Press, 1990.

Liddle, Joanna, and Rama Joshi. *Daughters of Independence: Gender, Caste and Class in India*. London: Zed Books, 1986.

Liehm, Mira. *Passion and Defiance: Film in Italy from 1942 to the Present*. Berkeley: University of California Press, 1984.

Lovell, Terry. *Pictures of Reality: Aesthetics, Politics and Pleasure*. London: British Film Institute, 1983.

MacCabe, Colin. *High Theory/Low Culture*. London: St. Martin's Press, 1986.

McIntyre, Steve. "National Film Cultures: Politics and Peripheries." *Screen* 26, no. 1 (1985).

Majumdar, R. C. *Historiography in Modern India.* Asia Publishing House, 1970.

Marglin, Frederique Apffel. *Wives of the God-King.* Delhi: Oxford University Press, 1985.

Mellencamp, Patricia, and Philip Rosen, eds. *Cinema Histories, Cinema Practices.* Baltimore: University Publishers of America, 1984.

Memmi, Albert. *The Colonizer and the Colonized.* Boston: Beacon Press, 1967.

Mercer, Kobena. "Third Cinema at Edinburgh: Reflections on a Pioneering Event." *Screen* 27, no. 6 (November/December 1986).

Metcalf, Thomas R. *Modern India: An Interpretive Anthology.* London: Macmillan Company, 1971.

Metz, Christian. *The Imaginary Signifier: Psychoanalysis and the Cinema.* Bloomington: Indiana University Press, 1977.

Micciollo, Henri. *Guru Dutt.* Avant-Scène du Cinéma no. 158 (1975).

Miller, Barbara Stoler. "Presidential Address: Contending Narratives—The Political Life of the Indian Epics." *Journal of Asian Studies* 50, no. 4 (November 1991): 783–792.

Mishra, Vijay. "Decentering History: Some Versions of Bombay Cinema." *East-West Film Journal* 6, no. 1 (January 1992): 111–155.

———. "Towards a Theoretical Critique of Bombay Cinema." *Screen* 26, no. 3/4 (May–August 1985).

Mukherjee, Meenakshi. *Realism and Reality: The Novel and Society in India.* Delhi: Oxford University Press, 1985.

Mulvey, Laura. "Visual Pleasure and Narrative Cinema." *Screen* 16, no. 3 (Autumn 1975).

Naipaul, V. S. *An Area of Darkness.* New York: Macmillan, 1964.

———. *India: A Million Mutinies Now.* Penguin Books, 1990.

Nairn, Tom. *The Breakup of Britain.* London: New Left Books, 1977.

Nandy, Ashis. *At the Edge of Psychology: Essays in Politics and Culture.* Delhi: Oxford University Press, 1980.

———. "An Intelligent Critic's Guide to Indian Cinema." *Deep Focus* 1–2 (December 1987–December 1988).

———. *The Intimate Enemy: Loss and Recovery of Self under Colonialism.* Delhi: Oxford University Press, 1983.

Napier, David. *Masks, Transformation and Paradox.* Berkeley: University of California Press, 1986.

Naremore, James. *Acting in the Cinema.* Berkeley: University of California Press, 1988.

Naremore, James, and Patrick Brantlinger, eds. *Modernity and Mass Culture.* Bloomington: Indiana University Press, 1991.

Nehru, Jawaharlal. *The Discovery of India.* New Delhi: Oxford University Press, 1946, 1981.

Nelson, Cary, and Lawrence Grossberg, eds. *Marxism and the Interpretation of Culture.* Urbana: University of Illinois Press, 1988.

Neumann, Erich. *The Great Mother: An Analysis of the Archetype*. Princeton, N.J.: Princeton University Press, 1972.

Nichols, Bill, ed. *Movies and Methods*. Vols. 1 and 2. Berkeley: University of California Press, 1976, 1985.

O'Flaherty, Wendy Doniger. *Women, Androgynes and Other Mythical Beasts*. Chicago: University of Chicago Press, 1979.

Oldenburg, Veena. *The Making of Colonial Lucknow, 1856–1877*. Princeton: Princeton University Press, 1984.

Pfleiderer, Beatrix, and Lothar Lutze, eds. *The Hindi Film: Agent and Re-agent of Cultural Change*. Delhi: Manohar, 1985.

Pines, Jim, and Paul Willemen, eds. *Questions of Third Cinema*, London: BFI, 1989.

Pritchett, Frances. "'The Chess Players': From Premchand to Satyajit Ray." *Journal of South Asian Literature* 21, no. 2 (Summer/Fall 1986): 65–77.

Quarterly Review of Film and Video. "Indian Cinema." Special issue, 11, no. 3 (1989).

"'Race,' Writing, and Difference." Special issue. *Critical Inquiry* 12, no. 1 (Autumn 1985).

Radhakrishnan, Sarvepalli, and Charles A. Moore, eds. *A Sourcebook in Indian Philosophy*. Princeton, N.J.: Princeton University Press, 1957.

Rajadhyaksha, Ashish. "Neo-Traditionalism: Film as Popular Art in India." *Framework* 32/33 (1986): 20–67.

———. *Ritwik Ghatak: A Return to the Epic*. Bombay: Screen Unit, 1982.

Ramachandran, T. M., ed. *Seventy Years of Indian Cinema, 1913–1983*. Bombay: Cinema India-International, 1985.

Rangoonwalla, Firoze. *Indian Cinema: Past and Present*. New Delhi: Clarion Books, 1982.

———. *Indian Filmography: Silent and Hindi Films (1897–1969)*. Bombay: Rangoonwalla and Udeshi, 1970.

Ray, Satyajit. *Our Films, Their Films*. Calcutta: Orient Longman, 1976.

———. "Under Western Eyes." *Sight and Sound* (Autumn 1982).

Report of the Film Enquiry Committee. New Delhi: Government of India Press, 1951.

Roberge, Gaston. *Another Cinema for Another Society*. Calcutta: Seagull Books, 1985.

Robinson, Andrew. *The Chess Players and Other Screenplays*. London: Faber and Faber, 1989.

Rosen, Philip. "History, Textuality, Nation: Kracauer, Burch and Some Problems in National Cinemas." *Iris* 2 (1984).

Ross, Andrew. *No Respect: Intellectuals and Popular Culture*. New York: Routledge, 1988.

Rowe, William, and Vivian Schelling. *Memory and Modernity: Popular Culture in Latin America*. London: Verso, 1991.

Roy, R. M., ed. *Film Seminar Report*. New Delhi: Sangeet Natak Akademi, 1955.

Rudolph, Lloyd, and Susanne Hoeber Rudolph. *The Modernity of Tradition: Political Development in India.* Chicago: University of Chicago Press, 1970.

Rushdie, Salman. *Midnight's Children.* New York: Avon Books, 1980.

———. "Outside the Whale." *American Film* 10, no. 4 (January/February 1985).

———. *The Satanic Verses.* New York: Viking Penguin, 1989.

———. *Shame.* London: Pan Books, 1983.

Said, Edward. "Intellectuals in the Post-Colonial World." *Salmagundi* 70/71 (Spring/Summer 1986).

———. *Orientalism.* New York: Vintage Books, 1978.

———. "Orientalism Reconsidered." In *Literature, Politics and Theory: Papers from the Essex Conference, 1976–1984.* Edited by Francis Barker et al. London: Methuen, 1986.

Sarkar, Kobita. *Indian Cinema Today.* New Delhi: Sterling, 1975.

Sarma, Gobind Prasad. *Nationalism in Indo-Anglian Fiction.* New Delhi: Sterling Publishers, 1978.

Schorer, Mark. "The Necessity of Myth." *Daedalus* 88 (Spring 1959).

Sen, Mrinal. *Views on Cinema.* Calcutta: Ishan, 1977.

Shils, Edward. *The Intellectual between Tradition and Modernity.* The Hague: Mouton, 1961.

Shohat, Ella. *Israeli Cinema: East/West and the Politics of Representation.* Austin: University of Texas Press, 1989.

Silverstone, Roger. *The Message of Television: Myth and Narrative in Contemporary Culture.* London: Heinemann Educational Books, 1981.

Smith, Anthony D. *Theories of Nationalism.* 2d ed. New York: Holmes and Meier Publishers, 1983.

Smith, Donald Eugene. *India as a Secular State.* Princeton: Princeton University Press, 1963.

Smith, Paul, ed. *The Historian and Film.* Cambridge: Cambridge University Press, 1976.

Sorlin, Pierre. *The Film in History: Restaging the Past.* Totowa, N.J.: Barnes and Noble, 1980.

Spivak, Gayatri Chakravorty. "Can the Subaltern Speak? Speculations on Widow-Sacrifice." *Wedge* 7/8 (Winter/Spring 1985).

———. *In Other Worlds.* New York and London: Methuen, 1987.

———. *The Post-Colonial Critic.* New York: Routledge, 1990.

Srinivas, M. N. *Social Change in Modern India.* Berkeley: University of California Press, 1966.

Stam, Robert, and Louise Spence. "Colonialism, Racism and Representation." *Screen* 24, no. 2 (January/February 1983).

———. *Reflexivity in Film and Literature: From Don Quixote to Jean-Luc Godard.* Ann Arbor: UMI Press, 1985.

Stam, Robert, Robert Burgoyne, and Sandy Flitterman-Lewis. *New Vocabularies in Film Semiotics: Structuralism, Post-Structuralism, and Beyond.* New York: Routledge, 1992.

Studies in Film History: D. G. Phalke. Poona: Film and Television Institute of India, 1979.

Thapar, Romila. *Ancient Indian Social History: Some Interpretations*. New Delhi: Orient Longman, 1978.

Thapar, Romila, Harbans Mukhia, and Bipan Chandra. *Communalism and the Writing of Indian History*. Delhi: People's Publishing House, 1969.

Thomas, Rosie, "Indian Cinema: Pleasures and Popularity." *Screen* 26, no. 3/4 (May–August 1985).

Vasudev, Aruna. *Liberty and Licence in the Indian Cinema*. New Delhi: Vikas, 1978.

———. *The New Indian Cinema*. New Delhi: Macmillan, 1986.

Vasudev, Aruna, and Philippe Lenglet, eds. *Indian Cinema Superbazaar*. Delhi: Vikas, 1983.

Vasudevan, Ravi. "The Melodramatic Mode and the Commercial Hindi Cinema." *Screen* 30, no. 3 (Summer 1989): 29–50.

Vieira, Joao Luiz. "Hegemony and Resistance: Parody and Carnival in Brazilian Cinema." Ph.D. dissertation, New York University, 1984.

Vitsaxis, Vassilis. *Hindu Epics, Myths and Legends in Popular Illustrations*. Delhi: Oxford University Press, 1977.

White, Hayden. *Metahistory: The Historical Imagination in Nineteenth-Century Europe*. Baltimore and London: Johns Hopkins University Press, 1973.

White, Miriam. "An Extra Body of Reference: History in Cinematic Narrative." Ph.D. dissertation, University of Iowa, 1981.

Willemen, Paul. "Negotiating the Transition to Capitalism: The Case of *Andaz*." *East-West Film Journal* 5, no. 1 (January 1991): 56–65.

Williams, Christopher, ed. *Realism and the Cinema: A Reader*. Boston: Routledge and Kegan Paul, 1980.

Williams, Raymond. "A Lecture on Realism." *Screen* 18, no. 1 (1977).

———. *The Sociology of Culture*. New York: Schocken Books, 1982.

———. *The Year 2000*. New York: Pantheon Books, 1983.

Wilson, James D. *The Romantic Heroic Ideal*. Baton Rouge: Louisiana State University Press, 1982.

Xavier, Ismail. "Allegories of Underdevelopment." Ph.D. dissertation, New York University, 1982.

Žižek, Slavoj. *Looking Awry: An Introduction to Jacques Lacan through Popular Culture*. Cambridge, Mass.: MIT Press, 1991.

Index

Aadmi, 274
Aag, 204
Aakaler Sandhaney, 246
Aakrosh, 236, 260–264, 267
Aandhian, 47, 103, 204
Aas ka Panchi, 219
Abbas, K. A., 62, 71, 88, 89, 93, 94, 131, 142, 166, 219
Adalat, 274–275
Adib, Prem, 2
Affron, Charles, 202
Afsar, 47
Alam Ara, 40
Albert Pinto ko Gussa Kyon Ata Hai, 236
Ali, Muzaffar, 287
Ali, Tariq, 23, 29
All India Radio, 76
Althusser, Louis, 14, 19
Amar Akbar Anthony, 200, 214, 230
Amar Prem, 270, 275, 294, 295–296
Amrit Manthan, 40
Anand, 228
Anand, Chetan, 46, 47, 89, 92, 219
Anand, Dev, 46, 48, 50, 133, 221
Anand, Mulk Raj, 61
Anand, Vijay, 30, 47, 52
Anandamath, 128
Anarkali, 168–169
Andaz, 131
Anderson, Benedict, 11, 12
Andha Kanoon, 230
androgyny, 146, 206, 276
Anhonee, 131, 142–144, 215
Annadata, 93
Aradhana, 219, 220
Aravindan, G., 236
Ardh Satya, 264–266, 267
Arnold, Alison, 167
Around the World, 210

Asif, K., 164
Attenborough, Richard, 183, 190, 192, 193
Aurat, 150–154
Aurobindo, Shri, 89, 100
Awaara, 131, 132, 134–142
Azmi, Kaifi, 248, 251
Azmi, Shabana, 184, 206, 301

Baazi, 47
Bachchan, Amitabh, 2, 3, 18, 60, 184, 201, 206, 214, 228–233
bahuru:pi, 6
Baiju Bawra, 168
Baker, Christopher, 128
Barnouw, Erik, 44
Barsaat, 131, 204
Barthes, Roland, 123, 203
Barua, P. C., 41, 111
Barucha, Rustom, 93
Bazaar, 245
Bedi, Rajinder Singh, 61
Benegal, Shyam, 10, 193, 236, 252, 260, 296, 301
Benjamin, Walter, 268
Bhabha, Homi, 11, 12, 27, 247–248
Bhatvadekar, Harishchandra S., 34
Bhumika, 270, 275, 296
Bhuvan Shome, 236, 243, 244, 267
Bilet Pherat, 40
biographical film, 191, 280
Blonde Venus, 276
Bombay Talkies, 42
Boot Polish, 104
Bordwell, David, 56
Bose, Debaki, 40
Bose, Nitin, 111
Bose, Satyen, 125
Bose, Subhash, 125
Bourdieu, Pierre, 238
Brecht, Bertolt, 268

Brennan, Timothy, 7
Bresson, Robert, 236
British, 22, 23, 24, 25, 26–29, 30,
    33, 42, 43, 58, 71, 74, 90, 93,
    126, 127, 169, 184, 186, 187,
    188, 191, 192, 194, 278, 279
Burman, S. D., 47, 48
Butler, Jeremy, 7

Campbell, Joseph, 202
Central Board of Film Censors, 72,
    78
Chakra, 236
Chambers, Iain, 8
Chandra, Bipan, 30
Chandra, Moti, 277–278
Chaplin, Charlie, 134, 205, 243
Chatterjee, Bankim Chandra, 86,
    128
Chatterjee, Basu, 236, 237, 243
Chatterjee, Kalyan, 163
Chatterjee, Sarat Chandra, 6, 29, 41,
    111
Chaudhari, Nirad, 55, 62, 63
Chetna, 270
Chinatown, 200
Chitra, 41
Chitralekha, 285
Chopra, B. R., 88, 131, 147, 274
Chowdhury, Salil, 77, 109
Chugtai, Ismat, 61, 248
Chupke Chupke, 200, 231
Coolie, 3, 214, 229, 230–231, 233
Corkin, Stanley, 90
Court Dancer, The, 42
courtesan, 269–305. See also prosti-
    tute; prostitution
Cyclopaedia of India, The, 168

dance, 78, 129, 147, 172, 189–190,
    239, 289, 298
Dasgupta, Chidananda, 21, 124–
    125, 242
Dastak, 270, 275
Deedar, 103, 105

Deewaar, 230
De Lauretis, Teresa, 188, 281
Denning, Michael, 5, 246, 311
De Saussure, Ferdinand, 188
Desh Premee, 200
Devdas (1935), 41
Devdas (1955), 141, 205, 270
Dharmaraj, Rabindra, 236
Dharti ke Lal, 85, 92–94
Dhondy, Farrukh, 133
Discovery of India, The, 18, 21–29
Dissanayake, Wimal, 224, 226
Do Ankhen Barah Haath, 131, 132,
    144–146, 149
Do Bigha Zamin, 69, 85, 89, 94–
    97, 106, 118
Don, 230
Doordarshan, 18
Dr. Kotnis ki Amar Kahani, 40
dream sequence, 139–140
Dutt, Guru, 10, 47, 133, 164, 173,
    204, 263
Dyer, Richard, 102

Ek Hi Raasta, 204
Eliade, Mircea, 127, 144, 161
Ellis, Havelock, 277
Ellis, John, 70
Elsaesser, Thomas, 159, 182, 295
Evening in Paris, An, 200, 210–212,
    213, 215, 218

Fanon, Frantz, 124, 247
Fearless Nadia, 59–60
Film Enquiry Committee, 66
Filmfare, 68, 69, 72, 73, 139, 230
Film Federation of India, 74
Film Finance Corporation, 44, 242,
    243
Film India, 69
Footpath, 103
Forster, E. M., 20
Foucault, Michel, 170
Franco, Jean, 199
Funtoosh, 47

Gandhi, 26, 183, 190–195
Gandhi, Indira, 19, 152
Gandhi, Mohandas, 20, 28, 29, 51,
   101, 125, 146, 167, 190–195,
   251; Gandhian, 92, 112, 113,
   166, 251
Garber, Marjorie, 201
Garbo, Greta, 150, 203
Garm Hawa, 166, 236, 241, 246,
   248–252, 267
Gavras, Costa, 260
gaze, 214–215, 273
Geraftaar, 230
Gerow, Edwin, 8, 11
Ghatak, Ritwik, 6, 128, 236, 237,
   238
ghazal, 44
Ghosh, Nabendu, 87
Ghunghat, 131
Godard, Jean-Luc, 236, 243
Godhuli, 241, 257–258, 267
Gopalakrishnan, Adoor, 236
Gramsci, Antonio, 121
Grindon, Leger, 171
Guide, 46–52
Gupta, Akhil, 30

Haqeeqat, 219
harem, 277, 280
Hare Rama Hare Krishna, 210
Heath, Stephen, 158, 164, 170
Holi, 235
Hollywood, 15, 33, 39, 56, 69, 71,
   73, 97, 98, 124, 273, 308, 311
House No. 44, 47
Humayun, 165
Hum Dono, 200, 219–224
Hum Log, 103
Humrahi, 89
Humsafar, 47
Huyssen, Andreas, 241

Illustrated Weekly of India, 72, 192
Imagined Communities, 11
impersonation, 4–7, 16, 48, 81,

   113, 118, 120, 142, 159, 160,
   163, 194, 195, 200, 201, 276,
   304–305, 309, 310–312
IMPPA, 75
Indian Cinematograph Committee, 66
Indian new wave, 235–268
India Today, 3
IPTA, 92, 93

Jaane Bhi Do Yaro, 267
Jagriti, 125–127
Jagte Raho, 85, 103, 106
Jaidev, 224
Jameson, Fredric, 14, 97, 98, 165
Jana Aranya, 270
Janus, 27, 28, 94
Jewel in the Crown, 26
Jhansi ki Rani, 71
Jogan, 204
Johnny Mera Naam, 200
Junglee, 205, 207–210

Kaala Patthar, 230
Kaalia, 230
Kakar, Sudhir, 120, 130–131, 133,
   140, 146, 161, 205
Kala Bazaar, 47, 103, 204
Kala Pani, 270, 275
Kalpana, 75
Kalyug, 252–255, 267
Kanch ki Guriya, 274
Kanoon, 131, 132, 147–149
Kapoor, Raj, 10, 47, 68, 131, 133,
   134, 138–144, 203, 205, 207,
   216–218, 224–228
Kapoor, Shammi, 60, 205, 206, 207,
   212, 215, 216
Kapur, Geeta, 237
Karanth, B. V., 257
Karnad, Girish, 10, 59, 85, 236,
   257, 281, 282, 283, 284
Kasaravalli, Girish, 236
Kasme Vaade, 230
Kaul, Awtar, 236
Kaul, Mani, 236, 237, 243

Kesari, 37
Keskar, B. V., 76
Khan, Ali Akbar, 47, 76
Khan, Mehboob. *See* Mehboob
Khilona, 270
Khopkar, Arun, 180
Kipling, Rudyard, 175
Kosambi, D. D., 122–123, 130
Kranti, 44
Kumar, Dilip, 29, 129, 169

Laawaris, 230
Lalit Kala Akademi, 63
Lanka Dahan, 35
Lannoy, Richard, 101
Levi-Strauss, Claude, 121, 188, 217–218
Light of Asia, 40
Love in Tokyo, 200, 210, 213
Ludhianvi, Sahir, 224

MacCabe, Colin, 158
McClintock, Anne, 288
Madan, Jamshedjee, 34, 39, 40
Madhumati, 128–131
Mahābhārata, 87, 162, 163, 171, 253, 254, 256, 297
Main Tulsi Tere Angan Ki, 270
Majumdar, R. C., 166
Mamta, 270, 274, 275, 294–295
Mandi, 270, 275, 296, 301–304
Manthan, 236, 241, 257, 258–260, 267
Manto, Sadat Hasan, 61
Mard, 230
Marglin, Frederique Apffel, 277–278
masquerade, 5, 7, 16, 32, 38, 48, 81, 121, 164, 190, 199–203, 210–214, 220–223, 233, 240, 270, 301, 305, 310–312
Masud, Iqbal, 236
maternal melodrama, 293–295
Maya Darpan, 236, 241
Mehboob, 86, 128, 131, 149, 150, 151, 155, 165, 204

Mehta, Ketan, 235, 236
Mera Naam Joker, 200, 216, 224–227
metamorphosis, 4, 45, 49, 155, 217, 295
Midnight's Children, 4, 119
Mili, 228
Mill, James, 160, 167
Miller, Barbara Stoller, 30
Minerva Movietone, 158
Ministry of Information and Broadcasting, 74, 192
Mir, Ezra, 165
Mirza, Saeed, 236
Mirza Ghalib, 158
Mishra, Vijay, 107, 163–164, 201, 215
Mississippi Masala, 3
Mitra, Bimal, 173
Mitra, Shambhu, 75
modernization, 118, 141, 257
Modi, Sohrab, 71, 165
Mohan, Madan, 77
Mohini Bhasmasur, 37
Morris, Meaghan, 308, 312
Mother India, 128, 132, 149–156
Mr. Natwarlal, 230
Mr. Sampat, 103, 105
Mughal-e-Azam, 164–173, 183
Mukerjee, Hrishikesh, 10
Mukherjee, Meenakshi, 82, 160
Muller, Max, 22, 23
multistarrer, 44
Munsterberg, Hugo, 21
Muqaddar ka Sikander, 230
music, 61, 77, 167, 168, 190, 221
myth, 36, 119–125, 131–133, 137, 138, 140, 144–145, 150–156, 159, 194, 267
mythological, 2, 36, 42

Nabanna, 93
Naipaul, V. S., 63
Nair, Mira, 3
Nairn, Tom, 11, 27

Namak Halaal, 230
Nandy, Ashis, 17, 76, 132, 200, 237
Napier, David, 6, 201, 202, 222
Narayan, R. K., 47, 49, 63, 105
Naremore, James, 201, 212–213
Nargis, 70, 134, 138, 139, 142,
    143, 150, 155, 215, 274, 275
Naseeb, 44, 230
National Film Archive of India, 34,
    44
National Film Development Corpora-
    tion, 44, 191, 244
Nation and Narration, 11
Natya Shastra, 87, 88
Nau Do Gyarah, 47
nautch-girl, 144, 176, 189, 269, 280
Navketan Productions, 46, 47
Navyug, 37, 38
Naya Daur, 204
Naya Din Nayi Raat, 200, 224,
    227–228
Neecha Nagar, 89, 91–92
Nehru, Jawaharlal, 16, 18, 19, 21–
    30, 101, 125, 203, 204, 219, 251
neorealism, 96, 97, 238, 241
Neumann, Eric, 152, 154
New Theatres, 41, 89, 111, 126
New York Times, 242
Nihalani, Govind, 236, 260, 264

O'Flaherty, Wendy, 156
Oldenburg, Veena, 279–280

Padosan, 200, 213
Padosi, 165
Pakeezah, 270, 275, 291–293
Panchsheel, 101
Parakh, 109–111
Pardesi, 71
Park, Robert Ezra, 202
Passage to India, A, 26
Patel, Jabbar, 31
Pather Panchali, 83, 94
Patil, Smita, 18, 206, 256, 259,
    261, 264, 272, 297, 298, 301

Phalke, D. G., 35–39
Phutane, Ramdas, 236
Prabhat Film Company, 40, 42, 67
Premchand, Munshi, 61, 84, 86,
    184, 186, 187, 190
Progressive Writers' Movement, 61
prostitute, 143, 144, 151, 269, 270,
    272, 274, 276–278, 290, 302, 304
prostitution, 49, 50, 93, 270, 275,
    277, 293–295, 300
Pukar, 158
Pundalik, 34, 35
Purab aur Paschim, 210
Pyaasa, 103, 107, 205, 263, 270

Radway, Janice, 98, 311
Rai, Himansu, 40, 42
Rajadhyaksha, Ashish, 57, 237
Raja Harishchandra, 35, 37
Ramachandran, M. G., 3
Ramāyana, 35, 162, 171, 233
Ram Teri Ganga Maili, 270
Rani, Devika, 42
Rao, N. T. Rama, 3
Ray, Satyajit, 3, 7, 21, 55, 80, 81,
    86, 124, 183–188, 190, 193,
    237, 243–244, 270
realism, 80–89, 97–98, 111, 117–
    119, 126, 163–164, 236, 241,
    297
Reddy, Pattabhi Rama, 236
Rehman, Waheeda, 47, 49, 50, 233
Renoir, Jean, 70, 243
Report of the Working Group on Na-
    tional Film Policy, 244
River, The, 70
RK Studios, 47
Roadarmel, Gordon, 84
Roberge, Gaston, 244–245
Robinson, Andrew, 242
romance, 68, 124, 130, 134, 158,
    164, 165, 168, 171, 172, 210,
    211, 213, 219–221, 224, 226,
    228, 283, 285, 286, 288, 289,
    299, 300

Rosen, Philip, 12, 159
Ross, Andrew, 14, 246
Roy, Bimal, 10, 86, 87, 88, 89, 109, 111, 117, 128, 204
Rudolph, Lloyd and Susanne, 30
Rushdie, Salman, 1–4, 85, 119
Ruswa, Mirza Mohammed, 287

Saat Hindustani, 219
Sadhana, 274, 275
Sagar, Ramanand, 131
Sahai, Malti, 224, 226
Sahib Bibi aur Ghulam, 164, 165, 173–183, 195
Sahitya Akademi, 63
Sahni, Balraj, 95, 96, 249
Salaam Bombay!, 270
Samskara, 246
Sangam, 210, 216–218
Sangeet Natak Akademi, 61, 63
Sangeet Samrat Tansen, 168
Sant Tukaram, 40
Sara Akash, 236, 243, 267
Sarhadi, Sagar, 245
Sarhady, Zia, 86
Sarkar, Kobita, 94, 242
Satanic Verses, The, 1
Sathyu, M. S., 236, 248–249
Savitri Satyavan, 37
Schorer, Mark, 120
Seema, 204
Sembene, Ousmane, 265
Sen, Mrinal, 236, 237, 243, 244, 246
Shah, Chandulal, 40
Shahani, Kumar, 236, 237, 252, 255, 276
Shame, 2
Shankar, Ravi, 76, 191
Shankar, Uday, 46
Shantaram, V., 40, 67, 86, 131, 144, 165, 274
Sharar, Abdul Halim, 278
Sharma, Kidar, 139
Shatranj ke Khilari, 183–190

Shaw, Bernard, 90
Shils, Edward, 85
Sholay, 44, 231
Shri 420, 103, 107, 137, 203
Sikander, 158
Silver Jubilee Souvenir, 59, 61
Silverstone, Roger, 123
Sircar, B. N., 40, 55
Sommer, Doris, 124
song, 5, 76, 77, 129, 131, 139–140, 147, 162, 172, 203, 221, 224, 239, 289, 298
Spivak, Gayatri Chakravorty, 19–20, 28
star system, 1, 7, 44, 97, 113, 203, 206, 213, 228, 239
studio era, 39–44, 64
stunt film, 3, 42, 58–61, 212, 299
Subarnarekha, 6
Sujata, 111–117
Suri, Surinder, 236

Tagore, Rabindranath, 21, 28, 86, 89, 131, 161, 163
Tarang, 252, 253, 255–257, 267, 276
Taxi Driver, 204
Taylor, Clyde, 247–248
Tendulkar, Vijay, 260, 264
Thapar, Romila, 160, 161, 162, 167
Third World, 8, 13, 14, 15, 17, 56, 194, 204, 309
thriller, 79, 147, 194, 260, 267
Torney, R. G., 34
Tribe, Keith, 158
Trishul, 230
27 Down, 236
Tyler, Parker, 120

Udayer Pathe, 89–91, 92
Umrao Jan, 275, 287–291
Uski Roti, 236, 243, 267
Usne Kaha Tha, 219
Utsav, 270, 281–285, 290

Vasudev, Aruna, 273
Verma, Nirmal, 31, 84
Victoria No. 203, 200
Vivekananda, Swami, 89

Wadia, J. B. H., 35, 40
Wadia Movietone, 42, 59
Wadkar, Hansa, 296
White, Hayden, 163

Williams, Raymond, 5, 21, 71, 83, 309, 311
Woolf, Virginia, 271

Xala, 265

Yeh Amrit Hai, 93

Zanjeer, 229, 230
Žižek, Slavoj, 11
Zubeida, 93